# SHEEP!

# SHEEP!

An Autobiography of Louise Turk,
Woman Sheepherder

## Louise Turk

Pentland Press, Inc.
www.pentlandpressusa.com

PUBLISHED BY PENTLAND PRESS, INC.
5122 Bur Oak Circle, Raleigh, North Carolina 27612
United States of America
919-782-0281

ISBN 1-57197-249-8
Library of Congress Control Number: 00-134883

Printed in the United States of America

*This book is dedicated to the memory of my husband Brookie and Pete Meike. They both had such confidence in my ability I had to keep reaching beyond what I thought I was capable of doing.*

*To Don and Peto, who, if they had any qualms about entrusting me with their valuable property, never let me know it.*

*To all the people who have waited so long and faithfully for this to be accomplished.*

*And last, but certainly not least, to my son Pete who spent years reading countless miles of my longhand material, editing and compiling my story, encouraging and prodding when I wanted to quit. Without him this book would never have been written.*

*Sheep*
*In my keeping*
*Sheep*
*In my sleeping*
*From morning to night*
*From darkness to light*
*Sheep*

—Debra L. Brown

# TABLE OF CONTENTS

# A Boy on Horseback
## November 1921

The last day of November 1921 was cold and blustery, with a raw north wind blowing swirls of dry cottonwood leaves along the frozen ground. Fourteen-year-old Brookie Turk was riding home after spending the earlier part of the day helping a neighbor move some cattle to winter pasture. He had been doing a man's work since he was nine years old and was a familiar figure on most of the ranches in the area. Because of the nasty weather he decided to leave the county road and take a shortcut through the Charlie Hall Ranch, cutting nearly a mile off the trip home to his family's ranch.

As he swung off his horse to open the gate into the Hall Ranch yard he saw Dan Brown, the ranch manager, working in the shop. Leading his horse, Brookie walked the short distance to get his blood circulating in his cold legs.

"Put your horse in the corral," Dan said after they'd exchanged greetings. "I've got the forge goin' so you can warm up before you go on."

Brookie accepted gratefully.

"Well, how's everything goin'?" he inquired as he held his stiff fingers over the glowing coals of the forge.

"Goin' great." Dan smiled proudly. "Just got word I'm the father of a baby girl born yesterday in Buffalo. We named her Helen after her mother and Louise after one of my sisters."

"That so? Congratulations!"

They talked about the topics ranchers were always interested in: the weather, livestock, winter feed prospects, and what was going on in the neighborhood.

"Well, I'm warmed up, so I better get goin'," Brookie said at last. He pulled his gloves on. "I've got all the chores to do tonight 'cause the folks and the kids went to Reuben Floyd's this afternoon and ain't comin' back 'till after supper. See ya," he called as he rode away. "And take care of that girl."

A grin spread across his face as he put the chilled horse into a gallop. "Someday I'm gonna marry that girl," he told himself.

At least that's the way I pictured it when he used to tease me about it years later after we were married.

# THE HALL RANCH

## (1921-1936)

"Adopt!" The word crashed into my brain, and panic welled up in me.

Now, suddenly, it was clear to me why Mr. and Mrs. Weeks had come to the ranch to have Sunday dinner with us, dinner being the noon meal in ranch country. Mom was well known as a better-than-average cook, and it wasn't unusual for us to have people drop in on Sundays to spend the day, but I was pretty sure the Weeks knew little about Mom's cooking ability. Dad knew Mr. Weeks as head of the Land Office in Buffalo, but he was certainly not a social acquaintance who would drive seventy-five miles to eat with us, so their arrival that morning had puzzled me.

I remember almost nothing about Mrs. Weeks, but her husband was a Scotsman who spoke very precise English, wore a three-piece suit, white shirt, and tie, and had a bushy gray mustache. They were childless, and it was very apparent that they had no idea how to interact with kids. To me they seemed downright stodgy.

After the meal was finished the men sat at the dining room table, talking and drinking coffee while Mom and Mrs. Weeks went to the kitchen to do the dishes. I was playing in my room across the hall when my attention was suddenly riveted on their conversation. Mr. Weeks had asked a lot of questions about me, and now I knew why! He had just told Dad that if they adopted me I would have a nice home, good clothes, and the opportunity for an excellent education.

I strained to hear Dad's reply, but his words were indistinct. He was agreeing, in a sad, low voice I thought, instead of in his usual outspoken fashion.

The rest of the afternoon I huddled in my room while a million thoughts raced through my mind. How could I ever endure being separated from my big, noisy family? And with two such humorless people! I tried to imagine what I would do to occupy my time and kept seeing myself sitting stiffly on the edge of a straight-backed chair with my hands folded (clenched?) in my lap.

What would my younger brother Fred, who was my best friend, do without me? Even my little sister Ruthie suddenly seemed very dear to me. The hours I spent looking after her while Mom cared for our baby brother Danny and cooked for our big family as well as two hired men took on the aspect of a great privilege.

My first thought was to hide somewhere, but I discarded the idea almost immediately. Where could a ten-year-old girl conceal herself indefinitely? Besides, if Dad gave his word he would have to honor it.

When Mom appeared in the doorway my heart almost stopped. "This is it," I thought. I would not disgrace myself or embarrass my family by making a scene. I would bid farewell to my loved ones with my head held high, a smile on my lips.

"Come say good-bye to Mr. and Mrs. Weeks," Mom's voice penetrated my martyrdom. "They're leaving for home."

I could hardly believe my ears! I was not going with them! Gladly I said good-bye.

For days after that I was uneasy, fearful that negotiations might be reopened. I did my best to give the folks the feeling that I was indispensable. Such distasteful tasks as washing and drying dishes, setting the table, and making my bed were performed cheerfully. I even looked after Ruthie without being asked. Gradually my fears subsided and I returned to normal behavior.

Because I felt I had been eavesdropping I never asked my folks about the circumstances leading up to the events of that day. They never mentioned it because they had no idea I'd overheard the conversation in the dining room. Years after Dad's death, when Mom was in her nineties, I asked her about it, and told her how scared I'd been that day. Too many years had passed and her recollection of the incident was fuzzy.

"Did you really think we'd have gotten rid of you?" she asked, and laughed.

So I never learned anything about the episode of my near adoption. It seems likely there had been a monetary offer made, but how the Weeks knew of our financial difficulties, or why they singled us out when there must have been dozens of families right in Buffalo in similar circumstances is something I'll never know.

For as long as I could remember I'd been hearing the grown-ups talk about something called "the Depression." I had no idea what it was, but I got the impression it mostly affected city people. Bread lines and soup kitchens belonged to a different world than the one I lived in, so I figured we were safe.

We lived on the Hall Ranch then, and what I remember most about my childhood there was being happy, even though by modern standards we would probably have been considered deprived. Of course there were disappointments and times of sadness, but I felt loved and secure.

Compared to Mom I led a pretty carefree life as I was growing up. Mom was third from the youngest in a family of eight girls and one boy. Her father died of tuberculosis in 1908 when she was twelve years old. Shortly after that their mother took Dorothy, the youngest, and moved to New Mexico, where she filed on a homestead. She left the older girls, who all had jobs, to support the younger children. Mom and her younger sister Julia were expected do the cooking and housekeeping.

In December 1910 they received a telegram saying their mother was very ill and for some of the family to come at once. Ruth, one of the older sisters, left immediately by train, arriving shortly before my Grandmother Skinner died. After making arrangements to have the body shipped back home for burial, Ruth and Dorothy returned to the family home in Topeka, Kansas.

Later, lured by the demand for schoolteachers out West, three of the older Skinner girls, Della, Evvie, and Margaret, migrated to the Kaycee area of Wyoming where all three married shortly after completing their first year of teaching. Della and her husband, Will Eldridge, homesteaded near Kaycee. As soon as Mom graduated from high school, Della sent for her to come live with them.

Mom left Topeka on May 1, 1915, coming by train as far as Sheridan, Wyoming. She and a blizzard arrived at the same time, and she was forced to lay over there for two days. The rest of the trip was made by horse-drawn stage, which took a full two days, with an overnight stay in Buffalo. For the next couple of years she worked as a hired girl on various ranches in the area.

February 1917 found her cooking at the John Cooper ranch. One of the ranch hands, Daniel Brown, was instantly attracted to the pretty new cook and began courting her. He must have been persuasive because they were married on Friday, July 13, 1917. The young couple continued to work for the Coopers until the ranch was sold a year later.

After the wedding, Mom asked Dad if he had let his family know he was married. He rather shamefacedly told her he'd had no contact with them since he ran away from home when he was fifteen years old. At that point Mom suddenly realized how little she actually knew about her new husband's life before he came to Wyoming. She knew only that he was born in Lake Mills, Wisconsin, on November 22, 1887, the next to youngest of four children, William, Louise, himself, and Ella.

About 1902 the family moved to the little village of Chile, Wisconsin. There was no high school in Chile, he explained to Mom, so when Ella entered seventh grade and he was ready to start high school they had to board with a family in the larger town of Marshfield, some twenty miles away. Because of the distance, and with transportation being what it was in those days, the only time they got to go home the entire school year was at Christmas. Dad vowed to himself when school was out in the spring that he would never go back.

Before the summer was over he "rode the rails" west into the Dakotas, where he helped harvest grain. From there he moved on to Montana and for several years herded sheep, worked on ranches, and even drove stagecoaches out of Cut Bank, Montana, one winter before moving down into Wyoming.

Mom immediately wrote to the address where he'd been raised, not knowing if any of the family was still living there. She was rewarded with a letter from his mother and very shortly after that, she heard from Louise and Ella. With no word of him in fifteen years they had assumed he was dead. They were overjoyed to learn he was alive and well.

Marshall, the oldest of us kids, was born July 26, 1918, at the home of Amelia Austin. There was no hospital in Buffalo at that time, but there were several women who took expectant mothers into their homes, where the babies were delivered by a doctor. The mothers and babies were cared for by the women during their confinement, the prescribed ten days in bed following delivery.

Dad couldn't understand why women in Wyoming needed ten days to recuperate. Unless there were complications, he said, the women in the German settlement he came from in Wisconsin were usually back at work twenty-four to forty-eight hours after giving birth. Mom maintained it was the only vacation ranch women ever got from working fourteen hours a day, seven days a week, twelve months a year!

When Charlie Hall hired Dad to herd his lambs the fall of 1918 the little family set up housekeeping in the bunk house, the only place on the Hall Ranch for them to live. About a year later, Charlie put Dad in charge of the ranch when the Hall family moved to Buffalo so their oldest daughter could attend high school. Mom and Dad were delighted to leave the little one-room bunkhouse and take up residence in the completely furnished two-story ranch house, which was considered one of the finest homes in the Powder River Valley at that time.

On the ground floor there were six rooms, plus an unfinished bathroom that served as a nursery, a walk-in pantry, and a closed-in back porch. Two large rooms upstairs were connected by a hallway that also gave access to the stairway. These two rooms had been designed as bedrooms, but in winter there was no way to heat them, and in summer they were stifling hot, so they served as storerooms.

When Dad brought home the year's supply of flour from the flour mill at Kaycee in the fall the bags were stacked in the south bedroom, along with a hundred pounds each of white and brown sugar in burlap bags lined with heavy brown paper. The brown sugar was very coarse compared with what I buy today, and I wonder if that isn't why it never petrified into a solid block. Once the bag was opened Mom would transfer a supply for the kitchen to a lard pail and the top of the sack was simply folded or rolled to keep the air and dust out. Today's brown sugar would set as solid as concrete if stored in a similar fashion!

The fall butchering was done after cold weather came, and the beef and pork carcasses were laid out on tarps spread on the floor of the north bedroom, where they kept as effectively as if they'd been in a refrigerated room.

The full basement had a big main room where Mom's countless jars of home-canned vegetables, fruits, pickles, jams, and jellies filled several rows of shelves. This room also served as storage for an amazing conglomeration of articles, from extra kerosene lamps to buckets of paint.

The rest of the basement was taken up by a coal bin and a furnace room. The monstrosity of a furnace consumed tons of coal each winter and never produced enough heat to warm one room, let alone ten. The big Majestic cookstove kept the kitchen, dining room, and Mom and Dad's bedroom livable in cold weather. The rest of the house was kept closed off, so going to bed in those icy bedrooms was a bone-chilling experience. Weekends when we older kids were home from school must have been pretty nerve-wracking for Mom, with all of us cooped up in such close quarters. That's probably why I can remember her having us put on our coats, caps, and mittens and go play in the unheated part of the house!

For a few years, we were the only people in the community who had cold running water piped into the kitchen. The fact that we never had hot water didn't bother us. I guess you don't miss something you never had. A windmill pumped the water from a well in the corner of the yard into a big galvanized steel storage tank housed in a small frame building just across the fence from the windmill. The tank sat on a cement platform with a fireplace under it. In cold weather a fire had to be kept burning so the water wouldn't freeze. The tank house, as it was called, was poorly vented and was always full of smoke in winter. Even though the top of the tank was covered with canvas and bridge planks, the water in winter always had a smoky flavor. I hated the taste of that water!

I seldom went inside because it was dusty, cobwebby, and smelled of smoke. The only light came from the door, and the building was just enough larger than the tank to provide a walkway around it. It always gave me claustrophobia.

Living so far from the ranch proved to be a real inconvenience for Charlie Hall. After several years of commuting back and forth on dirt roads in a Model T, he decided to close out his ranching operation on Powder River. He offered to lease the ranch to Dad and sell him enough sheep to give him a modest start in the sheep business. Dad jumped at the chance. Along with the lease and the sheep, he also bought the work horses, farm machinery, milk cows, and tools. He and Mom embarked on their career of raising farm produce, sheep, and kids—the human kind!

Most of the time our only form of transportation was by team and wagon, or by what Mom always referred to as "shank's mare"—in other words, on foot. Occasionally one of the bachelors who frequented our place would leave a car there while they were on a seasonal or short-term job. Though Dad had the use of them, he seldom drove unless it was an emergency.

Dad had to depend on the neighbors to get Mom to Buffalo for the births of Marsh, myself, and Fred, but at the end of March 1928, as the time drew near for the birth of their fourth child, Dad, for once, was completely confident that he had the means of getting Mom to Buffalo. A few months earlier he had bought a new Dodge touring car, the first car the Brown family had ever owned.

Expectant ranch wives usually went to Buffalo at least a week before their due date. Even though ranch life was pretty dull on a day-to-day basis, no one wanted the dubious excitement of trying to outrun the stork on the seventy-five miles of dirt road in the transportation available! During the wife's absence some older neighbor girl or an elderly woman who wasn't needed at home was hired to come in and stay with the family until the new mother and child returned home.

"Grandma" Stockham, a widow in our community who made her home with her grown son, Hugh, had been hired to care for us while Mom was gone. She had come a few days early to learn the routine.

One morning she looked Mom up and down and proclaimed, "That baby is going to be born before the day is over."

Dad panicked. There had been a soaking rain for twenty-four hours, followed by wet snow that was melting on top of the mud. Mom assured

Dad that she didn't feel any different than she had the day before and begged him to wait, hoping for better road conditions. Dad was insistent.

The main road was dirt and made a big dog-leg west to Kaycee, then north to Buffalo. The Four Mile Cut-off road was dirt, too, but it went more or less straight to Buffalo from our community, so that was the way they went. Mom said every low place had a big mud hole full of high centers and they got stuck in every one. Dad had the foresight to take a shovel, and he must have shoveled tons of mud that day. I can remember what terrible shape his hands were in when he finally got home a couple of days later. They looked like raw beef steak. He had worn blisters and the blisters had broken, but he had doggedly kept on shoveling.

And Mom had still not had the baby.

James Walter finally arrived on April 15, 1928, two weeks after Grandma had predicted his birth. When Dad came home after being summoned to town he told us the baby had died shortly after birth from a defective heart. I felt no sorrow because the baby never seemed real to me. No one ever talked about babies before they were born, so it wasn't as if we had anticipated the arrival of it.

When Dad came home from Buffalo and announced the birth of baby Ruth on May 29, 1929, I was ecstatic. At last! A sister to play with me! I could hardly wait for Mom to bring the baby home.

How wrong I was! It didn't take me long to figure out that Ruthie and I were never going to be playmates, not with eight years' difference in our ages, and when new baby Danny came home a year later it became my job to look after Ruthie.

"You can go swimming if you take Ruthie with you," Mom would tell me. Or, "Put Ruthie down for her nap, then you can go play."

Wherever a headgate diverted water from the Sahara Ditch Company's big supply ditch to the irrigation ditches in the fields, there was a wooden box, called a drop, built across the ditch. It created a waterfall and the force of the water as it came rushing out of the box eroded the ditch below it to form a nice swimming hole. Our favorite was about halfway between our house and our neighbors, the Jepsons.

There were six girls in the Jepson family. The next to the youngest, Margy, was my age and my best friend. If she didn't have work to do at home she and her younger sister, Millie, would meet Fred and me at the swimming hole for an afternoon of fun.

Ruthie wasn't allowed in the ditch because Mom was afraid we'd forget to keep an eye on her and she'd drown. She hated "going swimming" because all she could do was sit on the bank in the hot sun and whine to go home. Whenever she realized where we were headed she would dig in her heels and I'd have to drag her the first hundred yards. It's a wonder she didn't grow up with one arm four inches longer than the other! Maybe, without being aware of it, I alternated arms.

The crib Ruthie slept in was a marvelous concoction of cross-wise coil springs that were just made for jouncing a baby to sleep. Oh, the hours I spent crouched over that crib, springing her up and down, singing to lull her to sleep. Slowly, slowly, the heavy eyes would close, the breathing slow, the fingers relax on the toy they had been clutching. Gently I would lessen the bouncing, soften the singing, stop, silently straighten my aching back, and tiptoe toward the door.

"Waaah!"

The whole process might have to be repeated several times before I'd make my getaway. Sometimes I wondered why Dad hadn't just drowned her when she was born, like he did the numerous barn kittens we couldn't keep. I would much rather have saved the kittens!

\* \* \*

Ruthie was born on May 29, 1929, and Danny arrived October 13, 1930, when Ruthie was sixteen months old. One night a few months after Danny was born I overheard the folks talking. James, Ruthie, and Danny had all been born so close together that none of them was paid for, plus there were unpaid funeral expenses for James. Young as I was, I recognized the worry in their voices, and I had the uneasy feeling the Depression might be closer to us than I had imagined. That was probably the reason Dad sold the Dodge to a neighbor shortly after that.

The only girls within walking distance for me to play with were the Jepsons. Since there were no boys in their family the older girls helped their father with the farm work and the younger ones were their mother's helpers. As a result, much of my time was spent with Marsh and Fred and their friends Bob and Bud Taylor.

They were not much interested in playing house, but then, neither was I. The things they did interested me a lot more. I suppose I was as much of a nuisance to them as Ruthie was to me. They had an inflexible rule: If I couldn't do whatever they did, I couldn't play with them. One of their favorite ways of getting rid of me was to climb up on the roof of the barn via the granary, march across the roof in single file, step off the edge into the small pile of hay Dad kept behind the barn for the teams of horses used on the hay machinery, and go on about their business while I crouched on the brink like a turkey hen, looking down at that small target and willing myself to jump. Usually, cowardice won and I ended up going back across to the granary, which was attached to the barn, sliding the lower half of my body over the edge of the granary until my toes found the sill of the small ventilator window in the side of the building, and dropping from there to the ground. By the time I accomplished all this, the boys had given me the slip, so I had to go entertain myself.

All my life I have been terrified of mice and bats. The boys used this to their advantage, too. By standing on the edges of the mangers, they could reach up and grab a rafter and go hand over hand to the center of the barn, then swing their legs up and pull themselves up onto the rafter. From there, they could reach up into the peak of the roof, where dozens of bats hung suspended in the dim light during the day. Whenever I saw this happening, I made tracks for the house, because the next phase of this game was to grab a bat, drop to the floor, and take after me, threatening to entangle the angrily squeaking creature in my hair!

In spite of these incidents, I grew up wishing I'd been a boy so I could do the interesting things boys did, instead of the dumb things girls did!

We could cut off quite a distance on our hike to and from school each day by going across the fields, but Mom frowned on our shortcut because it entailed climbing over three barbed wire fences in our good school clothes. We usually followed the road, which went through Waugh Murphy's barnyard to connect with the county road. If Waugh and his hired man, Paul Lahitte, were out doing their morning chores as we passed by we would stop and talk for a few minutes. Waugh had crazy nicknames for all of us, and he loved to tease us. Paul, a Frenchman, seldom said anything, and if he did, his English was so mangled he might as well have been speaking Chinese as far as we were concerned.

Imagine our surprise when we returned home from school one evening the fall of 1930 to find that Paul had moved into our bunkhouse, bedroll, suitcases and all. With winter coming on, Waugh no longer had work for him and had let him go. Dad felt sorry for him, so he told Paul he could stay in our bunkhouse for the winter and work for his room and board. He was the most totally inept person I ever knew. He could harness a team and drive it, but only barely. Dad, realizing this, felt he couldn't kick him out into the worsening economic situation to fend for himself, so when spring came, he had Paul help put in the garden and begin taking care of it.

Paul ended up spending the rest of his life with the Browns. He became as much a part of the family as if he'd been born into it, sharing our trials and tribulations, the good times and the bad. As closely as we lived with him, I'm surprised we learned so little about his life prior to the time we knew him. He was a small, wiry man with graying hair when he began living with us. It never occurred to me to wonder what his age was at any given time; he always seemed old to me. How or when he came to the United States I never knew. He was proud of being a citizen, though I have no idea when he got his naturalization papers. He filed on a homestead on Meadow Creek, but I'm not sure whether he ever proved up on it.

When he first arrived in the Powder River country he went to work as chore boy at the H. W. "Hard Winter" Davis ranch, carrying in wood and coal for the stoves, buckets of water for the cook, emptying slop pails from the kitchen and chamber pots from the bedrooms. He tended the garden and the chickens, milked the cows, and served as chaperone for the Davis girls as they were growing up. When the Davis ranch was sold to the American Cattle Co., Paul stayed on for a while working for the manager, Cy Blair. When that job ended he went to work for the youngest of the Davis girls, Madge, and her husband, Waugh Murphy.

One thing we did learn was that Paul had served in the French Foreign Legion as a young man. Apparently he was released from service after suffering a bayonet wound in his side, fighting in "Mad-i-gas-CARR." On several occasions he showed his scar to Marsh and Fred, but I never got to see it. The wound was between his rib cage and hip bone, and it would have been most indecent for him to have bared his body to the belt so I could look at it! How I yearned to be able to see it! Once I asked Marsh to describe it to me. "What does it look like?" I asked avidly.

"A scar," was his enlightening reply.

Paul shaved every Sunday morning, a ritual we kids usually witnessed. I was not allowed in the bunk house (it was not lady-like), but no one said I couldn't stand in the door and look inside, so I did.

As soon as Paul returned to the bunk house from breakfast he began heating water, a tea kettle full and a wash basin half-full. While the water heated he began his preparations. First he removed his shirt. His torso was covered by "longhandled" underwear buttoned clear to his Adam's apple, so he was decent. The next step was to get out the razor strop and hone his straight razor, which he did with great flair and precision, as if he really knew what he was doing. Either he didn't, or he had an exceptionally tough beard because no matter how long he took or how sharp the razor appeared to be, he no sooner began to shave than he nicked himself. He always laid a cigarette paper close to hand before he began to shave. As each new nick appeared, he tore off a small piece of paper and stuck it on the cut to stop the bleeding. By the time he finished shaving, his face was bristling with little pieces of paper glued on with blood. He never removed them; they just stuck until they dropped off and fluttered away.

When safety razors began to replace straight razors we thought we would eliminate the blood-letting by getting him an Enders Safety razor and a package of blades for Christmas. The blades were single-edged with a heavy piece of metal along one side. Instead of buying new blades when those became dull, he used that original set of blades over and over again for years, faithfully stropping them every Sunday morning. The nicks continued.

We all got along well with Paul, though Fred and I used to argue with him a great deal. I realize now he deliberately incited many of the arguments just to make us think.

"You're wrong," we'd tell him.

"I am-a right. Look in the en-CEE-coplia," he'd reply.

We'd look up the subject in the encyclopedia and triumphantly prove him wrong.

"The enceecoplia is wrong," he'd say smugly and go on about his business, leaving us fuming.

About the only time Paul didn't have a Bull Durham cigarette hanging from the corner of his mouth was when he was eating or sleeping. He didn't actually smoke as much as it seemed because he rolled a cigarette just like he did everything else: inexpertly. Each cigarette had to be relit countless times before he got it down to a stub and started rolling another.

*   *   *

I'm sure if anyone had asked him, Paul would have said April 5, 1933 was the worst day of his life; worse, even, than the day he was run through by the bayonet. That was the day the last of us kids, Julie, was born. I was twelve years old at the time and had learned while I was at school that Mom was expecting yet another baby, though no one had ever mentioned it at home.

Dad made arrangements ahead of time to use Murphy's Model A Ford pickup to take her to town when the time came. It came, as I recall, shortly before noon. Dad hot-footed it to Murphys' for the Ford.

At that time, there was a working phone system among the ranches on Powder River. We were beginning to wonder what was taking Dad so long when the phone rang. It was Madge. She reported that they were having trouble getting the pickup started. Time passed and about every half hour, Madge would call with a nonprogress report. Mom retired to the bedroom to lie down and keep as still as possible. The situation became pretty tense as evening approached. Poor Paul spent the entire

time walking, first to the big window in the living room, which looked
north to the Murphys', back through the dining room and kitchen to
peer anxiously into the bedroom at Mom's still form, then back to the
living room again.

At suppertime, Mom instructed me how to fix something for the
family to eat. I can't remember about the rest of them, but I know Paul
and I didn't eat a thing. Paul had a habit of humming tunelessly to
himself no matter what he was doing, but by this time, he was so
distracted he was silent. Finally, long after dark, the phone rang and
Madge announced triumphantly that the pickup was running and that
she and Dad were on their way. We all rushed to the front room
windows and gave a concerted sigh of relief to see headlights
approaching. Quickly, we got Mom and her suitcase out to the pickup
and they chugged away into the night.

Aunt Della Eldridge lived just outside of Kaycee on the Sussex Road.
By the time they reached there, it was obvious that Mom could go no
farther. Dad left her and Madge with Aunt Della and hurried on into
Kaycee to get Cena Gibbs, who was a registered nurse and a midwife.
When they got back to Eldridges, Aunt Della and Madge had already
delivered Julie.

*   *   *

By the time we had lived around Paul for a few months, his garbled
English was as understandable to us as our own speech. When he
learned the Browns were getting ready to move to Washington in
February 1942, he walked the short distance from the Happy Jack Miller
Ranch, where he was working at the time, up to the schoolhouse. He
rapped on the door and asked to see Ruthie. They stood just inside the
schoolroom door to talk, and Ruthie confirmed that, yes, they were
leaving in a few days. Paul said to tell the family he was going with
them, and he left to collect his pay and clothes.

When school broke for recess, Ruthie was promptly surrounded by
impressed classmates.

"Gosh," said one girl in admiration. "We didn't know you could
speak French!"

"Oh, yes," Ruthie replied with cool aplomb, and never told anyone
differently.

Paul worked diligently for Uncle Sam in the shipyard in Seattle
during World War II as a scaler. The scalers ran push brooms and mops,
carried material for carpenters, welders, and riveters. He was good at it
because it was not much different than being a chore boy; he was
waiting on people and cleaning up after them.

Paul never mentioned any family, and the few times anyone asked, he said, "I have no family."

When he was an old man, living in California with Marsh, I finally heard from his older brother in Basses Pyrenees, France. I'm not sure how he traced Paul to me after so many years, because his first letters were in French. A lady in Kaycee, who came from French ancestry, could "sort of" read French, and she did her best to interpret for me, but I'm sure we had a less than accurate account of what he wrote, so I'm pretty sketchy about those first communications. Later, he had a grand-niece write his letters in broken English and read my answers to him. He wanted desperately to contact Paul, saying there had been a bad misunderstanding when they were young, but all was forgiven. When I forwarded this information on to him, Paul stoutly maintained he had no brother. There the matter rested until they both died in the same year, about 1950.

I remember clearly the day my older brother, Marshall, started school, but for some reason, I have no recollection at all of my own first school day. Mom said I returned home that afternoon crying bitterly because they hadn't taught me to read! Four months later, the schoolhouse burned to the ground one weekend. The other kids rejoiced at the unexpected holiday, but I worried that I might never have a chance to learn to read.

School was resumed in the three-room teacherage, where the teachers normally lived, as soon as supplies and equipment could be gathered, with the teachers setting up housekeeping in a vacant building at Sussex. As soon as weather permitted in the spring, a man from Midwest named Bates was awarded the contract to build the new school, and construction began at once. The new building was ready for occupancy by the time the fall term opened.

By country school standards, the completed building was quite large and modern. There was a cloakroom across the south end, with a doorway opening to the basement stairs. Five large windows ranged along the west side of the school room, all with honest-to-goodness window shades to pull down when the afternoon sun shone in.

Those window shades were one of the fringe benefits of the school. Some child would raise a hand to ask the teacher for permission to pull a shade down when the afternoon sun was shining in. What fun it was to get the shade almost to the bottom of the window, then "accidentally" let it go up with a zip and a crash that made everyone in the room jump!

The basement housed a furnace to supply heat to the upper building, and an adjoining coal bin was filled every fall with coal from one of the mines in the nearby Pine Ridge. That furnace didn't work any better than the one in the Hall House, and the interior of the school was never more than a few degrees warmer than the outside temperature when winter came.

The cloakroom had a row of coat hooks along the south wall, with a long bench underneath where one sat to remove or don one's overshoes. Our lunch pails and overshoes were placed under the bench directly beneath the coat hook assigned to that person. In very cold weather, the sandwiches and apples in our lunches were frozen solid by noon, and when it was time to go home, the overshoes were all frozen to the floor.

There was no playground equipment, but we played running games at recess and noon whenever the weather allowed. As soon as we had snow, we marked out a fox and goose ring. The ring became worn into the ground so deeply that even after the snow was gone in the spring we continued to play until school was out for the summer.

The school played an important role in community life. Every June, the annual school meeting was held in the schoolhouse. Patrons of the school district aired grievances, the mill levy was voted on, and new board members were nominated and voted in.

Sometimes a Halloween or Thanksgiving program would be put on by the school, but the really important event of the school year was the Christmas program. There was almost always a three-act play that required a lot of ingenuity on the part of teachers and mothers alike to come up with costumes. Recitations were delivered, skits acted out, and frightened preschoolers got up to race breathlessly through the little verses they'd learned or have their minds wiped clear by stage fright and exit in humiliated tears.

All of the old traditional carols were sung by the whole school, with an occasional solo or duet by the better singers. Usually, the audience joined in the singing at the end of the program while we awaited Santa's arrival. Meanwhile, some poor, reluctant father was backstage being padded with pillows and suited up to make his grand entrance with a less than hearty "ho, ho, ho," clutching nervously at the ratty cotton beard that constantly threatened to fall off. As the jolly old saint doled out Christmas goodies in cheese cloth bags sewed by the mothers and bought with donations from parents, the older kids speculated on who Santa was. One year, as a very noticeably knock-kneed Santa walked out on the stage, his eight-year-old son proclaimed in a loud voice from the front row, "That's my dad!"

When the school wanted something that was not covered by school funds, we raised the money ourselves. When I was in the sixth grade, we kids decided the school needed a phonograph. Our teacher found a secondhand one for sale for seven dollars, so we older kids, with her permission and guidance, gave a dance and pie social at the school on Halloween to raise the money.

Our local orchestra consisted of Smoky Brosius's wife, Merle, at piano, and Frank Heltzel, who played a hammered dulcimer, the only one I ever saw. Since they donated their services for our dance, the only expense we had was for a wash boiler full of coffee to be served with the pie.

For days before the dance, the older girls discussed what kind of pies they'd bring. Each of the women and older girls brought a pie—luscious creations like coconut custard, banana cream, pecan, and so on. There was never any doubt in my mind about the kind of pie I would take. My Mom's sour cream raisin pie, as far as I was concerned, was the absolute ultimate in pies, and though I was rankled by the reaction from the other kids ("Sour cream?! Yuck!"), I was not swayed from my decision.

At midnight, the pies were auctioned off with the men and older boys bidding on them, each pie going to the one who was high bidder. He and the pie's maker were paired for the pie supper. The identity of the pie's maker was not revealed until after the pie was sold. On this particular night, I ended up partnered with a middle-aged, one-armed man who had herded Dad's sheep at one time. What a terrible disappointment! I was hoping one of the older boys would share my pie!

Following the pie eating, the dance resumed and all of the kids gathered outside to share what was left of our pies. My supper partner had eaten only one small piece of my pie, so I had most of it left. It vanished rapidly after it was sampled cautiously by the skeptics. The next day, a neighbor boy arrived at our house, announcing he had not come to play; he wanted a copy of the sour cream raisin pie recipe so his sister could make him one!

At any rate, we raised enough money to buy our phonograph. What a beautiful thing it was, with its graceful legs, the gleaming, reddish-brown wooden cabinet where the records were stored, and at the top, the machine itself. The inside of the domed wooden lid proclaimed it to be a genuine Victor Victrola. There was the picture of the dog with his ear cocked, listening to an old-fashioned gramophone and the words, "His Master's Voice." The turntable was covered with green felt, and there was a little receptacle for the extra needles. The silver handle for winding the mechanism was inserted through a small opening in the side and could be removed and stored in the top by the turntable in a little clip.

There were several stirring marches in the records our teacher had chosen. We did calisthenics to these to get our blood circulating when the interior of the schoolhouse was so frigid we could see our breath. We did penmanship exercises to "Under the Double Eagle," "The Washington Post March," and "The Stars and Stripes Forever."

With the acquisition of the Victrola, our teacher, Gladys Westover, joined the Record of the Week club, and every week we had a new record to listen to. The records were made of thin cardboard coated with celluloid and were only about half the size of the regular 78 rpm records the Victrola played, about six inches in diameter. The only title I can remember was "Love Letters in the Sand," a much earlier version than the one Pat Boone popularized.

With our limited means of transportation, trips to anywhere except the neighbors were out of the question. By the time I was a teenager I could count on the fingers of one hand the times I'd been to Buffalo, our county seat seventy miles away. Kaycee, where we did our trading, was seventeen miles back up Powder River from the Hall Ranch, and even the times I got to make the trip there were so few they stand out in my memory as great events!

The homes were the center of rural life, and people created their own entertainment. Neighbors visited neighbors, shared meals, and spent evenings playing cards or just talking. The women discussed homemaking and all the related subjects: babies, children, cooking, and sewing. The men shared farming and ranching problems, asked advice or offered it, and told of the experiences from their past. My dad was a gifted storyteller, and I would always try to blend unobtrusively into his group so I could listen to his yarns. They were much more exciting than listening to a discussion of what to do for diaper rash and colic or a new way to prepare sweet corn for canning!

Even though I heard his stories countless times over the years, I never tired of hearing Dad tell about the life he'd led, the places he'd been, the people and animals he'd encountered in his travels. Dad told his stories without fancy words, but he wove drama and humor into them, filling his listeners with anticipation or hilarious laughter.

The aroma of burning leaves brings memories of the huge bonfires we kids had every fall. If the weather was cooperative, we celebrated Halloween by burning big piles of leaves in the middle of the garden and roasting apples in the fire. An apple roasted in a leaf bonfire had a flavor unlike any other! Juice oozed through cracks in the blackened skin, which we peeled off to get at the meat, which was steaming hot and smoky flavored.

Reading was the main form of entertainment on long winter evenings or rainy, house-bound days. One of the great accomplishments of my life was learning to read; having something to read was one of the greatest blessings. My parents both loved to read and instilled that enjoyment in all six kids at an early age by reading aloud to us. We had a bookcase full of books by Zane Grey, Gene Stratton Porter, Peter B. Kyne, and Grace Livingston Hill, to name a few. They were all dear friends to me, and I read my favorites at least once a year and never grew tired of them. Thanks to my Aunt Ella in Wisconsin, we also had subscriptions to several of the popular magazines of the day.

We had no access to a church, so I grew up without any formal religious training. I suppose there must have been a church in Kaycee, but it may as well have been a thousand miles away for all the good it did us. My mom was considered by the neighborhood kids to be religious, the implication being that she bordered on fanaticism because she didn't drink, smoke, or swear, believed implicitly in the Golden Rule, was truly an honest person, and read the Bible, this latter setting her apart as nothing else did. Mom had attended church before she moved to Wyoming, and it worried her that we were growing up like a bunch of heathens. She often read to us from the big book of *Children's Bible Stories* my aunt sent us. I loved that book because of its vivid illustrations. My favorites were Moses being rescued from the bulrushes and Absalom hanging from the oak tree by his hair with a very pained expression on his face!

The only exposure to formal religion I had was through the Jepsons. They were Catholic and twice a year, Father Brady came down from Buffalo and spent several days at the Jepson home ministering to all the Catholics in the community. I was invited to attend one of these sessions, and even though I was only an observer, I was immediately caught up in the whole thing. I left, armed with a copy of the catechism and fired with religious zeal, which probably lasted for at least fifteen minutes after I got home!

Prayer has always been an important part of my life, though I have no recollection of where or when I learned to pray. I only prayed when I thought I needed help from the Lord, such as asking Him to keep the latest litter of barn kittens hidden so Dad wouldn't drown them. These prayers were almost never answered, but I was never discouraged or disillusioned because deep down, I realized we could not have an uncontrolled population of cats.

When our friend and neighbor, Grandma Stockham's son Hugh, lay in the hospital dying of stomach cancer, I prayed for his recovery with childish confidence that God would answer my plea. Hugh was a big, friendly man, and all of us kids looked forward to his visits, which were fairly often, as he used Dad's shop when he needed to work on his truck.

When the local folks were still living in the horse and wagon era, Hugh was already looking ahead to the motorized age. As soon as a vehicle was developed that he could modify to haul freight, he bought it. Before long, he had completely replaced the big, heavy freight wagons drawn by four or six horse teams that hauled all the supplies to the Sussex store. If conditions were good, the wagons made the round-trip to Buffalo and back in five days: two days in, empty, and three days back, loaded. Hugh could make the trip in two, in one day and back the next, depending on road conditions.

Mechanical difficulties could add considerably to the road time. The story was often told of the time the truck quit Hugh at night, miles from anywhere, and all his tinkering and threatening were to no avail. At last, he gave up and began the long walk to civilization. A short distance down the road, he turned for one last look at the defunct truck. Its headlights reflected the bright moonlight like two eyes. Retracing his steps, Hugh picked up a monkey wrench he'd left lying on the running board, walked to the front of the truck, and smashed both headlights.

"You may leave me afoot," he told the truck, "but you're not gonna sit there and watch me walk away."

Hugh used to cut Dad's and Marsh's hair if he happened by and they were in need of a barber. According to Mom, his haircuts were jut one step above a "bowl cut," but he was available and his services were free.

One forenoon, he finished cutting Dad's hair and Dad went on about his work. Hugh was about half through cutting Marsh's hair when Mom stepped into the bedroom where he did his barbering and announced that dinner would be ready as soon as he finished with Marsh.

A lot more time elapsed than she expected, and just as she was about to go see what was taking so long, Marsh sauntered into the kitchen and informed her Hugh would be there "just as soon as he finishes cutting Weezie's hair." Mom dashed to the bedroom, but she was too late. I'd already been shorn. I don't recall the hair-cutting episode at all, but Mom had no trouble remembering it! Her blond-headed girl looked like a little boy. When she asked Hugh why he did it, he said I had watched with great interest while he was trimming Marsh's hair. He asked me if I'd like to have my hair cut, and I had said yes, so he obliged!

Hugh's death shattered me. It was my first experience with the death of someone close, and it caused me to lose faith in the power of prayer for a number of years. "How could God let a good man like Hugh die?" I asked myself. The only answer seemed to be that He didn't hear prayers from little people like me. After that, I didn't waste my time wasting God's time with pleas for this, that, or the other thing.

Then a girl named Rosie Gratz came into my life. She had been raised in a German community in Wisconsin and couldn't speak or write

English. When her parents died, she came to live with her sister, Ellis Olheiser. Ellis, her husband, Amos, and their numerous kids were neighbors of ours.

Poor Rosie! That first day at our school must have been a traumatic experience for her. I can remember all of us kids clustered around staring at her as the teacher introduced us and explained who Rosie was and why she was there. Even though it was a mystery to us that she couldn't speak English, we agreed to help her all we could. She was friendly and outgoing, and we all liked her. In no time at all, it seemed, she learned to read and speak English and she spoke with very little accent. She and I became very good friends, even though she was older.

The first time she came to stay all night with me, I was surprised when she knelt by the bed and said a prayer before crawling in beside me. She was just as surprised that I had not prayed. Snuggled down in the warm blankets in the dark, we discussed the subject at some length. I told her why I didn't pray. She explained that God does not answer all prayers and sometimes the answer comes in a much different way than we expect. Her simple sincerity renewed my faith. I began to pray again when I was troubled or something seemed worthy of prayer. Prayer has continued to be an essential part of my life, comforting me in the bad times and bringing me blessings at all times.

Threshing, to me, was the most exciting thing that happened on the ranch all year. There was such a fever of activity, with all the men of the surrounding area coming with their teams and hay racks to haul bundles, several of the neighborhood women coming in to help Mom cook and serve the mountains of food required to feed a threshing crew, and best of all, Frank Heltzel coming with the threshing machine, or separator, as it was also called. The threshing machine was moved and powered with a big gasoline engine, and we could usually hear the rumble of it long before we could see it. He parked it wherever Dad wanted the straw piled, and that's where the threshing took place.

I can't remember threshing ever taking place on a weekend, so we could have all day to be involved in the fun, but we were allowed to go to the field and watch after we got home from school and changed our clothes. I didn't appreciate until years later how much labor was involved in what always seemed to me to be a holiday! I must have gained this impression from the continual round of good-natured joshing and heckling that went on among the men at mealtime. If there were any frictions, I was unaware of them.

There were several bundle wagons. As a wagon drove through the field, the two men with it threw the bundles of shocked grain onto it with pitchforks. Frank always waited until there were at least two wagons of bundles ready to unload before he fired up the engine and started the separator, because the separator would throw its belts if it had to run empty for very long. The men made sure there was always a loaded wagon ready to drive into position beside the machine as soon as one was unloaded.

A long spout on one side of the separator spewed out straw, forming a golden mountain that would be a playground for us later in the fall. If hogs were turned loose in the fields, they burrowed into the base of the stack, making dens where they could get out of the wind and snow, and later on, have their babies. In addition to wheat and oats, Dad raised bearded barley. The straw from it was guaranteed to give you a bad case of the prickles because the barbed beards were all through it and would work their way into clothing where they were almost impossible to remove.

The grain wagons were plain box wagons with strips of flattened-out tin cans nailed over any holes or cracks to keep the grain from leaking out. An empty wagon was driven under the grain spout on the separator as quickly as a full one pulled out for the granary. At the granary, the grain was emptied by hand with scoop shovels into a window high up on the side of the building.

Meanwhile, the women had been working since early morning, baking and cooking for all the hungry men. And oh, the food! Huge quantities of it, and all of it Sunday-dinner quality: baked hams, chicken and noodles, mashed potatoes and gravy, baked beans, vegetables and salads, pies and cakes. The women and kids always ate last, after the men, usually two big tables full, had been fed and were on their way back to the field. We kids always missed the bounteous meal at noon, and I always worried that everything would be eaten and we wouldn't get the leftovers for supper, but I don't remember ever going hungry!

As a rule, the noon meal, dinner, was the only one the crews ate where they were working, but if they could finish a job by working past quitting time, the rancher's wife was expected to feed the men supper before they left for home.

One threshing day when Rosie had come home from school with us to spend the night, Dad sent us back to the house to tell Mom she would have at least part of the crew for supper because they wanted to finish. All but one of the women had gone home after the dinner dishwashing was done, so Rosie and I got pressed into service helping with the meal. About half the men went home to tend livestock before dark. We fed the rest leftovers from dinner, and that was once we kids got only small samples of the food and not even a taste of some things.

By the time I graduated from the eighth grade in May 1935, the Depression had worsened instead of improving, and things were really bad. We knew of several families who were living on relief, as welfare was called then.

A few years after the new school was built, a small, frame two-room house was moved onto the school grounds to provide housing for transients or people with school-age children who were too isolated to have access to the school. One of the relief families, a young couple with three small children, the oldest six and the youngest only a few months old, had moved into the Transient House, as it was called. The man worked wherever and whenever he could find a job during the summer.

There was no way I could go to high school in Buffalo when the fall term started, so I was at loose ends. I felt really adrift and began riding my old horse, Snip, over to the school and visiting this young mother. One day I arrived to find her crying as she nursed the baby. She told me she didn't have enough milk for him, and he was hungry all the time. They didn't have any money to buy canned milk to supplement hers, she explained tearfully.

We always milked no fewer than three cows, so milk was a plentiful commodity at our house. Snip and I headed home at a lope and I explained the situation to Mom. When I returned to the school, I carried not only a gallon lard pail full of milk liberally laced with cream, I had a gunny sack tied on my saddle containing fresh-dug potatoes, a cabbage, carrots, turnips, and onions.

Suddenly my aimless life seemed to have a purpose. For several weeks I continued to deliver not only milk and vegetables to the grateful young mother, I also took her eggs, an occasional loaf of Mom's home-baked bread, plus a big lump of fresh-churned butter now and then.

Then the father found a winter's job working in one of the Pine Ridge coal mines and he moved his family to a vacant building at Sussex so he would be closer to his work. I missed feeling like Lady Bountiful, the Good Samaritan, and Santa Claus all rolled into one, and I missed the visits with my new friend. At the same time, though, I felt a sense of relief that I no longer had to make that ride two or three times a week because winter was definitely approaching.

The winter of 1935–36 turned out to be one of the coldest ever for our area. In January 1936 the temperature plummeted to record lows and stayed there, until it seemed it would never be warm again. According to a diary I kept, we had two mornings when it was fifty below zero and for two weeks the night-time temperatures hung around minus forty, with very little warming during the daytime.

On one of those bitter-cold mornings, Dad and Paul hitched up Sam, a big, iron-gray gelding, and Ruby, a snow-white mare, and went to the field after a load of hay for the horses and cattle. The hayrack was usually backed into the stackyard until the first row of stacks had been used, clearing an avenue to drive in one end and out the other.

That morning, Dad was backing the rack into position to begin loading when Ruby fell against the stack alongside, then collapsed to the ground. For an instant, Dad thought she had slipped and fallen, but she didn't try to get up.

Paul, who had opened the gate and walked into the stackyard, got to her first.

"She's dead!" he exclaimed in a stricken voice as Dad jumped to the ground and ran around to her.

Dad walked back to the barn and harnessed a horse from another team and led him back to the stackyard. They hooked onto Ruby with a chain and dragged her out of the enclosure. Dad and Paul speculated that she'd had a heart attack, but later, someone told them she'd probably frostbitten her lungs in the extreme cold.

When they finally arrived back at the house and told us what had happened, it was such a shock I could hardly believe it. Beautiful Ruby, dead! She was gentle as a kitten and I thought she was the prettiest horse I'd ever seen when Dad bought her. In a way, I guess her death was an omen of things to come.

*The Hall Ranch buildings where I lived the first 14 1/2 years of my life. The garage at the left, the tank house with the windmill behind it, the bunkhouse in the foreground and the two-story ranch house. The outhouse is at the far right.*

*Dan and Helen Brown on their honeymoon at Cooper's sheep camp, 1917.*

*Mom and Grandma Stockham with Hall house in the background, 1922.*

*At the Charlie Hall Ranch, Sussex, 1922. From left to right: Grandma Stockham, Dan Brown, "Cap" Jones, Hugh Stockham.*

*Baby Louise, 1922*

*Louise, 1924. This shows the boy-haircut Hugh Stockham gave her.*

*Louise and Marsh, 1928. The parasol Louise is holding was sent to her from China by her great uncle Ed Skinner, who, along with his wife, was a missionary there for many years.*

# Homesteaders

# (1936-1938)

"Weezie! Wake up! Time to get up!" Mom shook me gently. I came awake reluctantly, my brain foggy with sleep. I opened my bleary eyes a crack and became aware of a lighted kerosene lamp sitting on the dresser.

"Why are we getting up in the dark?" I asked in confusion.

"Today is the day we're moving, and we need to get an early start," Mom told me. "Would you get the little kids up while I fix breakfast?"

Then I remembered: Today was the Big Adventure! We were moving to the homestead! Never mind that it was only nine miles from where I'd lived all my life. We were going pioneering! I had been so excited when I went to bed the night before I was sure I'd never sleep a wink. Now, here it was morning and I'd slept the night away after all.

The little kids were sleepy and resentful of being rousted out of their warm beds in the early morning darkness. I got very little cooperation from them as I got them dressed, but at last the job was finished.

Dad had filed on a homestead on Four-Mile Creek before he met and married Mom, but he later relinquished that filing and refiled on land on the north side of the Pine Ridge, an extremely rough range of low, mountainous hills south of Powder River. He renewed this filing several times over the years, as provided by the Homestead Act, but by 1936 he either had to prove up on it or let it revert back to the government.

Our departure date was March 15, when the lease ran out on the Hall place. Mom and I began packing in February. What a nearly impossible undertaking that must have been for my mother! How do you pack the accumulation of nineteen years of marriage, the contents of a ten-room house, the belongings of six kids and two adults with an eye to moving into a twelve-by-eighteen-foot one-room cabin? She did it somehow.

Now, at last, the day had arrived! As soon as everyone had eaten breakfast, the men began loading our box wagon and the farm truck Dad had borrowed from Cy Blair. Mom and I washed the dishes, stripped the beds and packed the last minute things that could not be packed the night before.

During the weeks we had been packing, the move had never been a real thing to me. How could I imagine living somewhere else when I had never lived anywhere else in my fourteen and a half years of life? While the rumpled bedding still covered the beds and a few pieces of clothing were strewn about, it still looked like home. Now, finally, the naked beds brought it home to me. Not one scrap of paper or stray, dirty sock remained in the usually cluttered, untidy room I had always claimed as mine. The clean, empty rooms were so alien a lump choked my throat and tears stung my eyes. I fled from the house that had been the center of my world.

We hadn't wanted to leave the Hall Ranch, but suddenly we were victims of the Depression, like millions of other people. I'd heard the grown-ups talking about the Depression for as long as I could remember, and though I wasn't sure what it was, I knew it was something bad. I figured we were safe from it, living out in the country because mostly it seemed to affect banks, businesses, and people living in cities. Then things began to happen that made me realize we hadn't escaped from it, either.

The years of 1933 and 1934 were terrible drought years for the Midwest and Rocky Mountain states. Dust blew into Wyoming from neighboring states and mingled with our own, depositing a fine layer of the stuff over everything. I can remember walking home from school in the afternoons when the air was so filled with dust the sun looked like a big, orange-red ball in the western sky. I hated the way things looked—no blue sky or clouds, just that pall of dirty air hanging over us. No rain fell to clear the air or water the parched earth, and always the wind blew.

I didn't realize until years later that sheep and cattle were dying of starvation. A lot of the livestock was in such poor condition they could not be shipped, and even if they could, there was no market for them. To the already faltering livestock industry, this was a staggering blow. It was, in fact, the beginning of the end for a lot of small ranching operations, including my dad's.

To keep ranchers from dumping their livestock on an already glutted market, the government set up slaughter programs and paid stockmen a token price, about fourteen dollars a head for cattle and two dollars each for sheep. Even though sheep and cattle were not yet starving in our area, ranchers took part in the program just to realize a little something for their older animals. It meant they would not have to winter them and could put what feed was available into their younger stock.

According to John Rolfe Burroughs in his book, *Guardian of the Grasslands*, in the fall of 1934 a government-operated cannery at Sheridan, Wyoming, employing 172 men and 64 women began processing the salvageable meat, which was then distributed to needy people through the Relief Program. A government-sponsored tannery opened in Casper, Wyoming, the following spring to take care of the accumulation of 11,517 beef hides, 340,644 sheep pelts, and 595 goat skins. The leather from this project was turned into 90,000 pairs of half-soles, 1,250 sets of harness, plus gloves, saddles, belts, etc., all manufactured in government work projects. A lot of the sheep pelts were turned into the "bomber jackets" worn by fliers during World War II.

The only way ranchers could get their livestock to market in isolated areas such as ours was to trail them. The government did not consider this feasible, apparently, so cattle were killed right at each ranch and left for the rancher to dispose of, while slaughter sites were set up at various locations for sheep. In our area, the sheep were killed at a site on the Meike Ranch, a short distance from Powder River.

I remember very well the day in September 1934 that my dad took all of our old ewes to be slaughtered under one of the government programs. I went to school that day sickened by that knowledge.

For some reason I have never understood, the mutton at the kill site on the Meike Ranch was condemned for human consumption. However the two government men who were overseeing the slaughter and skinning saved the hind quarters from all the ewes that were in good condition and hung them in two big cottonwood trees growing on the bank of the draw where the carcasses were being dumped. When the government men left that night, they said whatever happened to the meat hanging in the trees was none of their concern, so everyone, including Dad, helped themselves.

Dad returned home that night in high spirits. Besides the monetary gain of two dollars a head, he had fresh meat and he was greatly impressed by the efficient way the slaughter had been handled. The sheep were killed by hitting them in the head with a small sledge hammer. An air compressor forced air between the skin and carcass through a needle inserted into the "arm pit." This separated the skin from the body so all the skinning crew had to do was cut around the neck and legs, split the hide down the belly, and lift it right off.

I was totally unimpressed; all I could think of was those poor, innocent ewes receiving a skull-crushing blow and dropping dead. I was filled with horror that anyone could wantonly slaughter all those sheep.

I realize now that it was probably more humane than letting them starve.

Even those measures did not save our herd. In the fall of 1935, Dad had to sell the sheep to pay the overdue lease on the ranch. We now had no way to make a living because the Hall place was too small to support itself without livestock to utilize the hay and grain. Dad decided to move to the homestead. We could live rent-free and perhaps he could find a ranch job or pick up some Work Progress Administration work.

Paul faithfully came with us, so three adults, six kids, and an assortment of cats, dogs, chickens, one canary, cattle, and horses made the move.

The Hall house had been completely furnished when the Brown family moved in, so we had very little in the way of furniture. The few things we had acquired made up the first load on the truck, including a black walnut bed and dresser and a bookcase, all beautifully hand-made by my Grandfather George Skinner, who had died when Mom was twelve years old.

All the things we would need immediately after we arrived at the cabin were loaded in the wagon: bedding, dishes, cooking utensils, food, and Dad's big Majestic range that had been used to heat the bunk house all the years after he and Mom moved into the big house.

Dad, Mom, and the little kids left in the truck, following our access road out through the Murphy Ranch to the county road. Marsh and Paul drove the team and wagon down across the field, taking a shortcut that brought them out on the county road several miles closer to their destination.

Fred and I had always played at being cowboys, so we were given the job of trailing our eighteen cows and a Durham bull to their new home. As we led our saddled horses out of the barn I had a few moments of near panic when I realized everyone but us had already left for the homestead, but I was soon too busy to worry about it. Neither of us had ever had any experience moving cattle on horseback, and we discovered that driving the cows away from familiar territory was a lot different than walking two or three old, gentle cows to the barn at milking time.

Another complication developed immediately. Dad had raised the bull from a calf and one of our horses, Shorty, had tormented him from the time he was born. As the calf grew, he learned to fight back and by the time he was a yearling, the contests were pretty one-sided. He developed a technique of getting his head between Shorty's front legs, and with a push and a shove, neatly upending the horse. Shorty had quickly learned to put distance between himself and the bull when the game began. As soon as we tried to drive the bull, he turned on our horses. All we could do was leave him behind.

We followed the same route the wagon had taken out to the county road, which was fenced on both sides, so we had a lane to follow as far as the long, narrow suspension bridge on Powder River. The Sussex store, post office, and gas pumps sat on the east side of the road, the dance hall on the west, not far from the north approach to the bridge. Our progress with the cows so far had been slow due to their reluctance to leave home, but when they reached the bridge they decided unanimously that they were not going to set foot on this unfamiliar contraption. We would have saved a lot of time and trouble if we'd simply forded the river with them, but we never even considered this alternative after all the stories we'd heard about sheep, cattle, and even horses trapped in the quicksand of Powder River and doomed to a slow death in the treacherous stuff.

We set about the business of changing their minds, and in the next several minutes I reached several conclusions about cows, none of them very complimentary. Though I had lived around them all my life, my association had been superficial at best. I often brought them in for milking at night, and once in a great while, even milked one of them. They furnished us milk to drink, cream to pour on our oatmeal, and butter to spread on bread. Until today they went about their business and I went about mine. The term "bull-headed" must have been coined to describe a balky cow, I decided, as they milled and circled, wild-eyed and hostile. Occasionally one or more would break away and gallop back up the road or circle the dance hall, tails in the air and cobwebs of slobber streaming from their mouths. We might never have accomplished our task if two men had not come from the store on foot and helped us crowd them onto the bridge. By the time they went clattering across, Fred and I were hoarse from yelling, and our horses were dripping sweat.

The county road swung in an easterly direction once it left Powder River and began the climb toward the Five Mile Divide. Three miles from Sussex a road branched off to the south to the Lohse homestead a quarter of a mile away. From Lohse's on to our homestead there was just a dim wagon road that ended a few hundred yards from our cabin at East Carpenter Draw.

A few days before our move a neighbor with a vehicle had taken Dad, Fred, and me out to the Lohse turnoff and Dad had pointed out a landmark in the profile of the Pine Ridge, telling us the cabin was just north of it. Now I was becoming uneasy. It seemed as if we'd covered a lot of miles since we'd crossed Powder River and still had not come to our turnoff. Just as I was convinced we were lost we came over a hill and there was the Lohse cabin nestled in the big cottonwoods that bordered East Carpenter Draw at that point.

We saw we could cut off considerable distance once we crossed Carpenter by heading straight for our landmark on the ridge instead of following the wagon road. Our herd had walked along in a pretty decent fashion after our battle with them at the bridge, but now they were tired and wanted to graze. Our progress slowed to a crawl. As we poked and prodded, trying to move them, we watched the truck make its way down the road to the west of us trailing a plume of dust as Dad headed for the ranch after another load of our belongings.

At the ranch I rode almost every day, but whenever I got tired I could just unsaddle my horse and do something else. Today, for the first time in my life I was committed to a job that I had to finish no matter how tired I was. And I was tired! And famished to the point of faintness! As my hunger and thirst grew, so did my irritation at those no-give-a-darn cows who paid little attention to our efforts to move them. I finally got off Snip, my horse, and walked to loosen up my cramped leg muscles. This also enabled me to whack the cows across the rumps with the ends of my reins and hopefully, move them three or four more steps. Then, in a fit of exasperation, I ran up and kicked one of them in the hind leg. She continued to graze while I sat nursing a toe I was sure was broken. It soon became so painful I was forced to ride again.

I was beginning to imagine myself growing delirious from lack of food and water when we topped a brushy hill, and there was the cabin a short distance away. This was the first time I'd seen it, and I must admit I was a little surprised at how small it was. But it was a welcome sight regardless.

For the first time since we'd left the county road the cows showed an interest in something besides eating. They all stopped, heads up, noses testing the air, and stared at the cabin. Then, as if at a signal, they marched forward. Actually, the cabin was not the focus of their interest, it was the smell of water that had caught their attention. Past the house they trotted, to the reservoir beyond. They crowded and jostled for position as they sucked up the water in long, noisy drafts. Satisfied at last, they bedded down with a cracking of joints and much groaning and sighing and began contentedly chewing their cuds.

We let our horses drink their fill, then rode back up to the cabin to be greeted by the little kids with such genuine pleasure that we felt quite the heroes! We picketed our horses on the scanty grass and entered the crowded cabin, which was to be our home for the next several years.

Mom had our belated dinner waiting for us and we fell on it like hungry dogs, though I have no recollection of what we ate.

Dad always said he wanted to live where he could see in all directions, and the site he picked for our homestead cabin certainly met those qualifications. Our little settlement huddled on a flat-topped hogback in a clearing in the sagebrush, sun-baked in the summer, blasted by blizzards in fall, winter, and spring, and in the path of every wind that blew. But no one ever sneaked up on us! We could see for miles in every direction, except to the south where the Pine Ridge crouched, bristling with stunted pines and cut by sharp gullies and canyons. A mile to the east, across a miniature bad lands, was the Five Mile Divide; six miles to the north was the Powder River Valley, then the long, gentle rise to the Dowe Divide twenty-five miles farther off. To the west we could see clear to the Big Horn Mountains forty miles away.

I'm not sure what kind of deal Dad made for the cabin. Most homestead cabins were simple one-room frame structures, easily moved. One cabin might be used to prove up on several different claims, and ours was one of these. Dad got it the fall of 1935. Billy Gibbs had used it to prove up on his homestead southwest of Sussex and the land had been bought by the Meike Ranch. The Meikes may have just given the cabin to Dad. Several neighborhood men, including Gus Chabot and Jack Andrew, helped Dad jack it up, put skids under it, and move it with tractors to its new location.

Wonders had already been accomplished by the time Fred and I arrived with the cows. The stove was set up and a fire burned in it; the big reservoir on the end alongside the firebox was full of water carried from a nearby waterhole. The banks on East Carpenter had been shoveled down so it could be crossed with team and wagon, but that was as far as the truck could go. Everything was unloaded and piled on the west bank, and Marsh and Paul hauled it to the cabin with the wagon. The dishes, pots, pans, and skillets had been unpacked and the furniture had been hauled over and installed. Boxes of clothing and household goods were piled everywhere and a growing pile of boxes, trunks, and crates were being stacked against the north outside wall of the cabin as Marsh and Paul continued to freight stuff from the unloading site.

Our first night on the homestead was memorable. Meikes had loaned Dad a sheepwagon to live in the fall before while he was building the reservoir and moving the cabin and it was still at the homestead site, so Marsh and Paul took possession if it. Mom and Dad slept on a three-quarter-size bed in the cabin, and the rest of us made beds on the floor using every bit of available space.

Ranged around the walls of the cabin were the big iron cookstove, a dresser, Mom's Singer sewing machine, the bed, Dad's big rolltop desk, a bookcase converted to a dish cupboard, a home-made kitchen counter and a home-made corner cabinet that held the water bucket and wash basin. A home-made dining table stood in the middle of the room. We had no chairs, so we used wooden apple crates to sit on. During the day, these were pushed back under the table to give more floor space; at night, they were stacked on top of the table so one of the smaller kids could sleep under it.

We were all so tired that first night we could probably have slept standing up. After a few nights I learned to sleep on my belly because there was a good chance of getting some vital part of your anatomy stepped on by someone fumbling their way out through all the bodies in the darkness to answer a call of nature!

This was a pretty drastic change from our two-story, ten-room house. I suppose it must have been harder on Mom than the rest of us. She had everyone under foot and everything crammed into a smaller space. One thing that was simplified was housekeeping. Once the bed was made, all the rest of the bedding was folded or rolled and stacked on the bed. The bare wood floor was quickly swept and scrubbed.

Another change we had to get used to was the isolation. Our only transportation was by team and wagon, horseback, or afoot, and we felt as isolated from civilization as if we'd been on the moon. But we were young and soon adjusted to our primitive lifestyle. We were twenty years late as far as homesteaders went, but being latecomers made it no less an adventure to us.

The morning after the move we set about getting organized. There was no fence, so all we could do was turn the cows loose and hope they'd stay. They did—until they got rested up from the trek out. From then on, Fred and I spent every day hunting them and bringing them back from wherever they'd strayed. We fought them all that summer. Dad sold them in the fall because we didn't have any winter feed for them.

Dad had always kept a supply of lumber on hand for repairs and small building projects, and this came in really handy on the homestead. Our first and most pressing project was an outhouse, followed by a lean-to built against the north side of the cabin to protect the stuff piled there. A great many boxes and a trunk were still out in the weather, so Dad constructed an open-fronted storage shed to take care of that problem.

Once these most necessary things were taken care of we concentrated on general improvements. The ground was as hard as cement, so digging a hole of any kind was a major undertaking. Using a crowbar and an adze, we excavated a root cellar, which gave Mom much-needed storage space for a lot of things, including all her canning jars and several eight-pound lard pails full of clean, rendered mutton and beef tallow. Dad had complained about her moving all that stale tallow to the homestead, but it turned out later to be a godsend.

At the Hall Ranch a large garden had been a very necessary part of our livelihood, so we turned our efforts in that direction. Sagebrush had to be dug out with grub hoes, post holes dug with a crowbar, and the area around the cabin and garden site fenced. Dad broke up the black-root sod with the team and plow. By the time all this had been accomplished spring had arrived, so with high expectations we put in the garden.

At the ranch, though, we had irrigated the garden from the Sahara Ditch. On the homestead, we carried water from our reservoir, and every step of it was uphill. As the weather got hotter and drier, our enthusiasm for gardening grew cooler. Every day the sun blazed down without so much as a sprinkle of rain, and every day the garden looked sorrier. Then, as the prairie grass dried up, the rabbits moved in to eat what green stuff there was. We moved the old army cot out into the garden, but the rabbits came right up and ate the vegetables under the cot with someone sleeping on it.

Water, or lack of it, was a never-ending problem. When we first moved to the homestead, some little grassy-bottomed potholes full of clean rain water provided us with good drinking water, and Dad had built a reservoir the fall before in a draw east of the cabin. It filled with clean snow water during the spring runoff and we used this for drinking water, too, until warmer weather came. Then we found our water supply inhabited by a variety of water creatures ranging from water dogs (as we called salamanders) to the many-legged black beetles that burrowed in the mud in the bottom.

We finally managed to acquire several sixty-gallon wooden vinegar barrels from the Sussex store and started hauling water from the American Ranch. Dad would load the empty barrels in the box wagon, hitch up the team, and make the long trip in to civilization and back. It took all day to make the sixteen-mile round-trip, and in hot weather, the water in the barrels was lukewarm by the time he got home. It was always slightly vinegar flavored, too.

We did have some moisture later that summer, though. One day when Dad went to haul water, I decided to ride along on my saddle horse. It was mid-afternoon by the time we made the trip to the American Ranch, filled the barrels, and got back as far as Sussex. It was very sultry, and thunderheads were building over the Big Horn

Mountains to the west. When we left the Sussex store, the clouds were starting to darken and the air was very oppressive. We could see an occasional flash of lightning along the mountains and hear the distant rumble of thunder.

The storm caught us about a quarter of a mile past Lohse's. The wind hit us first, with big raindrops in it that stung when they struck. Then, even above the noise of the wind, we could hear a louder, more ominous roar.

"Hail!" Dad yelled. "Get off your horse!"

He jumped down from the wagon, but there was no time to unhitch the team before the storm hit. My horse turned his rump to it when the first hailstone pelted him. I got under his neck and used his body to shield me, but I stuck out enough on both sides that the hailstones really peppered me. Dad let the team turn tail to the storm, pulling the wagon off the road as they did, so it was kind of quartered to the wind and offered Dad some shelter on the leeward side of it.

The rain came down in torrents along with the hail and in a matter of seconds, the ground was awash. Hail was drifted up against the grass clumps and sage. Usually, a storm of this kind would be over with in a few minutes and the sun would be shining again, but this time it settled down to a drizzle and a chilly breeze took the place of the wind. Our wet clothing stuck to us, making us thoroughly miserable since neither of us had a coat. Once Dad swung the team back around onto the road, the chilled horses struck off at a brisk trot that soon had us all warmed. We were relieved to note that the hail had done very little damage to any foliage.

We soon learned not to waste one drop of water, and I often thought of the lady who told Mom about how careful she had to be with water when every drop had to be hauled. She said she bathed the baby in a dishpan full of water, then rinsed out the baby's clothes in the same water. After that, she scrubbed her cabin floor and finally, poured it on a small cottonwood tree she was trying to grow in the yard. When Mom asked her if that dirty water wouldn't kill the tree, she said, "Oh no! It's thriving. There's lots of nourishment in that water when I get done with it!"

In winter we kept a water barrel in the cabin next to the big range to keep it from freezing. There was always a dishpan full of clean snow melting on the back of the stove. As the snow was converted to water, it was added to the barrel. We always strained it through a clean cloth, since there was apt to be some foreign material, such as rabbit droppings or sage leaves in the snow.

As soon as warmer weather came, Fred and I moved outdoors with our beds. I was afraid of snakes so I made my bed on the old army cot that we later used unsuccessfully against the rabbits in the garden. I knew that metal attracted electricity, and I was deathly afraid of lightning, so I set each leg of the cot in an old rubber overshoe and had complete confidence in my insulators!

One night we decided to sleep on the roof of the shelter Dad had built over the big pile of stored items north of the cabin. The roof had just enough slope to drain off rain water, but we didn't think it was steep enough to create any problems for sleeping. After a restless night of crawling back from the edge of the roof, I woke to find Fred and his bed gone. I climbed down from the roof, which was only about four feet high at the back, and found Fred rolled up in his blankets, wedged between the back wall and two big mountain pine poles that had been used as skids under the cabin when they moved it to the homestead. For a second, I thought he must be dead, but his gentle snoring reassured me. When I woke him, he looked around puzzled and demanded to know how he got down there. He had rolled off the roof in the night without ever waking up.

Just a few days after we became homesteaders, Fred, Ruthie, and I decided to go exploring in the Pine Ridge. After we climbed around a while, we finally crawled the last few feet to the top of a sharp ridge in the best Daniel Boone style and peered over cautiously. Several deer were grazing in a big, bowl-like valley that lay before us. The wind was carrying our scent away from the deer, so they were unaware of being spied on.

A sudden movement in a big clump of cedar near the deer exploded them in all directions. It was a mountain lion. We could see the big cat very plainly as he stood there, angrily switching his long tail as he watched his supper vanishing over the far horizon. In a moment he faded back into the shadows of the cedar. We headed for home, bursting to tell the folks of the drama we had witnessed.

On the way home, we found a petrified tree lying across a small washout. Fragments of limbs and twigs littered the ground around it, and the trunk was large enough that we walked across on it. Because we were completely unfamiliar with the area, we weren't sure when we got home where we'd seen either the lion or the tree. We hunted that petrified tree all the years we lived on the homestead, but never found it again. Years later, my husband told me he'd seen the tree, too. He said he came across it one day when he was riding through the area, but like us, he was never able to find it again.

Dad scoffed at the idea of a lion, saying it was more than likely a big bobcat. We decided he was probably right, since we'd never seen either animal before. It never occurred to us to wonder why a bobcat would have a long tail.

Jimmy Iseminger and his family lived on their homestead to the west of us. He mined coal in the Pine Ridge and drove the school bus, using a pickup with a home-made cover on the back. Since there was no passable road to our cabin, Fred and Ruthie had to catch the bus at Lohses', three miles to the north of us. Ruthie had never ridden horseback, so Mom was afraid for her to ride one of our two horses alone. Apparently, Fred was not trusted to share his horse with her, so every morning, I had to ride to the Lohses' with Ruthie riding behind me, leave the kids to catch the bus, and ride home again leading Fred's horse. In the afternoon, back I went to meet the bus, leading the extra horse to bring the kids home. I was as glad as they were when the last day of school arrived. Before school began the following fall, Dad, Marsh, and Paul built a road to our cabin so the bus could pick the kids up at our door.

During the summer, Dad sold the Durham bull and with the money bought a tent large enough for the army cot and a three-quarter-sized bed to fit in. When fall came, Dad boarded up the sides of the tent and we made a stove out of a metal barrel. As luck would have it, 1936–37 turned out to be as cold as the previous winter. Our barrel stove could be white-hot when we went to bed and in an hour it would be stone-cold. Fred and Danny slept on the bed, and Ruthie and I shared the cot. I think we would have frozen to death if we hadn't been sleeping two to a bed! Even worse than going to bed at night was getting up in the morning. Looking back, I wonder how we ever survived.

There was no bank near the cabin where we could build a dugout, so the next summer we dug a large hole out away from the cabin, put a cellar-type roof on it, and built a stairway down into it with a cover to keep the snow off the steps. Before winter came again we were snugly housed in our dugout, and we kept warm even if we didn't build a fire in our barrel stove.

One night after we blew out the kerosene lamp in the dugout, Ruthie complained that something was biting her. I lit a match and to my horror, I saw bedbugs disappearing into the dirt walls everywhere I looked. In those days, bedbugs were almost as common a plague as flies and every fastidious housewife loathed them. Dad used to laugh and say that no matter what else they talked about whenever women got together, they always got around to the subject of bedbugs. Because bedbugs were easily transported in bedrolls and suitcases, our bunkhouse at the Hall Ranch was infested with them, but Mom always managed to keep them out of the house. When we moved to the homestead, Paul transplanted them from the bunkhouse to the sheepwagon.

Paul claimed bedbugs never bit him, but Marsh got very upset about them. Every so often he would wage all-out war on them, spreading all the bedding on sagebrush and turning it every little while so the hot sun would run out any lurking bugs. The mattress was given a similar treatment. The bed springs were liberally doused with kerosene, which brought bugs out of all their hiding places. While all this was going on, a pan of sulfur was ignited on top of the stove and the wagon tightly closed so the fumes would penetrate every crack and crevice. These efforts never did get rid of all the bedbugs, but it did give them enough of a setback so that they were tolerable for a while.

The next morning we held a strategy meeting and decided the only thing to do was burn them out. We carried everything up out of the dugout except our barrel stove, and gave the bedding, mattresses, bed springs, and clothing the usual treatment. Meantime, Fred fired up the gasoline blowtorch and we went over every inch of the walls with it. We'd apparently had the little varmints for quite some time because the cracks in the walls alongside our beds were literally alive with them. When the heat of the flame came near a crack, the bedbugs boiled out and we cremated them with sadistic glee. We must have done a good job because we were never troubled by them again.

In the early spring of 1937, Dad's bank in Buffalo contacted him and offered him a deal on a small band of old ewes that the Eychener Ranch was selling. Dad agreed to their terms, and once more we were in the sheep business.

The timing couldn't have been worse. We got them in early spring before they lambed, and it began to rain almost immediately. These ewes had wintered poorly and being old, I suppose their teeth were bad so they weren't faring too well on our short grass. Our land was gumbo, which when wet, sticks and clings in huge clumps to whatever comes in contact with it. I can still see those poor, old ewes, heavy with unborn lambs and weighted down with wet wool, slogging stolidly through the mud, trying to find something to eat. Every little bit, one would collapse and lie there in the mud, rolling her eyes in despair. Once they went down, no amount of urging would get the ewes on their feet again, and attempts to stand them up were futile; their legs just simply would not hold them up. Most laid there and died, and we took a loss right off the bat. As it turned out, that was the last rain we had all summer. Then the grasshoppers moved in and ate what little grass hadn't already burned to a crisp.

That summer I was introduced to smoking, and I never smell the dry, dusty odor of pines on a hot day without thinking of my first cigarette.

Louie Strentz, who had a homestead east of us and also had sheep, was in the same predicament we were. He and Dad decided to put their sheep in one herd and trail them to some lease range over in the Salt Creek Oilfield. Once they were there and settled in, Louie would come back to his homestead and Dad would stay and herd the sheep.

Louie and his wife, an attractive, French war bride, had no children. Marguerite had never really adapted to homestead life, and she was afraid to stay alone while Louie helped trail the sheep to Salt Creek. Dad volunteered me as a companion for her. I thought it sounded like fun, and it would only be for four or five days.

The men left at daylight with the herd, Dad and Paul trailing the sheep and Louie following along with his pickup with a camping outfit on it. They were barely out of sight when Marguerite said, "We clean the house! It is dirty from everyone!"

We had arrived the afternoon before and spent the night there, but I didn't realize we'd gotten the house dirty because the men were out with the sheep until dark. They came in and ate, and as soon as the dishes were done, we went to bed in anticipation of their early start next morning. The three-room house looked spick-and-span to me, but we got busy and cleaned it anyway.

Strentzes hauled water from a neighboring homesteader who had a well, but it was used strictly for drinking and cooking. Water for other purposes was carried about a hundred yards from a reservoir.

"I am not so well," Marguerite said. "You are young and strong; you carry the water."

So I carried the water, quite a few pails of it because she decided to do the laundry first, then use the wash water to clean the house.

When the clean laundry was on the line at last and we had scrubbed the whole house, I was ready for a break—and I was hungry! It had been hours since we had eaten breakfast by lamplight with the men.

When I finished emptying the wash water, Marguerite met me at the door. "Take off your shoes," she ordered. "Keep the floor clean."

I learned that we never wore our shoes in the house. I took off my shoes and stepped inside. The kitchen and living room floors were completely covered with newspapers. She explained that another neighbor who raised chickens dropped by from time to time to deliver eggs. There was a rivalry between them as to whose house was cleanest.

Marguerite said that when she heard Minnie's car coming, it gave her time to gather up the newspapers and put them out of sight so her house was spotless.

Marguerite asked me if I was hungry and if I liked tomato soup. Of course, my answers to both questions were yes. She opened a can of Campbell's tomato soup and heated it. She divided it into two bowls, doled out four crackers to each of us, and we ate. This was only an appetizer for my teenage appetite, and I hoped there was going to be something more. There was: two store cookies and a glass of tepid water. Now I knew why she was so elegantly slim.

She said she usually followed her noon meal with a couple of hours of napping and resting, so would I not make any noise? I looked around for something to do that wouldn't make any noise. There was nothing in the house to read, a situation I could hardly believe because my family read constantly, anything they could lay their collective hands on. There was a wind-up phonograph that she said I could play when she was not resting, so I spent half an hour going through her sizable record collection. To my amazement, I found not one Gene Autry record, nothing by Carson Robinson, no bum songs or Two Black Crow records. The music was all opera, classical stuff that really left me cold, but by the time she'd finished her nap, I was so bored I was ready for anything.

I was debating what to play when she said, "Play Harry Lauder. He is my favorite."

What a surprise that was! Instead of a romantic voice crooning about love, he bellowed! And about love, too! It wasn't until I began seeing Nelson Eddy-Marie MacDonald movies several years later that I had it proved to me that you really could bellow about love from atop a mountain, on a castle wall, or astride a horse!

After several Harry Lauder records and Marguerite clasping her hands on her bosom and rolling her eyes and proclaiming her love for Harry, I switched to something else. I was glad when Marguerite finally told me I'd better carry some water while she fixed supper.

Supper! I could hardly wait!

Supper turned out to be better than dinner. She made us each a cheese sandwich and she put several slices of bread on the table, plus peanut butter, so I went to bed satisfied.

After a good breakfast of toast and eggs the next morning, we washed up what dishes we had dirtied the day before. Already, the day stretched ahead of me with hours of emptiness to fill.

Then Marguerite said, "You will wash my hair, please?"

I was a little taken aback that a grown woman would expect someone else to wash her hair, but at least it was something to do. She had pretty hair and when I had toweled it almost dry, we went out in the sun and she had me brush it until it was dry.

With a twinkle in her eyes, she said, "You pluck your eyebrows. It is wicked to do." She grinned. "You pluck my eyebrows, maybe? The tweezers are in the top dresser drawer."

I opened one of the two top drawers, since she hadn't indicated which, and was amazed to see dozens of tailor-made cigarettes loose in the drawer, plus several unopened packages. My first thought was that they were Louie's, but then I remembered him putting a carton of Lucky Strikes in his camping gear before he left, and these were Camels. They must be Marguerite's! Suddenly I saw her in a new light: the rather dull, uninspiring woman was actually glamorous, chic, a woman of the world!

I located the tweezers in the other drawer, and stood looking at all those cigarettes. Smoking was the "in" thing to do. All the magazines carried full-page ads of sexy, fashionable women lighting up. I had to try it! Quickly I took three cigarettes with trembling fingers.

"Stealing!" my conscience said.

"No, swiping," I retorted. "It's not stealing."

As I went through the living room, I concealed the cigarettes in my box of clothes I'd brought from home.

After I plucked Marguerite's eyebrows, she fixed lunch, a replay of yesterday's, but with a different flavor of soup. I could hardly wait for her to go to her bedroom and close the door for her nap. Quickly I extracted one of the precious cigarettes from my box, took a few matches from the box on the kitchen stove, and made my escape.

The Strentz homestead house was right at the foot of the Pine Ridge, so I hiked up into the pines until I could conceal myself from the cabin. It was breathlessly hot on that north slope of the ridge, and the dusty, pungent smell of the pines filled the air. I sat down on the mat of dry pine needles, scratched a match on the sole of my shoe, and lit up.

I'd heard some of the boys telling how they got sick the first time they smoked, so I was careful not to inhale. I put the cigarette between the first two fingers of my left hand the way the models did in the cigarette ads, being very nonchalant and debonair. I practiced putting the cigarette to my lips in a casual, elegant manner and blowing the smoke in a similar fashion. Although I was disappointed in the taste, it was amazing how that one little cigarette changed my whole outlook on life. Instead of being an awkward, unsure teenager, I had just been transformed into a glamorous woman!

For the next two days, I sneaked off during Marguerite's rest period and was transported into another world for the length of a cigarette!

Then Louie came back and took me home to my cigaretteless existence on my family's homestead, and all my pipe dreams went up in smoke.

Even with the leased range, conditions continued to deteriorate and we finally lost the sheep. By the time the bank foreclosed on them, we were relieved to see them go, as they had netted us absolutely no income and many hours of grief, not to mention the expense of the leased pasture at Midwest.

It seemed as if Mother Nature was always waiting to test us with one thing or another. About the only thing we weren't bothered with was floods, because the cabin was on top of a high rise of ground. We had blizzards in winter and terrible thunderstorms in summer. In between there were always rattlesnakes to watch out for and once even a rabid dog.

One summer evening, Fred and I returned from a hike just at dusk to find the younger kids playing a very noisy game. They were running around and around the cabin in the near dark. Every time they passed over the door step, they made a big leap with lots of laughing and yelling. We asked them what the object of the game was. They said there was a June bug alongside the step and every time they jumped over it, it buzzed. Fred and I investigated and found a very large and very irritated rattler coiled by the step. We promptly killed it, which ended the game!

In the spring of 1937 I worked for Mrs. Orange Taylor for a month. Their ranch was right along the main road to Kaycee, and in addition to raising turkeys, geese, and chickens and planting a huge garden, she collected bum lambs from the trail herds that passed by on the way to the mountains. With so much outdoor work, she needed someone to do the housework and cooking. I told her I didn't know how to cook, so she did the actual cooking while I did all the potato peeling, vegetable preparations, table setting, and dishwashing as well as the housework.

One of the sheep outfits passing by abandoned a female puppy, and it showed up on Taylor's doorstep hungry and lost. Orange was going to kill it, but I told him I'd take her home with me since my job was nearly over. Mom was less than overjoyed when I brought the puppy home, but we kept her. She was an ugly little dog, sort of reddish brown, slick-haired with black speckles scattered over her. We named her Pepper because of the spots.

One Sunday afternoon in September when Dad was working away from home, Fred and I were walking back up to the cabin from the dugout garage Dad built along the same draw our reservoir was in. Pepper was lying in the shade along the north side of the cabin. Suddenly she sprang up and ran toward us, her hackles raised, her mouth dripping saliva, and her lips drawn back in a snarl. There was something so menacing in her appearance that we both ran in panic to the only refuge we could see, two empty gas barrels sitting out away from everything, but close to where we were.

Mom came to the cabin door when she heard the ruckus, and when she saw the snapping, snarling dog, she was terrified. She often told us of the horrifying experience when their dog went mad one summer during the "dog days" back in Kansas, and she realized that Pepper was mad, too. Fortunately, Ruthie, Danny and Julie were all in the cabin with Mom.

She called to us to stay where we were. The dog's attention was immediately diverted by the sound of Mom's voice and she abandoned us and rushed at the screen door. Mom slammed the door and the dog went around to the shade where she lay panting and watching Fred and me. Finally, she seemed to be asleep and we decided to make a run for the house. As stealthy as we tried to be in getting down from the barrels, we must have made some noise, because Pepper came charging back down the hill, snarling and snapping, and we barely had time to climb back on our perches.

The hot afternoon seemed to last forever. Pepper retreated to the shade again, but she kept us under surveillance every minute. At last, after what seemed like an eternity, she got up and staggered around behind the house out of sight. As if on signal, we leaped off the barrels and dashed for the cabin. Mom had the door open when we got there, and we crashed into the room out of breath and nearly hysterical.

We were prisoners in the cabin. For a while after our successful escape, we felt very adventuresome, but the confinement soon began to wear on our nerves. We had to ration what water was in the water bucket, since we didn't dare go outside to the barrels for more. Mom found something to read to us and that helped pass the long evening.

The next morning when Jimmie Iseminger drove in with the school bus, we yelled at him from the window not to get out of the bus because we had a mad dog running loose. He always carried a rifle in the bus, and when Pepper came around to the front of the cabin he shot her.

After Fred, Ruth, and Dan began the fall term of school in 1936, I was so bored I decided to go back to school and review the eighth grade. It was understood when I started that I could not compete with the eighth graders or recite in class, so I was in a grade by myself. It filled my empty days, but with no interaction of any kind, I had no motivation. After Christmas vacation I quit.

The following autumn, Anna Patrick, who was teaching at the Long School several miles on down Powder River from Sussex, contacted the high school principal in Buffalo and arranged for me to take high school courses under her supervision.

I was delighted to have such an opportunity, so on Mondays, Wednesdays, and Fridays I rode the bus to the Sussex school so I could study. On Tuesdays and Thursdays, I got off the bus at the Sussex store and Anna picked me up there on her way to her school. I spent those days each week reviewing with her what I'd studied, having lessons corrected and new assignments made.

On the nights we had to make connections with my bus, she let her school out ten minutes early. It always worked out about right as the bus had to make two or three stops between the school and the store. One evening we came over the Sussex hill just in time to see the bus crossing the bridge. Afterward, the kids on the bus said they saw us coming and hammered on the cab of the pickup and yelled as loud as they could that I was there, but the driver only speeded up. Later, we learned that he resented having to haul me because he was not getting paid for it.

Whatever his reason, I was faced with a six-mile walk home. It was sunset, the late fall evening temperature was dropping, and I was not very warmly dressed, even though I was wearing the warmest clothes I owned. Anna was quite upset, but I assured her I'd be fine because I didn't want her to try to take me home. Our road was definitely not for a driver used to driving on a gravel road.

As I was leaving the store, Jack Andrew and another man pulled in with a team and wagon. They were living at the mouth of Carpenter Canyon in a dugout and mining coal in the Ridge. They were on their way home from delivering a load of coal, so they offered me a ride.

It seemed like a good idea at the time, but I could have made better time by walking, and by the time they let me off to walk the last mile, I was so cold and stiff I could hardly stand. It was pitch dark, but I soon got my night sight and was able to make out dimly the seldom-traveled road that ran from the Carpenter road to the homestead. I don't know how I kept from dying of fright, because I was always terrified of the dark. But I made it, and the brisk hike had me warmed up by the time I reached the cabin, where I was warmly received by my worried family.

When school resumed after the Christmas vacation, I had to go to Buffalo for four weeks: three weeks to review the material I had studied the first semester, followed by a week of tests. I boarded with Gladys Westover, the county superintendent of schools.

My Aunt Winnie in California sent me the money for my room and board, but I needed enough money to buy two skirts, so I borrowed that from Marsh. The school did not have a uniform code, but girls were restricted to skirts of a dark color and plain, shirt-waist blouses or sweaters. I had no winter coat and it was a cold January. My friend Nora Miller, who was also boarding with Gladys Westover, had a light coat for spring and fall that she let me wear.

Studying at the two rural schools had been almost as boring as trying to review the eighth grade. What a revelation that month at Johnson County High School was! I had barely been getting by in history and arithmetic, but both the teachers were such gifted instructors that both subjects came alive for me, and I passed the semester exam in history with a 95 percent grade. I don't remember what my grade was in arithmetic, but I did well in it also.

The letdown of going back to the homestead and the Sussex and Long Schools was too much for me. I quit. Anna returned my books to the high school, and that finished my higher education.

Things had been bad at home when I left for my four weeks of high school in Buffalo, but I got back to find the situation had gotten much worse. Keeping the wolf from the door had been a constant battle, but during the early years on the homestead, Dad and Paul had had a few government work program jobs, using our team of horses. Finally, even those jobs fizzled out, so we had no income at all most of the time. We lived for the most part on beans and cottontail rabbits.

About a quarter of a mile north of the cabin was a big, flat-bottomed draw that was full of brush and had lots of banks where the rabbits seemed to really thrive and multiply. Fred and I hunted them with the .22 rifle until we ran out of shells and had no money to buy more. Then we took Marsh's muskrat traps and trapped the rabbits at their dens. It must have been an exceptionally good time for rabbits, because there seemed to be an endless supply of them. It was a good thing for the Browns that they were so plentiful!

The second year we were on the homestead, Mom started a lot of tomato plants in the house in window boxes, then decided it would be a waste of time to set them out, so she gave them to Pete Meike. That fall, he brought us two bushels of tomatoes ranging from green to ripe, so we had tomatoes over quite a span of time. He also brought us several of the biggest squash I ever saw. They looked like huge pumpkins except that they were more yellow than orange in color. Dad was leaving on a temporary job, so he took what money he had left from a WPA job he had had earlier and bought us a five-pound box of cheese and a slab of bacon. We feasted like kings for a while. Big chunks of squash baked with strips of bacon on them were a taste treat beyond imagining after the diet we had been on. The cheese and tomatoes were almost too good to be true.

Later in the fall, about the time our bonanza of food ran out, the Isemingers brought us several heads of cabbage from their garden, and a dry farmer from out in the Fifteen Mile area brought us a hundred pounds of dry navy beans. After the cabbage was gone, we were back to beans and rabbits.

When I got back from high school, the family was living on boiled beans and what few rabbits Fred could trap. We had run out of flour, so Mom could no longer bake bread. The government had given big bags of bran to anyone who wanted it for feed for milk cows. We no longer had the cows, but we still had two bags of bran. Mom mixed it with salt and water and fried it in patties in the mutton tallow she brought from the ranch. The tallow was very stale, but clean, so even though it wasn't tasty, it did add a necessary element to our diet.

When I hear young people complaining they don't like this or that, I always think that a month's diet of beans boiled with no flavoring except stock salt, and bran "dough-gods," as we called them, fried in stale mutton tallow would probably make a difference in their food preferences!

Keeping the kids in school got to be our biggest problem. All they had for lunches was rabbit and the fried bran dough-gods. Our credit had been shut off at the Sussex store because we owed the incredible amount of eighty dollars, and until something was paid on it, we couldn't buy anything more. My heart nearly broke because the kids came home every night vowing they would not go back to school the next day because the other kids teased them about their lunches.

Mom kept the kids nicely dressed because she was a good seamstress, and she had plenty of material to work with. My aunts sent cast-off dresses and coats that Mom ripped up and made over into dresses, shirts, pants, and coats for them.

Shoes were the biggest problem. I had taken some of my wages from the Taylors and bought a pair of English riding boots of black leather with flat soles. Even though they were the cheapest ones in the catalog, they were sturdy and well built and I was still wearing them after I got married. Dad always wore what were called policeman's shoes, black leather lace-up shoes, and I recall that he always had at least two pairs when we lived on the Hall place, one pair for dress and a pair for every day. Mom was well supplied with shoes, too, but the kids were a real problem. Not only were they hard on shoes, they were growing as well.

Dad had a cobbler outfit complete with different-sized lasts, tacks, awl, waxed thread, and a big piece of sole leather. Fred became the family cobbler; with practice he eventually became quite expert at shoe repair. As he became more skilled at repairing shoes, he became more desperate for something to put on his own feet. Someone had given us a pair of cowboy boots that were too small for me and too big for him. One day he got them out, cut the stitching that held the soles to the uppers around the toes, measured them against his feet, and cut the toes to fit. When he sewed the soles back to the uppers, instead of fairly pointed-toed boots, he had neatly square-toed boots that he wore until he outgrew them.

He resoled Dad's shoes and my boots once, but he patched and resoled the kids' shoes until there was just nothing left to work on. At last, the day came when Mom was forced to keep the kids home from school because they were the same as barefoot. She told the bus driver not to come for them any more.

Of course, it was only a matter of a few days before the teacher notified the county superintendent that the Brown children had been withdrawn from school. The Superintendent, in turn, passed the information on to the proper authorities. The next thing we knew, a man from the Relief Office arrived at the homestead. When he departed, his briefcase held a completed questionnaire bearing all the information about the destitute Brown family: how many people, their names, ages, places of birth, and what the nonexistent family income was.

Dad had steadfastly refused even to consider relief. Having to ask for welfare was a shameful thing to him, an acknowledgment of failure to care for his family, and his pride simply would not let him do it. However, when the decision was taken out of his hands, I think he must have been greatly relieved to know his family would be fed and clothed. Mom must have felt as if a terrible burden had been lifted from her when we received the first month's check, amounting to nineteen dollars.

A week later, sporting new shoes from Montgomery Ward, the kids were back in school.

Marsh was working away from home quite a lot of the time, so he was not living the day-to-day homestead adventure the rest of us were. During the summer, he stacked hay at the Meike Home Ranch, the old original place that Pete's dad had settled on in 1901. It was being managed by Pete's younger brothers, Emil and Mick (Harold).

In the late fall and winter when there was no water in the Sahara Ditch, maintenance work was done on it. During the summer, willows sprang up by the millions along the banks and had to be chopped out and burned. Wherever there was a draw, the water was carried across in a flume, a galvanized steel waterway, like half of a culvert, supported across the draw on a trestle. The bolts that held the big sheets of flume steel in place had to be checked, loose ones tightened, and missing ones replaced. The flumes leaked, creating swamps beneath them, so the trestle timbers were constantly needing replacement as they rotted.

Marsh worked for the Ditch Company whenever they needed him, so he was making enough money to buy clothes and save some toward his eventual "escape" from the homestead. In the late summer of 1938, with the help of Aunt Julie, his dream came true and he left for Seattle.

I knew how much he wanted to go where he could make something of himself. He was never cut out for ranch work. He didn't like working with livestock, and his interest in machinery was not in using it but in what made it run and creating better ways of doing things. I was glad he was going to have a chance to do the things he had a talent for, even though I wondered if we'd ever see each other again. Seattle was so far away!

In the early spring of 1938, Jimmie Iseminger was hired by the Sahara Ditch Company as a ditch rider. His duties included monitoring the big headgate at the J-U Ranch where the water was diverted from Powder River to the ditch, and checking the headgates of users to be sure nobody was taking more than their share of the available water. The water was scheduled to be turned into the ditch the first of May, so he had to be there several days before to be sure the headgate was free of trash and working properly. He also needed a couple of days to move his family to the small house provided for him at the headgate. School ran to the last week of May, so he asked Dad to finish out the school bus term for him.

When Dad began working away from home, he traded our team of horses for a pickup and taught me to drive it, so Fred and I could use it to haul water. The inner tubes were so thin the air was showing through, and it seemed we spent the entire summer patching them. I don't think we ever made a trip without having two or three flats. The poor old tubes looked like patchwork quilts. By the fall of 1937, we not only had nothing left to patch, we had no money to buy gas, so we just parked it. It was late enough we had snow, so we no longer needed to haul water.

In addition to a month's pay for driving the bus, Jimmie gave Dad enough money to fill our pickup with gas and buy a couple of inner tubes. Dad constructed a "dog house," as he called it, on the back of the pickup and he was in business. The first day Dad hauled the kids, I made the trip with him. On the way home that evening, he stopped at the Sussex store and on the strength of his job, the storekeeper, Sid Gering, let us have a hundred pounds of potatoes and a twenty-four-dozen case of eggs.

I could hardly wait to get home. Even with the relief check, we had been living mostly on beans. We had bought flour, yeast, salt, and lard so Mom could bake bread for sandwiches for the kids' lunches. They were able to have cheese and peanut butter, but we hadn't had potatoes in months, nor eggs since we left the Hall Ranch. Our chickens had survived that first summer on the homestead, but with fall coming on, we had no place to keep them and nothing to feed them, so we ate them, one by one.

As soon as we got home, Mom and I prepared a big iron skillet full of fried spuds. Even before they were completely done, she began frying eggs in another big skillet. Once, eons ago when we lived at the Hall Ranch, Fred and I thought we could not eat an egg unless the yolk was cooked to a hard-rubber consistency. On this particular evening, we each scooped an egg out onto our plates as soon as it would hold together enough to slip a pancake turner under it. Of all the meals I have eaten in my lifetime, none compares with that one. Dad said we could eat all we wanted, so when the skillet of potatoes was emptied, we fried another pan full. I suppose Fred and I must have eaten a dozen eggs between us that night.

From that point on, things began to look up for the Browns. When the bus job ended, Dad went to work for Jim "Pop" Comfort. Pop was getting up in years and needed help on the small farm they had just west of the Sussex store on the north side of Powder River. Dad did the irrigating and when haying started, he and Pop traded work with two old bachelor brothers, Sim and Art Taylor, who owned a small acreage between Pete Meike's ranch buildings and the Sussex store. After receiving three relief checks, Dad was able to tell the Relief Board we no longer needed charity.

During the summer, Mrs. Comfort hired Mom to come in and help her clean house and wash all the quilts and blankets. Mom usually took the three younger kids with her, so Fred and I were alone on the homestead. One morning we emptied a syrup can at breakfast and the empty can was still sitting on the table as I stacked the dishes and put away the breakfast things. Syrup came in square, metal gallon cans with a screw-on cap, much like the can Coleman fuel comes in today. In one corner on the top was the spout with a screw-on cap. Fred was still sitting at the table drinking coffee and for some reason, he stuck his thumb into the pouring spout of the can. There was a flange around the inside, and when Fred tried to withdraw his thumb, the flange wouldn't let him pull the thumb joint back out past it.

He began trying in earnest to get free from the spout, but all he accomplished was irritating the flesh where the flange kept biting into it, and soon his thumb began to swell. We tried everything we could think of: soapy water to lubricate the point of contact; immersing his hand and the can in cold water; slipping a thin-bladed knife in alongside the thumb for a shoe-horn effect. Nothing worked.

The whole situation was so ridiculous I wanted to laugh. "Of all the dumb things to do!" I kept saying.

"I know it was dumb! Just help me get it off!" Fred pleaded. He was so distraught by this time I had to feel sorry for him.

Suddenly I had an inspiration: our old-fashioned can opener! If I could slip the point of the thin, crescent-shaped blade in alongside his thumb, I might be able to slit the flange in several places and bend it away from the thumb, thus releasing its grip.

I warned Fred it was probably going to cause some damage, but the embarrassing alternative of trudging the six miles to Sussex with a gallon syrup can dangling from his thumb gave him courage.

Each time I slipped the blade in alongside his thumb and exerted enough pressure to cut the metal I drew blood. I was ready to give up, but he said it didn't hurt and urged me to go ahead. I think there was so much swelling by that time that his thumb was numb.

By the time I made enough cuts so I could bend the metal and free him, I was weak in the knees and my hands were shaking. Fred's thumb looked terrible, swollen and covered with nicks and cuts both from the can-opener and the can, but he was jubilant. We coated the wounds with mercurochrome and in a few days, he was as good as new. I don't think I ever told anyone about our interesting episode. I was probably under threat of death if I did!

When the bus route came up for bids that summer, Dad bid on it, as did Jimmie, even though his ditch job would prevent him driving for the first six weeks, and he would have to hire a driver. When Jimmie learned he was going to be in competition with Dad for the job, he cut his bid so low that the school board didn't even consider it, since there was no way he could even meet expenses.

There were no other bidders, so Dad got the job. Not only had he had an income through the summer months, now he was assured of a regular monthly wage all winter. He traded the old pickup for a newer model and built a neat enclosure on the back for the kids to ride in. He began paying off the debt at the Sussex store, so we no longer had the shame of that to live with. We felt like millionaires.

*The Browns' place at Sussex, the homestead cabin.*

*The six Brown kids on the homestead in 1938, shortly before Marsh moved to Seattle.*

# MARRIAGE

## (1938-1940)

As regularly as Saturday night came around, a dance was held at the Sussex hall. It was these dances which led me (and through me, the rest of the family) into disgrace. I became involved with a married man.

The dances were put on by the Sussex Women's Club, which appointed a dance committee to be responsible for the upkeep of the hall, hiring the orchestra, and furnishing the midnight suppers, which usually consisted of two sandwiches of ground chicken, a doughnut, and all the coffee you could drink. The coffee was brewed in a copper boiler on one of the stoves that provided heat for the hall in winter. People came for miles to visit, drink, fight, and seek romance, and some of us even went to dance! No one had ever heard of baby-sitters in those days, so the whole family came. Two or three long, narrow tables normally used for suppers or bridal and baby showers were ranged along the wall at the end of the hall to pile coats on, as there were no coat racks. The dances usually lasted from 9 P.M. to the wee hours of the morning, and as babies and small children succumbed to sleep, they were nested among the coats.

Over the years, the orchestra changed from time to time, as did the type of music played. Merle Brosius and Frank Heltzel played old-time hillbilly music, and that was what I learned to dance to. How well I remember Marsh playing "Red Wing" on the harmonica while Paul taught me to dance in the living room at the Hall House!

Like so many of the old bachelors that seemed to have ended up in our area, Frank had an unquenchable thirst once he began trying to slake it. I never knew of him to show up drunk when he was running the threshing machine, but whenever he played his dulcimer for a dance, he ran on alcohol. Probably the only reason he lasted through the night was because he only got to take a drink between dance numbers. Sometimes the supper break did him in, though, and the remainder of the night, Merle's piano thumping kept the crowd dancing.

When he was sober, Frank was not very talkative, though he was by no means surly. But the drunker he got, the more morose he became. Russ Streeter often told of an incident at one Sussex dance. He had been outside having a drink and was heading back to the hall when he passed Frank, also out having a snort.

"How's she goin', Frank?" Russ asked sociably as he walked by.

"None a yer damn business!" growled Frank. "And if you weren't such a good friend, I wouldn't a told ya that much!"

About 1938, a modern dance band, Floyd Coping and his Orchestra, was employed. Floyd played saxophone, accompanied by piano and drums. In addition to the old traditional music, they did all the popular music of the day. We younger dancers, at least, thought they were great!

Women attended the dances free, but all males who entered the dance hall door either had to buy a ticket or leave. A snippet of bright-colored cloth was pinned in a conspicuous place on the shirt so the ticket seller at the door could see at a glance if persons coming in were legal. Later, a purple stamp on the back of the hand replaced the cloth patch because it was too easy for several men to use one ticket by taking turns wearing the same ticket into the hall.

The hall was on the bank of Powder River and next to the Sussex Bridge which spanned it. It is nothing short of miraculous that no one ever staggered off into the river and drowned, or fell from the girders of the bridge where they had climbed in a fit of exuberance. One tipsy lady attracted quite a lot of attention one night by calling repeatedly from the top of the bridge, "Somebody help me! I'm somewhere up above the moon!" She had managed to climb to the top and was lying on her belly, clutching the girder in a death grip with arms and legs, and looking down at the reflection of the full moon on the water. A quickly formed rescue squad, employing more enthusiasm than technique, managed to bring her down without anyone being injured.

At midnight, the orchestra leader would announce the "supper dance." We girls waited nervously to see if some eligible male would ask us to dance. The men were expected to buy supper for whomever they danced with. There was a small charge for the lunch and the orchestra was paid out of the money taken in from tickets and suppers sold.

The married men usually paired off with each other's wives on the dance floor while the unattached males tended to seek single girls as partners, so I was quite pleasantly surprised one night when Brookie Turk asked me for a dance. I had had a secret crush on him ever since I started attending the dances, but he was not only much older than I, he was also married.

The first time I was ever really aware of Brookie as a person was when I was about eleven or twelve years old. He had been around all my life, but he had always been just one of the four Turk boys. It was late fall and Dad and Marsh, accompanied by Jimmie Iseminger and Brookie, had gone to the river bottom to cut bee trees and lay in a winter supply of honey.

A bee tree was a live cottonwood with at least part of the trunk hollow. The bees filled the cavity with honeycomb and honey, along with their intricate community system. The trees were located and marked during warm weather while the bees were working. When cold weather rendered the bees dormant, the trees were cut. After the tree was felled, a sort of doorway was cut out to provide access to the honey. The honeycomb was lifted out in big chunks and put in wash tubs and copper boilers, loaded into the wagons and brought home. Dad always insisted that enough honey be left for the bees to winter on and a piece of tree trunk fitted back into place in the "doorway" so the bees would not freeze or, in their dormant state, fall prey to mice. Mice could decimate a swarm of bees in short order.

Brookie and Jimmie ate supper at our house that night before going home with their share of the honey. Mom made a big pan of baking powder biscuits to go with the fresh-harvested honeycomb, dripping clear, golden, unbelievably sweet nectar. What a feast that was!

During supper, I kept noticing how witty and good-looking this Brookie Turk person was. I was beginning to be aware of boys at this stage, and something about Brookie really caught my attention. He was only five feet ten, but he had such a tremendous chest, about forty-seven inches, and was so muscular that he always made me feel he was much taller than he was. He was wedge-shaped, tapering down from his big chest to no hips at all. For years, he wore thirty-two-inch-waist Levis. He *always* wore Levis. No other brand would do, and they had to be shrink-to-fit, button-fly Levis. He only owned one pair of zip-fly pants in his life and that was a pair of western dress pants I bought him about five years before he died. He was buried in his beloved button-fly Levis.

I always thought he was a handsome man, but I was probably prejudiced. For as long as I knew him, he had silver-gray hair that was thin enough his scalp showed through, but as he later pointed out, his hair was just as heavy when he was seventy as it was when he was twenty!

Brookie received a boundless sense of humor from his mother. Not that his dad didn't have a sense of humor, but Mary Turk was a natural-born wit, with the ability to mimic people, including their mannerisms. This trait had been inherited by Brookie. He remembered every funny incident he'd ever been involved in or that had happened to people he knew. Whenever he was with other people he had them laughing. Over the years I heard him tell the same stories many times. Each time, he delivered them so spontaneously I felt the same delight at the conclusion as I did the first time I heard them.

He had a photographic memory for poetry and songs and could recite Grey's *Elegy* in its entirety, which amazed me because, for some reason, I cannot retain poetry or words to songs. He had a whole repertoire of silly, catchy songs he'd learned from his mother, plus all the limericks and short, funny poems that had caught his fancy over the years.

I was awfully shy that first time we danced, but he kept asking me questions and teasing me, and I finally began to relax and enjoy myself. He was such a good dancer, despite his life-long protest that "women who dance with me either don't know me or they feel sorry for me, because when I dance, I look like I'm trying to move a heating stove!"

We danced several more dances during the night. Brookie had to give Vernon Lohse, who lived with his uncle and aunt, Al and Helen Lohse, a ride home. I'd told him earlier that no one had taken me to the dance and that I was walking, so when the dance finally began to break up he asked me if I'd like a ride as far as Lohse's. After dancing all night, three miles less to walk had its appeal, so I accepted. He couldn't take me all the way home because the crossing on Carpenter Draw by Lohse's house was very sandy and there was too much chance of the car getting stuck in it.

In the weeks that followed, we enjoyed each other's company at the dances and learned a lot about each other. I found out Brookie was separated from Elma, his wife, who lived in a house he'd moved into the river bottom about half a mile southwest of Sussex. He lived wherever he happened to be working.

They had been married in January 1927, when he was twenty and she was nineteen. After their wedding, Brookie took a short-term job baling hay at the American Ranch. Like many large ranches, it put up a tremendous quantity of hay, which was sold during the winter. The hay was put up loose and if it was to be trucked, the buyer would move a baler in next to the stack and bale the hay to make it easier to haul. Brookie and Elma were living in a house at Sussex, and since he had no transportation, he walked the three miles in the dark winter mornings to the job, worked all day pitching hay off the haystack into the baler, then walked home in the dark in the evening.

In the next few years, he worked wherever he could find a job and they moved constantly. Times were hard, and it was a continual struggle to make a living. He worked at various times with the sheep for his brother-in-law Rol Streeter at the ranch where Elma had been born, and for the Sahara Ditch Company in the winter months. One winter, Brookie and his sister Evelyn's husband, Claude Key, took a contract to cut fence posts in the Pine Ridge for the Meike Ranch.

Their first child, named David Harvey after his grandfathers, was born the year after Brookie and Elma were married. He died from pneumonia a few weeks after birth. On May 24, 1930, Raleigh Earl was born, followed six years later, on August 14, 1936, by Vivian Luverne. By that time, the marriage had been in trouble for several years.

In 1936, when he was twenty-nine, Brookie went to work for Pete Meike, who was married to Elma's sister Naomi. With the exception of a two-year period during World War II, he continued to work there for the rest of his life.

Brookie himself was born October 24, 1907, in Boscobel, Wisconsin. His father, Harvey, a barber, had suffered from bronchitis all his life, and after several bad spells during the winter of 1915–16 his doctor advised him to move to a higher, drier climate. In early spring he left Mary, who was pregnant, and their four boys, Brookie, Halsey, Berlyn (Bo), and Carleton, at their home in Bell Center, Wisconsin and came west looking for a place to relocate. He found what he was looking for in Johnson County in north central Wyoming. He filed on a homestead on Nine Mile, a more or less dry creek about ten miles north of Sussex.

Harvey arrived back in Bell Center in mid-August, just in time for the birth of his and Mary's only daughter and last child, Evelyn. The winter was spent preparing for the move to Wyoming and disposing of several pieces of property Harvey owned, including his barber shop. By the time they left for Wyoming in early spring they had been joined by Harvey's brother Walter, his wife, Nellie, and their four children, and sister Etta, her husband, Rob Reistadt, and their eight youngsters.

They engaged an "emigrant car" to haul their livestock, household goods, and machinery. The railroad allowed one male member from each family to ride fare-free in the car to look after their livestock, so the three men traveled in it. Rob's three teenage stepsons also rode in the car as stowaways. Between stations the boys had the run of the car, but whenever the train stopped for water or freight the boys were concealed behind the pile of hay taken along to feed the work horses. Meanwhile Mary, Nellie, and Etta were trying to cope with fourteen kids on the passenger train that brought them to their destination at Buffalo. They arrived to find the entire area still buried under the winter's snow. There seemed to be no housing available anywhere and the three families ended up sharing two unfurnished rooms over a tailor shop next to the

Myer's Hotel. It is remarkable that this period of togetherness didn't result in lifetime estrangement!

The roads were still far from dry when Bud Hawkins, who had also filed on a homestead on Nine Mile, Harvey and Mary, and their family headed for the homestead sites. Freight wagons were bogged the full length of Six Mile Lane south of Buffalo, but Harvey's and Bud's wagons, loaded with lumber and the bare essentials for camping, somehow managed to get through. When they reached the homestead the two men set up a tent for Mary and the kids, decided on locations for the cabins, and left for the Big Horns to start cutting and hauling house logs.

Mary, who had lived in town all her life, suddenly found herself set adrift miles from any neighbors, living in a tent, cooking over a camp fire fueled by sagebrush, and carrying water from Nine Mile, which, fortunately, was full of pools of clean snow water. Years later, when she recounted her homestead experiences to me, I tried to imagine how she must have felt that day when the men, teams, and wagons finally vanished into the foothills of the mountains.

She laughed. "For a few minutes I considered throwing up my hands and screaming my head off, but I couldn't take the time right then. There were too many things to do."

Things like feeding the kids and keeping a fire going to wash diapers for baby Evelyn. Sagebrush makes a clean, hot fire, but burns rapidly. Brookie and Halsey were kept busy gathering and carrying dead sage to the campsite. When night came on, Mary was pretty unnerved, but she was a staunch Christian and decided she would just have to put everything in the hands of the Lord. She felt she was fortunate that the moon was in its full phase so at least she wasn't faced with the prospect of pitch-black darkness. The second night she was awakened from a restless sleep by a great rush of wind that struck the tent and threatened to blow it away. Quickly she shook Brookie awake and told him there was a terrible storm coming and they needed to try to make the tent more secure. They stepped outside and were astounded to find bright moonlight, with not a sign of a cloud anywhere.

"We had just been introduced to the Wyoming wind," Mary chuckled when she told me about it years later.

Mary was an old hand at camping out by the time a sufficient amount of logs had been hauled from the mountains and the cabins constructed. As it turned out, her experience came in handy. They had barely finished freighting the remainder of their possessions from Buffalo and gotten settled in the new house when they moved to a summer's job at the Henry Winter ("Hard Winter") Davis Ranch on Powder River.

A man named Robinson contracted to put up the Davis hay and hired Harvey, Brookie, and Halsey as part of the haying crew and Mary to cook for everyone. The haying crew consisted of about fifteen men as a rule, but there were usually grub-line riders and men looking for work so she often fed as many as twenty people at a meal. There seemed to be a big turnover of men on the crew, but there was always someone right there waiting to grab the job of anyone who quit. The crew had the bunk house to sleep in, but it was up to Robinson to provide a cooking facility for Mary. It turned out to be a large tent, complete with a new Majestic range to cook on! The Turks had brought their tent from the homestead, so they set it up next to the cook tent for their private living quarters. Once again Mary was camping out! At least she didn't have to cook on a sagebrush camp fire.

Brookie changed off driving a mower and a buckrake while Halsey drove the stacker team, which always seemed to be considered a kid's job. It's interesting to note that Brookie wouldn't have been ten years old until that October, and Halsey would have celebrated his eighth birthday in July while they were on the job. The boys weren't tall enough to harness their own teams, so Harvey did that for them.

When haying was over Harvey stayed on as Davis ranch foreman and Mary and the kids moved back to "hatch out" the homestead. The Majestic range went with them. Brookie and Halsey had taken part of their summer wages and bought it for their mother.

That winter must have seemed endless to Mary. There were no near neighbors, and Walter Turk and Rob Reistadt and their families had settled on Lower Four Mile, so they were too far away to visit. There was no school on Nine Mile at that time, so she tried teaching the three older boys at home. She had no school materials of any kind to work with, so she soon gave up on that project.

The Turks' mail came to Peckville, a store and post office a considerable distance north of the homestead. Occasionally Brookie made the trip on horseback taking Mary's letters to send to the folks back home and picking up mail that was waiting for them. Until winter set in, Harvey sometimes rode out to the homestead in the evening after work, spent the night, and rode back to the ranch early the next morning before work started for the day.

Things did not look very promising as the first Christmas on the homestead approached. Harvey had not been home for several weeks, and there was nothing Mary could do toward the holiday. A few days before Christmas the boys decided they could at least have a Christmas tree, so they went out and got a nice bushy sagebrush and brought it to the cabin. Everyone but baby Evelyn gathered red berries from the thorny wild rose bushes that grew in profusion along the creek bank. Strung on thread they made a pretty garland for the makeshift tree.

December 24 was sunny and mild. On an impulse Mary told Halsey and Brookie if they could harness the team they would go to Peckville. Inspired, the boys accomplished the feat by standing on Mary's two washtubs while they hoisted the harness onto the horse. Then one of them held the harness in place while the other ran around to the other side and pulled everything into position.

What an adventure that must have seemed after being confined to the cabin area all those months! And when they got to Peckville, in addition to a handful of letters there was a large package from Mary's mother. The excitement and anticipation helped shorten the long trip home.

As soon as the horses were cared for and the evening chores done, Mary opened the package. Gaily wrapped gifts for everyone were soon heaped around the sagebrush tree. There were homemade mittens, socks and caps for everyone, as well as cookies, candies, and dried fruits. Best of all, at the bottom of the box were magazines and books! These were a veritable treasure for Mary, who had read the small library of books she'd brought west at least twice.

Later that night there was a commotion outside the door and there was Harvey, home for Christmas. He had ridden horseback from the ranch, carefully carrying a burlap bag full of goodies from Mrs. Davis. There was a fat, dressed hen ready for roasting; cream and butter; and half a dozen precious eggs carefully packed in newspaper in a small wooden box to keep them from freezing or breaking. This memorable Christmas was to become a part of the Turk family history.

The following summer, Brookie returned to the ranch for haying, but Mary and the rest of the kids stayed on the homestead, with Halsey as man of the family. Before school started that fall Mary and the kids moved to the ranch so the older kids could attend the Sussex school. Mary was hired as ranch cook, which meant they had the use of the "cook shack," a two-story building with the kitchen and dining room downstairs and living quarters on the second floor.

The next spring, Harvey, Bud Hawkins, Claude Byler, and Ira Gibson built a schoolhouse to accommodate the increasing number of homesteader children. Some of them lived a considerable distance from the school, so it was decided to have a three-month summer school so there would be no danger of anyone perishing while trying to get to school in a blizzard.

Harvey gradually built up a small herd of cattle to run on the homestead, but the Turks continued to work at the Davis ranch, spending only enough time on the homestead to take care of the cows and meet the requirements for proving up on it. Consequently the Turk children got most of their schooling at Sussex, attending only two terms of school at Nine Mile.

During the summer of 1920 Harvey quit as the Davis foreman to go into partnership with Jack McPhillamy on a ranch adjoining the Hall ranch. McPhillamy was already ranching on Dry Fork on farther east, so Harvey and his family took over the place at Sussex, where they were living when I was born in 1921.

From that first year they worked for Hard Winter Davis, Brookie continued working for ranches in the area on a regular basis, in the hayfields and as cowboy. With the exception of the war, he spent the rest of his life working with livestock in one way or another, although he did train to be a barber with his dad as instructor. While he never did take the state exams to get his license, his barber training stood him in good stead and he did a lot of barbering in the years to come. Until we moved to Washington during the war, Harvey and Brookie cut each other's hair. Brookie refused to buy a haircut, so when we moved to Washington I got initiated (forced?) into the barbering profession and after his death, I inherited his customers and continued to act as the sheepcamp barber.

I was sixteen when Brookie began courting me, and even though I was tremendously attracted by his charm, wit, and good looks, I was very unsure of the relationship because he and his wife, though separated, were not divorced. I was like a giddy moth fluttering around an irresistible flame. I felt I should forget him and get involved with boys nearer my own age. I even tried, but they seemed too juvenile to me after being exposed to his more mature personality. Life without Brookie Turk would be too dull to even consider, I finally realized, so I agreed he should ask Elma for a divorce.

Prior to his involvement with me, she had suggested divorce on numerous occasions. He had been cool to the idea because he thought that as long as they were married, he would be free to go home and check on the kids' welfare. When she learned he wanted a divorce so he could marry me, she refused to even consider it.

The two years that followed were a time of unhappiness and frustration for us. Elma became the injured party in a marital triangle, and I became "the other woman," a home-wrecker. Gone was the easy friendliness of people I had known all my life, replaced by a thinly veiled hostility. My folks disapproved, of course, but once Brookie assured them he meant to marry me whenever Elma gave him a divorce, they gave us their blessing. The fact that they were supportive, I think, eased the aura of scandal that surrounded us.

Brookie was constantly plagued by guilt concerning his kids. He felt he would be abandoning them if we ever did get married, and at times we considered giving up and going our separate ways. We tried staying apart, but that didn't work at all with both of us living in the same community. Brookie wouldn't have left because of Raleigh and Vivian, and I couldn't leave for the simple reasons that I had nowhere to go, no money to go if I'd had a destination, and no training for any kind of a job. The situation dragged dismally on.

In April 1940, a sheep shearer named Bill Anderson, who had sheared at Sussex several springs, contacted Brookie and wanted him to come to Colorado, where Bill had a little sheep ranch. He told Brookie they could make good money shearing, as that entire area was made up of small herds of sheep that needed only a two-man shearing crew. Brookie had learned to shear sheep when he was working for Rol Streeter and later sheared at the Meike shearing pens. It was dirty, back-breaking work, but it paid better than anything else in the ranch country, so a lot of men worked at it for a few months in the spring to make some quick money. Brookie reasoned that if he could offer Elma a cash settlement, she might agree to a divorce, so he took a leave of absence from Meikes and headed for Colorado.

Colorado had one of the coldest, wettest springs they'd had in years, according to Bill. Whenever they were working too far from Bill's ranch to drive back and forth, they had to pay for meals and lodging, and if they couldn't shear for several days at a time, they soon used up the profit. After a month, Brookie gave up and came home, almost as broke as when he'd left.

Then a sheep shearer in Kaycee claimed he had several good jobs lined up in southeastern Montana if he just had transportation, so Brookie decided to give it one more try. That proved to be a worse fiasco than the Colorado venture because everywhere they went, another crew was already there working. At last, Brookie headed home in disgust, leaving the other man working temporarily with a Montana crew.

Colorado wasn't the only place to have bad weather that spring. One late April afternoon I was standing at the west window of the homestead cabin watching for Dad's school bus. I often rode the bus route with him just for something to do, but that afternoon I stayed home. There was one place just south of Lohse's where the road followed along a hog-back and was in sight of our cabin for about a quarter of a mile.

"I see the bus coming up from Lohse's," I announced to Mom, who was fixing supper.

In the same instant, I noticed an ominous black cloud just visible over the distant Big Horns to the northwest of us. In the time it took the bus to disappear from sight, the cloud had boiled up in an alarming fashion, and I could see it all along the northern expanse of skyline. I called Mom to look at it and even while we stood watching, it spread across the sky, hiding the mountains and then the foothills. In a matter of minutes, the inky black wall of clouds was blotting out the road where the pickup had passed a short time earlier.

There was such a dead calm where we were that I felt as if we were in a vacuum as we watched the storm approach. Suddenly there was a blast of north wind that caused the cabin to creak, a scattering of icy pellets spattered against the north window like buckshot, and then we were engulfed in a shrieking maelstrom of wind and snow that darkened the room to dusk. For a few awful moments I thought the cabin was going to be carried away. My next thought was for Dad and the kids, Fred, Ruth, Dan, and Julie. Surely Dad couldn't see to drive, and the engine would soon be packed with snow so the pickup would die. I stared out the west window hoping for a break in the storm so I could see the road approaching the cabin, but the wall of snow whistling past shrouded the window. For a moment, above the roar of the storm, I thought I heard the sound of a motor, but I knew it was wishful thinking.

Then the cabin door crashed inward and a cloud of snow sizzled and hissed against the hot stove in the corner by the door. Mom and I both ran to try to push the door shut against the storm, thinking the sheer force of the wind had blown it open. Before we reached it, five snow-crusted figures stumbled into the room. Mom helped Dad shove the door shut, then she grabbed the broom and began sweeping the snow off them while I wiped snow from their faces with a towel. We all began talking at once until everyone finally calmed down and Dad told us what happened.

He saw the blizzard coming about the same time I did and drove as fast as he could on the rocky, rutted dirt road. They had just come in sight of the cabin, with only about a quarter of a mile to go when the storm hit. Dad opened his door and looked down at the hard-packed track of the road and kept driving. The door was open on the side toward the storm, so it was blowing snow into the cab of the pickup, but all four of the kids were in the closed-in back, so he didn't worry about that. He almost ran into the side of the homestead shack before he realized he'd made it home.

The wind was not quite so bad on the leeward side of the cabin, and he got the kids out and walked them along the south wall to the corner. When they rounded the corner and headed along the east wall, the full fury of the storm hit them, and they had to cling to each other to keep from being blown away. When Dad found the door he turned the doorknob and the wind blew the door in so violently they all just blew in right behind it.

By nine or ten o'clock that night, the storm moved out as suddenly as it had come in. We had to shovel out the door to our dugout before we could get in to go to bed.

The next morning we awoke to a world of huge drifts and warm sunshine that soon began melting the snow. When we turned on the radio, we learned that two men had perished in the storm at Midwest. Their car stalled, and instead of staying in it, they got out and tried to walk a short distance to some dwellings. They became disoriented instantly, with eyes and nostrils plastered with wet snow. Then they got separated from each other. When searchers found them after the storm, they were a short distance apart and only about a hundred yards from a house.

About that time, an occurrence in the community created such shock waves that our scandal dropped into oblivion. A young woman of rather loose morals, a schoolmate of mine, was discovered to have contracted a venereal disease. She was informed by the county health officer that she must turn in the names of every man she'd had contact with so they could be checked in order to curb an epidemic. The list she provided had about ten names on it from the Kaycee-Sussex area and two of the names from Sussex were married men! The suspects all pleaded innocence and suggested she had turned their names in for spite. Only one man checked out as positive and he had infected her, so everyone else was given a clean bill of health. Even so, the little seed of doubt had been planted and it was a long time before that stain on the community completely faded.

After helping shear Meike's sheep, Brookie spent the summer tending camp for Pete Meike. He lived at the sheep camps on the mountains and only came down once a week to pick up supplies, visit the kids, and spend a few short hours with me. Even widowhood has not compared to the loneliness I endured that spring and summer. When it was time to bring the sheep off the mountains to the winter range at the Meike Ranch, Brookie moved Wes Stanley's camp down, so I didn't see him for almost a month. Then, just when it began to seem I'd never see him again, he arrived at my folks' homestead in a state of jubilation.

Elma had finally agreed to a divorce and was going to start proceedings immediately.

We decided, for reasons I don't remember, to be married in the sleepy little cow-town of Gillette, Wyoming. Two weeks before the date, we made the hundred-mile trip, only to learn that Brookie had to have a blood test taken before we could get our marriage license. We went to the only doctor in Gillette and explained what we wanted. He took the blood specimen from the inside of Brookie's elbow, pulled the needle out, and pulled the sleeve of Brookie's white shirt down without so much as dabbing any alcohol on the puncture. The sleeve had a blood stain till the shirt wore out. In about ten days, the report on the blood test came back from Cheyenne where it had been sent for evaluation. At long last we could get married! We had waited almost three years for this day!

I had supposed we would have to get someone off the street to witness for us, so I was pleased and happy the morning of the great day when Brookie said we had to go through Kaycee and get his parents to take with us for that purpose. They had openly approved of our relationship, and their support had meant a great deal during the difficult times.

We picked up Harvey and Mary and stopped in Edgerton to eat an early dinner. Though I don't recall what any of us ordered in the tiny cafe, I do have a vivid memory of the side dish being boiled navy beans, and Mary whispering, "Don't eat the beans; they're soured."

I could see the tell-tale little bubbles rising to the surface, and I knew she was right. Apparently the cafe had no refrigeration because when the waitress brought dishes of canned, purple plums for dessert, they were fermented, too.

We arrived in Gillette about 1:30 and went directly to the court house and got our license. The clerk who issued it told us where to find the justice of the peace. He ran a secondhand furniture store on the outskirts of town and we would probably find him there.

After all these years, I'm sure my memory has distorted my recollection of the building. To me, it seemed to be a huge structure with a ceiling so high I almost expected to see clouds forming above us. Along one side ran a counter piled with stacks of old, dusty magazines, lamps of all kinds, and a motley assortment of odds and ends found only in secondhand stores and country auctions. There were stacks and boxes of mismatched, chipped china, pots and pans, butcher knives, fruit jars, and bushel baskets full of miscellaneous junk. The rest of the building was piled with upright pianos; dusty, faded, overstuffed chairs and davenports; bedsteads and stained mattresses; wobbly chairs; and rickety tables.

A huge, pot-bellied stove stood in the middle of the room. Several men were sitting around it, even though we were having August weather that October day. They all gave us a good looking over as we came out of the bright sunlight and blinked uncertainly until our eyes adjusted to the dim interior of the building. Brookie told the men we were hunting the J.P. so we could get married.

This brought even closer scrutiny from the men, since I must have looked quite juvenile in spite of my nearly nineteen years, and Harvey, who was the deputy sheriff of Kaycee at the time, was wearing his badge on his shirt pocket.

Somebody volunteered the information that the J.P. was at an auction but should be back after a bit. We went back outside to wait— and wait some more. The sun was beating down and the temperature must have been nearly ninety degrees.

I had ordered my plain brown wedding dress with shoes to match from the National Bellas Hesse catalog. When the order arrived, the shoes were too small but there wasn't time to exchange them, so I wore them anyway. As the day progressed and the temperature rose, my feet began to swell. The stiff, too-tight shoes were terribly uncomfortable, but I was afraid to take them off for fear I'd never get them back on.

The sun was low in the west when a truck loaded with more of the same type of stuff the building was full of backed up to the door and two men got out. The men who had been warming the stove consulted with them in low voices and a cocking of heads in our direction. One of the new men came over and introduced himself as Mr. Robert P. Ennis, the J.P. He seemed quite flustered and uncomfortable. After he made sure we really did intend to get married, he said he would go home and change his clothes and asked us to wait inside for him.

Mr. Ennis arrived back at the warehouse looking ill at ease in a suit, and carrying a paper that turned out to be the marriage ceremony, plus a marriage certificate bordered by fancy scrollwork designs. He got behind the counter and we faced him across the clutter. We stood side by side: Mary, Harvey, myself, and finally, Brookie. There was no electricity in the building, so there were no lights and by now it was getting quite dusky inside. Brookie was nearly concealed behind a pile of junk, and I always felt that Mr. Ennis must have thought he married Harvey and me since he couldn't see Brookie.

I have no recollection of the words of the marriage ceremony. As the dusk deepened, Mr. Ennis had more and more difficulty reading. He peered closely at the printed page, stumbling over the words he could only half see. Meanwhile, the other men were busy unloading the truck, furnishing background noise for the ceremony and adding to Mr. Ennis's confusion.

"Where do you want this piano put, Bob?" one of the men called at one point.

He gave them instructions and continued the ceremony, more flustered than ever.

At last it was official. Brookie placed the $1.98 Montgomery Ward wedding band on my finger and kissed me: we were man and wife. Harvey kissed me on the cheek and shook hands with Brookie while Mary gave us an affectionate pat. Then he lit matches so Mr. Ennis could see to fill out the marriage certificate.

During our forty-one years of marriage, Brookie always referred to the ceremony as our "secondhand wedding." He claimed it was appropriate because he was a secondhand husband when I married him in a secondhand store.

Before starting the long trip back to Kaycee, we ate supper in a railroad car that had been converted to a short-order cafe. I don't recall what we ate. I only remember that the water in Gillette was so unpalatable that I ordered buttermilk to drink. Brookie paid for the supper, which just about used up the last of the ten dollars he had when we started our journey that morning. So, we began our married life about as broke as two people could be, but we were young and nothing seemed impossible as long as we had each other.

Three days after the wedding we went to work for Pete Meike. We had arrived back at Kaycee along in the night, too tired to worry about the fact that we had no money, no job, and no place to live. We set up our teepee in the Turks' back yard and rolled our bedroll out in it, creating an instant honeymoon suite.

The next morning Brookie went downtown to inquire about jobs. He came back to report that no one seemed to be looking for a ranch hand, a situation which didn't surprise us, since ranches traditionally lay off people in the fall rather than hire them. The second morning he went back to check again and returned shortly in high spirits. The first person he ran into was Pete Meike, who asked, "When are you coming back to work?"

Fred Lohse was taking a month off from his herding job and we would take over in his absence—relief herding, it was called. The sheep had just come off the summer range in the Big Horn Mountains, and they were mouthing the old ewes and making up the winter herds at the Meike shearing pens just south of the Sussex Bridge.

Until I married Brookie, I'm not sure I was even aware of what docking meant. I knew lambs had their tails cut off for sanitary reasons. A sheep can't lift its tail like a horse or cow, and during the summer when they are on green feed, their tails can get awfully messy, inviting fly eggs that hatch into maggots, which can kill an animal if they aren't tended to promptly. At docking time, in addition to getting their tails cut off, the male or ram lambs were castrated, making wethers out of them, and the ewe lambs were ear-marked for age. One year, the tip would be cut off the left ear; the next year, the right ear would receive a similar mark, followed the third year by a left split, and so on. When a rancher had used up all the possible combinations, the sequence was started over. A record was kept of what ear mark was used each year so the sheep owner could tell at a glance the age of a ewe by her ear mark.

By using ear marks, they cut out all the ewes that were over a certain age and checked their teeth. If a ewe had bad teeth, a daub of paint on top of the head indicated she was to be shipped. If their teeth were so-so, they were put in a herd by themselves and kept in the meadows for the winter where they could be fed hay. The young ewes and the old ewes with sound mouths were put in herds that wintered on the range with a herder to look after them.

The morning we went to work, Brookie went to the shearing pens and worked sheep all day. I drove our Nash car out to my folks' homestead and left it. I gathered up a flour sack full of my clothes and several books, tied it behind my saddle, and rode Dad's little bay saddle horse, Shorty, back to where Fred's sheep wagon was parked on a long divide east of Chalk Butte, southeast of Sussex with the Pine Ridge rising up to the south.

When I was a girl on the Hall place, I seldom played house or mothered dolls. My dream was to live in a sheepwagon and be a sheepherder. In the fall, after the sheep were brought in from the range and the herder let go for the winter, the sheepwagon became my domain. Until cold weather forced me into the house for the winter, I indulged my fantasy of being way out in the hills with just my faithful dog and horse, a herd of sheep, and a cozy sheepwagon to live in. Now my dream was about to come true. When Brookie came from the shearing pens that evening, he brought our herd with him and my life as a sheepherder began.

Sheepwagons tended to be built to a standard plan, though dimensions varied somewhat from wagon to wagon, depending on who built them. Our wagons averaged around twelve feet long and a little over six feet wide. At that time, all sheepwagons were covered with canvas. Whenever a top began to leak, it was removed and the wagon was recovered. Before the new canvas was put on, oilcloth was stretched over the bows in the front half of the wagon so smoke and cooking grease could be wiped off. Then a double-length cotton blanket was put over the entire top for insulation and the canvas went on last.

The body of the wagon was bolted to the solid-axled running gears, "dead exxed," as it was called. As the wheels were only about four feet apart, the wagon body had to be narrow enough at the bottom to go between them. The result was like a pickup camper, with "overjets" where the body of the wagon extended out over the wheels, about eighteen inches on each side. These overjets served double duty: as benches to sit on, and inside them between the front and rear wheels, storage space.

The wood-burning stove sat just inside the door, with a narrow space between the side of the stove and the end of the wagon. This space was lined with heavy metal sheeting for insulation and served as a wood box. The firebox of the stove was on the opposite side of the stove from the woodbox, so there was no fire hazard from it. Long metal rods with threaded ends and nuts ran down from holes in the four corners of the stove top through holes in the floor to fasten the stove securely so it was held in place no matter what happened to the rest of the wagon while moving over rough terrain. Part of the space directly behind the stove was closed in like a small closet without doors and utilized as storage space. This held pots, pans, lids, and skillets, and an open storage space on top held coffee, soap, lard, and so on. The end facing the bed at the back of the wagon was a closed cupboard that held the dishes and a drawer for cutlery.

At the end of the overjet directly across from the stove was another cupboard that the water pail sat on. In a lot of the wagons, this cupboard held a tip-out flour bin and any time water got slopped out, it immediately ran into the bin, creating lumpy flour.

The bed, about the same size as a modern three-quarter sized bed, took up the back third of the wagon and was a little over waist high. It was simply a boxed-in area deep enough to hold springs or mattress and bedding. The table pulled out from under the bed and filled up most of the area between the bed and the stove. The tables were designed so they could be pulled completely out and used for an extra bed by laying them across from one overjet to the other.

A lot of the old wagons had a very narrow table that was supported by a leg that dropped down from the center front when the table was pulled out. Nothing locked the leg in position, and it was not an infrequent occurrence for someone to accidentally kick the leg out from under the table. The ensuing crash of cutlery and dishes, the instant

blending of food and coffee and curses was enough to ruin a
sheepherder's or camptender's day. Brookie widened the tables in all
the Meike wagons and built tracks for them to run in so no leg was
necessary.

The area under the bed was called the "cubby hole" and was often
just an open storage area with a four- or six-inch board across the front
to keep things from sliding out. This was where the herder kept his
suitcase, extra footwear, canned goods, potatoes, and miscellaneous
groceries, among other things. Some wagons had the space split
between drawers on one side and a storage space on the other.

The wagons were equipped with kerosene lamps that fit in a metal
bracket on the wall between the bed and the stove. In one of the Meike
wagons, the lamp bracket slid along a board that was set between two
of the bows so you could position the lamp to shine on the stove while
you were cooking. Then, if you wanted to read in bed, you slid it to the
other end and presto! A bedside light! When the wagon was being
moved, the glass lamp chimney had to be packed so it wouldn't get
broken. A wagon always had at least one spare chimney because it was
so easy to drop one, especially if a herder was fumbling to get the lamp
lit with fingers numb from being out in the cold all day.

A sheepherder had just the bare essentials in his wagon: a few pots
and pans, a couple of skillets, enamel-ware plates and cups, and an
enamel or aluminum bowl for mixing pancakes. A butcher knife, paring
knife, meat saw, several table knives, forks and spoons and a big mixing
spoon, a pancake turner, a pan for baking biscuits or corn bread, a coffee
pot, and a dishpan completed the equipment in a wagon.

There was very little floor space, especially with the table pulled out,
but after being out all day with the sheep most herders were glad to sit
down to prepare a meal! The wagons were designed for only one man
to live in, so to accommodate the two of us, we had to utilize every
available space.

Our supper that first night was canned soup and crackers. I hadn't
ever really admitted to Brookie that I didn't know how to cook; now I
was forced to, and he learned the awful truth! I knew Brookie was a
good cook, so I was terribly embarrassed to have him find out my
shortcoming. He took it surprisingly well, although he told me in no
uncertain terms that I was going to have to learn. I felt better when he
said he would teach me. In later years, he loved to tell people he married
me so young so he could teach me to cook the way he wanted it done.

The second day we kept the sheep north of the ridge until afternoon,
then we started them up through Carpenter Canyon. Our camptender
was moving another herder and his sheep out that day and wouldn't

catch up with our wagon until the next day, so we would trail our herd through the ridge to the Cow Camp and spend the night there.

Shine Devoe was our camptender. He was christened Lawrence, but few people knew him by that name. The story I always heard was that when he first came to the Meikes' looking for work, he was riding a horse so thin you could see the sun shine through it. Thus, he got the nickname "Sunshine." Somewhere along the way it got shortened to "Shine," and Shine he remained. He was well over six feet tall, a big, powerful man with dark, curly hair and a big, friendly grin. He had big hands to match the rest of his frame, and years later when he became a TV repairman, Brookie always marveled that Shine could "go into the guts of a television and sort through all those little wires with hands that looked like two stalks of bananas!"

He had a great sense of humor and loved a practical joke as much as Brookie did. Each of them was always trying to put something new over on the other, and when they got together with Pete Meike, a person could never be sure what might happen! They could come up with more horseplay than three kids.

One spring Pete loaned Brookie to Rol Streeter for a few days while Rol was waiting for a new hired man to come to work. Brookie was looking after the sheep out in the hills north of Rol's ranch when he found an Indian skull that had washed out of the bank of a draw. When Brookie returned to Meike's, he brought the skull with him and put it in the jockey box on the front of Shine's supply wagon, then waited for the reaction.

It was several days before Shine had any occasion to look in the jockey box, and Brookie was pleased that he happened to be nearby when he did. Shine lifted the lid with one hand and reached in with the other. Suddenly he froze and stared into the box as if hypnotized, then with a yell of pure terror, he almost fell over backward! How Brookie loved to tell that story, especially when Shine was in the audience to enjoy it!

The Cow Camp was Naomi Meike's homestead cabin, a nice, four-room log house north of Meadow Creek. There was a good, soft water spring there, quite some distance from the house, but it was downhill coming back with a full pail of water. The cabin was kept stocked with nonperishable groceries and there were always bedrolls there, so it was ready for occupancy at any time.

Our unusually warm fall weather had continued, and this day was no exception. It was as hot as summer time in the canyon, and the sheep jammed up on the narrow road until it was almost impossible to move them. The only dog we had was Rex, a small, red dog that was three-footed. He had jumped a fence one winter, tangled in the wire, and hung there until his foot froze. Handicapped as he was, he soon played out in the heat and the rocky terrain.

By the time we worked the sheep out of the canyon on the south side of the ridge, it was almost sundown. It was still about two miles to the Cow Camp, so Brookie suggested I ride on over to the cabin and take care of my horse before dark. I could carry wood and water and start supper while he brought the sheep.

The cabin sits down in a sort of bowl, and when I rode over the rim, it was already in shadow. I hurriedly unsaddled Shorty and picketed him with the rope I had on my saddle. There was something spooky about the deserted house, which by now was almost dark inside. It was so quiet! The only sounds were Shorty cropping grass and the coyotes tuning up for their nightly concert. My boots sounded unnaturally loud on the porch floor.

I opened the door and forced myself to step into the shadowy kitchen. The water pail was just inside the door, upside down on the washstand to keep it clean. As I grabbed it, I noted with relief that the wood box was full. I headed for the spring in the near dark, feeling like a spooked horse. Every clump of sagebrush, every rock, was crouched along the path ready to leap at me till I got near enough to see what they really were. When I finally reached the spring my knees were so weak I wasn't sure I could manage to carry a bucket of water back to the cabin, even if it was downhill.

I had always been terrified of the dark, but I had tried hard to overcome this phobia as I grew up. Now I knew I was letting my imagination run wild, so I forced myself to calm down. It was reassuring to hear Shorty munching grass as I approached the dark cabin.

I cussed myself for not lighting a lamp before I went to the spring. I groped around in the dark and found the jar of matches that was kept on top of the warming oven of the stove. The only thing there was for light was a kerosene lantern with a smoke-blackened chimney. It was too dark to see to clean it, so I had to use it as it was.

I hung the lantern above the stove, got a fire started, and put water on to heat in the tea kettle. I peeled potatoes and put them on to boil and cut several slices from a big, home-cured ham that was hanging in a flour sack from a nail in the ceiling.

The lantern made a small circle of light around the stove, but ten feet away the shadows hovered, waiting for me. I tried to keep busy and ignore them. Then the noises began. The place was overrun with mice and pack rats and, as soon as they got used to me being there, they went busily about their nocturnal affairs. They pattered across the attic above my head; they rattled around in the wood box; they rustled things in the drawers and gnawed in the cupboards until I was afraid to move away from the stove.

Where was Brookie? He couldn't be trailing the sheep in the dark. My overactive imagination began to picture all kinds of disasters. Maybe his horse had fallen on him and he was lying out there somewhere in the dark, needing help. Just as I decided I couldn't stand another minute of this, I heard Shorty nicker a welcome to Bingo, the horse Brookie was using. I never let Brookie know till years later how scared I had been.

The next morning, Shine brought our wagon and set it on a high divide south of Meadow Creek called Six Horse Hill because it took six horses to pull a loaded freight wagon over it. We would camp there for the next two weeks. A little draw headed a short distance from where Shine set the wagon. He and Brookie pointed it out to me as the place where a fellow named Billy had committed suicide several years before. He went to one of the sheep camps, took a rifle from the wagon, and rode into this isolated piece of country. After turning the horse loose, he sat down in the washout with his back against the bank, and blew his head off. It took searchers several days to find him after his saddled horse came in to the Meike ranch. The story made me shudder, and I was nervous at living so close to the site of the tragedy. It didn't help matters a bit when Shine and Brookie assured me that his ghost wandered the hills at night.

Before we went to bed that night, I went out to relieve myself. I was scared of the dark, as usual, and my imagination had plenty of material to work on. I had just squatted when Brookie stuck his head out the back window and exclaimed, "Billy's ghost is right behind you!"

I cleared the distance from where I was to the back of the wagon in one leap, with my pants around my ankles! The window was too small for me to get through, so there I clung with my head in the window until Brookie came around and rescued me.

We settled into a sort of routine, but each day was a new experience for me. We got up each morning at daylight, which wasn't too early in mid-October, ate breakfast, then headed the sheep off the bedground whichever way Brookie wanted them to go that day. Then we left them to themselves while we explored the country.

Brookie knew every nook and cranny of the entire area, so he was able to show me many interesting things that most people didn't even know existed. There were campsites of ancient people, gone long before the Indians that the early trappers encountered lived here. Sandstone cliffs bore the names or initials of soldiers, cowboys, and sheepherders, many of them dated in the late 1800s. There were beds of dinosaur bones and fragments, and we sometimes found fossils embedded in sand rock formations.

While the sheep were nooning on water, either on Meadow Creek or Salt Creek, we would let our horses graze while I read out loud from one of the books I had brought from home. We usually carried some dried fruit in our pockets and we would munch on that. Our lovely Indian summer weather continued to hold, and we even went skinny-dipping in Meadow Creek a few times.

When the sheep began to graze off water, we would head them back toward the wagon, circle them, and ride on to camp as they grazed the rest of the way to the bedground by themselves. The divide we were camped on was so high we could see for miles in any direction, so we could glance out from our supper preparations and check on the sheep.

The coyotes were so numerous that hardly a day passed without us seeing several. They would go loping off across the country and blend into the sagebrush or vanish into a gully. As soon as the sun got low in the west, a coyote would start to yip. Soon, another would answer and in a few minutes dozens of them were yip-yapping and howling. After dark it sounded like they had surrounded our camp.

Poor Rex was deathly afraid of them and cowered under the wagon when they began their nightly songfest. Once in a while, the sheep would spook and run on the bedground in the dark, their hooves making a low roar. Whenever that happened, Brookie poked the rifle out the back window and pulled the trigger. There would be a blaze of fire and a blast that rocked the wagon, then silence. In the mornings, we sometimes found a dead ewe on the far side of the bedground where the coyotes had pulled her down before being scared off by the rifle.

One evening as I was fixing supper, Brookie looked out and his exclamation of surprise brought me to the door. About a quarter of a mile away, a coyote was moving back and forth across the far side of the sheep, herding stragglers along just like a good sheep dog. The sheep showed no alarm, only respect, moving ahead of him whenever he passed behind them. Before long, he disappeared into a coulee, apparently deciding his job was finished.

The evening after we got settled at our camp, Brookie butchered a mutton and from then on, we practically lived on mutton and potatoes. I have never eaten anything that tasted better than a plate full of fried mutton and fried potatoes and onions after being out in the open all day with nothing to eat but some dried fruit. Sometimes we cooked up a big kettle of stew during the evening to have the next night and for a day or two after. Fresh meat was kept in camp by hanging it up at night so the cool air could get to it, then rolling it in a piece of canvas in the morning and putting it back under the wagon where it was shady.

It was customary for the camptender to come to camp once a week with a barrel of fresh water, wood, groceries, mail, and grain for the horses. Because it was so far out to our camp, Shine made the trip out one day with the supply wagon and four horses, stayed all night and made the return trip back to the ranch the next day.

The supply wagon was just what the name implies. It held a barrel of drinking water and wood for the cook stove in the sheepwagon if we were on trail, kerosene for the lamp and for starting the fire in the stove, hay and grain for the horses, salt for the sheep, the teepee and bedroll of the camptender, and numerous other odds and ends. On the front of the wagon, a "jockey box" held a complete horseshoeing outfit, plus a can of axle grease for the wagons and a special wrench for the nut in the wheel hub.

The day before Shine was due, Brookie suggested it would be nice if I made a pie to have when he came. I didn't have the foggiest idea how to make a pie crust, but I tried. I made a dried peach pie and the filling tasted pretty good, but the crust had all the better qualities of a piece of ceramic ware! Shine was kind enough not to make fun of my pie, but Fred Lohse told me the next fall that even his dogs wouldn't eat my biscuits! And it was the truth.

When Shine came to tend camp, we learned from him that the movie *Boom Town*, starring Clark Gable, was playing at the theater at Midwest that weekend. I had seen only a few movies in my time, and this one had been so widely publicized that I longed with all my heart to see it. Brookie suggested we ride to Midwest horseback Saturday night after the sheep were bedded, and I eagerly endorsed the idea. From our wagon on the divide, we could plainly see the lights of the different camps in the Salt Creek Oilfield at night, and they looked quite close. Brookie said he had ridden to many a dance in Kaycee in years gone by, and that was a ride of close to twenty miles. This wouldn't be nearly so far.

Saturday evening the sky was overcast and there was a softness in the air like a spring evening before a rain. This was the first stormy weather we'd had since we came out with the sheep. I was young, though, and even the possibility of rain couldn't dim my enthusiasm for the big adventure. As soon as the sheep were bedded, we set out flares made of tin cans half full of sand saturated with kerosene. We placed them at intervals around the bedded sheep and ignited the kerosene-soaked sand. These would burn most of the night, barring heavy rain or high wind, and would presumably frighten the coyotes away. Brookie said he thought the flares made it easier for them to pick out the fattest sheep!

It was almost dark by the time we got away from camp. We were wearing our best shirts and overalls and our spurs, of course. No bona fide cowboy or sheepherder would be caught dead riding into town on a Saturday night without his spurs!

It was a good thing Brookie knew the country like the back of his hand. There was a deep canyon with sheer walls that had to be crossed and there was only one crossing on it. Darkness had set in when we reached it, and it was probably just as well that I couldn't see the narrow, steep trail.

Once we got the canyon behind us, we were on an honest-to-goodness dirt road, so the traveling was much easier. At least, it was until we began meeting cars coming to a party at the Tobin ranch. Their lights blinded our horses, and we found we could not get off the road because of a deeply cut wash on each side. As each car approached, we stopped our horses as close to the ditch as we dared and hoped the driver would see us in time to miss us. We finally reached Midwest all in one piece, to my considerable relief.

The legs of a big signboard provided a hitching post for our horses. We let our spur straps out a notch or two so the rowels would touch the sidewalk. With our spurs jingling in the best Western fashion, we made our grand entrance into the lobby. We were just in time for the midnight show, and for the next couple of hours, I was transported to another world.

That world ended abruptly when the show was over and we walked out of the theater. The night was black as pitch and a light, misty rain was falling. The horses were chilled from standing in the rain and pranced and shied at shadows till we got away from the lights of town. Once we were away from civilization, they got their night sight and settled into a mile-eating jog.

Anticipation had made the trip to Midwest pass quickly, but going back to camp was another story. The darkness and rain soon eliminated any sense of adventure, and boredom and weariness overtook me. In spite of myself, I drowsed and Shorty was quick to take advantage of a chance to drop to a walk.

"Billy's ghost is right behind you!" Brookie called back whenever he realized I was no longer with him.

I'd wake with a start, spur Shorty to a lope and catch up, only to repeat the whole process in a few minutes. After a seemingly endless trip, we finally reached camp just as it was getting daylight. We grained the horses, fixed breakfast, and began our usual day without ever going to bed.

What a long day that was! It was overcast and drizzly all day, so the sheep wouldn't steady down. They didn't noon on water as they did when it was warm; consequently, there was no chance to cat-nap. I decided that one trip was enough to last me a lifetime!

That stormy spell marked the end of our beautiful fall weather. We had more nice days, but there was a definite feel of fall in the air, and it began to freeze hard at night. There was always a thin layer of ice in the water barrel every morning. When Shine made his next trip out, he moved us north to the head of Carpenter Canyon. We camped there until Fred came back from his vacation, then we moved to the other Meike sheep camp and relief-herded for Wes Stanley so he could spend some time with his wife and kids.

The day before Thanksgiving, I rode over to visit my family. I spent the night, then rode back to our camp Thanksgiving morning. When I arrived at the wagon, I found Brookie roasting a chicken, and a beautiful cranberry pie was cooling on the table. Pete Meike had sent Shine out to the sheep camps the day before with some goodies for the holiday. The roast chicken and dressing was a real treat. Brookie's pie was delicious and the crust was very good. I asked him how he made the crust.

"It's really very simple," he grinned. "It's an old family recipe. I just line a pie pan with a paper plate and put in the filling and bake it! That's all there is to it!" Paper plates in those days were not the flimsy affairs they are now. They were thick, coarse, compressed fiber, about the shape, size, and thickness of a pie crust.

That's all I ever found out about his crust, too. In all the years we spent together, he always maintained that was how he made a pie; and in all our years together, he never baked another. Maybe his good crust that long-ago Thanksgiving Day was a once-in-a-lifetime fluke!

When we finished relief herding we were once again homeless. Brookie had a winter's job at the Pete Meike ranch, so we moved in with my family on their homestead. Brookie drove our Nash back and forth to work. After a few days he brought the good news that Jean Indart, a neighboring sheep rancher, had an extra sheepwagon he would let us use for the winter if we could clean it up. Someone had tipped the wagon over while moving it off the mountains that fall. It wasn't damaged, but the interior was a mess! Ashes from the stove had mixed with flour, syrup, coffee grounds, eggs, and dirt. This conglomeration was held together with a base of sourdough, which had dried to a cement-like hardness on every surface.

We moved in and I started cleaning. I couldn't scrape the sourdough off because it took the paint with it, so I had to soak it loose. Finally I got most of it off, and our wagon home looked really nice and cozy. The wagon was parked on the north side of Powder River about a hundred yards west of the Sussex Bridge. Before the ground froze we built a small dugout in the bank by the wagon so Raleigh, who was ten by that time, would have a place to sleep when he spent the weekends with us.

Brookie ate his noon meal at the ranch, so I was alone all day. Once I got the wagon cleaned up, I spent my days reading, writing letters, and doing the chores that were part of everyday living: chopping wood, carrying water, filling the kerosene lamp, emptying ashes and washing the dishes I dirtied in my cooking efforts. After my embarrassing attempt to make a pie crust, I vowed to myself that I would learn the cooking basics that winter if I didn't do anything else. I copied a lot of my Mom's old stand-by recipes in a composition book, which I still have. Brookie started a sourdough "jug," a two-gallon crockery jar, and taught me to make sourdough pancakes and biscuits. Brookie could always make much better pancakes than I could, and our camptender, Shine, made the best sourdough biscuits I ever ate. My dad used to tell us kids about a sheepherder he knew in Montana whose sourdough pancakes were so light he had to keep the sheepwagon door shut so they wouldn't float away! Mine were never anywhere near that good, but they were passable.

Powder River was our only source of water, and the trail from the top of the bluff where our wagon sat to the edge of the river was almost straight up and down, so I used water as sparingly as I could. I had no wash tub or wash board, so I did our laundry by sudsing out a few things at a time in the dish pan. On washdays I made numerous trips down the steep trail to the river and labored back up with buckets of water. I kept an ax at the river to chop the ice out of the hole where I dipped the water pail. We were having a very cold winter and I had to break the ice every time I got a bucket of water because it froze over in just a short time.

When it was snowy, icy, or muddy, the path was very treacherous. On one washday, my trips up and down the trail had packed it to a solid glaze of ice. I slid down the last few steps. When I got to the edge of the water hole, I was unable to stop and slid feet first into the river. It was only a couple of feet deep so I jolted to an abrupt stop, lost my balance, and sat down hard on the ice at the edge of the hole.

To this day, I can recall vividly the shock of the icy water and the feelings of outrage, indignation, and self-pity that swept over me. I scrambled out onto the ice, and the moment the cold air hit my wet overalls they began to freeze. I doubt if the temperature had gotten much above zero that day, even though the sun was shining brightly. In the few seconds it took me to get out of the river and onto my feet, the fast-running water had cleared, so I dipped up a bucket of water and headed up the trail, my feet squishing in my shoes at every step.

I had three resting places on the trail where it was level enough to set my bucket of water while I caught my breath, but the legs of my overalls now felt like stove pipes, so I kept climbing. I arrived at the wagon completely winded and in such a state of mind I didn't know whether to laugh or cry, so I did a little of both. I felt better immediately, but I'm sure the warmth from the sheepwagon stove had more to do with it than my little fit of hysteria!

One night Brookie asked me if I would like to go with him the next day to haul a load of barley to Fred Lohse's camp south of the Pine Ridge. Instead of feeding cake, a protein supplement in cube form, the herders were feeding the sheep barley. They scooped it out of a wagon in five-gallon buckets and poured it on the ground in long, narrow windrows before the sheep got to the bedground in the evenings. The sheep would pick up every kernel of it before bedding down for the night.

It was bitterly cold when we went up to the ranch the next morning. Brookie had loaded the barley the afternoon before, so all he had to do was harness the horses, hitch them to the wagon, and go. He dipped each bridle bit in the water trough, which was kept from freezing with a coal-burning tank heater. The instant the cold air hit the wet bits, it froze a film of ice over them. Brookie explained to me that this would prevent the bits from freezing to the horses' lips and tongues when he put the bridles on.

It took a four-horse team to pull the heavy load of grain up through Carpenter Canyon. A four-horse team, or "four-up," was made up of two teams of horses. The wheel team was hitched next to the wagon and the lead team was hooked on in front of them. Our wheel horses that day were big, powerful horses named Fred and Sleepy. Mike and Bally, the lead team, were a bit smaller than most work horses, but what they lacked in size they more than made up for in spirit and stamina. Once they were hitched up, they fidgeted and jigged with impatience, and I expected them to run away with the wagon before we could get in. There was no seat, so we sort of burrowed down in the barley and Brookie kicked the brake off. The horses lunged away at a gallop, but he soon pulled them down to a trot. They settled down to a walk when we left the county road and climbed toward the Ridge.

The road snakes its way up Carpenter Canyon with rock walls on one side and a sheer drop-off to the canyon floor on the other. I was surprised at the way Mike and Bally automatically swung wide on the sharp curves to compensate for the other team and the wagon. When we reached the top of the canyon the horses were sweating, and their shaggy winter coats were frosted with moisture. Vapor from their breath had transformed the long whiskers on their muzzles to pipe cleaners.

The Meike ranch had built a drift fence a short distance south of the ridge to keep the cattle from drifting back into the river during the summer months. When we reached the gate in the drift fence, I was so numb from the cold I could scarcely move. I managed to climb down from the wagon, but my legs almost refused to hold me up as I clumped woodenly to the gate to open it. Needles of sensation began to stab up my legs as I swung the gate open and then closed it after Brookie drove through.

Just as I turned from the gate, Brookie hollered, "Mike! Bally!" And away they went!

I broke into an awkward lope trying to catch up, but he kept the wagon just far enough ahead of me I couldn't quite grab hold of the tailgate. Finally he stopped and I stomped up alongside the front wheel, panting and red-faced from exertion.

"Why'd you do that?" I demanded furiously.

"Are you warm?" he asked, grinning as he gave me a hand up into the wagon.

I was not only warm, I was hot under the collar! After I cooled off, I realized the exercise had gotten my blood circulating and probably saved me from frostbite. I couldn't stay mad at him.

Then I remembered one of the stories Dad told about driving the stage out of Cut Bank, Montana. Cut Bank is only a few miles from the Canadian border, and the winters can be quite severe. The winter he drove the coach route, about 1912, was an especially bad one. His description of the bitter cold, the wind piling up huge snow drifts, and the stage teams laboring through them, was always so vivid I felt as if I was right there with him. I don't know where the route took him to from Cut Bank; apparently the name wasn't distinctive and didn't stick in my memory, but the episode surely did.

It was a bitterly cold day when Dad loaded the tipsy woolen salesman into the stage, climbed aboard, firmly gripped the leather lines of the four-horse team in his heavy, sheepskin-lined mittens and headed out of town. The temperature continued to fall as the shaggy horses put the snowy miles behind them, loping where they could, trudging when necessary.

Several times Dad stopped to check his passenger, and each time he became more concerned about him. Finally, Dad climbed into the stage and began shaking the man, pumping his arms, lightly slapping his face. When the salesman responded enough to become irritated and then abusive, Dad ordered him out of the stage. When he hesitated, Dad dragged him out forcibly. He took the man around to the back and pointed to a reinforcing rod that stretched across from side to side.

"Hang on to that," Dad ordered him, "and don't let go, no matter what, or you might not live to see another day!"

"I started the horses at a brisk walk and the farther he walked, the madder he got, and the madder he got, the warmer he got!" Dad always recounted. "When I figured he had his blood circulatin', I let him ride the rest of the way. He was stone-cold sober when we got into town and so grateful I'd saved him from freezin' he bought my supper and gave me a heavy wool shirt from his sample case to boot!"

I fully appreciated that story for the first time.

When we got to Fred's wagon, we unhitched the horses and tied them to the empty wagon we would be taking back to the ranch. Fred was out with the sheep, but we found a kettle of mutton mulligan so we built up the fire, heated the stew, and ate. How good it tasted after the long, cold drive!

After we washed up the dishes, we hitched the horses to the empty wagon and started for home. They were cold and wanted to run, but Brookie held them to a trot until we got through the gate and were starting down the canyon. Then he loosened the lines and the horses stretched out in a lope.

I was too terrified to do anything but hang on for dear life. There was no seat in this wagon, either, and we stood in the bottom. The wagon jarred the living daylights out of me as it bounced over rocks and small washes in the road, and it seemed to me we were plunging down the canyon to certain destruction! Then I noticed Mike and Bally were swinging out on the curves just as they had when plodding up the canyon with the loaded wagon, and I realized they weren't running out of control at all. I looked at Brookie. He was balanced on the balls of his feet and riding each bump without any jolt at all. And he was laughing! I began to laugh, too, and turned loose and tried it. From there on, it was one of the most exhilarating rides I ever took. I was sorry when we leveled out at the mouth of the canyon and the horses dropped to a jog. Steam rose from their sweaty sides in clouds. They had really warmed up, and so had we.

The winter sun was low in the west when we clattered across the Sussex Bridge on Powder River. Brookie stopped at the top of the Sussex

Hill and let me off. I walked the short distance up the river to the wagon and got the fire going and did my chores while he went on up to the ranch and took care of the horses.

The Meikes had built an addition to their house in the fall, and during the coldest part of the winter, Brookie and Ray Bock worked on the interior. Whenever Pete and Naomi were going to be gone for the day, I walked to the ranch and cooked dinner for the men. Brookie also did the evening milking, and I sometimes helped with that.

Almost every ranch had a big shed built of straw in those days. They were inexpensive and serviceable and quite easy to build. A framework of posts and woven wire or saplings was built, with a second framework a foot or two out from the first, depending on the desired thickness of the wall. The space between the two frameworks was then filled with straw. The roof was made the same way except that it usually had only the inner framework to hold the straw.

The sheds were popular with animals. The straw just naturally attracted mice, and sparrows loved nesting in it. The livestock stuck their noses through the mesh of the wire and munched on the walls of their shelter, making nice holes for the hens to lay eggs in. Checking the straw shed for nests was part of the daily chore of gathering eggs. Occasionally a hen successfully hid a nest in the wall and one fine day she would appear with a clutch of little peepers!

Every winter before shed lambing started, the year's accumulation of manure and bedding straw would have to be cleaned out of the shed. When Brookie started that job I helped him. The shed was large enough that the horse-drawn manure spreader was driven right in and loaded by hand with forks. It was a smelly, back-breaking job, but it was the first really hard physical labor I had ever done and it gave me a great feeling of accomplishment. After the first couple of days, my muscles toughened up and I realized that being in good physical condition gave me a great sense of well-being.

In March, Brookie helped shed lamb the older ewes that had wintered in the meadows. I would have loved to help, but that was not even to be considered in those days. After all, women were delicate creatures and had to be protected from the stark reality of the birthing process!

As soon as green grass came, the shed ewes and their lambs were moved out on the range, and we got the job of herding them. We moved our personal belongings into one of Meikes' wagons and returned Jean Indart's wagon to him. We moved our herd of ewes and lambs to the Leitner homestead north of the Pine Ridge at the mouth of Carpenter

Canyon. There was a good soft-water spring under a ledge of sand rock for camp use and good stock water for the sheep.

Working with ewes and lambs was a new experience for me, completely different than herding dry ewes the fall before. I took great pride in the lambs. Almost overnight, it seemed, they changed from wobbly legged babies into fat, sassy juveniles. In the evenings when the ewes were bedding down for the night, the lambs started their games. Any kind of a bank, low hill, or rocky outcropping was a invitation for the fun to begin. A few lambs would begin to run and jump and in seconds, dozens of others would join the group. As if on signal, they would stampede along a bank, leaping and bouncing stiff-legged, and just as suddenly, they would stampede back to the herd. This would go on until dark, with a few of the ewes bleating anxiously at their rowdy children.

We slept in a bedroll in a teepee wherever the sheep bedded. They left the bedground at first daylight, so we had to be ready to leave with them. By the time we had our horses saddled, I was usually awake enough to appreciate the beauty of the new day with the birds twittering, sleepily at first, then beginning to sing with enthusiasm as the eastern sky brightened from pale pink to gold. Getting up at the crack of dawn, though, was the one thing I didn't like about working with sheep, and I never did get used to it.

We herded the sheep the direction we wanted them to go, staying at a distance so they would spread out and graze. When they finally settled down to feeding, we rode to the wagon and fixed our breakfast. After we ate, we rode back to the sheep and brought them to water, where they stayed for several hours, drinking, resting, and digesting their morning's feed. Shortly before they left water in mid-afternoon, we ate our second and last meal of the day. After the sheep grazed away from water, we picked up our bedroll and teepee if we planned on bedding the sheep in a different place that night. We let the teepee down with the bedroll still inside, rolled the whole thing lengthwise, and slung it over my horse ahead of the saddle so I could steady it while we transported it to wherever we would sleep that night.

One afternoon we were down on our knees, rolling our portable bedroom when a sinister buzz almost directly under us startled us into frantic action. Brookie jumped backward, landing on his feet; I lost my balance, sprawled on my back, rolled over, and scrambled on my hands and knees to what I considered a safe distance. Brookie gingerly slid one of the teepee poles under the teepee and gave it a flip, revealing a very perturbed rattlesnake, which he dispatched with the pole. We were never sure if we had slept on the snake the night before, or if it had crawled under the teepee to get out of the heat of the sun during the day. From that day on, I had an aversion to rolling up a bedroll in rattlesnake country.

One morning when we rode back out after breakfast, we were confronted by a grisly sight. Eighteen of our pretty lambs lay scattered up a flat-bottomed draw, their blood-soaked throats grim evidence that we had been visited by coyotes. Only two carcasses had been torn open. Brookie said it was probably two grown coyotes getting food for their pups. He explained that they had eaten the milk-filled stomachs, the livers and hearts of the two lambs and drunk the blood of all of them. When they got back to their den, they would regurgitate the whole mess for the pups to eat. I was absolutely enraged at such wanton killing, and I wanted vengeance!

We herded the sheep toward water, got a shovel, and went hunting the coyote den. Brookie had done a lot of trapping and had a lot of know-how about coyote behavior. He reasoned that the coyotes would never bother sheep close to their den. That would draw attention to their presence and jeopardize their pups. He thought they had probably come down Carpenter Canyon from somewhere south of the ridge, so that's where we went looking for tracks. Sure enough, there were the fresh tracks of two coyotes heading right up the canyon. We had no trouble tracking them because the canyon floor was sandy with a trickle of spring water running down it.

We found the den in a sandy bank at the head of the canyon and Brookie began to dig. Soon we could hear the pups whimpering, and suddenly I was filled with pity for them. Poor little things! They didn't kill our lambs!

No, cold logic said, but they would as soon as they were old enough. I turned my back and covered my ears as Brookie dragged seven pups out of the den and killed them, one by one.

Since there was a ten-dollar bounty of each of them, Brookie tied them on his saddle and we rode back to our camp, where he skinned them, leaving the scalps attached to prove that each was a coyote and not just a piece of coyote pelt. After the sheep were on water the next day, we rode the six miles in to the Sussex store and left the skins with Harry Jones, the storekeeper. He would turn them in to the County Commissioners' Office the next time he went to Buffalo and collect the bounty money for us. Later, Brookie used the bounty to buy a much-needed new saddle, but I always felt it was "blood money."

Shortly before time to take our herd in for shearing, Russ Streeter asked Brookie to help him shear his brother Hial's sheep. My family's homestead cabin was only about a quarter of a mile east of our camp, so we hired my brother Fred to herd for us while we were gone. We moved our wagon away from the water to a hill overlooking one of our bedgrounds. We hoped this might discourage coyotes from bothering the sheep at night since Fred was going to sleep at home and just stay with the sheep during the day. We loaded our bedroll and teepee, a few clothes, a Coleman gas stove, and Brookie's shearing tools in our Nash, bought a few groceries at the Sussex store, and moved to Hial's lambing camp.

The only machine shearing I had ever watched was at the Meike shearing pens, where the shearing was done in a long, wooden-floored shed built just for that purpose. Up to twelve men could shear at one time, with power for the machines furnished by a big gasoline motor that ran a drive shaft with a big pulley at each stall. A drive belt ran from the big pulley down to the shearer's rig. The clippers, like an oversized, heavy-duty version of a barber's clipper, ran from a jointed, geared shaft, much like the shaft of a dentist's drill, but larger. Each shearer had his own stall, which was simply a five-foot doorway covered with woolsack curtains. The shearer sheared in front of it, while behind it was a five-foot-by-five-foot pen that could hold up to six sheep.

The wranglers kept a constant flow of unsheared sheep moving through the alleys and pens to the shearers, and the sheared sheep out to where they were branded. Most of the shearers could shear over one hundred sheep a day, so it had to be a fast-moving, smooth-running operation with no wasted motion anywhere.

As the clippers made the final pass down the sheep's body, the creamy fleece seemed to flow from it to join the heap of wool on the floor. Without ever breaking rhythm, the shearer turned the shorn sheep back out of the stall, shoved the fleece out the opposite side with his feet, and reached for another woolly sheep.

The wool tier gathered the fleece into a bundle and tied it with special wool twine, making a package of it. The precut strings, made of twisted paper, were hung on the front of each stall so all the tier had to do was grab the end of a string and pull. The hanks of strings were counted before they were hung up as a means of keeping track of how many sheep each man sheared.

In a smaller operation, the tier carried the tied fleeces to the wool rack where a big, burlap woolsack was suspended in a frame. For a large operation with a fast crew, such as at the Meikes', there could be as many as three tiers and a wool wrangler to carry the fleeces. The fleeces were thrown into the sack for the wool tromper, who was in the sack, packing the fleece with his feet. When the sack was full, the circular clamp that held it in the frame was released, the end of the bag was sewed shut, and it was rolled into the wool shed ready to be hauled off to a warehouse somewhere.

At Hial's, the men were shearing on an open floor with portable panels forming the stalls. Russ had a small, portable shearing plant that could handle two or three machines. Brookie and Russ were the only shearers, and Hial did the wool tromping, using a portable frame. I had only gone along to cook for Brookie, but they needed someone to tie fleeces. Before I knew what was happening, Brookie volunteered me for the job! He showed me how to gather a fleece into a neat pile, slip the twine under the wool, cross the twine and flip the fleece all in one motion, cinch up the string and tie it in a square knot. He told me to wear gloves, but I insisted I couldn't tie a knot with gloves on.

I was always a very squeamish person; the sight of blood made me sick, bugs made my skin crawl, mice scared me to death, and I couldn't stand to have my hands dirty. That morning, I learned that if I was going to work with sheep, there was not going to be much room for either being fastidious or having a weak stomach! After the first fat, repulsive sheep tick crawled up my arm, I could feel ticks all over me. In a few minutes, my hands were dirty and greasy from the wool fat in the fleeces, but after the first hour, I was more concerned about the blisters that were forming where the strings cut into my hands than I was about ticks and grease. My hands were in terrible shape by the time we broke for noon.

Hial's wife, Mamie, had a delicious hot meal ready for us, and I was ravenously hungry. What a remarkable person she was! She cooked for six of us in a sheepwagon, helped with the wrangling, and gave their old sheepherder a hand with the lambing. How she managed it all I never knew. She was a little woman, slim and very pretty, with more energy than anyone I've ever known. When I saw how easily she coped with all kinds of dilemmas, made spur-of-the-moment decisions, and managed to keep her sense of humor no matter what was going wrong, I knew I wasn't going to complain about the wool being greasy, sheep ticks crawling on my neck, or my hands being sore because I was too bull-headed to wear gloves. Before I went back to work, Mamie doctored my hands with some sort of salve and gave me a clean pair of gloves to wear. I learned I *could* tie a knot with gloves on!

I was more than ready to quit when quitting time came. I was bone-tired, my clothes were slick with wool grease, and my back hurt from the constant bending over. But I felt good! I was doing a real job, a very dirty job, to be sure, but real, honest-to-goodness work! When Brookie told me I really had the hang of tying the fleeces and was doing as good a job as an old pro, I nearly burst with pride!

We had set up our teepee by the river, so we heated river water on the Coleman stove and scrubbed off the day's accumulation of grime before we went to bed. It seemed I had hardly gone to sleep when it was time to get up and go to work again. I was so stiff and sore I didn't think I'd be able to get out of bed, but when I found out Brookie was just as bad off as I was, I felt better.

That morning, I passed another milestone in the making of the new me.

"Louise, come here! I need help!"

I knew by the tone of Brookie's voice that something was seriously wrong. When I got to him I saw he had cut an artery in the hind leg of the ewe he was shearing and her blood was pumping out onto the floor.

"Hold her leg while I sew the ends of the artery," he said calmly.

The sight of all that blood sickened me, but I knew I had to do as he said or the sheep would bleed to death. I grasped the ewe's leg and held it firmly and watched with fascination as he inserted the big, curved needle into the flesh on one side of the artery, brought the thread out on the other side, and neatly tied off the severed end. The wool on the ewe's leg was saturated with blood, and when I turned loose of her, my hands were dripping with it. There was no way to wash them, so I wiped off as much as I could on my greasy pants and went back to work. I was really making progress!

A couple of days after that, we got word that our wagon had burned. We were almost through shearing Hial's sheep, so we left Russ to finish by himself. Hial paid me in fleeces for my work, enough to fill two burlap bags (about six fleeces).

Baron Woolen Mills in Utah put out a catalog showing the beautiful wool blankets they made and telling how many pounds of wool it took to make each one. You could either have your own wool made into blankets of your choice or trade your fleeces for blankets already made up. Later, we shipped my fleeces to them and had them made into beautiful blankets, which lasted us for years.

There was nothing left of our wagon but the iron rims of the wheels, a few scraps of wood that hadn't burned, and some blackened and twisted pieces of metal. The wagon had burned during the night, so no one ever knew for sure what caused the fire. It was almost impossible to keep mice out of the sheepwagons, and we assumed that mice had started the fire by chewing on matches.

Fred had already taken our herd in for shearing, which was to begin the next morning, so our herding job was finished. Brookie was supposed to help shear the Meikes' sheep, so we decided to go to their shearing pens at Sussex and set up camp that evening. We still had our teepee, bedroll, stove, and groceries we'd taken to Hial's.

We ate supper with my family at their homestead, gathered up a few clothes we had stored there, and left for Sussex. When we tried to cross Carpenter Draw at Al Lohse's place, our car got hopelessly stuck in the sandy bottom. There was no one home at Lohse's and when they still hadn't come home at dusk, we decided to roll out our bed on the grassy bank of the draw and get some sleep. We figured we could get Al to pull our car out with his pickup the next morning and still get to Sussex before they started shearing.

Brookie undressed and put his hat, shirt and overalls in the car, but wore his boots back to the bedroll because there were dry cockleburs in the grass along the bank. I undressed in the bedroll and put my clothes under the pillow instead of in the car. Al and Helen came home shortly after we went to bed, unaware that we were bedded down almost in their back yard.

There had been some thunderstorm activity to the south of us during the evening, so far away the thunder was only a distant mutter. We were half asleep when we were roused by a strange rushing sound like water swirling and gurgling.

"Flash flood!" Brookie yelled.

He grabbed the flashlight from under his pillow and by its beam we watched the Nash, hit broadside by a wall of water, teeter for a moment, then go rolling over and over down the draw, carried along by the force of the flood. Fortunately, our bedroll was spread out above the high-water mark. The Nash finally lodged against a tree down around the bend, almost directly in front of Lohse's house. It dammed the creek, which spread out almost into their yard.

I dressed and ran over to the house and pounded on the door. I don't know which surprised them more: me gibbering like an idiot on their doorstep, or a car lodged just beyond their yard with floodwater rushing past.

Helen gave me a pair of overalls and a shirt for Brookie to put on while Al hunted up a rope. We got the rope tied to the car and anchored it to the tree so it wouldn't wash any farther down the draw. Then the flood subsided almost as suddenly as it began. We went back to bed but didn't do much sleeping.

When daylight came, we could see that our car and everything in it was a total loss. It was almost completely buried by sand, silt, and debris, and the interior was filled with mud to the windows. Between the fire and the flood, everything we owned was gone except our bedroll, and the two bags of fleeces, which we had left at the homestead the evening before because they took up so much room in the car. Without his shearing tools, Brookie didn't even have a job. We felt pretty desperate.

Brookie caught a ride to Sussex with Al, and I hiked the three miles back to the homestead. Later that day, Brookie came with the good news that Pete Meike had hired us to herd one band of sheep for the summer. I felt a great weight lift from me. That meant we had a sheepwagon to move into. All of the wagons were completely furnished with dishes, cooking utensils, ax, washtub, and washboard.

Since we still had our bed, all we needed was clothing. Pete gave us an advance on our wages and we bought shirts, overalls, underwear, socks, jackets, hats, and slickers. Some of our good friends gave us hand towels, dishtowels, and pillowcases, and my Aunt Julia sent us some clothing and a pair of scissors, which turned out to be one of the most useful gifts I ever received. With our misfortunes behind us at last, I hoped, we would be leaving for the mountains as soon as our herd was sheared.

*Louise and Mickey, 1938*

*Louise's stepson Raleigh and her brother Danny holding the dog on their bike in front of the dug-out bedroom stairway entry.*

*Brookie, 1939, about a year before he and Louise were married.*

# SHEEPHERDERS I

## (1940-1941)

If a long or difficult morning of trailing lay ahead of a herder, he left with the sheep before it was good daylight in order to make it to where he would "noon" before it got too hot to trail. Sheep simply will not trail during the heat of the day. They bunch up in clusters with their heads together and their noses to the ground and seem to go into a stupor until it cools off. This is referred to as "bogging" and has nothing to do with quicksand! An old Armenian who herded for the Meikes for several years always referred to these very early morning starts as "Three o'clock, up!" It was a term that stuck locally.

The first morning of trail was such a three o'clock up morning. It usually took a long time to get sheep across the Sussex bridge, especially with young lambs. The bridge was a long, narrow suspension structure that vibrated and swayed when the sheep got on it. The noise and motion alarmed them and made it very difficult to get them started across.

Brookie had told me so much about trailing sheep to the mountains I could hardly wait to get started. Shine had already left with two herders and their sheep, and there was some difficulty in finding someone to "pull" us, as moving the wagons was called. Finally a teenaged boy named Orville was hired. He had no experience as a camptender, but he had worked with horses enough that he knew how to harness and drive a team. Orville would only pull us until Shine got his herds to camp and could come back to meet us to take us the rest of the way. Raleigh was going with us, so he and Orville shared the bed in the wagon while we slept in the teepee.

I was so excited the night before we left I could hardly sleep. It seemed I had barely closed my eyes when Brookie shook me gently awake. "Come on, kid, three o'clock up!"

It was chilly, and I shivered as I fumbled my clothes on by the light of the flashlight. We woke Raleigh and Orville and left them to harness the horses and get the camp ready to move while we saddled up and rode to where we had bedded the sheep. It was barely light enough to see, but already most of the ewes were up nursing their lambs. As soon as we began to move them, the lambs got separated from their mothers and the cries of the unmothered ewes and lambs became a deafening uproar.

I had already had some experience with the bridge when Fred and I drove our cows out to the homestead. Now I learned why everyone dreaded crossing it with sheep. We bunched the herd up against the south approach and tried to force them onto the bridge. All they did was mill in circles as the ewes searched frantically for their lambs, which were running and leaping in panic. After what seemed like hours, we finally got some of the ewes started across the bridge and the herd followed.

When ewes and lambs are crossing a bridge, going through a gate, or trailing through a narrow lane, the lambs keep filtering through to the back of the herd. When it is separated from its mother, a lamb's instinct is to go back to where it last saw her. Suddenly, there you are with a lot of lambs that have no intention of going along with the herd. They are going back to where they came from to look for mama, and you've got trouble! If one lamb breaks away from the herd, it is immediately joined by others and away they go. This is called a runback and is something every herder dreads. It is next to impossible to turn them back to the herd once they start to run. The only practical way to bring them back is to take some ewes to the lambs and then drive them all back.

Brookie knew better than to let this happen, so when we began to get down to the tail-end of the herd, we really jammed them onto the bridge.

After we got the sheep across the bridge and past the Sussex store, they were in a narrow lane as far as the Sussex school. From there on, the lane widened out enough so they could graze a little as they went along. Raleigh and Orville worked their way through the sheep with the supply wagon and the sheepwagon, which were hooked together, and went on to the American watergap to make camp.

The American stockrest and watergap derived their names from the American Ranch, which adjoined them. A watergap was formed by fencing across a section of river or creek so that it was included in the stockrest to provide water for livestock stopping there. In this case, it was the Sahara Ditch. By the time we trailed the sheep the six miles from Sussex to the watergap it was getting hot. The sheep were jug-headed and had to be pushed every step with the dogs.

I was hot, tired, hungry, and thirsty, and I wondered what had given me the idea that trailing sheep to the mountains was going to be so romantic! My enthusiasm returned, though, after a good breakfast, several hours' rest, and a swim in the big irrigation ditch running through the watergap.

There was a sameness to the days, yet every day was different. Each day began at first light and ended at dark. We always trailed to where we would noon before having breakfast, which meant that breakfast was usually about ten o'clock. During the heat of the day, we napped or read. If we had a late breakfast, we usually didn't eat again until we got to where we would spend the night.

Trailing in hot weather was simple because the sheep were easy to manage. It took good dogs and a lot of hard riding to keep the lambs in the herd the first morning of trailing, but after a couple of days, they got used to being scrambled and didn't panic. They soon learned to "mother up" once they reached a stockrest where they could spread out a bit. A large part of the lambs would be in the rear and soon ewes would start working back through the herd looking for them, bleating and listening for answering cries from their offspring.

It still amazes me that they can pick out each other's voices in all the uproar that is part of the mothering-up process. Once a ewe finds her lamb, she always smells it to make sure there's no mistake, because a hungry lamb is not too particular about whether a ewe is its mother or not. As soon as a lamb starts to suck, the ewe smells its tail. If the lamb is hers, she will begin to chew her cud. If it's not, she will kick it loose in no uncertain terms, and if the lamb is persistent, she is liable to give it a good boot in the rear with her head.

A spell of bad weather could mean a lot of extra work. The sheep would not steady down when they were wet and cold, so the herder had to stay with them all day. On those days, the camptender would ride out to the sheep and herd them while the herder went to the wagon to eat and warm up. We had no bad weather that first spring I went to the mountains, probably because it was after mid-June and our stormy season was past.

Once we got past Kaycee, we hit the Mayoworth Stock Trail. We would follow it to where it joined the 33 Mile Trail at Bear Trap, then follow the 33 Mile Trail in a southerly direction until we turned off to our summer camp on Blue Creek.

The evening we pulled onto the Brock Mesa to spend the night, Orville announced we were out of wood and asked Brookie what he should do. We were camped right along Brock's fence, so Brookie told him to go along the fence and pick up an old post or two to do us till we could stock up on firewood on the slope of the mountains. When we got in from bedding the sheep, we discovered that Orville had chopped a big pitch post right out of the fence, not realizing that Brookie meant old, discarded posts that had been replaced with new ones!

The view from Brock Mesa was so spectacular I wondered if any other could ever compare with it. We were so close to the mountains now that I could see every detail: sheer-walled canyons, dense timber patches, long, grassy slopes rising upward to the very sky. The North Fork of Powder River ran along the east base, forming a barrier between the mesa and the hay meadows of the Brock Ranch. The mesa itself was long and narrow, sagebrush covered, with a scattering of gnarled, stunted pines and cedar.

The western side of the mesa broke off into an area that looked like something from another planet or a science fiction movie set. It was referred to as the Soap Holes by the local people, and the next day I learned to dread it after I nearly bogged my horse on what looked like solid ground. The Soap Holes were bentonite deposits. A sickly green, parched-looking surface covered a treacherous, viscous substance that could trap and hold unwary animals, as evidenced by bleached bones at some of the larger holes.

The whole area was made up of narrow hog-backs with the valleys between them cut by sharp, uncrossable gullies and soap holes. What little vegetation there was consisted of sparse grass, stunted sagebrush, and rabbit brush. The ground was littered with a sort of shale that looked as if it had been exposed to extreme heat in the dawn of creation. The only things that seemed to flourish were large clumps of bushy cedar trees and cactus.

Everything dropped away sharply to the north in this no-man's-land to Alkali Creek which was more of a slough than a creek. Rank salt grass, sedge, and cattails marked its sluggish way to where it drained into the North Fork, and in the spring, it provided a nesting place for large flocks of redwing black birds.

We nooned on Alkali the day after we bedded on Brock Mesa, and in the afternoon when we moved the sheep off water, I could see that we were beginning to climb sharply. We were again on a sort of mesa or ridge that ran west toward the mountains. The top was covered with mountain mahogany, a gray-green foliage bush that ranged from low, scrubby growth up to near tree-sized, taller than a person on horseback. The terrain was very rough and rocky, a rock-hound's paradise with a multitude of fossils of various kinds.

When the sheep moved off the west end of the mesa ridge, we were confronted by the Red Wall, which sloped upward from the east to drop off in sheer walls of blood-red rock on the west. The east side was densely covered with mahogany except for a bare slope where the road and trail angled up and through a gap in the wall. Before us a valley of red earth seemed to drop away to the foot of the mountains—an optical illusion I discovered when we reached the foot and looked back. I saw that the valley sloped sharply back to the wall and the gap was actually lower than where we were camping at what was called the Gyp springs. The springs were little more than seeps with barely enough water for the horses and totally unpalatable for humans. The whole area was a gypsum formation that sounded hollow under the horses' hooves, and I had the uneasy feeling that it might crack like an eggshell and let us go crashing down into some bottomless abyss. Brookie assured me it was solid.

Just after dark the dogs began to bark. Soon we could hear the jingling of a harness. Shine came riding in leading one of the teams he had used to pull the other two herds to the mountains.

The next morning was another "three o'clock up" morning. Orville started back to the Meike Ranch on his saddle horse, and we started the sheep up the slope just as soon as it was light enough to see. The slope was very steep and I could see why Shine needed four horses to pull the two wagons.

It seemed as if we were climbing into a different world. In spite of the shallow, rocky soil, grass grew abundantly and there were wildflowers everywhere. Even the rocky outcroppings were covered with delicate rust, green and yellow lichen, and tiny flowering plants grew in the crevices.

By sunup we were nearing what Brookie called the Little Park. We turned and gazed back at the world below us. What a fantastic sight! The view from Brock Mesa paled by comparison. We could look across all the miles to the Pumpkin Buttes rising up far to the east, hazy with distance. Every reservoir and water hole shone like mirrors in the first rays of the sun. Ridges and hills stood out in sharp relief against the shadowed gullies and valleys.

We could now look back at The Horn, a big, lone mountain that jutted out at an angle from the main mountain chain, so heavily timbered it fairly bristled with trees. It had been looming to the north of us since we topped Brock Mesa. The broad North Fork valley ran to the northwest between The Horn and the mountains proper.

We entered heavy timber after we left Little Park. The trees grew so close together I could only see a little way in any direction, and it was hard to tell where the sheep were going. We followed the road for the most part because the trees were too dense to ride through horseback. Just as I was sure we had lost most of the sheep, we came out into the open and Brookie told me we were in the Big Park, where we would noon.

In the days that followed, I saw all the places that up to now had just been names to me: Snow Cave, the Pole Patch, the Slip, and Arch Creek Hill, where the camptenders tied trees to the backs of the wagons to act as brakes going down the steep hill. In years to come, the strange names of all these places would be as familiar to me as my own, but for now, I was intrigued by what each day brought.

I was not very impressed with Snow Cave, which was between the Big Park and the Pole Patch. It was a hole that filled with snow in winter and due to the fact that it was situated in such a fashion that the sun could never shine into it, the snow never did completely melt. It really was a cave, a sinkhole in the flat top of a mountain, about fifteen feet across and twenty feet deep. Caves branched out from the bottom and went back into the limestone, but I'm so claustrophobic about caves I never did anything but look down into it.

The Pole Patch was an area of dense timber which had been devastated by a fire that burned most of the branches but left the blackened trunks standing. This was where Brookie's dad and Bud Hawkins hauled logs from in 1917 to build their cabins. As nearly as they were able to determine, people had been hauling logs and poles from there since the area began settling up many years before. When I made my first trip through the Pole Patch some twenty-four years later there were still a lot of stark skeletons standing. Most of the trees, though, had finally rotted through at the base and fallen in jack-straw fashion every which way, so you had to pick your way through them on horseback.

For some reason, very few new trees had grown up in the years since the burn, and even though there was always lush green grass in the spring, it gave me a feeling of being in a dead landscape. Even a light breeze caused the clusters of dead trees to move and create a medley of groans and rasps where naked trunks and branches made contact, and on occasion, I even heard the crash when one of them finally gave up and fell to earth.

The Slip was at the top of Arch Creek Hill, an extremely long and steep hill where a mountain dropped off to the west to the Arch Creek Valley. At some time, the side of the mountain had slipped right at the point where the road dropped over and started the long grade to the valley floor below.

When we reached the top of Bear Trap Hill the morning after we bedded at Mud Springs, another breathtaking view met my eyes. The sun had barely risen so the hill was still in shadows, but far below I could make out the sparkling creek that was Bear Trap winding its way through swamps and meadows before entering the canyon. Great, rocky walls topped by evergreens bordered the western edge of the valley, and the rising sun bathed everything in its path with pale gold.

The herd poured over the rim and spread out on the mountainside where we sat our horses. The wagons and the four-horse team looked like toys far below us on the rocky road. We watched while Shine crossed the creek and made camp on the west side. When the sheep were about two-thirds of the way down the hill, we rode on to the wagon and ate breakfast.

This was as far as we would go today. We had been pushing the sheep every day since we put them across the bridge at Sussex, so this layover would give them a chance to rest and feed. It also meant I could do the laundry, we could refill the water barrel, which was nearly empty, and the horses could rest and graze, too.

After breakfast, Brookie and Shine rode back up around the sheep to push them down onto water. Raleigh busied himself playing in the creek and I got busy on the laundry. I spread the wet clothes out on the thick grass to dry, then heated more water and washed my hair. How extravagant I felt, being able to use water unsparingly after the days of rationing every drop we used.

Dawn the next morning found us on the trail as usual. I kept wishing I could have slept an hour later, but I soon forgot that as we pushed the sheep through the narrow Sawmill Lane and across Sawmill Creek.

We were going south on the 33 Mile Trail now. At the Community Corrals I was surprised to find only a jumble of rotting corral poles marking what had been a large corral. It had once been maintained and used by all the sheep outfits in the area, but one by one, they began building corrals on their camps so they didn't have to trail to the big corral. In a few years, it began to show the effect of neglect and finally collapsed.

The day we nooned at Con O'Brien's, I found my first arrowhead. Brookie had the knack of finding Indian artifacts without even looking for them, or so it seemed to my inexperienced eye. He would dismount from his horse, lean down, and pick up an arrowhead or scraper without a break in the conversation. He told me I ought to be able to find something at the springs at Con's because the ground was littered with chips. I wasn't even sure how to go about looking for them. We walked slowly up the little creek toward the springs, looking at the ground. Suddenly, there it was! A perfect, opaque, white arrowhead! I let out a whoop and pounced on it. From that moment on, I was hooked on hunting relics.

The next day was our last full day on the trail. We camped at Chittem Springs that night, and for once I was anxious for morning to come so we could get to our summer camp. Almost three weeks had passed since the morning we crossed the Sussex bridge, and I was getting pretty trail weary.

The next morning we left the 33 Mile Trail and followed a wagon road in an easterly direction. When we topped a high mountain, named Gray Mound I later learned, the view before us was almost too vast to comprehend. Off to the east, tiny in the distance, were the Pumpkin Buttes. Far to the southeast, I could see a mountain range running east and west. This, Brookie said, was Casper Mountain. When I looked north, I was surprised to see that I was looking at the snowy western slopes of the Hazelton Peaks and Cloud's Peak. Brookie explained that this was because the Big Horns lie in a great, gradual curve to the southwest. Behind us, out over the Big Horn Basin, was the low, blue lines of the Owl Creek and Carter Mountains, and the Absarokas, behind which, on a clear day, we could see the white tips of the Tetons.

Just east of us to the left, the headwaters of Beaver Creek meandered down a valley that quickly became a canyon. On the right lay a broad valley bordered by steep, grassy mountains crowned with patches of timber. To my untrained eyes, it seemed to stretch for miles in an easterly direction before making a bend almost due south and disappearing behind more mountains.

"That's the Blue Creek Valley," Brookie told me. "Our camp will be about a mile on down around that bend on Wes Stanley's homestead."

Many of the people who took up homesteads sold the land to ranchers in the area as soon as they proved up on it. This was particularly true on the Big Horns, where deep winter snow rendered the land useless except for summer grazing. After Mick Meike homesteaded on Beaver Creek, the Meike Ranch added to it by buying some of the nearby homesteads, including Stanley's, thus giving them enough summer pasture for their sheep.

It took us most of the day to trail our herd to where we would camp for the summer. Shine parked our wagon by the Stanley homestead cabin, which was only a few feet from where a big, cold spring gushed out. The cabin was sturdily constructed of mountain logs, with a rough lumber floor. The roof was of the same rough lumber, covered with tar paper.

The cabin would make a good bedroom for Raleigh while he was with us, we thought. In the first rainstorm, the roof proved to be leaky, so Brookie set up an extra teepee right inside the cabin. He tied the top to a spike driven into the ridge log and fastened the four corners to spikes driven into the floor.

We were set for the summer.

Raleigh stayed on with us for a couple of weeks after we arrived at the summer camp. We were sleeping out with the sheep, so he was alone at the camp at night. Looking back, now, I'm amazed to think we left an eleven-year-old boy alone at night, but at the time, we thought nothing of it. He was used to playing alone and entertaining himself. He was not allowed to use the kerosene lamp, so when it got too dark for him to see to read, he went to bed. He hated getting up in the morning, so he was usually still asleep when we got back to camp.

Sheep were fairly predictable in those days when they were used to being herded. Brookie would start the sheep toward the bedground when they left water, while I fixed supper. Once they were headed toward the bedground, they spread out and grazed. By the time we finished eating and had the dishes done the sun was getting low and the sheep were approaching the bedground.

Several evenings a week, we had to carry salt up to the bedground, a job I disliked. The mountain water is lacking in the soluble minerals and salts that livestock need and get from the water on the flats. Therefore, it is necessary to give them salt or salt-mineral supplement during the summer on the mountains. Many of the poisonous plants present have a salty taste, which attracts salt-hungry sheep and cattle if they don't have the supplement. Also, many stockmen believe that feeding salt produces a more solid animal at shipping time.

After I got on my horse, Brookie handed me two fifty-pound bags of salt and I stacked them in front of me in the saddle. He piled a couple more sacks at the front of his saddle, mounted, got them positioned in his lap and we were on our way, circling the grazing sheep so as not to disturb them. By the time we reached the bedground, my legs were asleep, my rear numb, and my stomach smashed against my spine by the weight of the salt pressing back against me as we climbed the steep mountain-side. The lead of the herd would be arriving as we poured the salt on the rocks, then went to our teepee to take care of the horses.

Over the summer I acquired quite a bit of knowledge about sheep behavior. When sheep were herded, they developed a herd instinct that made them feel safe in a bunch. There were definite leaders that pretty much controlled the entire herd. Occasionally a ewe became a renegade or bunch-quitter. She was usually very cunning, managing to sneak away with a few followers. When a ewe made a habit of this, Brookie herd-broke her. He waited until she and her bunch thought they'd made their escape, then he sent the dog, using hand signals so the sheep wouldn't be alerted. The first thing they knew, the dog was charging into them from out of nowhere, and several of them got nipped before they got back into the main herd. Just as the dog hit them, Brookie hollered "Ho!" in a voice that could be heard for miles! After the sheep were herd-broken, all he had to do to turn them was holler. When his voice reached them, the ewes in the lead would throw up their heads and listen, then one would turn and start to run back to the main herd and the whole lead followed suit like dominoes falling over.

There were no fences on the mountains in those days, so each herd of sheep had a herder with them to keep them on their own camp. Most of the herders respected the boundaries, and as long as they did, everyone got along fine. Occasionally there would be a clash of personalities between herders, or a herder would be a moocher, letting his sheep graze over on another camp. The feud might carry on all summer unless one of the parties rolled his bed and left the mountains.

The victim of one of these boundary disputes is buried in an unmarked grave on the south slope of Torrance Ridge, a long, low mountain on the north side of Blue Creek Valley. A camptender on his weekly visit found the herder's saddled horse and his dogs at the wagon and the sheep on water. After a quick look around, he went after the sheriff who brought up a search party. The badly decomposed body was finally found at the base of Torrance Ridge. They rolled the remains in the herder's bed tarp, buried him in a shallow grave on the side of the Ridge, and piled rocks on the grave to discourage predators.

Because the camptender knew there was bad blood between his herder and the neighboring herder, the sheriff questioned the neighbor who, naturally, denied any knowledge of the death. Several days earlier, he said, there had been a bad thunderstorm and "that dumb Mex was probably settin' up on those rocks and got struck by lightnin'."

The case was closed, even though other nearby herders said there had been no storm.

The week before Raleigh went home, Pete Meike, who was tending our camp, brought my sisters and my youngest brother up to visit. Dan and Raleigh slept in the teepee in the cabin and Ruth and Julia slept in the wagon in our tarp bed.

While they were there we bedded the sheep on Seashell Mountain, a big, steep, smooth mountain with a rocky outcropping on top and surrounded by scattered pine trees. The limestone outcropping was embedded with fossil seashells, hence the name. We set up our teepee in the only level spot we could find, a buffalo wallow just under the timber, where we could see down to the wagon from the bedground.

The early part of the summer, the weather followed an almost predictable pattern. A very warm, sunny forenoon nearly always brought some sort of thunderstorm activity in the afternoon or evening. The clouds would billow up out of the Big Horn Basin to the west and soon there was wind, followed by lightning and thunder, then rain, sometimes accompanied by soft hail. The storms passed quickly, leaving a fresh, rain-washed landscape behind. Once in a while, a thunderstorm would hit during the night. Those always scared me the worst because the lightning was so much more vivid.

Sometime during the first night on Seashell we were jarred awake by a tremendous clap of thunder and rain began to spatter against the side of the teepee. Lightning lit up the inside with an eerie, blue-green glow, followed by another rending crash of thunder. Then we were engulfed by the incessant flash of lightning and the deafening sound of the almost constant crack of thunder and the wind-driven rain battering the teepee. The lightning was so close that each *flash! crash!* jolted the ground under us. There was such a tremendous volume of water falling from the sky that our teepee was soon flooded. Brookie and I had a double sleeping bag and two air mattresses to sleep on, and our bed, buoyed up by the air mattresses, was actually floating!

The storm ended as quickly as it started. We huddled in our wet bed and worried about the kids. I wondered if our horses had been struck by lightning and what had happened to the sheep. Finally the water seeped away and our body heat warmed the wet blankets and we slept—until one of us moved. Any shift in position put some part of our anatomies in contact with cold, clammy bedding with an unpleasant shock.

That was once I was more than ready to get up when morning came. Our clothing, which we always put under our pillows, was as wet and cold as the bedding. As soon as we were dressed, we dragged the soggy bed out of the teepee and spread the blankets and sleeping bags on the nearby sagebrush to dry. We undid the corners of the teepee from the stakes and emptied out what water was still trapped in the bottom, then draped it on the sagebrush next to our bed.

Our horses were cold but unharmed, and none of the sheep were dead, but as we rode to the wagon, we found drifts of rocks ranging in size from pebbles to boulders weighing several hundred pounds that had washed down the steep slope. We found the kids none the worse for the storm. In fact, Dan, Raleigh, and Julia had slept through it!

About the only people we saw after the kids left were Pete Meike when he came to tend camp and Fred Lohse, who was herding on the upper part of Blue Creek. Pete made a camptending trip from the ranch once a week, bringing mail, groceries, news of the Sussex community, and a week's supply of stock salt in fifty-pound burlap bags. He kept a drum of kerosene in the back of his pickup to refill the five-gallon kerosene cans that were standard equipment with each wagon. Nearly everyone referred to it as coal oil and it was used to fuel our lamps, start the fires in our stove, and for firing dead trees on the bedgrounds to scare away predators.

The Meike Ranch furnished eggs, home-cured hams and bacon, home rendered lard, potatoes, and butter. Pete always had a big burlap bag full of fresh vegetables from his garden. They were a real treat after eating canned vegetables all winter and spring.

Our grocery needs were simple, and we bought only the basic staples. I baked my own bread and we seldom had any kind of dessert. If we did, it was usually stewed dried fruit. We had a choice of Palmolive or Lifebuoy toilet soap and Fels Naphtha or White King laundry soap in bars. You applied it directly to the "ring around the collar" and the dirty cuffs as you scrubbed merrily away on your old washboard! First-aid supplies usually consisted of aspirin, Epsom salts, Vicks or mentholatum, and some sort of liniment. Every sheepwagon had a can of carbolic salve for saddle and harness sores on the horses. Since it was "good for man or beast," it was often the only medication some of the herders had.

One day, Fred Lohse rode down to our camp while the sheep were on water and invited us to come to his wagon for dinner the next day. We arrived at his camp about the same time he did, so I offered to help fix the meal, but he wouldn't hear of it. He was the host!

He built up a roaring fire in the sheepwagon stove, and asked me whether I preferred tea or coffee. I said tea, and watched in amazement as he filled a battered aluminum coffee pot with water and threw in enough bulk tea to make several gallons of tea the way I made it. While it was coming to a boil, he cut several mutton steaks, peeled spuds, and sliced them into a skillet of hot grease. The tea began to boil, so he moved it back where it could continue to simmer while he fried the meat and potatoes. He opened a can of peas and heated them and added water to the tea, which had boiled down considerably by this time. By the time he got plates, cups and cutlery on the table, the tea was boiling again. Brookie said he preferred water, but I had already specified tea, so I drank tea! And I drank two cups of it! When I finally managed to gulp down the last of the first cupful, I had a refill before I could unpucker enough to decline. The stuff would have made wonderful post dip, and he could have tanned a cow hide in it. Years later Fred underwent ulcer surgery in which part of his stomach was removed.

That really surprised me. I figured the lining of his stomach must be just like a piece of saddle leather!

After Raleigh and my family went home, we spent less time at the wagon. There was so much for Brookie to show me and so many things for me to learn. The Indians had camped all over the Big Horn Mountains, so there were artifacts just about everywhere. The area right around the camp yielded many an arrowhead and scraper that summer as I avidly pursued my new hobby.

I soon recognized the boundaries of our camp and all the landmarks. Hopefully, I wouldn't get lost if I got separated from Brookie. Irish Creek Rim and McCullem Gap formed our western boundary, with all the mountains and valleys running in an easterly direction from there. The big valley that began at the Gap and ran eastward separated Stanley Mountain and Seashell Mountain, running the full length between them, then looped around the east end of Stanley, where the camp was, to become part of the Blue Creek Valley.

The east end of Seashell Mountain looked directly down on a cluster of buildings and corrals nestled in a sort of three-sided bowl opening to the east. This was Johnson's cow camp, situated about a quarter of a mile east of our camp at the head of the North Fork of Keith Creek, which meandered down a big, rough valley to the southeast, then plunged into Keith Creek Canyon to eventually join Powder River. Mitch Johnson and his wife, Jean, lived there during the summer months and looked after their cattle while they were on their mountain range. Their winter range and ranch headquarters lay east on the slope of the mountains and on down onto the flats in the Barnum country. There were no fences, except for Mitch's horse pasture where he kept his saddle stock, so their cows drifted over onto the Meikes' range as often as not. To equal things out, they allowed us to graze our sheep over onto their range whenever we wanted. This was a good arrangement for everyone concerned because cattle preferred the coarse grass of the swamps and creek bottoms, while the sheep would only eat it when the feed on the hillsides was gone.

A few of the mountains in the Blue Creek drainage were heavily timbered on top, but most of them, including Stanley and Seashell, were too rocky to support more than a few clumps of trees. Most of the trees were dwarfed from lack of nourishment from the shallow soil and twisted by the strong winds that howled across the Big Horns eight months out of the year. Seashell had only a scattering of trees the entire length of it. Right across the valley on the southern side of Stanley was dense sagebrush and numerous trees, where deer browsed and sage chickens nested and hatched their chicks.

Irish Creek Canyon was spectacularly beautiful. It was deep and narrow, and the silver line of the creek at the bottom wound through stands of spruce and slabs of rock deposited there probably when the canyon was formed. The canyon followed a southeasterly direction for several miles to where it joined Powder River Canyon. From McCullem Gap south, sheer rock walls and almost perpendicular slopes of loose shale formed the rim. Below the rim, which varied in height from a few feet to several hundred feet, the northeast side of the canyon was made up of a series of benches with great heaps of boulders resulting from rock slides, springs, and swamps bordered by willows, and grassy meadows scattered haphazardly everywhere. On the southwest side of the creek, the entire drainage had its origin from one high mountain called McDonald Hill. Except for a few patches of timber and some rock outcrops, the whole mountain was densely covered with grass with wide benches dissected by gushing springs below which were willow-choked swamps. Emerald green marked the paths of the water courses as they tumbled down the side of the mountain to the canyon.

We sometimes rode through the gap and followed the animal trails down the steep canyon side to the creek and went fishing. We carried our fish lines wrapped around the crowns of our hats, and fishhooks hooked in our hat bands. When we reached the creek, we tied our horses to a tree or a bush and cut a fish pole from a clump of willows or alders. We tied on our line, attached a hook, caught a grasshopper, and we were in business.

The mountain soil is very shallow, for the most part, and the almost daily watering from thunderstorms is what maintains the lush growth of vegetation in the high country. The slopes are covered with several kinds of grass, dozens of varieties of flowers and weeds, sage, and low-growing bushes and shrubs. I always imagined that sheep lived on grass, but I learned that, like deer, a large part of their diet is made up of other plants.

The area abounded with wildlife. Deer and elk concealed themselves in the trees during the day, coming out into the open in the evening to feed. There were blue grouse and sage chickens everywhere, so we had fried chicken and grouse quite often after the young ones were frying size. Game wardens were almost nonexistent, and so were poachers. We never considered ourselves as poachers; we were users! The game was there, so we took what we needed without wasting it. If a sheepherder butchered a deer or a mutton, he shared it with his neighbors, and they returned the favor. Besides deer, elk, and the ever-present coyotes, there were bobcats, badgers, rock chucks, jackrabbits, gophers, and mice.

There were even bears and mountain lions, both of which I had experience with before the summer was over.

The sound of the sheep stampeding in panic woke us one night. The horses ran back and forth on their picket ropes and snorted in terror. Brookie quickly pulled on his overalls and boots and ran out with the flashlight. Across the milling herd, the beam of the flashlight picked out a large, dark object that kept moving around the outer edge of the sheep. As Brookie circled around the sheep toward it, the animal kept moving away from the light. Every few seconds, it lunged into the sheep, scattering them as they ran for their lives. Brookie was close enough by this time to see it was a large bear. I'm not sure what he intended to do if he caught up with it, but he didn't have to make that decision, because the bear vanished into a timber patch that grew right to the edge of the bedground.

In the remaining hours till daylight, we rested uneasily, half expecting the bear to return. The horses and sheep finally quieted down, but were very nervous, spooking at every sound or movement in the dark. I wondered why the dogs were so quiet. When morning came, we discovered they had left us and gone down over the end of the mountain to the wagon. Daylight showed seven ewes lying dead on the far side of the herd. Brookie cussed himself for leaving the rifle at the wagon the night before, and from then on, he carried it in the saddle scabbard everywhere we went.

We had just finished breakfast that same morning when our neighbor, Jamesy Arnold rode in. Jamesy was an old-country Irishman, and I really had to pay close attention to understand his English under ordinary circumstances. This morning he was wild-eyed and almost incoherent. It seemed that just as he was about to get his sheep on water, a large, black bear came crashing down the mountainside and headed straight for the herd. He had no gun, so he tried to intercept the bear on his horse. When the horse realized it was being asked to herd a bear, it went into a fine state of hysteria! It snorted, plunged, then stampeded. Jamesy managed to stay aboard and got the horse stopped about the time the bear reached the sheep. According to Jamesy, the bear was mad—not angry mad, but crazy mad! It lurched through the frightened sheep and when one was unfortunate enough to get in its way, the bear made a vicious swipe with a forepaw, crippling or killing it. The bear continued out the other side of the herd and disappeared down Keith Creek canyon. We never saw it again, thank goodness!

Bears were fairly numerous in the Big Horns at that time. We frequently saw bear signs, usually rotten logs they had torn apart looking for bugs and grubs. A few times we saw their tracks at the edges of creeks. Except for that one, they were shy creatures and preferred not to be seen. I liked it that way!

The mountain tops where we bedded the sheep all had timber patches on them, so there were always dead trees handy for fires for coyote scares. We would tie a rope onto a dead tree and drag it with one of the horses to the edge of the bedground. In the evening we poured kerosene on a small area and set it on fire. The bedgrounds were rocky, and the sheep grubbed a bedground right down to the dirt, so there was no danger of an uncontrolled fire. It took several days for one of the trees to burn completely, because it would blaze only if the wind came up. The rest of the time, it smoldered and made a lot of smoke, which was what we wanted because coyotes had a natural fear of smoke or fire.

One evening in August after the nights began to get chilly and we began sleeping at the wagon, we were herding the sheep to the bedground on Stanley Mountain. Brookie looked back and saw that a little bunch had broken off the main herd and were climbing to the Seashell bedground. He left me to set our coyote fire while he rode across the valley to get them.

It was sundown as I tied my horse to a scrub tree and I hurried to light the fire, hoping to be done before dark. Quickly I piled pine needles and twigs against the log. I got the bottle of kerosene we had cached in some rocks and doused some on the log above the kindling and touched a match to it. It burned briskly until the kindling turned to ashes, but the log hadn't ignited, so I had to repeat the process. Finally the log caught, making a cheerful little blaze in the dusk.

It was too dark to see across the valley, but I assumed Brookie had sent the wanderers back across and gone on to the wagon to take care of his horse. Shorty was picking his way carefully through the rocks and brush, now in total darkness. As usual, I was jumpy about being out in the dark. Suddenly, an agonized scream came from the valley below me. Shorty threw up his head and snorted in alarm, and the hairs on the back of my neck stood up like porcupine quills. Almost before my brain registered the first cry, a second one came from farther up the valley. A third scream sounded still farther away, and I sat there almost in a state of shock.

My first thought was that Brookie's horse was dragging him. Then common sense came to my rescue. If Brookie's horse had thrown him and his foot was caught in the stirrup, the frightened horse would almost surely have come to Shorty. Even if it had bypassed me in the dark, I would have heard hoof beats and my horse would have nickered at it. I decided that it must have been an animal of some sort—an animal I wasn't very crazy about meeting out there in the dark!

Shorty was spooked and wanted to run when we reached the floor of the valley, but I held him to a fast trot. When I rounded the end of the mountain and saw the light at the wagon, I was weak with relief.

"That was a mountain lion," Brookie proclaimed when I described the sound to him, and he proceeded to tell me some stories about "Salt Creek Bill."

Salt Creek Bill was a mountain lion that had been terrorizing Dolly Tisdale, who was living on her homestead on the V where Salt Creek ran into Powder River. Every night the light in Dolly's cabin would attract the big cat, and he would prowl around outside screaming.

One dark, drizzly autumn night when he was a kid, Brookie and his brothers, Halsey and Bo, took a kerosene lantern and went to dig out a skunk den on the bluff on the north side of Powder River. Suddenly, Salt Creek Bill, apparently drawn to the light of the boys' lantern, let out a scream right across the river from them. They stood there a moment, paralyzed by fright.

"Run!" one of them yelled.

Run they did! Brookie said he could always outrun Halsey, but that night, Halsey fell down and still outran Brookie on his hands and knees.

Another time, a school friend of his, Dutch Morgareidge, was riding his bicycle to a dance at Sussex one Saturday night. It was about an eight-mile ride, and as he pedaled along, cars kept coming up behind him and passing him. He was still about two miles from Sussex when he heard Salt Creek Bill give forth with one of his awful screams. Dutch said by the time he reached Sussex, he'd passed every car that had passed him earlier!

In the valley beyond Seashell Mountain was the Trapper's Cabin, a snug little cabin and a neat pole corral that had been built a number of years before by a man who made his living trapping. We often rolled our bed out in it and slept there when the sheep were bedding in the area. The gate was kept closed on the corral so range animals wouldn't get trapped in it; consequently, there was always luxuriant feed in it. All we had to do was put our horses in the corral and shut the gate without worrying about picketing them.

Later in the summer we grazed our sheep over on the area north of Powder River Canyon, east of the Irish Creek Rim and west of Keith Creek. It was beautiful country, with big, open, grassy slopes leading down to the west branch of Keith Creek, which headed some distance below the Trapper's Cabin.

My first view of Powder River Canyon made Irish Creek Canyon seem like a little gully by comparison. Every time I looked into it from the north rim, the sheer width and depth of it completely overwhelmed me. Many people have compared it to a miniature Grand Canyon. Brookie always said all the deer and elk that ever lived down in there died of old age because no one could get one out if he killed it in there.

The canyon was a jumble of rocks, brush, trees, dead timber, springs, swamps, and gullies. It was about a mile wide at the widest part, and perhaps a half mile from the river to the top of the high walls on the north. The south side was considerably lower, smooth mountains rather than the rock walls of the north rim. The north rim walls were broken by crevices full of huge slabs of stone; boulders as big as houses; steep, tree-grown slopes; and gaps where animals trailed in and out of the canyon. The river itself was seldom visible from the north rim. It ran along the bottom of the south side of the canyon, often between narrow rock walls. Cattle grazing in the canyon looked like so many ants.

Brookie was a great explorer, and one morning he suggested we ought to make an expedition into the canyon while the sheep were grazing toward water on Keith Creek. We picketed the horses at the Slide, a narrow crack in the rock wall that was almost straight up and down and filled with rocks of all sizes and shapes, and hiked the rim to where Keith Creek ran into Powder River, then headed back up to the Slide inside the canyon.

Brookie thought it would be simple to follow game and stock trails back up the canyon, but inevitably, they wandered into swamps where you suddenly bogged to your knees, or vanished into a clump of alders or willows so dense you couldn't fight your way through. A detour usually intercepted another trail that would bring you to a twenty-foot drop-off on a slab of rock or head directly off down to the river, which was not where we wanted to be.

Ages later, we finally arrived at the foot of the Slide. I was young, active and resilient. I was also scratched, foot-sore, wet, muddy, and absolutely pooped! We had not had anything to eat since early supper the day before. About the time we reached the Slide, we discovered our very pregnant sheepdog, Johnnie, who had come with us, was missing. We had no idea when she left us. Brookie decided she had gone back to the horses by an easier route.

After we rested a bit, we began the climb up the slide. It's hard to describe what it was like, because I become speechless just thinking about it! Big slabs of rock, more or less standing on end, were embedded in loose, round stones that dislodged and rolled down the steep chute we were attempting to climb. Talk about using tooth and nail! After climbing forever, we reached the top to find a six-foot, solid rock drop-off with some variety of bush growing along the top. Brookie was able to pull himself up by grabbing a gnarled tree root that was protruding from the rock and then gave me a hand up.

All during the climb, I had the unhealthy feeling that we would find the horses had broken their picket ropes and left us afoot two miles from camp, but they were dozing in the sun when we finally emerged from the crevice. There was no sign of Johnnie, though. It was mid-afternoon by this time, so we headed the sheep off water up toward Seashell and rode on to camp. When we got there, Johnnie was under the wagon, looking a little apologetic but proudly nursing a litter of pups.

In the last few days of August, our summer abruptly ended. We awoke one morning to find ourselves in an eerie, gray world of dense fog. We ate breakfast, saddled our horses, and went to look for the sheep. As soon as we left the wagon I was lost. I don't know how Brookie managed to keep oriented, but soon we could hear sheep bells and make out the dim forms moving ahead of us.

We stayed all day with the sheep. The trees and grass were dripping from the fog, so there was no need for the sheep to go to water. We wore our slickers, so we were warm and comfortable, but the fog never lifted, making it a long, strange day for me. I was really glad when we bedded the sheep, took care of our horses and holed up in our snug, warm wagon. I was hungry enough to eat my saddle strings—almost!

I expected to wake up to a normal, sunshiny day the next morning. Instead, we had a repeat of the day before. The fog fascinated me, yet there was something about it that gave me an uneasy feeling. It was too much like the dark. I almost expected some monstrous creature to come creeping up behind me. There was always the feeling that something was lurking out there just beyond where my vision penetrated.

The fog held on for two more days. The sheep were cold and miserable and wanted to walk instead of graze, so we had to stay with them all day. I never knew where we were in relation to our camp. It was a good thing Brookie knew, or we might have fallen off a canyon wall or wandered aimlessly into the misty netherworld.

At last the sunshine returned, but it was no longer summer. Every night we had frost. Though the days were warm, the air had a different feel to it—sort of a crisp tang you could almost taste. The sky was so blue it hurt my eyes. A few days later, we had our first snow. It barely covered the ground and was gone in a few hours, but it was definitely fall. Shine came and moved our wagon to the upper end of the Blue Creek Valley, where Fred Lohse was already camped. As soon as Shine made a trip to the ranch for supplies, we hit the trail.

Fred was in the lead with his herd, and Shine pulled both camps. At noon we all ate together. Later in the afternoon Shine dropped our wagon where we would spend the night and went on with Fred's wagon and the supply wagon to where he and Fred would stay. Instead of moving before breakfast, as we did on the trail up, we ate an early breakfast before we pulled out. After breakfast, Shine rode back leading one team, hitched onto our wagon, and took it up to Fred's wagon where it was again hooked on with the others.

We were getting well into September and the days were noticeably shorter, the nights colder. Most of the other sheep outfits had already left the mountains, so there were only deserted campsites where a few weeks ago there had been wagons, herders, sheep, horses, and dogs. Somehow, it made me feel sad and lonely. We rode to a few of the camps that were close to the trail and looked through the summer's collection of trash. Nearly every abandoned camp we visited contained discarded magazines of one kind or another, so we had a fresh supply of reading material as we went along. At one old cabin we found five issues of *Life* magazine, a veritable treasure! The morning we trailed the sheep down the slope of the mountains to the foothills I was suddenly filled with a sense of relief. Without being aware of it, I guess I had felt really cut off from civilization after passing all those empty sheep camps.

Even though it was September, the Mayoworth country was hot, dry, and terribly dusty. Before the day was over, I heartily wished I was back on Blue Creek, but when I thought of the fog and snow, I decided I was satisfied right where I was. I had enough happy memories to last me through the winter and with any luck at all, we would be going back to the mountains when spring came again.

As soon as we reached the ranch, the usual fall sheep working took place. The wether lambs were cut out to be trailed to the railroad at Clearmont and shipped to market. The ewe lambs were put in the meadows, where they were fed hay during the winter because out on the range, tender lamb was too much of a temptation for the coyotes.

After the ewes were mouthed and the winter herds made up and moved to the hills, we spent October and November relief-herding again. When the other herders got back from their vacations, we moved to Pete's ranch and lived in the sheepwagon we'd had all summer. We parked it about a quarter of a mile east of the top of the Sussex Hill on top of the river bluff.

Brookie and Pete worked at all the various and endless jobs that were part of ranching: repairing buildings, mending harness, and fencing stack yards to keep the livestock out of the haystacks. Pete was a skilled wheelwright and blacksmith, and he rebuilt and repaired all the wagon wheels for the ranch. This was a process I never got to see, unfortunately, because the shop was off-limits to women the same as the lambing shed was. He bought the spokes ready-made and fitted them into slots in the hub and the wooden rim. The iron tires were heated, slipped on the rim, then cooled with water to shrink them onto the rim.

The bucks were grained every day to get them in top shape for the bucking season on the range. Barley was carried in five-gallon buckets from the granary and poured into long, low wooden troughs. At that time, the Meikes used Rambouillet bucks with great, curled horns very similar to wild bighorn mountain sheep. It paid to keep an eye on them, because some of them were mean and to get hit by one of them could be downright dangerous. When two of them fought, they would back off, put their heads down and charge. When they connected, it sounded like a rifle shot, and it was not all that uncommon for one to die of a broken neck.

Dad had a Rambouillet buck that we named after his former owner, Smoky Brosius. He was a treacherous beast. Once he treed Fred and me on Frank Heltzel's threshing machine out in the middle of the field where Frank had left it for the winter. Smoky grazed off quite a way from the thresher, but if we made a move like we were going to escape, he charged right back. We yelled till we were hoarse, trying to attract attention, but no one heard us. At noon, when we didn't show up for dinner, our absence was finally noticed because almost nothing short of death would keep us away from a meal. Dad finally saw us and came to our rescue armed with a length of pitchfork handle.

Later, Pete bought the buck from Dad. Brookie was graining the bucks and he learned never to turn his back on Smoky. One day Brookie was going to do some riding, so Pete grained the bucks. Dad had warned Pete that the buck was mean, and Brookie warned him again about Smoky. Pete jokingly said the buck only attacked people who were afraid of him and he wasn't afraid of any buck.

Brookie was just leading his saddled horse out of the corral when a commotion accompanied by a lot of hollering took place in the buck pen. Pete was flat on the ground and every time he tried to get up, Smoky charged again. Brookie armed himself with the club he kept handy for the purpose and drove Smoky off so Pete could escape. Pete never turned his back on that buck again!

On December fifth, Shine took one bunch of bucks to the herd of ewes on Salt Creek and Brookie and I took the others to Fred Lohse's herd on Spring Draw. We knew we weren't likely to get anything to eat at noon, so we stopped at the Sussex store as we passed by and got some candy bars. It was a clear, cold morning and by the time we got to the foot of the Pine Ridge, my feet were numb. There was snow on the ground, so the trail up the steep north slope of the ridge was pretty treacherous, especially after the bucks packed it into an icy glaze with their hooves. The horses had trouble keeping their feet, so we got off and led them. Scrambling ahead of my horse on the really slick places soon had my blood circulating, and I was sweating by the time we reached the top.

Once we were over the ridge, we let the bucks spread out to graze and rest before we made the last leg of the trip. We found a spot under a clump of pines where there was no snow and sat in the sun eating our candy bars.

Fred knew we were coming with the bucks, so he threw his herd north to meet us. We declined his invitation to ride on to his wagon to get something to eat. The pale winter sun was already sliding toward the horizon, and we had a long, cold ride back to the ranch.

Two days later, Harvey and Mary came from Kaycee and stopped at our wagon. A turkey shoot was being held at Sussex, so Mary stayed with me while Brookie and Harvey went to have a try at winning a turkey for Christmas dinner. When they returned, they brought the shocking news of the bombing of Pearl Harbor. I have no recollection of whether either of them won a turkey. Pearl Harbor was so unexpected as to be almost unbelievable, even though we had all been following the war news from Europe with the feeling we were sitting on a time bomb. I think most people were in a state of shock at first, followed by outrage, just as we were.

Shortly after that, Pete's sister, Anna, and her husband, Dale "Pat" Patrick, went to Kansas City to visit Pat's family. Pete asked us to move into their house while they were gone, to fuel the oil heater and look after things. Since Patrick's house was only a couple of hundred yards down Powder River from where we had our sheepwagon, this worked out fine for us. Living in their house was quite a step up from our wagon! I loved the convenience of hot and cold running water, a kitchen sink that drained, and a bathroom complete with all the niceties, not to mention real carpet on the living room floor! There was even a good log barn where we could keep our horses.

Brookie was feeding hay to the ewe lambs every day, so I went with him in the forenoons to drive the team while he pitched the hay off the hayrack to the ewe lambs. In the afternoons, we drove to one of the stack yards and loaded the hay for the next morning's feeding. Brookie taught me how to arrange the hay on the hayrack as he pitched it off the stack. There was a knack to loading it so it didn't all slide off when we started moving. The hay came off the haystack in big slabs up to six or eight feet across and a foot or two thick. The slabs were laid along the edges of the rack, extending over the sides three or four feet. Then a layer was put down the center of the rack, locking the sides in place. The process was repeated over and over until the rack was loaded. The top of the load was tapered by drawing in the lap-over until a couple of center rows held it all in place.

The weather turned extremely cold, and I nearly froze every day, but I wouldn't have stayed at the house if I'd known I was going to freeze as stiff as a poker! Pitching hay used just about every muscle in the body, so I kept warm while we were loading it. The long, plodding trip back across the snowy fields to Patrick's was another story. We burrowed down into the hay, making a nest that Brookie could just see out of so he could guide the team, and that was some protection. Even so, I would be almost too cold to stand up by the time we reached the barn.

The Patricks got home just after Christmas, so we moved back into our wagon. Jumping out of bed every morning onto the ice-cold floor to start a fire in the cold stove and climbing back into the bed with chattering teeth took some getting used to! I didn't really mind, though. There was almost no housekeeping involved in living in a wagon, so I had a lot more freedom. Whatever Brookie worked at, I went along and helped him, except when he worked in the shop, of course.

I don't think the horses missed the barn any more than I missed the house. We parked the loaded hayrack by our wagon and tied the horses on the downwind side at night. The load of hay made a very effective shelter from the wind, and they could munch hay all night.

Very shortly our lifestyle changed again. Halsey came to our wagon one night after we had gone to bed and said we were needed at the ranch to stay with the Meike kids. Pete had left for the hospital in Buffalo with Naomi, who was hemorrhaging from the throat.

The fire had been out long enough that the wagon was cold, and I shivered as I dressed with fumbling fingers. By the time we got in Halsey's truck for the short ride up to the ranch, I was shaking, partly from the chill, but mostly from shock at the news. The kids were in bed when we got there, but they were awake and very worried about their mother. We did our best to reassure them, and finally everyone settled down and went to sleep. The next morning brought news that the hemorrhaging had stopped and Naomi was resting comfortably. The doctor had been unable to find the source of the bleeding, so she would remain in the hospital while they did further checking. Suddenly, I found myself the stand-in mother of four Meike youngsters, Don, Barbara, Peto (Pete, Jr.), and Emmy, plus Raleigh who stayed with us when it became apparent we were going to be at the house for some time, though he usually spent the weekends with his mother and Vivian.

I guess I had missed my own big, noisy family of brothers and sisters because I really enjoyed the kids. They were all in school except Emmy, so we had her with us all day. It took me a while to get used to being tied down with a "youngun," but she was a good-natured little thing and was very little bother.

The days became weeks, and still Naomi was hospitalized. Pete came from Buffalo frequently and visited the kids, picked up the mail, and checked to see how things were going. We settled into a routine that went smoothly: on school days, if the weather was nice, Emmy and I went with Brookie in Pete's pickup to haul and feed baled hay to one of the herds of sheep on Four Mile Creek; bad weather meant she and I stayed at the house and I baked, cleaned house, and did the laundry. On the weekends, I stayed home with the girls, and the boys often went with Brookie to feed. He was still feeding the ewe lambs in addition to the Four Mile herd he had taken over from Pete. He fed the baled hay on Four Mile in the mornings and in the afternoon he hauled the loose hay to the lambs.

One evening, Don brought a book about Paul Bunyan home from school. After supper, Brookie settled himself in a big armchair and began reading it to the kids. I can see them still: Peto and Emmy on Brookie's lap; Don, Barbara, and Raleigh draped on the arms and back of the chair, and everyone completely spellbound by the tale. Brookie was just naturally a clown and a mimic and when he read out loud, the characters came alive. The kids loved it and after that, he read to them nearly every night from the books they brought from the school library. Looking back, it seems like it was a lot more fun than watching television.

From babies to teenagers, almost all kids loved Brookie, and the Meike kids were no exception. He seemed to operate on their wavelength. Every one of his nieces and nephews adored him, and as they married and raised families, those kids, in turn, became Brookie fans.

Years later, whenever some of the in-laws were up at our camp for a weekend, he and as many small fry as could crowd onto the bed in the wagon held forth. He would recite for his audience and was repaid by their giggles and sometimes their hysterical shrieks as one of them was the recipient of his bee story.

"Once upon a time, a long, long time ago," Brookie would intone, "there was a big old bee and he lived in a big, hollow tree in a big forest. Every day, he would come out of his hollow tree in the big forest and he would fly around looking for pollen. Bzzz-bzzz-bzzz!" As Brookie buzzed, his index finger described a circle above all the spellbound kids.

The circle grew smaller and smaller above the tensed watchers as he continued to buzz. Suddenly with a loud "ZZZZ!" the finger descended and poked some kid in the tummy.

On one of his visits, Pete thought Emmy looked a little "peaked" and he decided she might have worms. He said there was worm medicine in the top of the cupboard over the sink if we wanted to worm her. That evening, Brookie got the worm medicine and read the instructions, but there were so many cautions about possible side effects we were afraid to give it to her.

The next morning, Brookie decided to give her a laxative. If she was wormy, he assured me, that would clean her out. He found the familiar blue Milk of Magnesia bottle in the cupboard over the sink and gave a very obliging Emmy a tablespoonful before we left to feed. I took along a roll of toilet tissue in anticipation of the probable results. When we arrived home several hours later, the Milk of Magnesia still hadn't worked, so Brookie decided she needed a follow-up dose. She was a little reluctant about taking it this time, so he told her if she'd take a spoonful, he'd take a spoonful, too. She agreed to that and took her spoonful like a good little sport, then watched while Brookie took his. A look of surprise and consternation crossed his face as he swallowed. Then he ran to the sink spitting and sputtering while Emmy looked on with great interest.

"That's not Milk of Magnesia!" he exclaimed when he finished rinsing out his mouth. "It's almond-flavored hand lotion!"

One of the recent projects of the Sussex Women's Club, we learned later, had been the making of hand lotion using a glycerine base and, among other ingredients, almond extract for scent. I'm not sure what effect it had on Emmy's worms, but she and Brookie suffered no ill effects from using it internally. She seemed to thrive despite the fact that she never did get wormed while we were caring for her.

Brookie moved our wagon from the meadow up to the barnyard while we were staying with the kids. When Pete finally brought Naomi home, we left it there since shed lambing would start soon and Brookie would be helping. I went over to the house every morning and did the housekeeping until they hired a neighbor girl to take over until Naomi was on her feet again.

After all this time, Emmy was not sure who Naomi was. Every afternoon, for several days, she ran away from home and came over to our wagon.

"You have to go back to your mama," I'd tell her.

"But I don't wanna!" she'd wail. "I wanna stay with you!"

We would both be in tears by the time I persuaded her to go home. After a few days, though, her life settled back to normal and she quit coming.

We had a late spring, and when shed lambing was finished there wasn't enough green grass on the range to feed milking ewes. This meant they had to be fed hay a while longer, so we moved them to one of the meadows at the ranch and Brookie and I took over the care and feeding of them. Vernon Lohse, who had fed the old ewes all winter, enlisted in the army, along with every other young man in the area. The wagon he had been living in was now vacant, and since it was larger than the one we had, we transferred our personal things to it and moved in.

Then I made an interesting discovery: either he couldn't cook, wouldn't cook, or he had a passion for corn flakes! He had been living on corn flakes and canned milk. And he must have detested washing dishes. About the only utensil in the wagon that didn't have corn flake remains cemented in with dried canned milk was the dishpan. What irritated me most, I think, was that everything was neatly stored where it belonged: cups, plates, and bowls in the cupboard; spoons in the cutlery drawer; pans, kettles, and skillets in the storage area behind the stove. As I soaked, scrubbed, and scoured corn flaky dishes, I hoped fervently that he got lots of K.P. duty in training camp!

Just about every able-bodied citizen in the United States had gone to war. The demand for war workers in the defense plants sparked a migration of people that made the Gold Rush look like a Sunday afternoon stroll! My aunt Julia had been a teacher all of her adult life, and it worried her that our educational opportunities were limited to eight years of grade school. After she persuaded Marsh to move to Seattle, he breezed through his upper-level schooling and went on to become a welder, and later, a welding instructor. He and Aunt Julie urged my family to move there so my younger sisters and brother could have the advantage of good schools. Dad, Fred, and Paul Lahitte could go into defense work and make good money. In February, Dad sold the homestead, bought a new Ford pickup, and the Brown family joined the westward movement. Dad gave me a bill of sale for Shorty, so he was now legally my horse. They loaded their personal things, a few household goods, and their dogs in the pickup and Dad, Fred, and Paul drove through while Mom, Ruth, Danny, and Julie made the trip by train.

I was glad to see them go. I knew I was going to miss them because we were a close-knit family, but there was certainly no future for them on the homestead. The six years they lived there were years of loneliness, privation, and drudgery for my mother. I felt she deserved to live where she could enjoy a few luxuries such as running water and electricity.

Finally it was time to trail to the mountains again. Shine was half a day's trail ahead of us with Fred Lohse's camp; Jack Andrew was our camptender. Everything went along routinely until we were climbing the slope of the mountains and one of the wheels on our sheepwagon hit a rock. The iron tire slewed off and the wheel broke, leaving our wagon disabled. There was nothing we could do but leave it and go on with the sheep. We threw some clothes in a flour sack, loaded our teepee and bedroll across one of our saddle horses, and caught up with Shine and his camp while Jack went back to the ranch for another wheel. For the next several days, Shine threw our bedroll off where we would bed for the night and continued on to his own bedground. We caught up to eat and drop our bedroll off with him for the next leg of the trail.

We were on Bear Trap when Pete and Jack caught up with us with our repaired wagon and the news that Jack had decided not to go on with us. He had been reluctant to pull us to begin with because he had a defense job waiting for him on the West Coast where his brother-in-law was, and he was planning on moving his family out there as soon as he got us to camp. Since we were already more than halfway there, Shine took over moving both camps as he had the fall before and Jack went back with Pete.

As we worked our way south along the 33 Mile Trail we met and passed several north-bound herds. This was a new experience for me because we had made the trail late enough the year before that the other herds were already on their camps. The camptenders always stayed ahead of the sheep with the wagons to make sure the trail was clear. When Shine saw an approaching herd, he rode ahead on his saddle horse, met the other camptender, and they decided the course of action. If we were at a wide place in the trail, it was a fairly simple procedure, but if we were passing where the trail was narrow, it was always a tense situation. Each herd was bunched up as tight as possible and kept that way while we passed, with herders, dogs, and camptenders hurrying the herds past each other and doing their best to keep any sheep from breaking away from one bunch and mixing with the other. If a mix-up occurred, the herd with the strays in it had to be held up while the culprits were caught, thrown, and their legs tied. As soon as the herd moved on to a safe distance, they were released and returned to their own flock, which was being held nearby.

We managed to get past the other trail herds without any problems and a few days later we left the 33 Mile Trail to go to our summer camps.

Fred Lohse was taken to the Blue Creek Camp at the Stanley Cabin where we'd spent the previous summer and we were given the Beaver Creek Camp, so I had to learn new boundaries.

Mick Meike's homestead cabin was just down the creek from our camp. It was one big room built of logs cut right there on the homestead. About a hundred yards below Mick's cabin was another homestead cabin belonging to Mark Davis, a Casper sheepman who ran several bands of sheep on the Big Horns. This was our eastern boundary on the creek. The north side of Torrance Ridge to the top was our southern boundary, and the big mountain north of Beaver Creek, later known as Mick's Mountain, was our northern limits. The west end of our camp took in most of the wide, flat valley of the headwaters of Beaver Creek.

In my opinion, the Beaver Creek camp didn't have the spectacular views or the feeling of space and vastness that the Stanley camp had. I soon learned, though, that it was a much easier camp to herd because of the main water source running the full length of it. At the Stanley camp, the only water was from the springs at the cabin, so the sheep had to be brought clear to the east side of the camp to water every day.

Shine and his wife, Gerry, and their four kids lived in Mick's cabin during the summer months and the other cabin was occupied by Davis's camptender, Dwight "Chub" Corn, his wife, Hattie, and their little girl, so we had none of the isolation we'd had the summer before. The camptenders always stayed on the mountains during the summers, but for some reason, Pete had tended our camp the summer before, so we had rarely seen Devoes. This summer we often rode down and visited them while our sheep were nooning on the creek. Gerry was a much better cook than I, so it was always a treat when we were invited to stay for a meal.

Almost before I knew it, the summer was over and it was time to leave the mountains. The trail down was as uneventful as the summer had been, but once we reached the ranch, things changed in a hurry.

*Brookie and Louise, 1940, in front of the wagon they lived in the fall they were married.*

Raleigh and Louise in a teepee at Seashell Rock, July 1941.

# WAR

## (1941-1944)

Our carefree life as sheepherders fell apart without warning the day we arrived at the ranch with the sheep, and Pete greeted Brookie with the shocking news that his ex-wife, Elma, was pregnant.

Early in the spring Elma had hired on as cook for two bachelors who had leased one of the smaller irrigated ranches in the community. They convinced her it would be simpler for her to move in with them, since they had an extra bedroom, than to drive back and forth in the car she had received as part of the divorce settlement with Brookie. Later in the summer the partnership dissolved when one of the men left the country rather unexpectedly. Elma and the kids moved back to the little house in the river bottom behind the store. Everyone assumed the two men had quarreled and agreed to part company.

Shortly before we left the mountains with the sheep, Harry Jones, the storekeeper, remarked to Halsey that he hadn't seen Elma in several weeks. She always sent the kids to pick up the mail and buy groceries, and he wondered if she was okay. Halsey went to check on her and was dumbfounded to see she was obviously pregnant.

Halsey was at a total loss for words. Elma, however, was not. Apparently she was so relieved to have someone to share her problem with that she poured out the whole sad story. As he drove away, Halsey had no idea what he ought to do, except he needed to tell Carol.

The logical thing, they decided, was to let Elma's family know of her dilemma, so Halsey passed the news on to Pete Meike. Once they were aware of the situation, her family came to her assistance. Arrangements were made for her to go to a home for unwed mothers several weeks before the baby was due in February. Her brother Clarence, who was a widower, said she could live with him in exchange for keeping house for him, until she left to have the baby. One condition was that he wanted no kids under foot, so we would have to take them immediately.

We spent a sleepless night weighing the situation from all angles. One thing was definite: there was no way we could keep the kids and continue to herd sheep. They would have to be where they could attend school. Vivian had just started first grade and Raleigh was beginning seventh. After much debate we decided the sensible thing would be to move to Washington. My folks had been urging us to join them ever since they'd moved in February, and get in on some of that big money that was to be made in defense work. When the war was over we'd come back to Wyoming with enough money to buy some sheep of our own.

Once we'd made our decision, everything began to happen so fast I felt as if I was caught up in a bad dream and couldn't wake up. Even after I wrote my folks and told them that we were coming it seemed completely unreal to me. I didn't want to move to Washington, or become the mother of two kids! I was just a kid myself! Why, I barely knew how to cook. How could I cope with all that responsibility? I just wanted to go on with my safe, predictable life in sheep camp. But I knew that was out of the question, and I was committed whether I liked it or not.

Arrangements had already been made for Shine's brother-in-law, Emil Digby, to take over our herding job, so our first priority was to clear our things out of the wagon so he could move in. Halsey and Carol and their three kids were living on the Horde ranch near the Sussex school, so we moved in with them while we made our preparations to leave. The next few days passed in a haze of activity and emotional shock for me. Raleigh and Vivian joined us along with all their worldly possessions and walked to school every morning with Howard, Jack, and Darlene. Raleigh seemed to take everything in stride, but I'm sure Vivian was as dazed as I was by the sudden disruption of her life.

I was grief-stricken at having to part with my horse, even though Pete assured me he'd be well taken care of and I could reclaim him as soon as we returned from Washington. There was no way we could take Mike, our young border collie, so Brookie gave him to Emil. Because we had the impression that Washington had a very warm climate, Brookie donated his wool underwear and sheepskin coat to Fred Lohse—something he lived to regret!

When we began looking for a secondhand car we got lucky. A used-car dealer in Edgerton had a fairly late-model tan Chevy coupe that belonged to a young man who had gone into the army. The price of $200 was almost too good to be true, so we borrowed the money from Pete and drove it home.

Right up to the moment we drove out of Halsey's yard, with the trunk of the coupe crammed with our clothes and bedding, and the four of us sandwiched into the seat, I couldn't believe we were leaving.

Before we reached Buffalo we had a flat tire, which was fortunate. Otherwise we might not have realized what bad shape the tires and tubes were in until we were in the middle of nowhere. Because of the war, tires and tubes were practically nonexistent.

We went to a filling station run by two old bachelor brothers who knew Brookie. When he explained our situation they literally built us three inner tubes and managed somehow to come up with some reasonably good used tires. Just to be on the safe side we invested in a plentiful supply of patches and cement. While all this was being accomplished we went to the county attorney's office. When Brookie and Elma got their divorce, she received full custody of the kids. Before we left we arranged temporary custody of them, thanks to a call from Pete Meike, and permission to take them out of state.

Since there was a nation-wide thirty-five-mile-an-hour speed limit to conserve tires and gasoline, both of which were rationed, late afternoon found us only as far as Hardin, Montana, on the northern border of the Crow Indian reservation. All of us were tired, and Raleigh was entertaining himself by aggravating Vivian. That was when we learned she had a vocabulary that would make a mule skinner blush!

It seemed like a good idea to make an early night of it and get a fresh start in the morning. As we ate supper at a small cafe, Brookie asked the proprietor about overnight accommodations and learned there was no such thing. A middle-aged Indian couple eating at a table next to us told us we were welcome to spend the night at their ranch. When we learned it was almost twenty miles back from the highway we thanked them for their kindness but told them we'd just keep driving.

At dusk we pulled off into the barrow pit, unloaded our bed tarp and bedding, and made one large bed for the four of us on the ground beside the car. There was almost no traffic on the highway, but we barely got bedded down for the night when a train came clattering by so close we nearly stampeded! In the approaching darkness we hadn't realized there was a railroad track just outside of the highway right-of-way fence. Consequently we spent a very restless night and were relieved when daylight came and we could resume our journey.

After all these years, only a few memories of the trip stand out in my mind. The mountains through Montana and Idaho were absolutely spectacular but so different from my beloved Big Horns they only made me more homesick. During my lifetime I had eaten so few meals in restaurants that it was truly a novel experience to eat three meals a day that someone else cooked. On the downside, the constant bickering of the kids and our restricted speed made it seem as if the trip would never end. But at last it did!

We arrived on Brookie's birthday, October 24, in a fog so dense we drove through a little village with the unlikely name of Falls City and never knew it! A sense of direction had been a very essential part of my life herding sheep, and now I felt completely lost and disoriented. When the fog finally lifted in February, the sun came up in the south and set in the north, and my directions were turned around all the time we lived there.

So many defense workers had flooded into the Seattle area that my folks weren't able to find a place to live when they first arrived. They were finally lucky enough to rent a big, three-story farm house thirty-five miles from Seattle in the foothills of the Cascade Mountains. Because the housing situation hadn't improved, we stayed with them when we got there.

It was nice to see my family again, but there was still a sense of unreality about everything, as if it wasn't really happening. Psychiatrists probably have a name for what happened to me, but all I knew was I couldn't quite convince myself it was real. My yearning for home became an obsession as the months passed.

Brookie went to work immediately at Associated Shipyards, where Dad, Paul, Marsh and Fred worked. He had to join the union, which took a lot of time and red tape, but was necessary if he was going to work. Except for Marsh, they were all working as scalers—a fancy name for the cleanup crews and the lowest-paid job in the shipyards. As soon as Brookie got squared away with the union, he and Dad enrolled in Marsh's welding class. When they finished the course and passed all the welding tests, they were full-fledged welders, which paid much better.

In the meantime, Mom and I were trying to cope with too many kids cooped up together on weekends, fixing nine lunches every weekday morning, and trying to dry laundry for eleven people in the bathroom and kitchen because nothing ever dried on the clothesline and there were no clothes dryers. On pay day, Mom and I rode the bus in to Issaquah, the small town where we did our trading. We bought mountains of groceries and waited for our men to pick us up on their way home from work in Dad's pickup.

We had to have ration stamps to buy sugar, meat, and butter. Leather shoes were also rationed, and this presented a real problem for a bunch of kids with growing feet. Tennis shoes weren't rationed, but fifteen minutes after the stores got in a shipment they were sold out. Being out in the country as we were, they were usually gone before we even knew about them. Finally, a friendly clerk in the little clothing store in Issaquah, aware of our predicament, took the kids' shoe sizes and put back shoes for them when they had them in stock.

While we were summering on Beaver Creek in 1942, Harvey and Mary, lured by the promise of defense job money, left Kaycee to join Brookie's sister, Evelyn, and her husband, Claude Key, in Oregon. Claude and Harvey were carpenters, so their days on the job were spent out in the cold and rain. By November, Harvey was having such a problem with arthritis in his hands and feet that he and Mary decided to head for home.

The Turks had sold their car when they got to Oregon because it was a liability with both tires and gas being rationed. We had decided to sell our Chevy coupe for the same reason, and since a car was an absolute necessity for them once they got back to Wyoming, it was agreed that they would come up to Washington on a bus and buy our Chevy from us to drive home.

How nice it was to see them again! When they left for home, though, I was completely bereft. I became so depressed I could hardly handle the day-to-day pressures of two newly acquired children, the nerve strain of too many people living together, and the homesickness that overwhelmed me all of my waking hours, plus the never-ending rain and fog. The last sound I heard at night before I went to sleep was rain dripping off the eaves, and it was the first sound I heard every morning when I awoke.

Just before Thanksgiving, we had the opportunity to rent a small, four-room house right across the garden from my folks' house. The people who owned it lived just across the highway in their own home. They had started to build the house for their son and daughter-in-law, but the war put a freeze on all building materials before the interior was finished. There were no doors on the kitchen cupboards and no fixtures in the bathroom, but we wanted a place of our own so badly that we didn't care. Once we were a separate family, things got better for me, although I was never completely happy. Every time we heard from anyone at home, I was so filled with longing for Wyoming I could hardly keep from crying.

Our old sheep-herding buddy Fred Lohse wrote quite often, and it was from him we learned that Mike had been run over and killed. I guess Mike was a one-man dog, because every chance he got, Fred said, he left Emil and went hunting for Brookie. He was crossing the Powder River bridge at Sussex when he was killed. I cried over that letter.

Mary Turk wrote every week. She knew how we longed to be back home; since that wasn't possible, she wrote letters that brought home to us. She was a gifted writer with amazing insight into human nature and one of the wittiest people I ever knew. Her letters about the people and the doings of the Kaycee-Sussex communities were a history of that time period. I saved almost all of her letters and still read them occasionally.

I was a fair seamstress, so I began making Vivian a wardrobe of new dresses, which helped pass the time. Mom still had the old Singer treadle sewing machine I learned to sew with when I was in the 4-H Club, so I felt right at home with it.

About a week before Thanksgiving, Ruthie was sent home from school with the measles. Mom immediately quarantined her in one of the second-floor bedrooms. Since she was a high school freshman, she attended a different school than the rest of the kids, and we hoped they hadn't been exposed. It would probably have worked, too, if we hadn't felt sorry for her on Thanksgiving!

Our men had to work on Thanksgiving Day, so we had our big feast that night. Ruthie was still quarantined, but we decided she surely wasn't contagious after this length of time, and it seemed a shame for her to be isolated on a holiday. Mom allowed her to come out of her room and eat in the upstairs sitting room, and we all went up to join her.

In due time, Julie, Danny, Vivian, and Raleigh all came down with measles. Fred and Marsh had both had them when they were kids, but I hadn't. When I didn't catch them from Ruthie, we decided I must be immune. Just as Raleigh and Vivian were ready to go back to school, my turn came! I was very ill, I guess because of my advanced age. Ruthie came over and nursed me through a couple of days of delirium, which I conveniently had on a weekend, so she missed no more school. My recovery seemed very slow to me, but by Christmas I was feeling better.

To me, Christmas was a dismal, disappointing affair. There was no metal available for the manufacture of toys; it was all being used in the war effort. The age of plastic had not yet arrived, so everything was constructed of cardboard or wood, and even those materials were in short supply. The kids were as pleased with their gifts as if they'd been well made, though, so that was what counted.

Because Elma was still the kids' legal guardian, Brookie's draft classification was 1-A, which meant that he could be called for service any time. I decided if there was a chance of losing him in the war, I wanted something to remember him by: a baby! In late January, the doctor confirmed that I was pregnant, and for the first time since arriving in Washington, I was truly happy.

The fog finally lifted in February, and we saw our surroundings for the first time. The mountains were beautiful, but so different from my mountains. I was used to the big, open, grassy Big Horns, which were smooth, rolling, and rounded, with gentle slopes, except in the canyons, and while the timber patches could be too dense to ride a horse through, they were scattered for the most part. Only the canyons were consistently timbered.

The Cascades, where we were, at least, were smaller, but steep sided, usually rising abruptly from the surrounding valley floors, and so covered with greenery there was no place where you could see the actual mountain surface. I would have liked to explore them, but that was impossible because swamps and underbrush covered every inch between the close-growing trees. A lot of the plant life was downright unfriendly. Devil's clubs, nettles, and wild blackberry vines abounded, along with a variety of thorny bushes and plants whose names I never learned. I loved the big, feathery ferns and the spectacular dogwoods and rhododendrons which grew in profusion everywhere. There were dozens of different kinds of trees, some of them growing to tremendous size. There was a lot of lumbering going on in our area, and during the summer we often heard the distant cry of "Timber!" followed by a rending crash as some forest giant fell to earth.

The big orchard on the Carlson place where my folks lived had just about every kind of fruit there was: sour, red pie cherries, two varieties of sweet cherries; apples; currants; raspberries; loganberries; and several kinds of plums. Years before, someone had planted blackberries along the fence line between the orchard and the pasture. They had been untended for years and had grown into a wild tangle of bushes armed with vicious thorns—and huge blackberries that made the punctures worth while!

When the weather turned warm in February it stayed that way. Mom and I started planting a garden in March, and I just knew we would lose it to frost. Instead, the weather got warmer and warmer, turning into one of the hottest summers the Pacific Northwest had seen in years. We were used to hot summers; what we weren't used to was the humidity, something that we Wyomingites had no experience with. That winter, Brookie had nearly died of hypothermia until we got enough money to buy him some warm clothing; now he was in danger of collapsing from heat prostration every day.

We finally realized that the house we were living in had been built in a swamp, and so had the outdoor toilet. On occasion, the water rose over the floor of the outhouse, a most unsanitary condition. Brookie suffered from bronchitis all winter because the interior of the house was so damp. Condensation on the walls ran down and kept the baseboards and flooring along the walls green with mold. Shoes that weren't worn every day grew green fuzz and the mattresses mildewed no matter how often they were turned. Body heat turned to moisture, so the bedding was always damp.

About a quarter of a mile down the road from us, an elderly couple named Reeves had a grocery store, tavern, filling station, and some tourist cabins. When we learned that they had a vacancy, we decided to move there. The cabin we rented had originally been just one large room until someone partitioned off a small area for a bedroom. It was so narrow there was no room to walk between the bed and the wall. In my pregnant condition, making the bed was a real challenge.

Big double windows looked out onto Raging River, and there was a walkway about four feet wide that ran from the door around under the double windows, with a railing to keep the unwary from falling into the water. Raging River was a fast-flowing river that frothed and boiled over huge granite boulders. It would have been a beautiful place, except that everyone who lived there before us had walked out on the balcony and heaved their garbage into the water. All the heavier stuff sank, so the river bed next to the cabin was full of rusting tin cans, broken glass, old tires, and other junk.

Our neighbors in the next cabin were a married couple with three children. They had a fairly new sedan, so when the man offered to provide transportation to and from work for Dad, Paul, Brookie, and Fred, it sounded like a good deal for everyone concerned. They would each pay him so much a week for gasoline and expenses, and it would be a lot more comfortable than the four of them crowded into Dad's pickup.

After a few days, the situation went downhill rapidly. It became apparent that the man, Cecil, was a practicing alcoholic. He worked in a different shipyard than they did and he began signing out after lunch every day. By the time they got off shift, he was usually so drunk he could hardly stand up. He was convinced that the drunker he got, the more his driving skills improved and he refused to let anyone else drive. One evening, with a near wreck the night before still fresh in his memory, Brookie grabbed the keys as Cecil was fumbling to find the ignition. Cecil refused to relinquish the driver's seat, and Brookie stubbornly kept the keys. They sat there for the better part of an hour. At last, Cecil passed out. They moved him over, and Brookie drove home. Several times, Cecil failed to put in an appearance at all and the men had to ride the bus, which didn't get out to our place until 11 P.M.

Then one night Cecil almost drove into the side of a train. The next day, Brookie skipped work, and we took the bus into Issaquah and bought a car. For some reason, long since forgotten, we dubbed the black Chevy sedan Old Minnie. It carried the name as long as it ran, even after we no longer owned it!

The Reeves' cabins weren't my idea of an ideal environment. The tavern was always full of lumberjacks and war workers in the evenings, and on Saturday nights it was a wild place. No matter how often it happened, I was always terrified when some drunk tried to open the door to our cabin in the middle of the night. A small building halfway between the tavern and the cabins housed the rest rooms we had to use, and I was afraid to go to them after dark unless Brookie went with me.

Finally, early in the summer we decided to build a small shack at my folk's place. Someone nearby had torn down a building, so we bought enough scrap material to build our "house." Right across the little creek that furnished the water for the big Carlson house was an open, grassy park on high ground, with a Royal Anne cherry tree at the edge of it. With the exception of oranges and apples, most of the fruit Brookie or I had ever seen was either dried or in a tin can, so we built our home right in the shade of that tree!

When we finished we had something that was a cross between a sheepwagon and a present-day camp trailer without wheels. One end had a built-in bed with a table that pulled out from under it, just like a sheepwagon, but because our shack was almost twice as wide as a wagon, we built a large clothes closet at the head of the bed and a big storage cabinet at the foot. A big bin with a hinged lid served as seating on one side of the table, and Brookie built a bench for the other side. At the other end of the house were bunkbeds for the kids, with closets at each end and drawers under the bottom bunk where they could keep their personal things. Along one side, Brookie built a table that folded up against the wall out of the way when it was not in use as a kitchen counter. We cooked and heated with a sheepwagon stove we'd had Harvey ship from Wyoming when they got home. We didn't have much room, but I was happier than I'd been anywhere else we'd lived, probably because it seemed so much like my wagon home in Wyoming.

Fred was inducted into the army in the early summer of 1943. I missed him dreadfully because he and I had always been buddies when we were growing up. Immediately following his basic training at Fort Riley, Kansas, and a short leave home, he was shipped to the South Pacific. During the bloody fighting there we expected every day to be notified that he'd been killed in action. By the grace of God he came through the whole thing with only one minor wound when flying shrapnel struck him in the leg above the shoe top.

During the long summer evenings, Dad and Brookie played ball with the kids out in the pasture. How I yearned to join them, but I was quite ungainly by this time, so it was out of the question. My pregnancy was starting to remind me of the trail to the mountains: a lot of fun the first half of the way, but the second half became a real drag, and I wished it was over!

Issaquah boasted a theater and we went almost every time the show changed, twice a week. Sherlock Holmes pictures must have been cheap and plentiful, because it seemed like every other movie we saw was a Holmes mystery. I liked mystery and suspense, and they always had lots of both, with the London fog drifting past the dim street lights and all manner of villains lurking about in the mist.

A small shed down next to the highway served as a garage for Old Minnie. It was so narrow that in my pregnant condition, I couldn't get the car door open wide enough to get out, so I always made my escape before Brookie drove in. One evening after an especially spooky Holmes movie, he let me out and I went up the dark path to the shack, expecting some horrible monster to leap on me from the shadows. I made it without anything grabbing me and was surprised to find the door open several inches. Then I remembered Vivian had run back after something as we were leaving. Probably she hadn't latched the door, I thought, and the wind had blown it open a bit.

I stepped into the pitch-black interior, reached up, and grabbed the pull-chain on the overhead light. At the same instant the light came on I heard a stealthy sound behind me. Almost rigid with terror, I forced myself to turn around and look. There stood a civet cat blinking at me. Since the cat was closer to the door than I was, I did the only thing I could think of: I stepped up on the edge of the bottom bunkbed and held onto the top bunk—a good, safe twelve inches off the floor! The cat ambled out into the darkness just before Brookie and the kids got there. When they stepped in the door, I was still clinging to the bunkbed looking exactly as I felt: eight months pregnant and foolish! I'm not at all sure they believed me when I told them there'd been a polecat in the shack. It certainly was a gentleman (or a lady) as there wasn't a trace of odor lingering behind.

A narrow suspension footbridge spanned the little creek, and like everything else in our part of Washington, it was covered with moss and mold. One rainy day when I was about eight months pregnant, I started across it at a lumbering gallop, slipped on the slimy planking, and made a most ungraceful landing on my bottom. No damage was done, though it gave me a jolt that encouraged me to travel at a more sedate gait in the future.

I went into labor in the early morning hours of October 5, and a few minutes after midnight, October 6, Brookie Peter (for Pete Meike) Turk made his debut into the world at Bronson Memorial Hospital at Renton,

Washington. I thought he was an absolute marvel from the top of his blond head to his perfect, miniature toes.

I spent the prescribed ten days in the hospital and because I was so far from home, Brookie only got to come and see me once during that time. I was pretty lonesome, so it was a great day when I finally got to go home. I felt like a queen on a throne, reigning from the old daybed in Mom's dining room with baby Pete sleeping in a basket nearby.

When the kids got home from school, they all passed me by to look at the new baby—all except Vivian. She leaned on the daybed and looked down at me. "I'm glad you're home," she said. "I missed you."

I got a lump in my throat and tears in my eyes. For the first time, I felt like a mother to her. She was not a rebellious child, and we had gotten along really well, but this was the first time she had ever shown any affection toward me. I was deeply touched.

When Pete was about six weeks old, Claude and Evelyn decided to move back to Wyoming to help Harvey run the farm he had bought. They came up the coast so they could visit us and see the new baby. They arrived driving an ancient Dodge sedan with all their worldly possessions piled on a little two-wheeled trailer made from a Model T running gear.

The night they arrived, Brookie complained of not feeling well. By midnight, he had a high fever and his right hand was swollen so badly it looked like he was wearing a boxing glove. He had scratched his hand at work a few days earlier and had it treated at the first-aid station in the shipyards. Now the scratch was an angry reddish-purple and an ominous red streak was starting to show on the inside of his wrist. We tried soaking it in Epsom salts solution, and Dad made a poultice of bread and milk and put on it, but neither remedy helped.

Brookie was delirious when Claude drove us to our doctor in Issaquah at daylight. He diagnosed it as Streptococcus infection and said we were in luck. A new drug, sulfa, had just been released for civilian use by the government. The red streak was halfway to Brookie's elbow by now, and Dr. Hillery said without sulfa to fight the infection, he would have had to amputate.

Dr. Hillery thought Brookie would be better off at home with me to nurse him than he would in the hospital at Renton, where they were continuously overcrowded and understaffed. I spent the next forty-eight hours keeping his arm packed in hot, wet towels and administering sulfa capsules. Slowly, the angry red streak that had finally reached from wrist to elbow began to recede, and Brookie slept in quiet exhaustion instead of tossing feverishly and muttering in delirium. I catnapped without ever going to bed and nursed the baby whenever Mom brought him to me. My hands were nearly cooked from wringing the almost boiling water out of the towels as I changed them. I was aware, in a dazed sort of way, that Claude and Evelyn had gone on to Wyoming, leaving the little trailer behind with about half their stuff, for us to bring if and when we moved back ourselves. Dr. Hillery made a house call the second day, said Brookie was on the mend, and ordered me to bed before I collapsed.

Brookie was laid off for nearly a month and when he went back to work, his hand was so stiff it made it difficult for him to weld. At the doctor's suggestion, I bought a rubber ball, about the size of a tennis ball, which Brookie used for therapy. Squeezing the ball loosened up the tendons in the back of his hand and strengthened the muscles. In a few months, his hand was back to normal.

Our second winter in Washington was an unusually cold one, which created all kinds of problems in a place that was used to mild, rainy winters. Fog froze on everything, creating a world of beauty wherever you could see it. It also broke power lines and tree branches and coated the highways with ice. Driving was extremely treacherous, especially since the natives had no experience with icy highways and streets, and absolutely no idea how to drive on them. Frost built up on the highways so that snowplows had to be brought over the mountains from Ellensburg to clear them. By late winter, the highways were bordered by huge piles of ice crystals that looked for all the world like snow banks.

Spring brought warmer temperatures, but we continued to have fog and very little sunshine. Whenever the fog lifted to treetop level, it rained so everything dripped constantly. It was chilly all the time and I doubted if I'd ever be really warm again. I wondered what it would be like to hang diapers out on a line in the sunshine instead of dodging them strung up in Mom's bathroom and kitchen.

All war workers had been frozen on their jobs shortly after we arrived in Washington and anyone who quit a defense job was subject to immediate induction into the Armed Forces. By the summer of 1944, though, the workforce for farms and ranches was so depleted by men going into military service and defense work there were no longer enough able-bodied people to keep things going. Farm production was a very necessary part of the war effort, so some defense workers were being released to return to work on farms and ranches.

In July, Pete Meike wrote asking Brookie to see if he could get a release to come back to the ranch. Brookie applied immediately, and we waited for a decision, hardly daring to hope. The August day Brookie came home from work triumphantly bearing his release was a day of jubilation. I think if he had been turned down we would have left for

Wyoming, anyway! I felt as if the weight of the world had lifted from me. We were going home!

We began packing immediately, a job which turned out to be a bit more involved than moving to Washington had been. Moving out of a sheepwagon had been simple, since all we took were our clothes and bedding, and all the kids had besides their clothes were a few toys and Raleigh's precious comic book collection. Now we had all the equipment it took to maintain a house, including our sheepwagon stove, plus several cases of my home-canned fruit, which I refused to leave behind. We also had a baby and all his necessities, not to mention the stuff Claude and Evelyn left for us to haul back to Wyoming. We had shipped some of their more vital things on to them already, so I condensed what was left into fewer boxes and we finally got everything piled on the little trailer except the stove, which Dad crated and shipped to us after we got home.

The morning of our departure it was raining—again. I was very depressed at leaving my family, but nothing could have kept me from going home. I wept and sniffled as we climbed the Cascades. Without warning, we drove up through the layer of fog and rain into bright sunshine. I was free at last, free from the unhappiness that had held me prisoner for almost two years!

My euphoria lasted until that afternoon. It was blistering hot in eastern Washington. The baby was fretful at being cooped up in such close quarters, and he was either climbing up me or climbing down me. I stripped him of everything but his diaper and still he was too warm. Raleigh and Vivian rode in the back seat and bickered like two stray cats. We finally pulled over so everyone could get out and stretch. Before we went on, we piled the bedding on the seat between them so they couldn't even see each other. Things progressed smoothly then. For a while.

Suddenly Vivian gave a shriek that would have turned a banshee green with envy! Brookie nearly lost control of the car and I was afraid to look back to see what awful thing had befallen her.

"Raleigh pinched me!"

Raleigh was the picture of innocence, his nose studiously buried in a comic book, both hands plainly visible.

"Did you pinch her?" I demanded.

"How could I? I can't even reach her," followed by a demonstration to prove he couldn't reach over the bedding, which was piled clear to the roof of the car.

After several more incidents, Brookie promised them, with feeling, that he was going to pull over and give them both a sound thrashing if there was any more disturbance from the back seat. They must have realized we'd reached the limit of our patience, because Raleigh quit sliding his arm behind the bedding to pinch Vivian, and Vivian even endured him leering at her around the blankets without giving a blood-curdling screech.

Late in the afternoon as we were driving through rough, hilly country, we rounded an especially sharp curve in the road. One of the trailer tires peeled off the rim and went cartwheeling down over the side of the road, jumped the highway fence, and continued on down the hill, leaping and bouncing until it struck a railroad track snaking across the valley floor. The tire lost its forward momentum, did a slow death whirl, and dropped. Raleigh sprinted down the hillside and retrieved the runaway tire, thus putting himself back in his dad's good graces.

Brookie remounted the tire and we continued on our way until it happened again. This time, it crashed into the highway fence and stopped. As Brookie mounted the tire again, he said he remembered that Model Ts had a habit of slipping tires on curves at high speed. Thirty-five miles an hour was apparently speeding for a Model T. We would just have to drive slower.

Late the next day as we drove through the mountains of Idaho, it began to rain and soon there was snow mixed with it. At dusk we stopped in a tiny village that had once been a mining town, but was now headquarters for a lumber operation. We found a vacancy at the only motel. The lady who ran it had a room with a double bed and a single, and she said she would set up a camp cot for Vivian.

"But what about the bybee?" she asked in her Southern drawl.

I told her he could sleep with us in the double bed.

"Do you have a pyad?" she asked.

I was baffled and asked her to repeat what she'd said.

"Do you have a pie-ad," she repeated, emphasizing the word. I still couldn't understand her.

After the third time, she stomped to the bed and gave it several irritated slaps and exclaimed, "To keep the mattress from getting stained! A pie-ad to put under the bybee!"

We had camped alongside the road the night before, but tonight, with the snow coming down, the cheery little gas heater in our room was certainly welcome. We had a good, nourishing supper in the little cafe next door where the lumberjacks ate. The next morning dawned bright and clear and the warm sun made short work of the snow on the highway as we continued on.

Before long, we were in hot, dry country again and pulling the heavily loaded trailer at twenty-five miles an hour, Old Minnie began to heat. By mid-afternoon we had poured our entire water supply into the radiator and still it boiled like a tea kettle. When we got to Three Forks, Montana, Brookie decided we would have to lay over and get the radiator flushed out. We found a nice park full of big cottonwoods and even a stream running through it. While I set up camp, Brookie walked to the business part of town to find a garage. In a short time, he came back and began taking the radiator off so he could carry it to the garage he'd located.

Meanwhile, I built a campfire from the abundance of twigs and limbs that littered the ground, carried water from the stream, and heated it. After washing out some diapers and draping them on bushes to dry, I heated more water and bathed Pete and Vivian. Raleigh stripped to his shorts and spent an hour or so playing in the creek in lieu of a bath.

I can imagine what the reaction would be now if an itinerant family set up camp in a city park like we did, but it was commonplace then, at least in the West. Farther east was another story.

The summer after Brookie and I were married, a fellow I knew only as "Boot," who worked at the Meike Ranch every summer, failed to put in his annual appearance. We learned later he had a very good reason: he was in jail in Omaha. He always spent the winter months traveling, living on his summer's wages. He had a late-model pickup with the equivalent of today's camper shell on it and he lived in it so he was not out much in the way of expenses. One spring evening as he was working his way back toward Sussex, he drove into Omaha, and when he spotted a well-groomed city park, he drove onto the lawn by a clump of trees and set up his camp.

About that time, a friendly deer came browsing by and Boot shot it for camp meat. When the law arrived, he had the deer dressed out and hanging in a tree and was heating a skillet on his Coleman camp stove preparatory to frying some fresh liver for supper. He was quite surprised that everyone was so upset about a little poaching!

Brookie returned with the radiator and reinstalled it while I was cooking supper. The break from traveling did us all a world of good, and we resumed our pilgrimage the next morning with everyone in much better spirits. Happily, the remainder of our trip was uneventful. The car ran without heating and the temperature had cooled enough to be bearable. We arrived at Harvey and Mary's ranch in good condition five days after we left Washington.

Our arrival at Sussex was an occasion! I was so glad to be home I don't suppose I'd have cared if no one noticed we were there, but the family, Harvey and Mary, Claude and Evelyn, and Halsey and Carol, made such a big thing of it, I knew how the prodigal son must have felt when he returned! Everyone made a great fuss over Pete, the latest Turk offspring, and we soaked it all up and beamed like the proud parents we were.

The next morning, Brookie went to the ranch. Pete told him we could go to work immediately. Jim and Lillian Andy, who had been herding on one of the mountain camps, had quit several days before we got home and Shine was herding until we could take over. We spent the rest of the day unpacking the little trailer. We stored the canned fruit and the household things we couldn't use in camp in a shed at Harvey's. The next morning, we packed our clothes in Old Minnie, left Vivian and Raleigh with Grandma and Grandpa Turk, and headed for my beloved mountains.

My eyes filled with tears when we drove up to the wagon at the Blue Spring on the north fork of Blue Creek. There was my old Shorty horse on a picket, looking no different than when I'd last seen him. He endured my overly affectionate greeting with bored indifference. The air was filled with the most heavenly aroma of roasting mutton! I hadn't eaten any mutton since we'd left Wyoming, and in those long, dreary months there were times when I wondered if I'd ever taste mutton again, or ever see a sheep again, for that matter!

Shine's tall, gangly form appeared in the wagon door and a big grin split his good-looking face when he saw it was us. It was hot in the wagon with the stove going full blast. Shine's face glistened with sweat and his thick, dark hair curled damply. He was glad to be relieved of his herding job, so as soon as we ate the delicious meal he had ready, he left for the cabin on Beaver Creek where his family was and we moved our things into the wagon.

Home! At last!

*Louise, Baby Pete, Vivian, Brookie, and Raleigh in Washington, early 1944.*

*First day out on the trail coming off the mountains in the fall of 1941. Fred Lohese's wagon behind. The Turks' wagon in front.*

# SHEEPHERDERS II

## (1944-1947)

Before long it was time for the sheep to leave for the flats. School started in a few days, and Shine moved his family down to their home at Sussex and brought a load of trail supplies back up. When we got the kids two years before, the problem of what to do with them while they were in school had been one of the main reasons we decided we couldn't herd sheep and have the kids, too. We were so eager to return to Wyoming that we hadn't given it a lot of thought.

Part of the problems fell into place without any trouble. Raleigh would be going to high school in Buffalo and boarding in town. Pete had already found a place for him. Harvey and Mary lived less than a quarter of mile from the Sussex school, so Vivian could stay with them and start third grade there. We assumed that Pete would bring up a camptender and Brookie would trail the sheep down while I took Old Minnie and the baby and stayed with them, too, until he got to the ranch. After that, we would handle things as they came.

We didn't reckon on Pete Meike. When Pete and Naomi arrived at our camp with no camptender, I decided Pete must be going to pull camp and Naomi had come along to drive his pickup back down. The men stayed outside talking and keeping an eye on baby Pete while she and I fixed dinner.

"Naomi will take your car," Pete said while we were eating, "and take Little Pete down to Halsey's."

Before I could gather my wits to ask why, "You're gonna trail the sheep down," Brookie announced between bites.

Finally I found my voice. "Oh, no!" I protested. "I've never trailed sheep alone before."

"Neither had I, the first time I did it," Brookie told me reasonably.

"But I don't know the trail!" I wailed.

"I'll be ahead of you with the wagon," he pointed out. "All you have to do is follow the road."

In the end I was outvoted and outargued. Halsey and Carol had already volunteered to keep Pete for us.

I was in a state of shock as I loaded Pete's clothes in the back seat of the car and put him in the front seat by Naomi. I had never been separated from him for more than an hour or two; now I wouldn't see him for nearly three weeks. I cried my heart out as she drove away with him howling at the top of his lungs.

Naomi told me afterward she almost turned around and brought him back. He climbed over into the back seat and crouched among his boxes of clothes like a little, frightened animal, sobbing pitifully. When she unloaded him at Halsey and Carol's house, he cried till he was exhausted. Whenever anyone tried to pick him up or console him, he screamed harder. I guess Halsey reminded him of Brookie, because he finally made up with him. Soon he made friends with the Turk kids, Howard, Jack, and Darlene. He accepted Carol last, his surrogate mother who was feeding, bathing, and clothing him, and changing his diapers! His acceptance was complete, though. Until he was grown, their home was a second home to him, their family his family. The problem of what to do with the kids never arose again, even after Pete started school.

When Brookie finally got me calmed down, he said we needed camp meat for the trail, so we saddled the horses and rode over to Deer Valley, where Brookie shot a nice buck. We dressed it out and hung the carcass in a tree to cool until morning. The next day, our preparations for leaving on trail kept me pretty well occupied, so I didn't have much time to brood. We brought our deer into camp, quartered it, and wrapped it in a tarp. The water barrel had to be filled a bucketful at a time and wood had to be hauled from the nearest timber patch. The sheep had to be herded, too.

Later that day, we moved up the west fork of Blue Creek to the head of Beaver Creek so we would be ready to leave early the next morning. Shine and Fred Lohse had left on trail a couple of days ahead of us because the trail feed was scarce and it gave the herds a better chance to graze if there was plenty of space between them.

After an early breakfast, Brookie started up the valley with the wagons and I headed the sheep out behind him. I was so unnerved I felt like screaming, but as the sheep spread out and grazed along, I calmed down. The morning was completely uneventful. The sheep knew where they were going and caused me no trouble at all. In fact, it seemed almost as if they were humoring me because I was a greenhorn!

"Why this is easy!" I thought to myself smugly. "Just like Brookie and Pete told me it would be."

Brookie was lavish with praise for the fine job I was doing as a herder, and I really lapped that up! Just about the time I was coming down with a bad case of overconfidence, which can get you in a lot of trouble when you're working with sheep, I got cut down to size.

One afternoon we started across Harriet's range. The camp was covered with dense sagebrush almost as tall as a horse. Brookie told me not to crowd the sheep when they hit the sage, because they don't like to trail through brush, especially if it is warm, and it was almost summery hot that day. This was the first time he had given me any special instructions about trailing, so I was a little uneasy as the sheep grazed up to the sage.

Instead of working into it and following the narrow wagon road, they spread along the edge both ways from the road. I rode around one side of the herd and headed them back toward the road, then did the same with the other side. Without intending to, and without realizing it was going to happen, there I was with the sheep all bunched up. To my relief a few of them worked into the brush, but then, instead of going on, they put their heads down and stood there. Sheep have a remarkable communication system. Within five minutes, the whole herd was bogged.

"Well," I thought, "they'll soon jar loose and go." So I sat and waited. They stood in clusters, noses to the ground, some chewing their cuds, all puffing in the heat.

Time passed. I kept watching hopefully for a sign that they had had their siesta and were ready to move. Nothing happened. I glanced at the sun and was startled to see how far down the sky it had made its way. I began getting the sheep stirred up, thinking they would go into the brush, but they milled around at the edge and went nowhere. Even the ones that had been shaded up in the brush came back out. In a matter of minutes, their attitude changed from lethargic to mad.

Now, I have never seen an angry sheep, but I have certainly seen a lot of mad ones! These all had their ears laid back and were scowling— and don't let anyone tell you animals can't scowl! Everything in their bearing said they weren't going into that brush! The dog worked back and forth behind them till his tongue nearly dragged on the ground, to no avail. I was stymied, and the sun seemed to drop toward the horizon with alarming speed. In that moment, I knew the meaning of total frustration and helplessness. Then I saw Brookie riding around a bend in the road. I was so relieved I burst into tears.

"No need to cry," he comforted me. "This is something that happens to every sheepherder sooner or later. We'll make it to camp before dark. Here, I'll show you what to do next time they do this."

As far as I was concerned, there wasn't going to be a next time!

Brookie moved the sheep back away from the brush a short distance and told me to just hold them there. He cut a small bunch off the lead and quickly crowded them along the road where it went into the sage. They had little choice but to follow the road, as he was right on their heels with the dog. As soon as he got them around the bend, he galloped back and cut off another bunch and did the same thing again. They knew the others were ahead of them, so they ran to catch up. Even before he got back out of the brush that time, sheep started running past him, following the others, and soon the whole herd was jostling to get into the narrow road. Up ahead, where the road was visible on a rise of ground, we could see the lead marching along with a solid stream of sheep behind them.

Shortly after sundown, we reached camp, bedded the sheep, and took care of our horses. I was pretty subdued as we fixed supper together. I learned a lesson that day that I've had to take a refresher course in a lot of times in the years since. About the time I'd get to thinking I knew all there was to know about sheep, I'd find out I didn't know very much at all about sheep.

Everything went smoothly the rest of the way. The weather was ideal, with chilly nights, warm days, and the bright blue skies of autumn. I really enjoyed myself now. It was a treat to ride up to the wagon at noon and find dinner ready. Brookie was not only a good cook but a creative one as well. I was always ravenously hungry, and everything tasted so good! After that one incident, the sheep handled fine, and I was learning to use the dog with a little more confidence. We met no trail herds; in fact, all the sheep were gone already, except for a few herds that wintered in the valleys off the west slope of the Big Horns. They usually stayed until the snow ran them off because a day's trailing would put them on their winter range.

I worried needlessly about losing the sheep in the heavy timber between the Big and Little Parks. Almost nothing grew for sheep to graze on in the subdued light under the trees and they literally poured down through on the paths made by the trail herds before us.

Pete met us in the Mayoworth country with more grain for the horses and didn't seem a bit surprised to learn that I had managed to bring his herd off the mountains without some catastrophe. He said he would let Halsey and Carol know what night we would be at the Figure 8 stockrest between Kaycee and Sussex so they could bring Little Pete up to see us.

For the next two days, I lived in anticipation. I thought the time would never pass. I could hardly wait to see my baby! When the big moment finally arrived, he took one look at me, began to cry, and clung to Carol like a burr. My own child had forgotten me! My heart was broken! They stayed about an hour, and he would have nothing to do with either Brookie or me. After they left, I let the tears spill over. "Do you supposed he'll ever remember us?" I asked Brookie. He hugged me and assured me he would, but I went to bed filled with doubt.

We reached Sussex in mid-afternoon two days later and they began cutting out the lambs, mouthing the ewes, and making up the winter herds, a job that usually took several days. Brookie parked our wagon south of the shearing pens, and I was relieved of my duties as a sheepherder.

During the time we were in Washington, Halsey and Carol bought a small acreage on the south side of Powder River, directly across from Sussex and right across the road from the sheep-working corrals. As soon as I got the wagon unpacked, I walked over and got Pete and Old Minnie. Pete was as scared of me as he had been of Naomi the day she hauled him off the mountains.

During the short time Pete was on the mountains with us, Brookie rigged up a way to picket him on the bed with a used kiddie harness someone gave me. Any time there was a fire in the stove I couldn't put him down on the floor, so the bed was his playground. Brookie attached a stout metal ring to one of the brace rods that ran across the back of the wagon just above the bed. He fastened a snap in each end of a small rope, so one end could be snapped into the ring, and the other into a ring in the back of the harness. The rope was just long enough for Pete to come to the edge of the bed. He used to crouch on all fours and look over onto the table when I was preparing a meal and beg little tidbits.

He was crying hysterically as I unloaded him at the wagon, put his harness on him, and turned him loose on the bed. He got as far away from me as he could and cowered there, sobbing. I kept up a soothing line of chatter as I began to fix supper. Suddenly, the crying stopped and I looked up as Pete reached the edge of the bed. He looked over at what I was doing, then looked at me with recognition lighting up his tear-streaked face in a big grin.

Oh, how I longed to grab him and hug him close to me, but I restrained myself! Instead, I gave him a bite of something and he sat there happily munching, while I went on with my supper preparation. From that moment on, he knew where he was and who we were.

After the winter herds were made up Shine pulled our wagon up through Carpenter Canyon to Lone Tree Bedground, which was about halfway between the head of the canyon and the Cow Camp. We would camp there for about two weeks before moving to a new bedground and fresh grazing for the sheep. Brookie trailed the sheep and I drove Old Minnie through the canyon to our camp. I used the car to store all the extra things that just simply would not fit into the wagon. It was amazing how much extra gear it took for a little person no bigger than Pete was.

A great event took place while we were camped at Lone Tree: Pete celebrated his first birthday! What a lot of changes had taken place in our lives in the past year! Pete had grown from a red, wrinkled, squally little mite to a cute, blond little boy with a sunny disposition and a grin that lit up his whole face. Being a parent was not a new experience for either Brookie or me, but becoming a natural mother was something that had to be experienced firsthand to appreciate. Someone can spend an hour telling you how it feels to jump from a plane with a parachute, about the anticipation, fear, exhilaration, and sense of accomplishment when you are safely back on Earth, but a person would have to experience it firsthand to really know what it was all about. Having a baby was much the same.

A few days before we were due to move to a new camp over on Meadow Creek, we had the first snowstorm of the season. Out in the high country where we were, it piled up some sizable drifts, so the day Shine came to move our camp, there was no way I could move Old Minnie. I sorted out the things I needed most and crammed them in the wagon.

Brookie had already left with the sheep, grazing them straight through the way the crow would fly. Shine had to make a sort of big half-circle, following the road with the wagons to get to where we would camp. It was too cold for Pete to ride in the supply wagon, so he and I rode in the sheepwagon. We were all bundled up in our coats, caps, and mittens, sitting on the bed. I had a fire in the sheepwagon stove and the door of the wagon open to help alleviate my claustrophobia.

The Meikes had bought a new camp team, a solid black horse named Jock and a blocky bay called Jum. Shine was using them as wheel team that day, with Fred and Sleepy as leaders. The road angled down a steep hill with a deep gully on the lower side. Wind had scoured the road bare of snow, and the ground was frozen as hard as rock. When the iron tires hit it, they began to slide like sled runners and the wagons started to jackknife. At that moment, Jock decided to balk, and it looked as if we were going over the edge. All I could think of was Pete and me trapped on the bed with all those live coals in the stove just inside the door.

Shine, God bless him, literally rose to the occasion. He stood up in the supply wagon, let out a ferocious bellow at the horses, and brought the ends of four leather lines down with a resounding whack across Jum's rump. Jum, Fred, and Sleepy lunged into a gallop and dragged Jock and the two wagons down the hill to flat ground at the bottom.

Shine called back to ask if we were all right. I managed to find enough voice to answer him, but it was a good thing I was sitting down or I would surely have collapsed. I kept thinking about what would have happened if Jock had fallen or thrown himself, something balky horses often did.

I never heard a logical explanation of what caused a horse to balk. One minute they would be going along in a completely normal fashion. The next, they would throw a fit and refuse to go another step. As far as I know, this is an affliction peculiar to work horses. I never heard of a balky saddle horse. One thing I observed in the years we drove Jock, he only balked going downhill, and then he only did it once in a while. Another balky horse the Meikes had only balked when pulling up a hill. I've always wondered if it was a form of claustrophobia. Sometimes, if a balky horse was allowed to stand quietly for a few minutes, he would go on as if nothing had happened.

Afterward, I told Brookie I thought it was downright strange, not to mention unjust, that Shine walloped Jum with the lines when Jock was the one who had balked. Brookie just grinned and said, "There's an old teamster's proverb: if you're about to get stuck, beat the horse that's pulling!"

Except for an occasional drift, the road was good the rest of the way to our new campsite, and we arrived in time for me to get dinner before Brookie got there with the sheep.

The coyotes were so bad the Meikes hired Haywood Waggoner to trap. He stayed at Naomi's homestead and trapped all the country surrounding the cabin. Whenever he checked traps in our area, he ate dinner at the wagon with us. Except for Shine, he was the only other person we saw for over a month.

During our stay on Meadow Creek, someone managed to retrieve Old Minnie and bring her in to Halsey's. While she was abandoned at Lone Tree the mice managed to get in and not only ruined some of the stuff I left in the car but had used the padding out of the car seats for nesting material as well.

The weather continued to deteriorate, and we finally had to leave Meadow Creek because all the feed was snowed under. Shine moved us in to Powder River, then on north to Lower Four Mile and Reno Hill. After we got settled in our new territory, we took Old Minnie to camp. In spite of the winter snow, we managed to move the car each time our wagon was moved to another bedground.

The winter seemed to go on and on forever, and at times I wondered if spring would ever come again. It was exceptionally cold and snowy, so Pete was trapped in the wagon most of the time, and he had never really learned to walk because there wasn't room. Usually, it was too cold for him to be down on the floor, so he spent most of his time picketed on the bed. He walked all over the bed, springing along like he was on a trampoline. When I saw the first TV pictures of astronauts walking on the moon years later, I knew I had seen that peculiar gait before, somewhere. Then it came to me: Pete walking the sheepwagon bed on his picket line!

Brookie ate breakfast before he left with the sheep in the morning, and he ate again in the evening after he brought the sheep back to the bedground for the night. Except for the chores of chopping wood, melting snow for water, and filling the kerosene lamp, I spent most of my time inside. I read, listened to the radio, cooked and baked, and played with Pete.

Doing laundry for a baby in winter sheepcamp was a real chore. I could melt enough snow one day to wash diapers. The next day I would repeat the snow-melting process and get the diapers rinsed. Then it usually took another day for them to freeze-dry. By the time all this was accomplished, it was time to start the whole process over. Shine came every seven days to tend camp. I always knew what day to expect him, but once I got my days mixed up and when he came to move us to a new bedground, I had a line full of diapers freeze-welded to my rope clothesline with no way in the world of getting them loose. We unfastened the line from the posts and I folded at every clothespin, making a huge stack of rigid diapers, which I laid on the bed while we were moving.

In winter sheepcamp a herder depended on melted snow for his water since all the water sources were frozen. The sheep ate snow as well. Cattle and horses, though, cannot survive on snow alone, probably because of their need for much larger quantities of water, so saddle horses were not used and the winter herders had to herd on foot.

In February the weather finally moderated, so Brookie had Shine bring out a young horse we had bought from Halsey's boys, Howard and Jack. Tony was the most unlikely looking horse I ever saw. His mother was part Shetland, and he had inherited his size from her. In addition to being small, he was rat-tailed, had almost no mane, and was pot-bellied to boot! As if that wasn't enough, he was ornery. He had no intention of being a saddle horse, and he wanted that clearly understood. He didn't mind being saddled, it was being ridden he objected to. Tony's small size was the only reason Brookie was able to ride him at all. They went through the same routine each time. Tony stood, half asleep, while Brookie saddled him, and led him into heavy sagebrush, rocks, or a gully. Then he took hold of the cheek strap of the bridle and pulled Tony's head around so it was almost touching the saddle. Quickly, he stepped on and if he was lucky, he could untrack Tony without him bucking. But a dozen times a day, Tony would buck if Brookie let down his guard for a minute.

Since the weather had warmed up, most of the snow was gone except for the big drifts on the northern exposures. Our wagon was parked right beside a huge drift I was using for camp water. As we finished breakfast one morning, I told Brookie I was going to do the laundry that day. While he went through his daily ritual of getting Tony saddled and under headway after the sheep, I began chopping chunks of snow out of the drift with the shovel and carrying them to the wagon to put in the washtub. I built up the fire in the stove and put water on to heat in the dishpan so I could wash the breakfast dishes while the snow was melting. I pulled the table out, set the dishpan on it, and was turning to go out and get the washtub when Pete lunged against his rope, the snap broke, and he sailed head first off the bed, skidded across the table on his belly, and onto the hot stove. I hadn't dressed him yet, so all he had on was an undershirt and diaper. Horrified, I grabbed him up. The skin was already slipping on his neck and chest and there were angry red stripes on one arm and his cheek.

Quickly I wrapped him in a blanket and ran to the car, praying it would start. Brookie had been parking it on the hill behind the wagon because the battery kept going dead. I put it in second gear, turned on the key and released the brake. Halfway down the hill I let out the clutch and stomped on the gas pedal. It was almost at the bottom before it fired. My mother instinct urged me to go, to get to where there was help for my baby, but my common sense made me sit long enough for the engine to warm a bit. If I killed the motor I'd be afoot.

It seemed to take forever to get anywhere following the old wagon road that meandered across draws, followed ridges, and detoured around sagebrush patches. When I finally reached the main road, I was astonished to find Brookie tying Tony to the highway fence. He climbed over to intercept me, slid into the driver's seat and asked me what happened. Together we looked at the burns, which by now were either blisters or shreds of skin. Pete's shrieks had abated to tired little sobs until I uncovered him. Now he began to cry again and so did I. Poor Brookie was trying to drive and soothe both of us. When I finally got a grip on myself it suddenly occurred to me to wonder how he happened to be there at the road waiting for me.

He said that from where he was with the sheep he saw me driving away from the wagon. He figured something bad must have happened because he knew I was planning to do the washing and he was sure only an emergency would have made me start the car with its dead battery. He rode cross country and got to the highway ahead of me. He always said that was the day he broke Tony to ride, when he knew I needed help. I suppose I'd have held myself together and made the trip to the doctor alone if he hadn't gotten there, but I was glad I didn't have to. I must have been in a state of shock because I can't remember anything about the seventy-five-mile trip to Buffalo.

The doctor assured us the burns were superficial, and they looked worse than they really were as he cleaned them and applied medication. He prescribed some kind of antiseptic cream to put on them and sent us home. His diagnosis was that there would be no permanent scarring, and he proved to be right.

It was mid-afternoon when we got back. Brookie had half-expected Tony would get restless and break the bridle reins and be gone, but we found him still standing where Brookie had tied him. Brookie began searching for the sheep while I drove on back to the camp. A short time after he left me, he overtook them grazing back toward the bedground.

Shed lambing was due to start the middle of March, so the forepart of the month Shine moved us to the ranch. This time we stayed so Brookie could help shed lamb. The herd we'd had all winter was turned over to another herder and moved south to Meadow Creek. It was nice to be camped in one place and not have to move every couple of weeks. I especially liked being able to go to Carol's and do my laundry in her gasoline-motored washing machine! Even though the water had to be carried by the bucketful into the house and heated on the stove, it seemed so much easier than the way I'd been doing laundry all winter. They had a good well with a windmill on it, so if the wind was blowing, we didn't even have to pump water.

With the end of shed lambing and the coming of green grass we moved to the Leitner place with the ewes and lambs. Never before had I appreciated the end of winter as I did that year. After the months of snow and cold and being confined to the wagon I enjoyed every minute of springtime. Wildflowers were beginning to bloom on the sunny hilltops. Pete was able to play outside and was finally learning to walk. We went with Brookie quite a lot herding the ewes and lambs. I carried Pete with me on a pillow on the front of the saddle.

Then, suddenly, on the night of May tenth, we were right back in the middle of winter! The wind came shrieking out of the north, bringing a barrage of snow flakes that spattered and hissed against the canvas wagon cover. The three of us huddled together in bed listening to the fury of the storm and hoped our sheep would be all right. I kept thinking of the newborn lambs and the ones that were being born in the herds south of the ridge where the rest of the Meikes' sheep were in the heaviest part of May lambing.

The storm blew itself out as quickly as it blew in. The morning brought clear skies and a drift halfway up on the bottom door of the wagon. The whole landscape was buried under drifts. An hour after sunup, the water was running away from them, and they settled rapidly in the shirt-sleeve temperature. By sundown all of the snow was gone except the biggest drifts on the sheltered north slopes. We found no casualties in our herd, but we learned later that all of the lambs that were born during the storm were lost.

The weeks passed quickly, and soon the sheep were being brought in for shearing. One of the herders was an Austrian by the name of Paul Pilch. He had lived in the United States for years but never became a citizen for the simple reason that he had nothing but contempt for the country and for the American people. When the war broke out and the government began rounding up undesirable aliens, Pete Meike stepped in and kept Pilch from being deported or detained by agreeing to be a sort of guardian for him.

At one time, Pilch had had money and sheep, but over the years he frittered both away by poor management and unsound business deals until the bank in Buffalo, where he borrowed money for running expenses, sent him a foreclosure notice through Pete. To keep him from losing the few hundred sheep he had left, Pete cleared up his debt at the bank and took a mortgage on the sheep and the small parcel of land Pilch still owned. The Meikes put enough sheep with Pilch's to make a herd and took him out to one of the winter camps.

To say Pilch was strange would be the understatement of all time. He lived like an animal. He owned a good sheepwagon that sat in the river bottom where he stayed off and on, but most of the time he lived out in the hills with his sheep, sleeping wherever night overtook him. He had no bed of any kind and was poorly dressed most of the time. I don't know how he survived. He built sort of dens back under rock outcrops out on the range where he holed up at night, and at some of these, long after he was gone, we found gallon lard pails blackened on the outside. He had used them in camp fires, probably to cook rabbits.

His sheep followed him anywhere. His main source of sustenance was milk from tame ewes that had lost their lambs. He told us once that some of his tame sheep slept in the shelters with him to keep him warm. Pilch left the bucks in the sheep the year-round so he lambed the year-round. Most of the lambs born during the winter died of the cold and the ones that lived had their feet, ears, or tails frozen off, so there were a lot of grotesque cripples in his herd.

When Pete sent Pilch out to herd he had Shine move his wagon out to where he would camp. Shine hated tending Pilch's camp. There was nothing to eat except what Shine took with him, and there were hardly any dishes or cooking utensils in the wagon anyway. Pilch's bed consisted of a few burlap bags strewn on the springs, so when Shine spent the night at his camp, he took his own bedroll with him. He rolled out on one half of the bed and Pilch curled up on the other half and shivered all night, keeping Shine awake.

At shearing time, Shine told Pete he would quit before he would pull Pilch to the mountains, so Brookie was given the job. Shine took over our band of sheep as herder and "Mary's Bill" Taylor was hired as Shine's camptender.

There were so many Bill Taylors in our immediate area that in order to designate which one was being spoken of, people attached some descriptive term to their names, such as Dry Fork Bill, Agnes' Bill, and so on. Wild Bill, as he was also known, came into this neck of the woods when I was pretty small, so I never knew how he came by "Wild Bill." After he was married, he was usually referred to as Mary's Bill.

They finished shearing Pilch's sheep at noon, so after dinner, we hit the trail for the American Stockrest and Watergap, leaving Vivian and Pete with Carol and Halsey. Raleigh was still in school. Pete Meike insisted that Pilch take a dog, a horse, and a new sleeping bag, and we equipped his wagon with dishes and cooking utensils. He was so mean to the dog it wouldn't follow him, so we left it at the ranch as we passed by with the wagons. Pilch refused to ride the horse, so he walked and led it.

We arrived at the stockrest long before dark, and I got busy and prepared a good supper. We waited quite a while for Pilch to come in, then finally ate without him. It was the camptender's job to go out and relieve the herder for meals if the sheep needed to be herded, but in this case, the stockrest was fenced, so there was no reason for anyone to stay with the sheep. I kept the supper warming, and as the hours passed and Pilch did not come to eat, I became more and more irritated. At 9 P.M., I was ready to throw his supper out, partly because it was no longer edible, but mostly because I was mad.

Brookie said, "Whenever you're tending camp, you're working for the sheepherder. Whatever he wants, he's the boss, and you do your best to get along with him."

At ten o'clock, Pilch finally came into camp, standing out in the dark and hollering for Brookie to bring him a pair of pants. Instantly I was concerned and remorseful. Had his horse thrown him and perhaps dragged him and torn his pants off? Had he been lying out there injured all the time I was sitting there grumbling? Brookie took a pair of pants out to him and learned he had used the ones he was wearing to flag the bedground so coyotes wouldn't bother the sheep!

Pilch refused to come in and eat as long as there was a woman in the wagon, so Brookie told me I could go out and go to bed. We had set up our teepee when we first made camp, so I did, gladly, while Brookie took care of Pilch's horse.

We always broke camp before daylight going to the mountains, because by the time the horses were wrangled, harnessed, and saddled; the wagon packed; the picket ropes and hobbles gathered; the teepee let down and loaded; it was daylight and the sheep were already moving out. That first morning when it got light enough to see, I discovered that Pilch had taken off afoot with the sheep in the dark and left his horse right where Brookie put it the night before. Brookie was busy hitching the work horses to the wagon, so I saddled Pilch's horse.

Brookie moved out with the wagons and I mounted Shorty and started to follow, leading the other horse. Then I made a revolting discovery. Pete had given Pilch a gentle old horse, but he was one of those miserable beasts that cropped up every so often among saddle horses: he wouldn't lead! He didn't pull back, but he followed so reluctantly it felt as if his feet were glued to the ground. His neck was stretched to the limit and so was my arm. Because the bridle bit pulled against his tongue, he plodded along lolling his tongue out his mouth, first one side, then the other, and rolling his eyes. He couldn't see where he was going so he stumbled over bushes and rocks. Brookie slowly pulled away from me with the wagons, so I tried to drag him into a trot, which I found to be a physical impossibility.

Because we were in the highway lane, we finally overtook Pilch, and I turned the horse over to him. If looks could kill, I'd have dropped dead the way he glared at me when I told him to take his horse. "He not my horse!" Pilch informed me in his high, shrill voice. "He Pete Meike's horse!"

In the days that followed, we developed a routine—a repeat of the first twenty-four hours. Pilch would leave with the sheep in the pitch dark in the mornings, so I had to drag that horse and try to catch up with him. He never saddled, unsaddled, or picketed the horse the whole trip. He continued to refuse to come in the wagon and eat until I went outside. The second meal I cooked for him was breakfast, and he ate the sourdough pancakes without comment. The third meal sealed our enmity for all time.

He never spoke to me directly, always talking around me to Brookie. I had tried my best to be civil to him, in spite of him always referring to me as "Dem damn vimmins," a term he used collectively for all females, I soon learned. But when he viewed my dinner and demanded, "Vat dis? At home ve feed dis kind of slop to dogs!" open warfare was declared between us. I quit trying to save supper for him because he would not come to the wagon till all hours of the night. The contest of "The Led Horse" reached the point of being ridiculous: he would run from me when he saw me dragging the horse to him, knowing I could not overtake him. I have never experienced such frustration in my whole life.

In the Mayoworth country he opened a gate and let the entire herd into a rancher's grain field. Brookie happened to see what was happening and galloped back on his saddlehorse and ran the sheep back out onto the trail.

After he shut the gate, he demanded an explanation from Pilch.

"Sheep hungry. No feed on trail," Pilch replied.

"The next time you try that, somebody's liable to kill you," Brookie told him. "And it will probably be me!"

Several times a day, Pilch told us what a smart woman his mother had been.

"If she'd been very smart," Brookie told him sourly one day, "she'd have drowned you when you were born and fed her milk to the hogs!"

When we began climbing the slope, Pilch declared he would go no farther with the sheep. He had never been on the mountains and didn't know where we were going.

"Pete Meike got no range up here," he growled. "You tryin' to lose me!"

We pulled into the Big Park with the wagons and made camp where we would be nooning. When Pilch and the sheep still hadn't come out of the timber at eleven o'clock, Brookie went back looking for him while I prepared dinner. He found him holding the sheep in the Little Park right where we'd left him several hours earlier.

Pilch refused to budge, so Brookie took the sheep and started moving up through the timber. Just as the sheep began breaking out of the trees into the open by our camp, Brookie looked back and caught a glimpse of Pilch skulking along behind him, and for once, he was riding the horse.

Just as we were getting ready to move on that afternoon, Pilch suddenly "discovered" his coat was missing from where he had tied it on the back of his saddle, so Brookie had to back-track looking for it. He found it lying, neatly folded, on a tree stump about halfway between the two parks, where Pilch had obviously left it.

"You old son-of-a-gun," Brookie told him when he got back to camp, "if you leave that coat again, either you'll go back after it yourself or you'll go without a coat this summer, and it can get mighty cold up here, even in summer!"

The next day, Pilch decided he'd gone as far as he was going.

"Okay" Brookie said. "We'll hold the sheep up here and you can sort yours out, and we'll take the Meikes' and go on. But I ought to warn you, that trail rider at Bear Trap is tough. He'll probably have you in jail by dark!"

The Bureau of Land Management had built a log cabin on Bear Trap Creek and hired Mike Streeter to headquarter there as he monitored the herds using the trail. His job was to see that everyone kept moving and didn't abuse the trail by grazing it into the ground.

For some reason, that threat really threw a scare into Pilch. Maybe he equated jail with concentration camp. Almost instantly, he changed from an arrogant, insulting banty rooster to a pathetically frightened old man. In the days that followed, if he lost sight of the wagons, he drove the sheep frantically along the trail until he could see us again ahead of him. Every day, Brookie had to convince him anew that he had to let the sheep spread out so they could graze.

Strangely enough, from that day on he rode the horse, though he still refused to take care of it. Brookie unsaddled and picketed the horse in the evenings, and I still had the job of saddling up for him every morning, but at least I didn't have to run Pilch down dragging that horse behind me!

When we reached the summer range, Brookie took Pilch to the Stanley place and showed him the boundaries of his camp. That afternoon Shine and Bill pulled onto Beaver Creek with their herd about the same time Pete arrived from the ranch. Bill, Brookie, and I all came back down with Pete. Bill had to go to a job he had waiting, and Brookie and I had to gather up our kids and household goods to take back up to the Meikes' cabin on Beaver Creek where we would be spending the summer camptending.

Old Minnie had developed an undiagnosed ailment before we left on trail, so Brookie decided we would not try to take her to the mountains. That meant we needed transportation back to camp. Pete had caught up with Shine on the slope to bring him the news that his wife, Gerry, had given birth to twins, a boy and a girl, so Shine was anxious to see his family. Shine's pickup had a homemade camper-type cover on the back, so we loaded all our stuff, as well as Gerry's, and piled all the kids—June, Larena, Leonard, Violet, Raleigh, Vivian, and Pete—in on top of it. Brookie drove and Gerry and I rode in front with him, each holding a baby.

It soon became apparent that the pickup was not running as well as it should, but it didn't do too badly until we started climbing the slope. Then it began to miss, sputter, and backfire. Periodically it died altogether, and there we sat. Brookie checked everything he could think of without ever finding anything wrong. Every time we stalled, all the kids had to get out because half of them were carsick at any given time, and the other half needed to go to the toilet. After each stop, Brookie would somehow manage to get the pickup started again and we'd go another few hundred yards, if we were lucky, before repeating the whole process. We left on our trip about 9 A.M.; by noon we were still miles from Shine's camp, so we dug into our groceries and made a lunch of sorts for everyone.

Shine had expected us to show by early afternoon, so he was beside himself with worry by the time we finally arrived after dark. The kids had all fallen into exhausted sleep and we adults were ready to drop from nerve strain and fatigue. The babies, who couldn't have been much over two weeks old, had been jolted, mauled, and their schedule disrupted, so they were howling their heads off.

Shine said he couldn't imagine what was wrong with the pickup because it was working fine when he left on trail with the sheep.

"Did Digby put the new spark plugs in after I left?" he asked Gerry.

She said he had. That gave Shine the clue he needed to find the trouble. By flashlight, he and Brookie checked spark plug wires. In no time they had the pickup running smoothly after they put the crossed wires on properly.

As soon as we got Gerry's bedding and clothing unloaded, we drove to the cabin and unpacked enough of our stuff so we could eat another lunch and go to bed. The next morning after Shine got the sheep on water, he rode down and got the pickup, leading his saddle horse out the window as he drove back up to his wagon.

It didn't take us long to get settled in at the cabin. It was just one big room made of native mountain logs, built right on the bank of Beaver Creek. There was no danger of flooding, because at that point the bank was twenty-five or thirty feet above the creek and almost straight up and down, with rocked-in steps to make it easier to carry water. A couple of herds of sheep watered above the cabin, so we made it a point to carry all of our drinking water for the day early in the morning while the water was clean.

A big Majestic range sat in the kitchen end of the cabin, and though the top was fine to cook on, the oven would not bake the bottom of whatever was in it. Since I baked all my own bread, it proved to be quite a problem. The tops of the loaves would brown beautifully while the bottoms stayed white and doughy. I learned to set the bread pans on top of the stove, toward the back where the heat was moderate, and leave them until the loaves were crisp and brown on the bottoms.

Sharing the end with the stove were built-in cupboards under a big, lazy window, a regular window that had been installed horizontally instead of vertically, that looked down the canyon to the Davis cabin. The west end of the cabin served as a bedroom with two double beds and a cot. A home-made dining table with benches completed the furnishings of the cabin.

Meat, butter, sugar, and leather were still rationed, but this did not present the problem it had in Washington. Vivian and Pete splashed in and out of the creek all day, so they seldom wore shoes, and Raleigh had pretty much finished growing. Whenever we needed meat, Brookie went out and killed a deer. He was an excellent fisherman and with a good trout stream running right past the cabin, we had all the trout we could eat.

That summer, oleomargarine went on sale in Wyoming for the first time. Prior to that, the dairy industry had been successful in keeping margarine off the market in Wyoming, and even then, they were able to keep it from being colored to look like butter. It was sold in a one-pound block that looked like lard and bore no similarity to today's margarine. Each package contained a color capsule so the consumer could color it for himself. After warming the margarine to room temperature, the capsule was broken into it and the color worked in with a spoon or fork, a job I detested. Apparently, a lot of other people did, too, because I kept seeing it served without the coloring that winter in some of the homes we visited. I always had to color ours, though, because the uncolored margarine looked so much like lard it turned my stomach. Even after butter became available again, margarine was a staple for sheep camp. We had no refrigeration, and stale butter had always been a problem. Margarine solved it. It was years before margarine was available in Wisconsin, though, and friends and relatives from there who came out hunting always brought their own butter with them, claiming not to like our substitute. Brookie always teased them about their "imitation margarine" and for years, "imitation margarine" was a hunting season joke.

The south slope of the canyon wall along the cabins had a sparse to medium growth of several kinds of evergreens as well as clumps of aspens. The tangles of shrubs beneath the trees turned out to be wild raspberry and gooseberry bushes. The growing conditions must have been just right that year, because we harvested of lot of berries. I made gooseberry pies and jam, and we ate big bowls of raspberries with sugar and canned milk on them. They were only about half the size of the ones we'd had in Washington, but it seemed to me they had a much better flavor. I was saddened when, over the years, the wild berries in Beaver Creek Canyon were destroyed by tent caterpillars, or web worms, as they are also known.

The summer camptender on the Big Horns was primarily responsible for moving the camps from place to place about every two weeks. When Shine tended camp, he sometimes took his pickup down to get supplies, but Pete Meike usually brought the supplies to the mountains and the camptender distributed them to the rest of the camps with the team and wagon. Because we had no transportation Pete made frequent trips up from Sussex that summer. After Pete left, the kids and I piled in the wagon and made the camptending rounds with Brookie just for a break in routine. We seldom saw Pilch, as he had a tendency to hide when he heard us coming. The only groceries he ordered all summer were case lots of canned orange juice, canned milk, and rice. He wanted nothing else.

The corral Mick used as part of the improvements on his homestead sat on the flat south of the head of the canyon. Brookie decided to rebuild it and add on some pens so we could work sheep in it if the need arose, since there was no sheep working corral within several miles. After figuring out the boundaries, Brookie stepped off the distances between the post holes that would need to be dug, marking each one by shoveling out a neat round of sod the size the hole was to be. He hired Raleigh to dig the post holes while we cut trees in the canyon for posts and corral poles and hauled them to the corral with the team and wagon.

The Big Horn Mountains are one of the many mountain systems that form the Rocky Mountain chain, and by the time Raleigh dug all those post holes, he assured us that the Rockies came by their name honestly! Nearly every post hole had to be dug with the crowbar to pry, break, or dig out the rocks. It was a good thing most of the posts we cut were crooked because the holes were, too! It gave us something to do all summer, and we all had a sense of accomplishment when it was completed. In addition to earning some spending money, Raleigh developed a lot of muscles, not to mention a couple of handfuls of calluses from his summer's work.

I was filled with horror the day we turned on the radio and learned of the bombing of Hiroshima. It seemed as if there would never be an end of the bombings, the slaughter, the devastation of war. During our stay in Washington we lived with constant reminders of it, day in and day out: the big Boeing bombers flying over, the blackouts at night within so many miles of the coast, the truck convoys of troops that moved past our house for hours at a time from Ft. Lewis, Washington, to Seattle, with boys shipping out to fight in the Pacific. Nearly every letter from Wyoming brought names of boys killed, captured, or missing in action. Back in Wyoming, and especially on the mountains, we seemed a little more removed from the war, simply because of the peace and quiet of our environment. But the news of the bomb being dropped on Hiroshima brought it all home a hundredfold. "Where would it all end?" I wondered. Would the whole world finally be destroyed?

The bomb was dropped on August 6, 1945. On August 14, we were celebrating Vivian's birthday. I splurged and baked a birthday cake with some of our precious sugar. I don't suppose we had any birthday candles, probably substituting the proper number of kitchen matches, which served quite well when lit. We finished eating the cake, and Brookie got up and turned on the radio. For a few seconds we couldn't imagine what was happening. It sounded like a Fourth of July and New Year's celebration combined. Then a nearly hysterical announcer babbled that Japan had agreed to the terms of surrender!

When the full import of the news hit us, Brookie and I went a little crazy. We grabbed each other and danced around the cabin. The kids didn't know what it was all about, but it looked like fun so they joined in. I was soon sobered by the realization that there would be families receiving word of the loss of a loved one long after the war ended, but at least the horrible war was over.

Shine and Gerry had bid on and been awarded the school bus contract at Sussex that summer. In late August, just before school started, Shine moved from the mountains and we took over his herd of sheep. Raleigh moved back to Buffalo to continue high school, and we sent Vivian down to board with Grandpa and Grandma Turk while she went to school. I carefully packed all my own things and stored them in the supply wagon under a tarp for the present, and we moved from the cabin into the wagon Shine had lived in all summer.

We already knew I would be trailing our herd down with Brookie pulling my camp, so we planned on sending Little Pete down to Halsey and Carol before we left on trail and intended to send my dishes and cooking utensils down at the same time. When Pete arrived, however, he brought the news that he had sold the wether lambs and in order to meet the delivery deadline we had to be at the Hibbard Ranch in the Mayoworth country by September 17 to cut them out of the herds. Pete came prepared to pull Pilch down because we would leave on trail the next morning. One of the Meike ranch hands came up with Pete to take the pickup back down. We didn't want to burden the poor fellow with not only our housewares but a baby as well, so Little Pete and the dishes went down on trail with us!

During the early part of the summer I had regaled Pete with my aggrieved accounts of our trip to the mountains with Pilch. Brookie didn't say much about Pilch to him, except that he could understand now why Shine said he would quit before he'd pull Pilch to camp. Pete remarked rather shortly that he couldn't understand why we all had so much trouble getting along with Pilch.

After Pete and the hired man ate dinner with us, they unloaded our share of the groceries and transferred several hundred-pound sacks of grain from the pickup to the supply wagon. As soon as they left for Pilch's camp, Brookie got on his horse and wrangled the camp teams and Shine's saddle horse, which Pete would use. He picketed our work horses, harnessed the teams he was taking to Pete and hitched onto the supply wagon. Leading the two saddle horses, he headed down the Blue Creek Valley to the other camp, which was only about a mile from us since Brookie had moved Pilch a couple of days before in anticipation of hitting the trail.

Brookie arrived at Pilch's camp to find an extremely irritated Pete Meike. He was busy soaking and scouring petrified rice off all the dishes, pots and pans, skillets, even the dishpan. Pilch had lived on cooked rice and canned milk all summer, and he never washed a dish apparently. We had a good laugh when Brookie got home and told me about it, and we relived my experience with the corn flakes. "Pete has had his first lesson in Pilch," Brookie remarked. It wasn't his last, either.

We hit the trail the next morning with Little Pete riding in the sheepwagon with Brookie while I followed with the sheep. Pete and Pilch were half a day's trail behind us when we started out, but this changed several days later. Brookie held up one morning waiting for Pete to catch up so he could get another sack of grain for our horses.

Pete was glowering when he drove up, and while they transferred a sack of grain to our wagon, he began cussing Pilch. It all started the first night Pete was at Pilch's wagon. By the time he got all the dishes clean, he'd worked up quite an irritation with his sheepherder. Pete cooked supper and waited for Pilch to come in. And waited; and waited. Finally he ate by himself and kept the rest of the food warming for Pilch. Long after dark, Pilch flung the door open and stood staring at Pete.

"What you doin' here?" he demanded.

Pete told him they were starting down on trail the next morning.

Pilch demanded to know where Pete was staying. "Right here," Pete replied, slapping his hand on his bed, which was rolled out on the mattress. "Where's your sleeping bag?"

"Gone."

Brookie and I had found the brand-new sleeping bag earlier in the summer hanging in tattered shreds in a dead tree on one of Pilch's bedgrounds where he'd hung it as a coyote scare.

"Supper's ready," Pete informed Pilch.

"Don't want any," Pilch growled, backing away into the dark.

Pete got up and scraped everything into a skillet and went outside and dumped it, then washed the dishes and went to bed. He waited for some time for Pilch to come in. Finally he opened the back window. "When are you coming to bed?" he called out into the dark,

"I'll sleep under the wagon," Pilch replied.

Pete immediately got up and locked the door and went back to bed.

Sometime in the night the wind came up out of the north, bringing a brief sleet storm with it. It blew on out shortly and turned crisply cold afterward. At the height of the storm, Pilch tried the door and when he found it locked, he called to Pete to let him in.

"Go sleep under the wagon, you old son-of-a-gun!" Pete hollered, and snuggled down in his bedroll and went to sleep.

The next morning, Pilch crawled out of the supply wagon where he'd hunkered down among the sacks of grain with a tarp over him. After that, Pete said, grinning maliciously, he had no trouble getting Pilch to come in to supper. In fact, after supper, he wouldn't leave the wagon for fear Pete would lock him out. Once Pete got bedded down for the night, Pilch curled up on the bare mattress in his clothes, but he kept getting up and roaming around outside half the night.

Then one day, Pete flipped the tarp back to open another sack of grain for the horses and discovered he only had two sacks left. Pete asked Pilch if he knew what happened to it. Pilch said defiantly that he'd been feeding it to his pet sheep at night to keep them gentle.

Pete was more than a little perturbed because grain was vital for the horses on trail, especially in the fall when grass was bound to be scarce. A lot of nights, a big feed of oats was about all the horses had to eat after of long day of pulling wagons or trailing sheep.

Then came the proverbial last straw! Pete had brought up about sixteen loaves of bread for the trail. He left us several, put a couple in Pilch's wagon, and stored the rest in a large pasteboard box under the seat of the supply wagon. The evening before he caught up with us, he opened the box to replenish the bread supply in the wagon and gazed in disbelief into the large, empty box!

Pilch had to be the culprit. "What did you do with the bread?" Pete bellowed at him.

"I feed to my sheep!" Pilch yelled back. "Sheep hungry."

"That's not all that's gonna be hungry!" Pete exclaimed.

"Would it be all right if we catch up at noon and eat dinner with you?" Pete asked Brookie plaintively when he finished recounting his woes with Pilch. "Then we'll drop back at night, and I'll fix supper and breakfast for us. But if I have to eat three meals a day with that old coot, I'm liable to kill him!"

"It's okay with me," Brookie told him, "only Pilch won't eat in the wagon unless Louise goes outside, and since she's the herder, I won't ask her to do that."

"Don't worry," Pete assured him grimly. "Right now, I don't care whether that old so-and-so eats or not. If he won't come in, he can go hungry."

For the next couple of days Pilch sulked outside while we ate dinner. Then one day he came in, sat down, and ate with us, and continued to do so the rest of the way to the Hibbards.

It was fun having Little Pete with us on trail. In the morning he rode in the wagon with Brookie and if the afternoon was warm, I took him with me on the horse, trailing the sheep. If it began to cool off before we got to where we would spend the night, Brookie would wait until we caught up and take him the rest of the way with him.

We were having beautiful Indian summer weather: clear, cold nights and warm, sunny, blue-sky days. We were pushing the sheep every day in order to make our deadline, but all the other sheep outfits were gone, so we had the trail to ourselves. I still didn't have the trail memorized completely, but I remembered it well enough that I was much more confident than I'd been the year before. I was learning to study the sheep and their behavior and for some reason, I found it fascinating. I've always said it doesn't take much to entertain a sheepherder!

Brookie had ridden Tony all summer, but he was still as unpredictable as a green bronc. Given any opportunity at all, he would buck, and he was always looking for something to shy at: a bird flying up, a leaf blowing in the wind, a butterfly, or a figment of his overactive imagination. He also had a bad habit of kicking. The dogs learned to stay away from his heels, and Brookie was careful never to walk behind him. In spite of his treachery, he had one good habit: he stayed ground-hitched. Wherever Brookie dropped the reins, that's where Tony would stay. He might graze in a small circle, but he would be within a few feet of where he was left. Of the numerous times he bucked Brookie off during the years to come, he never ran off and left Brookie afoot.

During the summer, the Meikes had bought a new camp team and brought them to the mountains, and we were using them. Brookie was picketing them rather than hobbling them since the trail was new to them and he was afraid they might leave us during the night. The evening we pulled into the Big Park to spend the night Brookie led Tony a little way from the wagon and dropped the reins, then unharnessed Jack and Jim and picketed them on some patchy feed a short distance away.

My herd was grazing contentedly toward the bedground, so I circled them and rode on down to the wagon. Brookie always left Pete in the wagon until the team was taken care of. Then, if the weather was nice, Brookie would put his harness on him and picket him outside the wagon on about twenty feet of small rope so he could play and get some much-needed exercise. Pete saw me coming and ran toward me shouting happily just as Brookie stepped out of the wagon. From where I was, I saw that Tony was grazing just around the corner of the wagon from Pete. When he heard my horse, Tony threw up his head and turned to face me just as Pete careened around the corner. He ran full tilt into Tony, and my heart was in my throat as he came to a stop right between Tony's hind legs with an arm around each leg. Tony sort of squatted and stood trembling, but he didn't kick.

"Whoa, Boy," Brookie said gently to the horse.

He reached down and grabbed Pete's picket rope. Still Tony held his frozen pose. With a quick yank on the rope, Brookie jerked Pete sideways away from Tony's hind legs. Tony jumped as Pete rolled away, but he still didn't kick. Snorting loudly, he whirled to face Pete, who was howling lustily at such rough treatment.

Brookie picked Pete up, brushed him off, and was cuddling and talking to him when I got off my horse. My knees were so weak I could hardly stand. Brookie said he had read once that animals usually won't harm a small child. We decided it must be true.

The rest of the trail to the Hibbards was uneventful, and we arrived on time. For the next two days the men worked sheep at the Hibbard Corrals. As soon as the lambs were cut out, a crew from the Meikes left with them, trailing them to Buffalo to deliver to the buyer. At that time, there was a spur railroad into Buffalo from Clearmont that was used primarily for shipping livestock. Pete went with the lambs, so Brookie was to pull both Pilch and me the rest of the way home.

The night before we left the Hibbards, one of Pilch's ewes died from poison. The next morning when Brookie packed Pilch's wagon, he discovered Pilch had loaded the dead ewe and put her in the cubbyhole back under the bed. The weather was still summerlike on the flats and already the carcass was grossly bloated and starting to smell bad, but Brookie figured Pilch must have a reason for hauling it along. At noon, he asked Pilch what he intended to do with her. Pilch answered that he was going to take her home.

Home was still almost three day's trail away.

"It's his sheep and his wagon," Brookie figured. "If he wants to take her home, so be it!"

Maggots were dribbling out from under the door the day we got home. Brookie never opened the door of Pilch's wagon again. I never did find out what happened after it was parked in the river bottom at his headquarters. I've always wondered.

The first order of business when we reached the ranch, of course, was sheep working. Pete had had his fill of Pilch, so he cut Pilch's sheep out and sent him back to his own range. It was not the last we saw of Pilch, however. He seemed to think the fact he had herded on Meike's range the winter before gave him full use of all of it now. After he and his sheep were run back onto his own land several times by Meike sheepherders, camptenders, and Pete himself, Pilch resorted to cunning. He would move thirty-five or forty head of his sheep in the dark and put them into one of the Meike herds where they were bedded. The herder would discover the next morning that he had picked up a few of Pilch's sheep in the night, but not enough to warrant trailing several miles to a corral to cut them out, so they were allowed to stay.

Every few nights, Pilch would slip in a few more, without the herder being aware of it. In a herd of two thousand or more ewes, it was hard to tell if you had fifty or a hundred and fifty stray sheep. He might have managed free range for at least part of his sheep all winter if he hadn't made a mistake one night.

We were camped north of Naomi's cabin just outside the horse pasture fence that enclosed the area around it. Brookie knew he had picked up some of Pilch's sheep when we first moved there. One morning as the sheep were leaving the bedground, he discovered he had an extra black sheep. The sheep outfits used black sheep as "markers," usually one "black" to every hundred sheep. A herder usually counted his blacks off the bedground in the morning and back on again in the afternoon. If he came up short any of his markers, it was safe to assume he was also short some white sheep as well. If he didn't pick them up during the next couple of days with his herd, the camptender would ride out horseback from the ranch and hunt until he found them.

The extra black in Brookie's herd wasn't hard to pick out. Not only was it a wether, as none of our blacks were, but it was long-tailed and unbranded as well, a sure sign of Pilch's sheep, since he did not believe in docking or shearing. Brookie was pretty sure he hadn't picked up a lone black, so he took a rough count on the strays as they left the bedground and discovered he had over two hundred head of them.

We had Old Minnie in camp, so Brookie made a quick trip in to the ranch to tell Pete we needed to work sheep. They decided they could rig up a corral by using a corner of the horse pasture fence and some panels that Pete would bring out. Pete said he and Naomi could come out the next morning and bring Pilch with them to trail his sheep back to their own range.

The next morning Brookie held the sheep close to camp in anticipation of the early arrival of the sheep workers, but it was almost noon when they finally showed up. Pete was exuding irritation as he got out of the pickup and explained why they were late. He had made the mistake of hunting Pilch up the day before to tell him they would pick him up early to go work sheep, and Pilch had been playing hide and seek with them half the morning.

The evening before, when the sheep came to the bedground, Brookie caught the black wether, killed it and butchered it, and draped the pelt prominently over a big sagebrush right out in front of the wagon. Pilch was strutting around in his usual arrogant fashion when he saw the black sheep pelt. He rushed over to it and once he was convinced his eyes were not deceiving him, he turned to Pete and Brookie.

"No wonder my sheep don't come home!" he screeched. "He can't! He dead!"

"He sure is!" Brookie told him. "And every time you throw a bunch of your sheep in mine, there'll be another dead one! You can keep the Meikes supplied with mutton this winter."

That was the last time we were bothered by Pilch's sheep.

We spent part of that winter out on the Five Mile Divide herding on the homestead land that the Meikes had bought up, including the Strentz place. Louie and Marguerite had sold out and moved to the West Coast to retire.

How different this winter was from the previous one! For one thing, Pete was potty trained so I no longer had to wash diapers. We had an open winter, so we were able to keep Old Minnie with us most of the places we camped. I often drove in to Carol's and did the laundry, and we spent an occasional evening with Brookie's folks so we could spend time with Vivian. We took her out to camp nearly every weekend, and she slept on the table or rolled out on the floor of the wagon.

Just after we got off the mountains, Harvey brought Pete a pup about seven months old. He was a beautiful little dog out of a Corgi sire and a sheepdog mother. He inherited her instincts, but he was pure Corgi in build: long-bodied and short-legged with silky red fur and black and white markings. Some months before the war in Europe was over, we heard a reference on the radio to Hitler's Bier Hall Putsch. The term caught Brookie's fancy and he named the pup the Beer Hall Pooch; the poor critter carried that name as long as he lived.

Pete and Beer Hall were inseparable and spent hours playing together. I always kept a pretty close watch on them, but one day when we were camped at Six Horse Hill they gave me the slip. They had been playing in a sand bank out behind the wagon, and when I looked again they were nowhere to be seen. When they didn't answer my calls I began looking for tracks. They had followed the road that ran along the divide for a short distance before angling off over the side to the valley floor. I couldn't believe how much of a head start they had on me when I finally got where I could see them still running down the road. It was amazing that they could cover ground so fast as short-legged as they both were! I was so winded when I finally overtook them I hardly had breath enough to scold them for running away!

With Shine no longer tending camp, the job fell to anyone at the ranch who was available. Brookie kept wishing he had some way to move our camp so we didn't have to depend on someone else to do it. Pete finally sent out an old tractor for him to use, the forerunner of mechanized camp moving.

Halsey had opened up one of the numerous coal seams on the north slope of the Ridge that fall and was mining coal for people in the area. While we were camped just south of the ridge we rode down to the mine one day to visit. Halsey and Pete were so glad to see each other we let Pete go home with him to spend the night. The next morning as we were riding through from our camp to pick Pete up at the mine, Brookie shot a coyote. He tied the carcass on behind his saddle and we continued our trip on over the ridge. Halsey and his boys, Howard and Jack, were already loading coal on the truck and Pete was "helping," tossing small lumps of coal into a big washtub used for gathering up the smaller pieces.

Pete looked up at the dead coyote. "Oh! Meat!" he exclaimed.

That really tickled Halsey's funnybone. "Makes you wonder what they've been feedin' that kid!" he always added every time he told the story.

As Christmas of 1945 approached, we moved our camp to the Heltzel place. The cabin was in pretty good shape, considering no one had lived in it since Frank proved up on the land and sold it. There was even a big cook stove and an iron bedstead. We cleaned the cabin out and fixed up the bed for Pete and Vivian to sleep in.

We drove in to Sussex for the school's annual Christmas program so we could watch Vivian perform and Pete could see Santa Claus. I guess he hadn't had enough exposure to the Santa Claus legend at age two, because he took one look at the jolly old soul and clung to me, crying hysterically. When we went back to sheep camp, Vivian went with us to spend the Christmas vacation.

There were some cedar brakes out north of our camp, so the next day we all piled in Old Minnie and drove as close as we could get, then hiked the rest of the way. It was a lovely day. The sun shone warmly from a cloudless blue sky, and the kids frisked along, jumping in the mud where little rivulets of water were draining away from the snow drifts. We soon found the tree, about four feet tall, covered with dusky blue berries and smelling so Christmasy I was overwhelmed with memories of my childhood Christmases.

"Tree! Tree!" Pete shrieked, jumping up and down and clapping his hands as Brookie sawed it off with the meat saw.

At last it was down. Brookie hoisted it over his shoulder. I picked up the meat saw, and our little band marched triumphantly back to the car. Brookie put it in the trunk and with part of it sticking out we hauled it back to camp. While Brookie built a stand for it, I popped corn to string into garlands since we had no ornaments. The kids helped by eating the popcorn as fast as I popped it. Brookie cut a star out of a piece of tin can for the top, and with the popcorn strings draped around it, it was a truly festive tree!

When we picked up our mail the night of the program, our Christmas order from Sears Roebuck wasn't there and we were getting a little uneasy. Pete told us that night he would come out to camp the day before Christmas to bring some goodies and our mail. When he arrived, he had our order and a dressed hen, fresh cranberries, a paper bag of mixed nuts, and another of mixed candy.

When the kids proudly escorted him to look at their bedroom and Christmas tree he was so impressed I imagined I saw tears in his eyes. Maybe I did, because later he told Halsey, "I have to admire those people. They can make something out of nothing!"

I should have been good at that; I'd had plenty of practice!

Before the kids went to bed Christmas Eve, Brookie drove a couple of nails in the wall next to the Christmas tree and they each hung up a stocking. They went to bed as soon as they ate supper, but it took them hours to fall asleep. When we were finally convinced they were dead to the world, we carried all the stuff to the cabin and began putting it under the tree and in the socks.

This would make up for last Christmas, I thought, as we whispered and giggled and fumbled in the shielded light of the flashlight. The year before, we had been invited to share Christmas with Claude and Evelyn and their kids and Grandpa and Grandma Turk. We drove in from camp after the sheep bedded. Both Brookie's and my families always opened gifts Christmas morning after Santa had put in an appearance during the night after all the children had gone to bed. On this occasion, everyone opened their gifts after supper, sat around a while amid the debris, then the protesting kids were sent to bed. We had to get up early the next morning and get back to camp before the sheep scattered. For days afterward I felt as if we'd been robbed of Christmas.

Christmas at the Heltzel place was totally satisfying for everyone concerned. The kids were thrilled over their gifts, especially Pete, since he had not experienced anything like this in his short life. He immediately named his teddy bear "Baby Bear" and no toy was ever the recipient of more love than Baby Bear, whose battered remains are still stored in my attic!

A few days after Christmas, I received one more present: a letter from my folks in California, where they had moved shortly after the war ended in Europe, saying Fred had arrived safely home December 24 after being discharged from the army. The war was finally over for us!

By now I should have been used to Brookie volunteering me for jobs I was completely unprepared to perform. Not so. When he told me matter-of-factly that Pete had hired him as lambing boss for the May range lambing operations and me as lambing cook, I was thunderstruck. I was still a mediocre cook at best, and the idea of cooking for a crew of seven in a sheepwagon put me on the verge of panic.

"I can't do it!" I protested.

"Sure you can," Brookie told me. "You don't need a lot of fancy stuff, or a lot of variety. Just keep it simple: meat and spuds and some kind of canned vegetable and dessert."

He made it sound so easy I should have been suspicious, but I swallowed the idea, hook, line, and sinker. Three days later, Brookie, Little Pete and I were in lambing camp. Never having cooked for a crew, I had no idea what to order in the way of supplies, or how much. It was a good thing Pete had been stocking lambing camps for enough years that he knew what I needed.

Whenever my meat supply began to dwindle, some of the crew butchered another mutton and hung it up for me. From there on, it was up to me to cut off what I needed for each meal, roll the mutton in a

SHEEP! 169

canvas during the day to keep it cool and away from flies, and hang it out at night. I spent my days cooking, serving meals, and washing dishes. I baked bread every other day, three loaves at a time, plus a big pan of hot rolls for dinner on baking day. On the alternate days I baked pies or cake, which disappeared like snow before a chinook wind! I varied the dessert with stewed dried fruit, bread pudding, and rice and raisins, always followed by rice pudding! After ten days I was bored silly trying to think of some way to vary the limited menu, and I'm sure everyone was as tired of eating the food as I was of cooking it.

All the time Brookie and I had been married, Shine was lambing boss. I didn't realize what a lot of responsibility went with the job, or what a complex operation it was until Brookie took the job that spring. I was surprised to find out that lambing supplies included a lot of things in addition to groceries. There was a big coil of rope from which lengths of picket rope would be cut. If the grass was still too short to make picket feed, there would be baled hay to supplement the grass. A big bundle of laths, square at one end and pointed at the other, a can of small nails and a bolt of fiery red lambing flag cloth were also part of the lambing supplies.

A plentiful supply of lambing flags was taken to wherever sheep were being bedded, both ewe and lamb bunches and the drop herd, as the pregnant ewe herd was called. The flags were made of pieces of the cloth at least a foot square and nailed to the squared end of the lath. The pointed ends of the sticks were stuck in the ground at intervals around the herd so a coyote approaching could not reach them without being in sight of a flag. A standard procedure was for the herder to urinate on the flags so a strong human scent would be present to discourage the predators, as well. I learned that making lambing flags was considered one of the jobs of the lambing cook.

Along with the lambing flag material would be a big role of quarter-inch sisal lambing rope. Each lambing hand cut off several six-foot lengths of this and carried them wherever he went, usually with a couple of pieces attached to his belt and the rest tied on his saddle. These were used to tie ewes to bushes or whatever was handy if they needed to be detained for some reason.

Finally, there was a clutch of sheephooks with extra handles and lambing tents. A sheephook consisted of a long, round wooden handle with a metal hook on the end, the idea being that you could reach out with it, either afoot or horseback, and catch the sheep you wanted. The hook was springy enough to slip over the sheep's leg, but would fit tight enough she could not pull it over her foot. Because of the very nature of

their use, sheephook handles were easily and often broken, so a supply
of spares was a necessity.

Lambing tents were designed to house one ewe and her offspring.
The floorless contraption was comprised of a simple metal rod
framework of four legs with a canvas shell. They stood about thirty
inches high by about forty inches between each of the four legs, which
extended below the edge of the tent bottom about five inches and were
pushed into the ground to serve as tent stakes. The four rods looped into
a metal ring at the center top so each tent could be folded flat for storage
or transport. Several of them could easily be carried horseback across a
person's lap.

We parked the wagons a mile or so down Meadow Creek from the
extreme eastern edge of the Meikes' range and began lambing. At that
time, the creek water was potable, so I had an abundant supply of water
for camp use.

There were always two men with the drop herd. The sheep watered
on the creek during the nooning period, then spent the afternoon
grazing slowly away from the creek to where they would bed. As ewes
gave birth, they were left where the lambs dropped to clean their babies,
get them up, and suckle them.

Brookie left the wagon every morning while it was dark so he would
be at the bedground by daylight. While I was cooking breakfast, getting
the rest of the crew up and fed, he was doing what was called working
the bedground. Every ewe that had lambed had to be cut out of the drop
herd as it left the bedground and left behind with all the lambs. Most
ewes would stay with their lambs no matter what, but there was often
one or more that wanted to follow the herd whether their lambs did or
not.

Brookie soon discovered that Tony had a natural ability to work with
sheep, and since Brookie was better than average with a sheephook,
they soon made an unbeatable team. Once Brookie singled out the ewe
he wanted Tony had an uncanny ability to pursue her, even in a whole
herd of sheep. He always worked with his head lower than his
shoulders, which gave Brookie a clear field for using the sheephook,
something you didn't have with a high-headed horse. You had to lean
forward to hook the sheep, and it was hard to be very skillful with a
horse's head in your face. Tony was fast and as agile as a cat, so a sheep
just simply could not outdodge him.

As soon as the drop herders arrived to take over, Brookie rode in and
ate breakfast with Pete and me. In the meantime, some of the crew
would be gathering up the ewes that had lambed the day before and
working them together into a bunch, checking to see if all the ewes had

lambs, if all the lambs had mothers and were nursing satisfactorily. The smaller bunches of ewes and lambs were combined little by little until they made up a bunch of about 500 ewes. They were then turned over to a herder who was left back with a sheepwagon to look after them until shearing in early June.

After breakfast, Brookie rode back to the bedground and began pairing up ewes and lambs. If there were any dead lambs the mother or mothers had to be caught, picketed, and given live lambs. Sometimes this necessitated riding some distance to another bunch of ewes and lambs to pick up a bum (an orphan lamb) or a "short milker," one of a set of twins belonging to a ewe that didn't have a plentiful milk supply, or a single whose mother didn't have enough milk to raise him.

Brookie would manage to get back to the drop herd in time to relieve the herders so they could come in for dinner. After they got back out, Brookie rode in and ate. I usually fed Pete after the men left, but I always waited and ate with Brookie so he wouldn't have to eat alone. The crew ate supper between five and six o'clock, but Brookie didn't eat until he had the sheep bedded for the night, usually around nine o'clock. As soon as the dishes were done we fell into bed, to rise again at four o'clock the next morning and do it all over again.

After they left the bedground, the drop herd was moved over far enough from the area they had covered the afternoon before so they wouldn't pick up yesterday's drop as they were moved slowly toward the creek for noon. In the afternoon, the drop herd would go the opposite direction from the creek when they left water so both sides of the creek were covered. The same routine would be followed every day: bed on one side of the creek, noon on water, and bed on the opposite side, never covering the same ground twice, and always working down the creek. One of the responsibilities of the lambing boss was to select each night's bedground, and make sure it was a sheltered location, preferably where there were depressions, rocks, gullies and brush so lambs born during the night would be out of the wind as much as possible. As the lambing operation progressed down the creek, the camp was moved to keep up with it.

In three weeks time we covered Meadow Creek, moved over onto Salt Creek, and were working our way in toward Dead Man, a small, seasonal stream. The drop herd had dwindled down to the stragglers and the pace had slowed considerably. I was so burned out with cooking by that time I fervently hoped it would be my last lambing camp cook job!

Soon lambing and docking were behind us, and we were at the shearing pens waiting for our herd to be shorn so we could head for the mountains. I was nervous because I was going to trail our bunch by myself with Brookie pulling camp. I knew trailing young lambs was a lot more tricky than bringing the older lambs and their mothers off the mountains in the fall had been.

We decided to take Pete and Vivian with us, so I went to Carol's house to do all the laundry so I'd be starting out with everything clean. The wash water was heating on the stove when a car drove up and Elma got out. I was stunned when she informed me she had come to take Vivian to spend the summer with them and she would come back that afternoon after the laundry was done and pick up Vivian and her clean clothes.

Elma had given birth to a baby girl early in 1943. The plan had been to put the baby up for adoption, but Elma decided to keep her. After they arrived home Elma was unable to care for baby Sandra, so her brother Hial and his wife, Mamie, who were childless, took care of her temporarily. Elma's brother Clarence had remarried and finally he and his wife, Amy, adopted the baby. Elma had remarried the year before to a railroad man and they were living down along the U.P. between Rawlins and Rock Springs in the southern part of Wyoming at a railroad siding called Aspen Tunnel.

When Brookie learned at noon what was happening, he was as dismayed as I, but since Elma still had legal custody of Vivian, there wasn't a thing we could do except comply with her demands. She agreed she would send Vivian back in late August so she would be here when school started. Within a few hours, Vivian was on her way to Aspen Tunnel, and I was still trying to absorb the sudden change to our plans.

Twenty-four hours later, our herd was ready to go, so we hit the trail. Brookie helped me get the sheep across the Sussex bridge, past the Sussex store, and into the lane. Then he went back and got Pete from Carol, hitched onto his wagons, caught up with me, and worked his way through the sheep to the lead.

Everything went remarkably well until the day we nooned at the bridge on North Fork up in the Mayoworth country. The livestock followed the main road from the Hibbard Stock Rest to the North Fork Stock Rest where we were nooning. As I came out of the lane, I threw my herd off the road, which followed the fence along the west side of the stock rest, so they could graze along a range of steep, rocky hills that jutted up abruptly along the east side. As the fence approached the creek, it narrowed down to become a lane again.

Brookie made camp far enough back so we would not interfere with the sheep watering on the creek and we could keep an eye on our back trail and watch for a runback. The creek was wide and shallow at this point, and some of the more adventurous sheep waded across to the west side while we were nooning. As we packed the wagon to move on after dinner, a few sheep began crossing the narrow bridge to join the "waders." In a matter of a few minutes the whole herd was jostling and pushing their way across the bridge. I could see an alarming number of lambs still sleeping back where the main herd had drained away from them, so I jumped on my horse and galloped back to gather them up and push them down to the mass of milling sheep at the creek.

If I hadn't startled them, everything would have been all right. As I circled them, I gave a yell to wake them up and in two seconds flat, I had started the most spectacular runback of my entire career as a sheepherder! Several dozen wild-eyed lambs leaped up and, completely oblivious to the uproar at the creek, headed back toward Hibbard's as hard as they could run. Every time I outran them and tried to turn them, they streamed past me like water. The dog was as ineffective as I was; they just ran over him and past him as he tried to head them off. I looked back and saw a veritable tidal wave of panic-stricken lambs pouring down the road behind me, threatening to engulf me as more and more lambs left the herd and joined the runback. I had no idea what to do except to keep ahead of them as much as I could and keep trying to turn them. It was the most helpless feeling I'd ever had in my life! If I'd had time, I would have wrung my hands and cried!

Then a strange thing happened. The lambs in the lead began to veer off the road and spread out in some confusion across the brushy flat toward the hills where I'd grazed the herd a few hours earlier. Just then, Brookie came thundering up on Tony, and between the two of us and our dogs, we finally got them turned. By this time, quite a few ewes were catching up, frantically searching for their lambs. When they were confronted by the dogs, they turned tail, and the stampede instantly reversed itself back toward the main herd. We were right on their heels as they approached the bridge, and we made sure they didn't stop until they were all on the west side.

Brookie was not a patient man as a rule, but during the years I was learning the sheepherding business, he never chewed me out for such blunders as the one I'd just made. He explained what I had done wrong and what I should have done instead. He was so kind it always made me feel worse. I used to think, in exasperation, that if he'd holler at me I could yell back and I'd feel better! I usually ended up crying, much to my chagrin. But I learned my lessons well and seldom made the same mistake twice.

"If you'd eased around the lambs and given them a chance to get their wits about them, they would have heard the sheep and probably gone to them," he told me now.

"What made them quit the road back there where you caught up with me?" I sniffed, wiping away the tears. "If they'd stayed on the road, they'd be clear back at Hibbard's by now!"

"That was because they didn't follow the road coming in this morning," he explained. "They came in over the hills. To begin with, they were running blind. Then suddenly they realized they didn't know where they were, so they turned off toward where their instinct told them they'd been before."

Then, for the first time, I wondered what had happened to Pete in all the commotion. Brookie told me that he had been about to hitch up the horses when he saw what was happening. He quickly tied the team to the supply wagon, shut Pete in the sheepwagon, and came to my rescue.

The rest of the trail was uneventful, thank goodness! Only one other incident stood out. The government had small parcels of land scattered all over the Big Horn Mountains, in the middle of deeded land as well as along the top of the mountains. Eventually, they traded isolated government land to private landowners for land that would form a continuous stock trail the full length of the Big Horns. In the meantime, where there were gaps in the trail, the trail herds had to cross private land, and some of the landowners were pretty touchy about it, because there were always sheepherders, and sheepmen, too, who would take advantage of a chance to mooch on someone else's range.

Brookie and Shine had told me several times what a tough customer Con O'Brien was with trail herds, so I sure wasn't looking forward to crossing his range. I had never seen Con, but their description of him had been very descriptive: tall (over six feet), rawboned (not an ounce of lard on him), tough. But surely he wouldn't beat up a woman! Would he?

The weather had been so nice Pete was spending almost as much time riding with me on Shorty as he was with Brookie. He was with me the day I crossed O'Brien's. I was hurrying the sheep as fast as I could when I saw a man on horseback approaching at a gallop. I could tell by the way he was riding that he was on the warpath. Soon he was close enough I could see his face was dark as a thundercloud. Then, as he drew closer, I could see his expression change from anger to puzzlement and then to wide-eyed disbelief.

He pulled up his hard-breathing horse a few feet from us and stared in amazement. Finally a big smile spread across his face and he doffed his hat politely. "Spread 'em out, ma'am," he said in his rich Irish brogue, "and let 'em graze!"

I heard Con relate the incident many times over the years. He always referred to Pete as "the youngest sheepherder I ever saw! Riding on a pillow, he was!"

We spent the summer at the Stanley camp, and though it was a different kind of summer than I'd spent on the mountains so far, it was not really very different from the past two winters. Pete and I occasionally rode out with Brookie in the afternoons when he headed the sheep toward the bedground, but more often we stayed in camp. I took advantage of the time to experiment and expand my cooking skills. Pete and Beer Hall were constant companions, playing away the long, summer days, and splashing in the little creek that ran away from our spring. When Brookie and I hunted Indian relics he picked up rocks, too, in his little sand bucket.

In July, Fred, Danny, and another young man arrived from California. I was happy to see Fred and Danny, but when they left at the end of a week's time to hunt jobs, I was just as happy to see them go. Pete was like a friendly puppy, pestering them all the time. When they got tired of him they tormented and roughed him up in self-defense. I could never tell from his ear-splitting shrieks if he was mortally injured or having a good time. It was a nerve strain cooking for three extra people, too, because where we might have eaten a sandwich, I felt I had to cook a meal for them. The boy with Fred and Danny had never had to rough it and had no idea how to cope with our primitive lifestyle. Coming from California he probably had never envisioned a meal without fresh fruits and vegetables, and his remarks about my cooking hurt my feelings.

The day before they left he dumped a big heap of soiled clothing on the grass in front of the wagon and informed me he needed his laundry done before he went job hunting. Fred, who had been used to doing laundry under less than ideal conditions in the jungles of the South Pacific, was pretty blunt: "There's the washtub and there's the washboard and there's the spring. If you want your laundry done, fly at it!"

Danny went to work for the Meikes immediately, and Fred and the other boy eventually found work on another ranch stacking hay.

In August, Elma wrote and said she'd decided to keep Vivian through the winter, and she needed her school records so she could get her enrolled before school started. The kids from the railroad camp rode a train into Rock Springs every morning and back again in the afternoon. Our hands were tied, so all we could do was comply with her request. We never heard from Elma again all winter, even though I wrote numerous times trying to find out how Vivian was, and how she was doing in school.

We brought our own herd of sheep off the mountains again, and when we got to the ranch, Pete told us Brookie would have a feeding job for the winter, plus a house to live in. Ralph and Bessie Sheperd homesteaded years before on Powder River below the Meike Home Ranch, raised their family there, and finally sold the place to the Meikes and moved in to Buffalo to retire that summer. We could move into their house for the winter.

I was thrilled beyond words at the prospect of having a house! It was a rundown, ramshackle place, but it looked like a palace to me. Like a lot of the houses built along Powder River, it was constructed of cottonwood logs cut along the river because they were the only readily available building material, even though they did not make good house logs because it was their nature to be crooked and knotty. I think it had originally been one large room, but rooms had been added on in a hit-or-miss fashion as the Sheperd family grew. We used one big room as a living room and two rooms on the north of it as a kitchen and bedroom. The bedroom was heated by the Majestic range in the kitchen, and the living room had a big heating stove in it that was supposed to warm it.

The whole place was in a terrible state of disrepair. There was a whole conglomeration of out-buildings, all of them in various stages of collapse. Brookie patched up the barn for the team he would use for feeding and salvaged some lumber from one of the old sheds and did some repair work on the house.

Our most immediate problem was lack of furniture. Brookie used some of the old lumber to build some kitchen cupboards and a built-in dining area. There were several old iron bedsteads complete with springs and old, stained, soggy mattresses, so we put up a bed in the room off the kitchen and set up another bed in the living room. We opened a charge account with Montgomery Ward and ordered linoleum for the kitchen floor, some curtains, and a rocking chair.

We didn't realize until cold weather set in that the old house was little better than being outdoors. The outside had been covered with tin sheeting made to resemble brick. It was so old the stuff was rusted through in a lot of places. We stuffed rags in the cracks between the logs, which helped some, but the floor was so cold all the time a person had to wear overshoes to keep his feet from freezing. Pete spent a lot of time on the bed in the living room because it was too cold for him to get down on the floor. Halsey hauled us several loads of coal so we didn't lack for fuel, but no matter how much we used, we couldn't keep the house warm.

Halsey also brought us a little Guernsey cow so Pete could have fresh milk. Brookie fixed up one of the out-buildings, a semi-dugout, for a shelter for her, and I milked her night and morning. Halsey kept the calf because the cow only gave about three pints of milk at a milking, but it was so rich we were eating cream on everything and I began churning our own butter to use up the excess.

I have never felt so far away from civilization as I did that winter. Old Minnie had developed a seemingly incurable ailment before we went to the mountains the spring before, so we had no transportation. Once a week Brookie rode to Sussex on Tony and got our mail and what groceries he could carry home in a burlap bag horseback. Carol and Halsey and Claude and Evelyn and their families came to visit once in a while and Fred took us to buy groceries once a month. Other than that, about the only one I ever saw was Roy Garrett. The Garretts lived a short distance from us and he frequently walked over to spend an afternoon and evening with us. I always enjoyed his visits. He was an entertaining storyteller and he had lead a fascinating life since leaving England when he was a boy.

It was a cold, snowy winter, so Pete and I were confined to the house most of the time. The Sheperd place sat on a long stretch of bare prairie on the bluff above Powder River. No matter which way the wind blew, the snow went sweeping ahead of it, and it seemed as if the wind never stopped. I often stood at the kitchen window and watched the endlessly swirling, smoking snow and wondered if spring would ever come again. On the rare occasion when it warmed up enough for us to go feeding with Brookie, I felt as if I'd been released from jail.

Brookie made Pete a stick horse which Pete named Pancho. He and Pancho galloped many a mile through the old Sheperd house that winter. One day when we were going with Brookie to feed, Pete insisted on riding Pancho. The snow was almost as deep as Pete's legs were short, so we told him Pancho would get awfully tired. Pete informed us that Pancho never got tired.

Away we went, the work horses plodding through the snow pulling the hayrack and Pete and Pancho bringing up the rear. Pancho, valiant though he was, began to flounder almost at once in the deep snow. We had barely traveled the length of the hayrack when Pancho lost his footing and he and Pete sprawled full-length and face down in the snow.

"Why can't Pancho keep up?" Pete demanded through his tears as we loaded them on the hayrack. He was soon smiling again as he discovered he and Pancho could trot back and forth on the empty hayrack as we moved along.

Brookie watered the work horses where he crossed Four Mile Creek on his way to and from the ranch. It was narrow, deep, and fast-flowing and I don't think it ever froze completely over. The little cow and Tony, though, had to be watered at the house, and I was truly thankful for the well. I had to pump the water by hand, but that was so much easier than melting snow.

In spite of the loneliness, I loved the place. Besides, I was only lonely during the hours Brookie was gone; whenever he was with me, I was complete, lacking nothing. We could look off the bluff right into the river bottom, which was a jungle of willows, tamarisks, sage, and young cottonwoods and willows. On cold, sunny afternoons, I could look out the living room window and see countless deer browsing and resting where the sun reflected off the bank directly below the house.

Cooking had become my hobby, and as I improved, I became more adventuresome. I learned that a person could take ordinary foods and turn them into something extraordinary with the use of seasonings and flavorings. I spent a lot of my time creating marvelous concoctions for Brookie to eat and pass approval on. Once in a while my experiments didn't turn out quite as tasty as I anticipated. I learned early on that sage is one herb that does *not* lend itself well to all foods!

For Christmas, Brookie bought me a nice set of Fire King glass ovenware: cake pans, pie plates, and casseroles with lids. After the old battered enamelware I was used to in the wagons, those dishes were things of beauty.

One afternoon I made a casserole for supper, and the house was permeated with the mouthwatering aroma of it. When Brookie drove in and began taking care of the horses I made one last check of my creation. "Ah! Perfection!" I thought, looking at the cheese bubbling on top of the macaroni, hamburger, tomato mixture. I set it back on the oven rack, closed the door and finished setting the table. I was reaching to take the casserole out of the oven when Brookie opened the door and stepped into the house. Suddenly there was a loud snap and before my horrified eyes, the dish broke neatly in half, and the halves parted enough so my supper ran thickly down through the rack to spread sizzling over the bottom of the oven! Over a supper of scrambled eggs and toast, we speculated on what caused the disaster, and concluded a cold draft from the opened door must have hit the dish.

In early February, a new dimension was added to our lives: skunks. We were roused from sleep one night by a loud thumping and bumping under the house, mixed with squeaks and squeals, and then the house was filled with the overwhelming odor of skunk, so strong it burned our throats and brought tears to our eyes. The cute little critters had evidently denned under the house before we moved in and slept there peacefully during the cold winter months. Now their blood was stirring with the instinct to mate, and they apparently did not go in for passive lovemaking!

By day I tried to air out the house, a futile effort because each night brought a repeat performance of the mating ritual. Brookie reasoned that in the middle of the night, most of them would be outside cavorting around, doing whatever skunks do besides mate, so he plugged their crawlway with planks, rocks, and chunks of wood. Morning revealed that they had simply dug under and were still with us.

Then someone told Brookie to sprinkle lye in their crawlway. The lye would burn their feet when they walked in it, they would lick their feet and get it on their tongues and in an attempt to escape from their misery, they would take off for distant parts. It seemed like a cruel thing to do, but we were desperate so we tried it.

It worked. After a few nights there were no more nocturnal orgies under the house. For days afterward, I hung all our clothes out on the clothesline, but a faint skunk odor clung to them for months.

Brookie was going to be in charge of the shed lambing that spring, so the latter part of February we prepared to move back into a wagon at Pete's. We planned to live at the Sheperd house again the next winter, so we stored everything except our clothes and groceries at the house. Brookie had built a nice storage bin against the kitchen wall for flour, sugar, and so on, and it had proved to be mouseproof during the winter. We piled all the kitchen equipment in it, took down the curtains so they wouldn't fade in the summer sun and laid them in the bin on top of everything else, closed the lid, and we were on our way.

*Brookie and the G.I. weapons carrier in the spring of 1947*

*Pete and his "dawg," Beer Hall, January 1946*

# RANCHERS

# (1947-1949)

Pete Meike had been scouting around for some kind of transportation for us and decided he had found just what we needed. As part of his mustering-out pay, a Buffalo area serviceman had taken an army weapons carrier, a vehicle that looked very much like a present-day Suburban. After the man got home, he decided a pickup would be more practical on his family's ranch than the weapons carrier, so he was looking for a buyer for it. Pete told him to bring it down so we could look at it.

"It's almost big enough for us to live in!" I thought as I gazed in awe at the immense vehicle while the men dickered over the price. At last everyone was in agreement and the man left it with us and rode back to town. The next morning, with an advance from Pete, we took the weapons carrier to Buffalo, completed the deal, and proudly drove our olive drab "GI" (for government issue) home again. From that day on, it was called the GI by everyone in the community. We didn't realize the day we bought it what a complete change in our lifestyle it would bring.

I wasn't aware until shed lambing got under way that they had bred a lot more ewes to lamb early. For the first time they hired a night man. This early in the season the nights were cold enough for a newborn lamb to chill to death outside, so the ewes were shut in the shed at night. The night man checked for ewes that were lambing and as soon as a ewe dropped a lamb he carried it to a jug, a little pen just large enough to hold a ewe and her offspring so she could concentrate on cleaning off her baby and getting it on its feet and nursing. A row of jugs was set up along one wall and ran the full length of the shed. Most ewes would follow their lambs right into the jugs when they were picked up. If one didn't she had to be caught and put in the jug.

Until now, the entire shed lambing had taken place at Pete's ranch. This time we soon ran out of space for ewes with lambs, so the drop herd was moved to Patrick's, where there was a shed large enough to accommodate them at night. As we moved the sheep we also moved our camp, first from Pete's to Patrick's, then, as lambing was winding down, to the place where Shine and his family lived about a quarter of a mile on down Powder River from the Patrick place. This was part of the Meike ranch, as was the Patrick place. Pete and Dan took care of the ewes and lambs we left behind at the ranch. Brookie lambed the drop herd during the day and I was allowed to help! Glen Lohse was our night man, and part of my job was to fix a lunch for him to eat at midnight. He ate in his pickup so he didn't have to disturb us.

When we moved to the Shine shed we parked our wagon behind the shed. Glen always drove his pickup in alongside our wagon and parked with the front bumper right up against one of the big pitch pine posts that held up the roof of the shed. One evening Glen arrived just as Shine was leaving after visiting at our wagon. I heard Brookie and Shine talking in low voices and doing a lot of laughing after Glen went in the shed. I should have guessed they were up to some kind of skullduggery!

After Glen's night shift was over he always ate breakfast with us before he headed for home and bed. The morning after Shine's visit Glen finished breakfast and went out to his pickup. Brookie followed him out, and I was a little surprised to find Shine standing in front of the wagon. He and Brookie watched with interest as Glen got in, fired up his engine, put the pickup in reverse and prepared to back away from the shed. Instantly the motor died. Glen started it again, and the procedure was repeated.

After several more tries Glen jumped out and told Brookie and Shine he thought the clutch had gone out of the pickup. They were keeping straight faces with great difficulty, and I knew then they had hatched and executed some dastardly plot the night before. Glen walked around the pickup to raise the hood and I saw a range of expressions cross his face: total disbelief, dawning comprehension, and finally chagrin followed by laughter. The pickup bumper was held hard and fast to the big post with a securely fastened log chain! Brookie and Shine were laughing so hard they had trouble outrunning Glen when he began grabbing up big chunks of dried cow manure to throw at them.

Little Pete was so excited at having the Devoe kids to play with that I realized how little contact he'd had with other children since Vivian left. Then, without any prior notice, Vivian was back. Late one afternoon, we came from tending the ewes and lambs at Patrick's and found Vivian sitting in the wagon, munching on an orange. Her mother had put her on the bus at Rock Springs and sent her to Kaycee without letting anyone know she was coming. Harvey and Mary had turned their ranch over to Claude and Evelyn the fall before and moved to Kaycee where they were working as custodians at the school. Vivian walked over to the school from the bus depot, and Harvey brought her home.

When we asked Vivian if she had her report card and school records so she could continue school at Sussex, we made some surprising discoveries. Not only did she not have any school records, we learned she had spent very little time in school at Rock Springs! Elma had just recently given birth to a baby boy. During her pregnancy, she kept Vivian home from school to help with the housework whenever she wasn't feeling well; apparently that had been most of the time. We consulted with the teacher at the Sussex school, who said since school would be out for the summer in less than a month, it would be kind of pointless to start Vivian now.

When shed lambing was done, someone else took over the ewes and lambs and we moved to the lambing camp on the range. Brookie was hired as lambing boss again and everyone just assumed I was the cook, so I never told anyone I wasn't! The fact that I was hired to cook again had a lot more to do with my availability than it did with my ability. Lambing cooks were so hard to come by that anyone with enough savvy to fill a teakettle could qualify as a cook. The arrangement of Brookie as lambing boss and me as cook continued every spring until the Meikes finally abandoned the range lambing operation in 1959 and began a full-scale shed lambing operation instead.

During shed lambing we used the GI to move our wagon, and we were so pleased with the results that for the first time ever, no work horses went to lambing camp that spring. The wagon had been mounted on the running gears of an old car, and in lambing camp we found out the rubber tires made it easy to pull. There was none of the jolting and jarring of the wooden wheels. With its four-wheel-drive and low range, the GI was not only tremendously powerful, but it could be geared down to a crawl for easing over rough country out in the hills.

By the time we left for the mountains that spring, the GI had replaced not only the camp teams but the supply wagon as well, since we were able to haul all our supplies in it.

It was the beginning of the end for the day of the horse-drawn sheepwagon. As four-wheel-drive vehicles became widely available, more and more wagons were mounted on automobile running gears instead of the high, wooden-wheeled, iron-tired running gears. Within a few years, practically every sheep outfit on the Big Horns had gone from horses to vehicles to move their camps.

Several kids in the community had the three-day measles just before we moved to lambing camp. Up to then, I had never heard of three-day measles; I just thought measles were measles. One morning in lambing camp, Pete woke up with a dry cough and complained of a sore throat. He felt as if he had a temperature, so I made him stay in bed until after the crew had eaten and left on their morning rounds. When Brookie came in for breakfast, I let Pete get up so he could eat with us. He began scratching his neck and upper arms and complained fretfully of itching. I knew before I looked what I was going to find.

"Oh, no!" I exclaimed. "You've got the measles!"

Pete flung himself on the bed and burst into tears. I told him it was nothing to cry about. "Lots of people get the measles," I assured him.

"Don't tell Jack and Peto," he kept sobbing. "They'll make fun of me." I promised I wouldn't tell.

When the crew came in for dinner, Jack and Peto barely reached the front of the wagon before Pete proudly and loudly announced, "I've got the measles!"

Right after breakfast, I had bathed him with soda water, which relieved the itching to some extent, and by noon, he was feeling better, though I made him stay on the bed for the day. In three days, he was feeling great, and the rash was gone except for a dry roughness on his skin where it had been.

Before lambing was over, I noticed an inattentiveness in Pete that was quite unlike him. He had always been so alert to everything that was going on around him that it bothered me, but I kept telling myself it was just a phase he was going through.

One day, I decided to test him. He was sitting with his back to me, busy playing with a toy.

"Pete," I said in a normal speaking voice, "would you like a candy bar?"

His total lack of response sent a chill through me as I realized he hadn't heard me. After I told Brookie of my fears we made numerous experiments to check his hearing ability. Sometimes it seemed as if he had no trouble hearing; then, sometimes he seemed not to hear at all. Before we left for the mountains we took him to a doctor in Buffalo for a checkup. The doctor said his inner ears looked fine to him and assured us it was probably just a phase he was going through to assert his independence.

We did a lot of work on the Stanley cabin that summer, putting on new roofing, replacing broken windows, and chinking up the cracks between the logs. There were two old cots in the cabin that the kids slept on the nights we slept at the wagon instead of with the sheep.

The sheep grazed to the bedground by themselves and Brookie hauled salt in the GI to the salt licks, set the fires, and at dusk came back to camp. The next morning, he left at dawn, drove to the bedground, and herded from the GI until the sheep headed for water, then came on into breakfast. We still set the teepee up on the bedground where we were bedding the sheep, and we set our fires for coyotes scares, but unless there was evidence that the coyotes had bothered the sheep, more often than not we slept in the wagon. On the nights we slept with the sheep we all bedded down in the GI. Vivian stretched out across the seat and Pete shared the bed in back with us. I don't recall ever sleeping in the teepee again after the GI entered our lives.

Through the summer Pete's hearing loss became quite noticeable, but we weren't sure what to do about it since he had no ear infection and the doctor had said his ears looked all right. We decided we would take him to an ear specialist in Casper as soon as we got moved off the mountains that fall.

When school started, Vivian came down and stayed with Claude and Evelyn. We still had no school records for her, so the teacher gave her a series of tests, which showed her grade level to be where she was when Elma came and got her, so she had to make up the year she missed.

Then our lives changed again: we became property owners! Halsey and Carol had decided to move to Buffalo that summer so Jack could go to high school. When they offered to sell us their place at Sussex, we jumped at the chance. The acquisition of not only a house but a little piece of land to call our own seemed too good to be true. It meant we would have a place to come to when we got off the mountains each fall and a sense of permanence for the kids, whose existence had been pretty rootless up to now.

When Halsey bought the property, the house on it, built of hand-hewn cottonwood logs, sat so close to the river that if there was any flooding at all, the house was flooded. The first thing they did was dig a hole on higher ground further south, tear down the house, and rebuild it over the hole in which they installed a monstrosity of a furnace. It consumed prodigious amounts of coal and produced no more heat than the furnace at the Hall house or the one at the Sussex school.

When we moved into it in the fall of 1947, the house consisted of a living room and dining room, two bedrooms with a walk-through closet between them, and a lean-to kitchen Halsey had built across the east end of the house from lumber left over from the old house.

The hole under the house was referred to as the basement, and Raleigh even slept down there during the winter of 1949, but to me, it was and is the Hole, a dank, airless den full of spiders and cobwebs, a place that could (and probably does) harbor all manner of creepy, crawly critters.

When we went to the Sheperd place to retrieve our things, we found a real mess. Our "mouseproof" bin was completely filled with mouse nests made of curtains primarily, with tufts of sheep wool, chicken feathers, and assorted bits and pieces of material they had gathered from around the house and barnyard. I was relieved to find they had not chewed pieces out of the seat or back of the rocking chair to add to their nest. As we sorted our dishes, utensils, and cookware out of the debris, we found how they had gotten in. Where there was an especially wide gap between two of the logs, the chinking had crumbled, leaving the mice a fine entry way. It was big enough that a pack rat could have made use of it, and it was lucky none had found it or chances are, we would have had to replace all the cutlery! If we had had the money I would have replaced all the dishes, because in spite of all my scouring and scalding, it was a long time before I could use those things without wondering if we would get the plague or some other horrible malady from them!

We took up the almost new linoleum, hauled it to our new home, and put it down on the kitchen floor there. When I had picked it out of the Montgomery Ward catalog, I thought it was the prettiest pattern of all the numerous selections they had to choose from: a bright, cherry red with off-white marbling swirled through it. On the floor at the Sheperd house, it had never really had any traffic on it because Pete and I spent most of our time indoors and Brookie always took off his overshoes before he came into the kitchen, so we weren't tracking in any mud. Besides, it was so cold there wasn't any mud! With the increased traffic at our "new" house, though, I soon learned it was impossible to keep it looking nice. Every dusty footprint showed even though I scrubbed and waxed conscientiously. Brookie swore I wore that linoleum out scrubbing and waxing it with such vengeance!

Pete Meike told us to take anything usable from the Sheperd place because the old house would probably just "melt down." We took the bedsteads and mattresses and several old kitchen chairs. When Carol moved she left a nice buffet, a round oak dining table, and a book case she said we could have. Without them, our lone rocking chair would have looked pretty forlorn!

Little by little during the winter we added to our furnishings, thanks to Mary and Harvey. Mary bought a well-used davenport and matching chair set at a sale for us, so at least we had something in the living room besides a cot masquerading as a daybed and the faithful rocking chair. Fifty years and several covers later, that chair is still inhabiting my living room! Like me, it's a little creaky, but still serviceable!

Our trip to the Casper ear specialist was a frustrating experience. We were treated with cool indifference as the doctor made a quick check of Pete's nose and throat, and we were told that he had enlarged tonsils that needed to come out as soon as possible. The procedure might or might not help the problem, the doctor told us.

The Casper specialist's diagnosis was so inconclusive that we took Pete back to Buffalo, this time to our family doctor who had been unavailable the first time we took him in. His examination showed a small amount of scar tissue in the inner ear, but not enough to produce any deafness. I told him Pete had an inner ear infection when he was four months old, but he had never had a hearing problem until after he had the measles in May of this year. The doctor said Pete's tonsils were enlarged, but he didn't think removing them would improve his hearing. So there the matter stood.

I have often wondered if Pete's hearing loss would have been easier for Brookie and me to accept if it had occurred gradually over a period of time. Pete adjusted remarkably well, partly, I think, because he had learned to talk before he became hard of hearing, and he was not totally deaf. I was angry at fate, bitter at God for letting this happen to my little boy, and I asked over and over in my heart: "Why? God, why Pete?"

Brookie's reaction was guilt, an idea that Pete was being punished for something that was our fault. Because he felt guilty, he had a tendency to be overprotective and try to remove all obstacles from Pete's path. Once, someone remarked that there were many things that people with a hearing disability could do. I was appalled when Brookie responded angrily that Pete would never have to work as long as he, Brookie, was able to! Later, I told him that Pete was deaf, not crippled, and we had a terrible row, with him accusing me of being unfeeling and uncaring. For the next couple of years our relationship went through some pretty rocky times, and our marriage had a great strain put on it. As Pete grew from a little preschooler to a school-age kid and proved to be as self-sufficient as most kids his age, Brookie began to develop a more relaxed attitude toward his ability to cope with life. After Pete got his first hearing aid, things began to fall into place, and our lives got back on an even keel again.

Brookie tended camp, fed the old ewes and ewe lambs in the meadows, and worked around the ranch that winter. At the same time, another dream came true: we cashed in our war bonds and bought a hundred head of mixed-age ewes from Pete. He made a verbal agreement with us the day we got them that was honored all the years we had sheep: we would run our sheep with the Meikes' and they would furnish all our range, hay, cake, and shearing expenses in exchange for our wool each year, while we got the lamb crop.

The spring of 1948 marked another milestone in our lives with Raleigh's graduation from high school. Keeping him in school had been a constant struggle, not only because he hated school but from a financial standpoint, as well. If country kids wanted to continue their education past the eighth grade, their families either had to pay tuition at Kaycee, since the Kaycee High School belonged to the town of Kaycee, or else take on the expense of boarding the kids in Buffalo to attend the county high school. On top of that were the problems of being transplanted into a whole new environment, and having to fit in with a family other than their own. After Carol and Halsey moved to Buffalo, Raleigh boarded with them, so he felt more at home, but he still disliked school so much I'm surprised he managed to graduate.

Like the Meikes, we planned to sell our wether lambs every fall at shipping time and keep our ewe lambs as replacements for death loss and old ewes that we sold. We sold our first lamb crop that fall for more money than either of us had ever dreamed of seeing all in one lump in an entire lifetime! We took a look at our new-found wealth and decided to take a month off and go visit my family. It seemed like such a long time since that dreary, rainy morning when we drove away from the Carlson place. So many things had happened since then, so many changes in our lives. What fun we had planning our trip! Mom, Dad, and Julie had left California and moved back to the Seattle area, so first we would go to California to see everyone there, then go on up the coast to Washington.

The first thing we did was buy a secondhand car. It was an Oldsmobile, a good buy, we were assured by our friendly used car dealer. I left Brookie to worry about minor mechanical details, such as if it would run. The color was what sold it to me, sort of a cross between brick orange and flamingo pink! Later, we learned it took a quart of oil every time we filled the gas tank! Brookie told someone we never wondered how many miles to the gallon we got; we were too busy figuring out how many miles to the quart!

We hired Raleigh to herd for us while we were gone. He was going to keep the GI in camp so he could do his own camptending. My brother Dan was relief herding the other Meike herd while Henry Hickey, the regular herder, took a month's vacation. Raleigh's and Dan's camps were about a mile and a half apart, so Raleigh tended camp for Dan, too, and the two boys had a lot of fun visiting back and forth, learning to herd sheep and sharing each other's inexperienced attempts at cooking.

At last the great day arrived. I had packed and repacked countless times, and I think I took everything we owned except our household goods! The trunk of the car was full of boxes of clothing and the back seat, except where Pete was riding, was stacked with folded blankets so we could furnish our own bedding. We planned our departure for Election Day so we could vote for Harry Truman before we left. We cast our votes at the Sussex hall and headed for Buffalo where we would stay overnight with Halsey and Carol and listen to the election returns on the radio. At eleven o'clock that night, we conceded that Thomas Dewey had won and went to bed. The next morning we turned on the radio during breakfast to see how the state and local races had gone and were surprised to learn Truman had won!

It was threatening to storm as we left Buffalo, and it began to snow lightly as we crossed the Big Horn Mountains to Worland. We drove in light snow all day but the highway was warm so the snow melted as it fell, and by the time we reached Rawlins, Wyoming, where we spent the night, it was clearing off. The next morning it was nineteen degrees below zero when we hit the road and that was when we discovered the heater in the Olds didn't work. We rode along dressed like North Pole explorers, and I thanked my lucky stars I had not left our winter clothes behind like we did when we moved to Washington.

When we stopped for breakfast at Coalville, Utah, it was still very chilly, so we continued our journey wearing our winter coats and gloves. Sometime during the early afternoon we began driving through scattered cactus of a sort unknown to us. Soon we were in a virtual forest of them, so we stopped to take some pictures. We should have realized we were in the desert with all those cactus plants towering over us. Nonetheless, I was unprepared for the drastic change of temperatures I encountered when I stepped out of the car. Brookie insisted on taking a picture of Pete and me bundled up like Eskimos standing in a cactus forest before we shed our coats in this balmy climate.

We had been snacking all day as we drove along, so when we ordered supper at a little cafe before settling down for the night at our motel in St. George, Utah, I decided a bowl of chili was all I wanted. The steaming bowl the waitress set before me looked and smelled delicious. It took a few seconds for the first spoonful to register, but when it did I got the message—from my lips to my stomach! Tears sprang to my eyes as I gulped down the entire contents of my water glass just as the waitress arrived with Pete's and Brookie's orders.

"More water?" she asked, giving me a sympathetic smile. Speechless, I nodded and drank half of Brookie's water, then half of Pete's before she returned with my own replenished glass.

"What in the world is in that?" I managed to gasp.

"Chili," she answered, "Mexican style. Some people find it a little on the warm side."

My supper consisted of crackers washed down with more water. After all these years, I have no recollection of St. George itself, but I'll never forget their chili!

We never ate breakfast where we spent the night because Brookie liked to drive far enough to work up an appetite before stopping to eat. The morning after our stay in St. George we drove out of Utah, across a corner of Arizona, and into Nevada to a place called Mesquite. It was hardly more than a wide place in the road, but there was a neat little diner and a filling station so we stopped for breakfast. The man behind the counter was cordial to the point of effusiveness and very apologetic as we tried to order breakfast. Once a week, he explained, he drove in to Las Vegas for a week's supply of food for the cafe and since this was his day to go, he was out of nearly everything. He had only enough pancake batter to make us each one pancake and though he was out of eggs, he did have ham. By the time he had the pancakes and ham in front of us he knew our life history. He was so interested in our lives as sheepherders that he asked endless questions.

Four cups of coffee apiece later, with matching ones for himself each time we had a refill, we finally convinced him we had to leave. When he tallied up the bill we paid it and walked out in stunned silence. He had never showed us a menu so we had eaten our small breakfasts, blissfully ignorant of the price which, he said cheerfully, came to three dollars each because Brookie and I each had two pieces of ham and Pete had a glass of milk. Also, the coffee was fifty cents a cup, he added happily. Several miles down the road we finally figured out he had not only charged us for the coffee we drank, he had charged us for the coffee he drank, as well. Brookie remarked bitterly that the man must have been sitting there waiting for some sucker to show up so he could raise enough money to go in to Vegas and when he found out we were sheepherders from Wyoming, he knew his prayers were answered.

"But why would he charge such an outrageous price for coffee?" I protested. The price for a cup of coffee was ten cents just about anywhere in the country then.

"We're in the desert," Brookie suggested. "He probably has to haul his water from Las Vegas."

A little later the guy passed us driving the late model pickup we'd seen parked at the cafe, waving enthusiastically as he went whizzing by. "It's a good thing I didn't eat that hot chili at his place," I muttered. "It would have cost us a small fortune to put the fire out!" The whole episode seemed so unreal I had the odd feeling that if we'd gone back to Mesquite the next day we would have found the little diner boarded up, with sand and tumbleweeds drifted up against the door!

We followed the truck route through the outskirts of Las Vegas, so I know we missed the glamorous part of the city, but I was so unimpressed with what we saw I've never had any desire to go back. The residential section we passed through either had sand drifted up on the lawns or the yards were edged with rusted, sand-blasted corrugated tin to keep the sand off the grass. We only stopped long enough to fill the tank with gas and buy several more quarts of oil.

We were nearing the California border when we stopped at a roadside stand and bought a bag of Delicious apples. They were rightly named, I thought, as we rode along enjoying the aroma as well as the taste. They were so crisp each bite produced a sharp snap and so juicy they almost dripped. Suddenly the highway ahead of us was full of activity at what looked like a road block of some sort. As we approached, a large sign informed us we were about to enter California and this was an agricultural check station. The older model car ahead of us bearing Oklahoma license plates was crammed to the roof with all manner of stuff and the small, two-wheel trailer it was towing was heavily loaded, too. A bewildered looking young couple stood by the car watching as two uniformed men quickly dragged everything out of the car and trailer and heaped it on the long, narrow tables that paralleled the road.

The car ahead of the Oklahomans was sent on and another inspector waved us around the car and trailer to an empty table. I had a vivid mental picture of all our carefully packed boxes being dumped upside down on the table and me refolding everything and trying to get it all to fit back in the boxes.

"Do you have any agricultural products with you?" asked the inspector.

To us Wyomingites, agricultural products meant cattle, sheep, hay, and grain, so we shook our heads.

"What's in the paper bag?" He indicated our bag of apples.

"Just some apples we bought right back down the road," I answered.

Without saying a word, he smilingly beckoned toward the sack and I reluctantly handed it to him. He opened the back door and surveyed the stack of blankets and Pete sitting there staring at him big-eyed. "If you've come from Wyoming in November, the only thing you'd be likely to have is snowballs!" he said as he slammed the door and waved us on into California.

Grateful not to have to unload and repack, we quickly drove off lest he change his mind. As I looked back, I saw the young people trying to stuff everything back into their car and trailer.

We were pretty indignant about losing our bag of apples. Brookie speculated that the people running the fruit stand were in cahoots with the people running the check station. "Every night," he said, "I'll bet the people at the fruit stand come and collect all the confiscated fruit and resell it the next day to all the unsuspecting tourists heading into California."

By the time we pulled into Tehachapi to spend the night, I was so sick of Joshua trees I hoped I'd never see another one, and to this day I haven't.

Madge and Waugh Murphy, our neighbors all the years we lived on the Hall place, had a farm in the San Joaquin Valley in California, so that was where my family migrated when they left Washington. Marsh, Paul, and Dad cashed in their war bonds and invested the money in a motel, grocery store, and filling station complex alongside Highway 99 near Selma. By the time my folks sold their share of the business to Paul and Marsh in 1947 and moved with Julie back to Washington, Ruthie and Marsh were both married and Ruthie and her husband, Doyle Lane, had a baby girl.

We had no trouble finding Ruthie and Doyle the next day. Even though the family no longer owned the business along 99, the Lanes still lived in one of the cabins.

"Just turn off at the big Richfield sign," we'd been told, "and that's it."

After our initial greeting, there seemed to be some restraint between Ruthie and me. I guess it was because she was still just a kid when we'd last been together. Since then, she'd grown up, married, and given birth to baby Margaret who, at one and a half years, looked like a beautiful, blonde doll. Brookie soon had us laughing with his teasing and before long, we were completely at ease. By the time Doyle came home from work, it was as if Ruthie and I had never been apart. The moment we met Doyle it seemed as if we'd always known him.

Our week in California was a whirlwind of activity. We visited Marsh and his wife, Muriel, at their home in Kingsburg where he had bought some land and built a welding and repair shop after he and Paul sold the business at Selma. Muriel was a red-haired girl who was as friendly as she was pretty. I was saddened that we did not see Paul. He was confined to his room in the last stages of emphysema and requested that we not come in. We spent an afternoon visiting Madge and Waugh at their little ranch, reminiscing about the good old days in Wyoming.

After our frigid departure from Rawlins it was hard to believe we were running around in our shirtsleeves, eating fresh tomatoes every day off the three vines Doyle had growing alongside the cabin, and buying just-picked melons from produce stands along the road. I had mixed feelings about California as we prepared to resume our journey north to Washington. I hated the smog, the first I'd ever seen, and there were far too many people to suit me. The traffic streamed by on the highway twenty-four hours a day, so thick you were taking your life in your hands to try to cross to the other side, but an endless supply of fresh fruit and vegetables certainly had a lot of appeal.

We had planned to follow the coast up through Oregon, but the morning we left the Lanes we heard on the car radio that a big storm was coming in out of the Pacific with gale winds and high seas. People were being urged to travel farther inland, so we adjusted our travel plans accordingly, going past Klamath Falls and on up to The Dalles, where we crossed the Columbia River.

Then we discovered there was no direct route through to Issaquah; we had to make a big loop either to the west or east. The east route would bring us to Ellensburg and we would follow the same highway we had driven when we went to Washington in 1942. We wanted to see new country so we took the western loop, which followed the Columbia to Kelso, then swung north and east to Enumn Claw, to Preston, where the kids had gone to school when we lived out there, and finally to our destination.

What a happy reunion we had! Pete and Dad became buddies immediately, and Mom began planning and preparing meals like she thought we hadn't been properly fed since she'd last seen us. My folks had bought a small piece of timberland next to the Boeing Ranch, cleared a spot where they built their own house, constructed a woodshed, an outhouse, and rabbit hutches. After all their "civilized" living during the war and later in California, they were right back to the same primitive lifestyle they'd left on the homestead! Mom always had a plentiful supply of rain water in her water barrel for everything but drinking. Dad worked at the Boeing Ranch, so he hauled drinking water from there. They did have electricity, but they continued to haul drinking water and use an outhouse until Dad's death in 1960. Their little house had a homey, friendly feel that had always been lacking in the big, imposing Carlson house, and the closed-in feeling I had when we lived there was not present here. Possibly I just felt more at home with an outhouse than I did with the trappings of civilization!

On Thanksgiving Day we feasted like royalty; the next day we left for Wyoming. We were becoming increasingly uneasy about all the mountain chains that lay between us and home. This time of year it could lay down a lot of snow in that high country. At least, we now had the benefit of the car heater. Marsh and Brookie had decided to work on it before we left California. When they pulled the hoses off, they found, to their surprise, that someone had inserted wooden plugs in both the inlet and outlet of the heater so no coolant could circulate through.

Other than some light snow in Idaho, we had good weather for the last leg of our trip. The closer we got to home, the more anxious I was to get there. I felt as if we'd been gone forever and at the same time, it didn't seem possible we'd been gone a whole month.

Our first order of business when we arrived at the house was to move Vivian home from Harvey's ranch where she'd been living with Claude and Evelyn ever since early September when we brought her off the mountains to go to school. After we got off the mountains with the sheep in October we were camped out on the Six Horse Hill Divide. Distance and almost nonexistent roads made it impossible to haul her in to school. Then our trip to the West Coast meant she had to stay another month.

Brookie went to the ranch and let Pete know we were home while Vivian and I got unpacked and settled in at the house. Raleigh had gotten along fine with his sheepherding job, Pete said.

The grass was short because we hadn't had much rain during the summer. Pete wanted to keep the ewes in good shape during the bucking season and into the coldest part of the winter, so he suggested Brookie and Raleigh might want to start working the herd north to fresh feed, ending up eventually on the Five Mile Divide where they could be fed cottonseed cake. My brother Dan had grazed the Spring Draw country and on down onto Salt Creek with the other band of Meike sheep while he was relief herding for Henry Hickey. When Henry returned from his fall layoff, about the same time as we got home from our trip, Pete moved him and his herd north into the Dead Man country for easier accessibility and began feeding cake to them as well. Dan moved back to the bunk house at Pete's and went to work feeding the old ewes and ewe lambs that were wintering in the meadows.

Once our sheep reached the divide a full-time herder was no longer necessary as there was a fence between the divide pasture and the Irvine Ranch. We only had to feed them every day and keep them from coming down through the Beecher Breaks to Powder River. Raleigh moved back to the house to spend the winter with us, and he and Brookie took over the job of tending Henry's camp. They fed Henry's herd in the forenoon because they knew right where he would have them. That left them all afternoon to locate and feed the Divide sheep because they were apt to scatter and be in more than one bunch.

"Would you like to ride up to the divide with me to check the sheep?" Brookie asked me late one Sunday afternoon. "We'll be right back. Raleigh can keep an eye on the kids."

I welcomed a chance to get out of the house, so I eagerly accepted the invitation. We took the Olds because Brookie said he didn't plan on getting off the road. He and Raleigh had fed cake to the sheep that day over on the east side of the pasture, and he wanted to be sure they hadn't come over to the rim because he didn't want them down in the Beecher Breaks.

Where the county road topped the rim of the divide and headed south to eventually join Highway 387, we turned north into the sheep pasture. The dirt road we followed ran parallel to and never more than a couple of hundred yards from the rim the full length of the pasture. We were at the extreme north end before we saw the sheep, bedding down for the night not far from where they'd been fed.

Brookie turned the car around to head for home when it suddenly coughed, died, and refused to start again. Brookie got out and raised the hood and tried to determine what the trouble was. I watched and kept thinking how glad I was this hadn't happened when we were driving through downtown Sacramento or coming through the mountains of Idaho when we were on our trip.

The sun was setting when Brookie gave up on the car. "I guess there's nothin' to do but make tracks," Brookie said, so we did. We hiked the short distance to the rim where a seldom-used wagon road skirted the north edge of the Breaks into the river bottom. From where we were it was about five miles to our house if we could have followed a straight line, but that wasn't possible because at one point the Powder River made a big curve almost up to the county road. If the river had been frozen solid it would have been simple but it had been mild enough that every day water ran on top of the ice, so we didn't dare risk it, especially in the dark.

It was dark enough by the time we were halfway to the river bottom that we were stepping off into the washouts that crisscrossed the road. There were also ruts to fall into and bumps to stumble over. Gradually we got our night sight, but we couldn't see well enough to take any shortcuts through the brush and down timber of the river bottom, so we had to follow the dim road's devious path. It was a pleasant evening for mid-December and I would have enjoyed the walk if I hadn't kept worrying about the kids. I knew Raleigh would be wondering what had happened to us.

We were just getting to where the road curved up around the big river bend when we saw a car light leave our house, go out to the road, and turn our direction.

"That's Raleigh coming to look for us!" Brookie exclaimed. "Maybe we can intercept him!"

I don't think either of us really thought we could because we were at least a half mile from the road and it was uphill all the way, but we tried. We started running. We were still a considerable distance from the road as, from our hands and knees in the washout that had tripped us up, we watched the car lights go past and disappear. Raleigh was driving slowly, apparently expecting to find us walking along the main road.

My imagination worked overtime as we walked on out to the road and started the last leg of the hike home. What if the kids, left alone, knocked over the kerosene lamp? Or put too much wood in the stove and started a chimney fire? Then I worried about Raleigh. We could tell by the sound of the vehicle as he went past that he was driving Old Minnie rather than the GI. Raleigh and my brothers had been repairing the car and had it running, but it only had brakes occasionally. A few days before I thought we'd had an earthquake when there was a loud "bang!", the house shook, and things fell off the walls. But it wasn't a quake. Brookie had driven in with Old Minnie and the brakes failed as he pulled up to the house. No damage was done, except to my nerves.

Not only was the walking much better on the road but it was mostly downhill so we made good time the rest of the way. The house was dark when we got there, and I wondered why. As soon as we walked in and lit a lamp we encountered two mad kids! Raleigh was so afraid to leave them alone he had banked the Majestic range, made the kids take off their shoes and get in their beds so they'd stay warm, and then blew out the lamp so there'd be no danger of a fire. And they'd had no supper!

Brookie left immediately in the GI to overtake Raleigh while I hastily began to prepare supper and explained to the kids what had happened. As soon as the meal was ready, I fed the kids, expecting Raleigh and Brookie to arrive any minute. From the dining room windows I could see to about where Raleigh had bypassed us and though I made countless trips to look there was nothing to see but darkness.

Tomorrow was a school day for Vivian, which meant an 8:30 bedtime. The kids pleaded to stay up till Brookie and Raleigh got home so they could find out why they were so late. At 9:30 I was rewarded by the sight of a car light coming down the road. I kept looking for a second light but there was none. I was so sure it would go past our place that I was quite surprised when it turned in. It was the GI, I could see by the light from the window, and both Raleigh and Brookie were climbing out of it.

As soon as everyone quit talking at once we learned "the rest of the story," to quote Paul Harvey. Brookie had followed the road out, expecting to meet Raleigh coming back. When he drove clear to where the Olds was sitting without any sign of Raleigh, he assumed he had followed the old wagon road down into the river bottom hunting us. As Brookie carefully picked his way along the washed-out road the lights reflected off something up ahead. As Brookie approached, he saw it was the rear end of Old Minnie, sticking up in the air like an angry stink bug. Too late, Raleigh had seen that the road made an abrupt turn to avoid a washout just as it dropped over a sharp little hill. The brakes either hadn't been working, or chose that moment to quit again. At any rate, all he could do was brace himself as Minnie nose-dived into the little gully.

There was no damage to either Minnie or Raleigh, but the car didn't have power enough to back up such a steep incline. After a couple of tries Raleigh abandoned it and headed off into the dark down the same road we had so recently traveled. When the road turned up out of the river bottom to go around the big bend, Raleigh left it and headed straight for home up the river.

He almost walked off a small cliff into the river before he saw starlight shining on the ice and heard the gurgle of water running under it. At the same time, he became aware of the sound of the GI on the road behind him. He thrashed his way through the brush trying to head Brookie off, and watched helplessly as the GI bypassed him and lumbered on out to the county road, disappearing into the darkness.

Brookie drove down the road to the bridge on Carpenter Draw before he convinced himself that Raleigh couldn't have had that much of a head start on him. He turned around and drove back to the turnoff to the river bottom and sat there debating which way to go. Just then, Raleigh came panting over the hill into the glare of the headlights, waving his arms.

Years later we began calling it "The Three Stooges Episode" after we saw some of their antics on TV!

Following the death of Mother (Emma) Meike in 1947 the six Meike heirs decided to divide up the ranch. All of them were married, and four of them had growing families, so it was the sensible thing to do. By January 1, 1949, the division of the livestock and all the land, both irrigated and rangeland, had been accomplished. All that remained to be done was the rebranding of the livestock, which was to take place as soon as possible. As it turned out, that was not accomplished until spring. Pete's youngest brother, Buster (Arthur), did not want any sheep so he traded his share of them for Pete's share of cows. Pete's kids already had a start in the cattle business with their purebred Hereford 4-H Club cows and over the years built their ranch herd from them.

Brookie and I worried about what was going to happen to our job and our little herd of sheep, but Pete told us we would go with him since he was the one who hired Brookie and the agreement on our sheep was still the same.

In their spare time Raleigh and Brookie hauled our winter supply of coal from Pine Ridge. In many places there were veins of coal lying exposed right on the flat ground, so it was possible to uncover endless amounts of good-quality coal with a minimum of digging. Halsey had built a coal chute into the basement so coal could be shoveled from a wagon or truck into the coal bin under the house. By the time the winter of 1949 was over, we had good reason to bless Halsey for that innovation!

During our first winter in the house we discovered it was not very airtight. The first storm that blew through blew right through our house. We awoke to find a snowdrift that reached from the door almost to the heat register in the floor above the furnace. Snow also sifted in around the windows and some of the cottonwood logs in the walls were so crooked and knotty that the cement chinking had loosened, letting wind and snow come through. This was our first chance to do any repair work. We all, even Little Pete, got busy at digging out the old chinking and mixing concrete to redo the job. Where the cracks were especially wide Brookie nailed narrow strips of wood along the lower edge to help hold the cement. Next we shoveled dirt up against the house all the way around so no wind could get under it.

Brookie and I slept in the smaller bedroom while Vivian and Pete shared the other one, with their beds on opposite sides of the room. It soon became apparent that this arrangement was not going to work. They squabbled and bickered over boundaries until Brookie gathered up all the old scrap lumber on the place and built a partition down the middle, creating two rooms no larger than jail cells. The kids were satisfied, though, to have their own space and I was relieved that the territorial war between them was resolved!

Halsey had floored the attic and Howard and Jack had slept up there, but Raleigh decided he would rather sleep in the basement. He put down a crude board floor in the west end away from the furnace and the coal pile and set the old army cot on it. He had the warmest place in the whole house when the winter of 1949 arrived!

We invited Carol and Halsey and their kids to come see the New Year in with us. Before they arrived for supper New Year's Eve I'd scrubbed and waxed the linoleum until it was glistening. It had been an unusually mild fall with only scattered light snow and people began to worry that our dry spring and summer were going to be followed by a dry winter. Between Christmas and New Year's we had a fairly heavy snowfall. Then it warmed up again and New Year's Day was unseasonably balmy. The snow soon melted in the warm sun, and we had mud and water everywhere. By the time we sat down to our big New Year's dinner the next day the linoleum was all one color: muddy! The weather was a major of topic of conversation, and we even speculated that probably the worst part of the winter was behind us.

After the Turks left for Buffalo about three o'clock I got busy and scrubbed the kitchen floor again. I was just finishing when a car drove in, followed by an army jeep. The men driving them got out and talked to Brookie, who was outside doing some chores. When they came into the house I saw that one of them was our used car dealer, Hank Mayor from Buffalo. He introduced the other fellow as Ezra Jones, an insurance man, also from Buffalo. Hank wanted to sell us the jeep. He said he'd taken it on a trade-in and thought of us immediately. It was just what we needed for herding sheep, and he was sure that as soon as jeeps were generally available they'd be replacing saddle horses.

We had seen jeeps in action on newsreels at the movies during WW II, fighting their way through the jungle and churning across sandy beaches. While we'd been impressed with them, and knew they had proved invaluable in rough terrain, Brookie kept telling Hank we already had our four-wheel-drive GI. We'd sold the Olds shortly after the "Three Stooges Episode," so we were a one-vehicle family again and we intended to stay that way. Besides, Brookie didn't really think jeeps would be practical for ranch work.

I had noticed a low line of dark clouds lying on the horizon toward Buffalo as Halsey's family left. Now, suddenly, the wind hit from the north with such force it made the house creak. Hank and Ezra exchanged uneasy looks as the lowering sun was suddenly blotted out by ragged black clouds scudding before the wind.

"Tell you what," Hank said, "I don't want to drive that jeep clear back to Buffalo this late in the day. I'll just leave it and you try it out. Drive it all you like, and if you decide you don't want it, bring it back in some day when you're coming and drop it off at the lot. If you decide to keep it, sometime when you're in we'll fix up the papers on it and that'll be that."

As they sped away into the gathering storm none of us dreamed we'd drive that jeep until late March without any papers or money changing hands.

The wind blew harder as night came on and it began to spit snow. The temperature kept falling, and soon the mud was frozen as hard as stone. The next morning we had a full-scale blizzard blowing which was not in itself surprising. What was out of the ordinary was the amount of snow that was piling up with the temperature at thirty below zero. Spring and fall blizzards can dump huge amounts of snow when the temperature is not much below thirty-two degrees. As a rule, the colder it gets, the less moisture there is, but the winter of 1949 proved to be a complete contradiction. Each storm that came roaring through piled up tremendous drifts on top of what we already had and most of the time the temperature ranged between thirty and fifty below.

The wind seldom stopped blowing. When it blew from the north it brought another blizzard. In the brief respites between storms it switched to the southwest and blew the dry, feathery snow into a whole new pattern of drifts so there was no way to keep roads open. Our well was east of the house and about twelve steps from the back door. The windmill tower was sturdily constructed of six-by-six timbers and the legs caused drifts to form that not only buried the pump but made it impossible even to get to it. Within a few days after the storms began I was melting snow for water, just like back in sheepcamp. We had to climb over big drifts to reach the outhouse, but some fluke caused it to blow bare in front of the door, no matter which way the wind blew.

Everyone was stunned by the bitter cold and the ferocity of the storms, but we all assumed it would blow itself out in a few days and we'd be back to more normal January weather. By the time it became apparent there wasn't going to be any immediate relief from the storms, the whole area was buried so deep in snow it was almost impossible to get anywhere. The ranchers spent all their waking hours fighting blowing snow, drifts, and unbelievable cold trying to get feed to their livestock.

I don't know how the Meike crew would have gotten to the livestock at all without the four-wheel-drive vehicles. In addition to our GI and the little jeep, Pete had brought a military truck with a canvas cab on it, which didn't do much in the way of sheltering the occupants from blowing snow, but the truck was great for hauling cake and fighting drifts.

We had one stroke of luck. The first storm blew the Divide sheep off into the Beecher Breaks. The draws and gullies led down into the river bottom, so the sheep all filtered down through, ending up along Powder

River in about the best natural shelter on the ranch. Large cottonwoods, clumps of willows, stands of tamerisks, heavy sage, and greasewood, plus lots of smaller bushes and shrubs cover the bottoms. The north bank of the Powder River is considerably higher than the south side, and the resulting bluff creates a natural wind break. It was also fortunate that Henry had been moved into the Dead Man pasture before the weather turned bad. Even so, it was a terrible struggle just reaching his camp, and after a few days Brookie, Raleigh, and Dan managed to move Henry's wagon north of the Pine Ridge by using both four-wheel-drive vehicles.

Little Pete and I were completely housebound, and since I was not taking an active part in the battle against the elements I'm not sure now if they had any set division of the work or if everyone worked together to get everything fed. The divide sheep were in the Beecher river bottom; the Meike cows were in the next river bend above that; Henry's herd was in the Dead Man pasture southwest of the ranch headquarters; and they also had the old ewes and ewe lambs at the ranch itself. All these animals needed feed every day.

Amazingly, the Sussex school was never closed during the blizzards of 1949, so Vivian was at school every weekday. Shine and Gerry Devoe still had the school bus contract. Shine's father died, and Shine left to attend the funeral in Washington State, so that left Gerry to drive the bus route alone. Her twins were only three and a half years old, so she had to take them with her. She said she shoveled a lot of snow, but she made every trip!

Una Skiles, who with her husband, Fred, were the mail carriers between Sussex and Kaycee between 1934 and 1954 also had memories of the winter of 1949. "The winter of 1949 was a test of man and beast. The government sent the Army Corps of Engineers into Johnson County to help the residents open roads and get feed to their stock. But Fred recalled he spent a lot of time rescuing the engineers as their maps did not coincide with the reality of the terrain of southern Johnson County. There were only two days during this period when Fred did not make it to Kaycee for the mail."

Finally there was so much snow on the level that Henry's sheep could not paw down to grass and were living on the cake that was being taken out every day. Everyone could see that the time was fast approaching when they would no longer be able to get through to feed them, so a concerted effort was made to move Henry and his herd in to Powder River so the sheep could be fed hay.

They did it in stages, using Meike's four-wheel-drive truck loaded with cake to lure the sheep and our GI to pull the sheepwagon. The truck would go ahead for a ways to break trail for the GI and wagon, then go back to break trail for the sheep because for the most part, the snow was so deep they simply couldn't get through it. It was late afternoon before they made it to the shelter of the trees west of our place, a distance of less than two miles. Brookie said there were times when he didn't think they were going to make it. What swung the balance in their favor was a quarter-mile stretch south of the river bottom where the wind had blown it bare so the exhausted sheep no longer had to plow through snow as deep as they were tall.

That night Raleigh, a gifted cartoonist, sketched a picture of a barely visible truck in the blowing snow and two hazy figures armed with scoop shovels in front of it.

"Do you think we're almost through this drift?" said the words above the first figure.

"What drift?" the second one was asking.

I made the mistake of loaning that cartoon to someone later and never saw it again.

Even though the trees provided a shelter for Henry's sheep, they caused such a drifting problem on the leeward side the crew couldn't find any place where they could feed them. They decided to move the herd across the road to our pasture where there were only a few scattered trees. Though there were a lot of drifts in the area south of our house, there were also places where the wind swept it bare.

The hayracks had been mounted on rubber-tired running gears about the same time the sheepwagons were so they could be pulled with the trucks. This sometimes proved to be a detriment in the deep snow because the axles were much closer to the ground, causing them to high center. Brookie said this was offset to some extent by the fact that they were more maneuverable so they could dodge around the drifts with them.

An interesting situation developed in the Beecher river bottom where Brookie and Raleigh were feeding cake to the sheep every day. Because of the snow, trees, and downed timber, it was not possible to drive the GI and scatter cake from the back of it. The men shouldered the hundred-pound sacks of cake and walked and poured it wherever the snow was packed down or had blown bare. The deep snow had driven numerous deer into the shelter of the river bottom from the surrounding hills, and they soon learned to eat cake with the sheep. Before long they lost their fear of Brookie and Raleigh and they would mob them when they started to feed. One morning a big doe reared up on Brookie, trying to get her head in the cake sack. He stopped and shoved her away. She ran past him, kicked, and caught her hind foot in the pocket of his coveralls, ripping the coverall leg from pocket to bottom.

No hay was ever airlifted to this area to my knowledge, and I don't recall any great loss of livestock, though I'm sure everyone must have had some stock die because of stress from the constant wind and the prolonged cold. Our daytime temperature seldom warmed above thirty below zero, and I recorded fifty-two below one morning. One day when the men were feeding hay to Henry's sheep in the river bottom by our house, Brookie saw a big jackrabbit crouched in a depression in the snow alongside the trunk of a cottonwood tree. As the GI passed near the rabbit, it jumped up, ran a short distance, and fell dead in the snow. Brookie and Raleigh were so surprised they stopped and examined it. They decided it died from the extreme cold because there was no sign of any injury.

The GI ran on a twelve-volt electrical system, which was furnished by two six-volt batteries. Every night Brookie and Raleigh unhooked the batteries and brought them in the house, along with the antifreeze, which they drained into a washtub. In the mornings one of them refilled the radiator and installed the batteries in the unbelievable cold, while the other one heated the oil pan with a gasoline blowtorch. Sometimes, in spite of all these precautions, the GI wouldn't fire. When that happened they jumpstarted it with the little jeep, which never once failed to start.

The jeep proved itself over and over during that terrible winter. Brookie used the GI to pull the hayrack because it was bigger and more powerful and handled the snow drifts better. The jeep was much more maneuverable, though, and being narrower could sometimes skirt the edges of the drifts with enough speed to get through where the slower GI often lumbered into them and bogged down. By the time the winter of 1949 was history we were so attached to the jeep we went to Buffalo at the first opportunity and bought it from Hank Mayor.

At last the storms ended and eventually the snows of the winter of 1949 began to melt. By the time we moved to lambing camp, there were only some glacier-like drifts left on the north slopes of the hills and in the deeper gullies, and the green grass was really coming on because of the moisture. I was glad to get away from the house after being cooped up for three months.

The full impact of the Meike Ranch split never really hit me until we moved to lambing camp that spring. I had such an intimate geographic knowledge of the entire ranch after camping on it from one end to the other and herding sheep the length and breadth of it, I felt a real sense of loss when I realized those days were gone forever.

*Louise and Brookie's house as it looked when they bought it from Halsey and Carol in 1947.*

# THE MARCH OF TIME I
## (1950-1959)

1950 always seemed to me to be the end of an era. The ten years since the day I said "I do" in that secondhand store in Gillette had brought many changes, some of them so gradual we were hardly aware of them, others so profound they took some getting used to. In that decade we had progressed from nomadic sheepherders possessing only our clothes, bedroll, and saddles to the owners of sheep, land, a house, plus three children who depended on us not only for the creature comforts of food, clothing, and shelter but for a sense of family, the making of traditions, and mostly for love.

Most of the work horses had been sold or put out to pasture, replaced by four-wheel-drive vehicles and tractors. The age of mechanized farming had arrived. In the larger sense, our whole world had changed, not only our immediate part in it. World War II had unleashed the awesome power of the atomic bomb so the world would never again be the same safe, sane world I'd grown up in.

The war turned us into a nation of wanderers—war workers and servicemen who never returned to the narrow confines of the old homestead after the war ended. Kids grew up on the move, without any real roots. Divorce became as common as marriage, with children shuffled back and forth with no real feeling of belonging anywhere. People grew up without any sense of home or permanence, without building any traditions. At least our kids led a fairly predictable if nomadic lifestyle with the seasonal migration to the summer range on the Big Horns in the spring and back to the Powder River Flats in the fall.

World War II also liberated women to work at jobs none of them would ever have dreamed of doing before and completely turned around the taboos concerning things females could do since the time I was growing up. That was driven home to me the spring of 1947 when I was allowed to help Brookie with the drop herd during shed lambing. A woman in the lambing sheds was unheard of until then. Besides the bunk house and the sheep and lambing sheds being off-limits for us, it was considered unseemly for a woman to be anyplace where three or more men were gathered, unless she was cooking for them, and a woman helping dock sheep was unthinkable.

I'll never forget the first time I helped dock. It was the spring after the Meikes divided up the ranch, and Pete was running his share on a shoestring trying to get it going. Brookie was the only full-time hired man he had. He had hired extra men for lambing but with lambing over, they had been let go with the exception of Trum Shaw. The docking crew turned out to be Pete and his family and Brookie and his family! When I was informed I was going to help dock I was horrified. I still had a tendency to get sick at the sight of blood, and I was afraid I might humiliate myself by actually vomiting.

We all arrived at the docking pen right after dinner and helped Trum, who was herding the ewes with the oldest lambs, corral them. A big pen held the herd, about 500 ewes plus lambs, with a smaller "catch pen" which we filled with sheep from the big pen. Along one side of the catch pen was the docking board or table, a one-by-ten or -twelve board nailed flat along the tops of the posts about three and a half feet off the ground.

The catchers and holders were in the catch pen with the sheep while the docker and brander were on the opposite side of the board, outside the pen. If there was enough crew, there were usually two dockers and branders. The kids who were too small to lift the lambs onto the board caught them for the holders.

There's a knack to holding lambs so they can't kick loose. Holding the lamb with its back against your belly and its head up alongside yours, you cross and grip the front and hind legs on each side, swing the lamb up onto the board so it is sitting on the rump with the tail hanging over the edge of the board in front of the docker. If it's a ewe lamb, he grasps the tail in one hand and severs it with a quick slash of the knife. There is usually a spray of blood, so to keep the docker from getting drenched with gore, in the instant the tail parts company from the lamb the holder flips the lamb forward enough so the lamb's head is toward the docker, who grabs the proper ear and earmarks it, if they are still using earmarks. Then the holder lifts the lamb and sidesteps to the brander, sets the lamb level, and the brand is stamped on its back with a branding iron dipped in sheep paint. The branded lamb is then turned loose outside the corral.

If the lamb is a ram, the holder first spreads the legs enough so the docker can grip the tip of the scrotum between thumb and finger and slice it off, leaving the ends of the testicles exposed. Holding the knife with the blade turned back toward the wrist, the docker uses both hands to push the bag down against the lamb's body, ducks his head, grips the testicles in his teeth and carefully pulls them loose, dropping them in a bucket on the ground directly under the docking board. The tail is cut off, the holder moves over to the brander, and another lamb is turned loose bearing the ranch's brand. When all the lambs have been caught out of the catch pen, the ewes are counted out the gate to the outside to mingle with the docked lambs. The pen is refilled from the corral, and the whole procedure is repeated.

When the last lamb is branded and the last ewe counted, the total number of ewes is tallied up and the lamb tails are counted into piles of ten tails to a pile. The little heaps of tails are counted to get the total number of lambs so the rancher can figure what kind of a lamb crop he has. The testicles, which are called Rocky Mountain oysters or lamb fries, are taken home and cleaned and fried. They are a real delicacy, let me tell you!

The day I learned all about docking lambs I know I must have turned pretty green, but I was soon too busy to even think about it, and my dinner settled back down where it belonged. By the time we finished docking the second bunch a few days later, I felt like an old hand at it. Years later, Raleigh showed one of our home movies of a docking to some of his Johnson's Wax colleagues in Racine, Wisconsin. One gentleman retched violently when Brookie, who was doing the docking, raised his head from the lamb's crotch and leered at the camera with a pair of blood-dripping testicles hanging from his mouth!

Someone in the group said, "Oh, that's just a posed picture! They don't really do it that way." And I don't think he ever believed any differently.

Actually, we don't do it that way much any more.

The discovery of oil on the Meike Ranch probably changed our lives more drastically than any other single event with the exception of the advent of four-wheel-drive vehicles. In a matter of days after the No. 1 Discovery Well blew in May 1948 we learned what an oil boom was all about.

Up to then most of the wagon roads out on the range were barely more than trails, following the hogbacks and ridges and skirting such obstacles as canyons, draws, rock piles, and the like. The oil company's first priorities, then, were roads and housing for their workers. A construction company from Cheyenne moved in and began building houses on the Linch homestead between Meadow Creek and the south slope of the Pine Ridge. Soon the quiet of the rangeland was shattered by the bellow of huge dirt-moving machines. Clouds of dust and diesel fumes filled the air as they ripped up the sod and rocks and piled them in canyons and gullies, following the lines of stakes that bristled behind the surveying crews swarming over the landscape marking out road and well sites.

Water trucks rumbled along hauling water pumped from Salt Creek and Meadow Creek to sprinkle the road bed so it could be more firmly packed. Gravel trucks followed, hauling red shale to surface the gumbo roads. Later, tank trucks labored by twenty-four hours a day, hauling crude oil to the Casper refineries until pipelines could be built. With the exception of well servicing, the pipelines probably created more jobs than anything else connected with the oil business, not just the laying of the lines but the constant maintaining of them. The lines were checked for leaks every day from a small plane flying out of Casper.

Oil leaks were fairly common, and the usual procedure was to construct an earthen dam ahead of the oil to prevent it getting into the creeks. Vacuum trucks then suctioned up all of the oil they could. What couldn't be salvaged was burned to keep the sheep and cattle from coming in contact with it. If livestock drank the oil it could be fatal. Sheep with their wool full of crude oil were frowned upon, too! In later years the EPA banned burning oil because of air pollution, and after an experience I had I could understand why.

When Brookie rode in to the lambing camp at the Heltzel place one morning he told me he had to ride almost to Salt Creek to cross East Spring Draw because it was full of oil. A bulldozer had already been trucked in and unloaded and was in the process of building a dam. Very shortly a crew of roustabouts and a couple of vacuum trucks had arrived.

Before Brookie went back out to the sheep he rigged up a makeshift clothesline for me so I could dry the laundry I was going to do when breakfast was cleared away. As I scrubbed, rinsed, and hung out clothes I kept an eye on all the activity going on at the oil pool. While I washed out the dirty overalls the brisk southwest wind was rapidly drying the clean clothes flapping on the line.

I heard a vehicle pull up in front of the wagon and stepped to the door to be confronted by a man yelling, "Ma'am, you might want to get your laundry off the line!" His message was too late! The camp was about to be engulfed by a huge cloud of oily, gray-black smoke billowing up from the draw. I hadn't even begun to get things unpinned from the line before the inky smoke swirled over me and my clean clothes, leaving little oily motes that looked like tiny black tadpoles clinging to everything. A little later I realized my hair, face, and clothing were also covered with them.

Flinging the damp laundry on the bed I grabbed our newly acquired home movie camera. Slamming the sheepwagon door shut behind me I dashed out of the path of the smoke to where I could film the scene before me. Up to now our home movies had consisted of friends and relatives either staring at the camera in consternation when they realized they were being filmed, or self-consciously making exaggerated movements after the camera person exclaimed in exasperation, "Give us some action! It's supposed to be a movie."

My only regret that morning was that I had no way of recording the tremendous roar of the burning oil as new pools ignited and huge tongues of orange flame licked up through the thick black smoke. The men ran in and out of the smoke, yelling to each other as they smothered grass fires as they flared up. The fire burned itself out quickly, leaving only smoldering clumps of vegetation along the edges of the draw.

I barely got myself cleaned up before the lambing hands rode in for dinner. I spent the afternoon redoing my laundry!

The more inaccessible an area was, the more likely the oil company was to drill a well there, it seemed. The resulting roads really simplified things for us, especially after they built a steel suspension bridge across boggy Salt Creek, giving us ready access to the Meikes' land west of the creek with both livestock and vehicles.

As the oil field continued to expand across the Meikes' west boundary onto the Davis Ranch, it was no longer feasible for pumpers working out of Linch to care for such a far-flung territory. Consequently, Continental Oil built what became known as West Sussex Camp between Salt Creek and the Meike-Davis fence.

West Sussex was a neat little community consisting of five or six white frame houses surrounded by pretty green lawn in the middle of a sagebrush flat. Brookie cautioned the people moving in that they needed to keep an eye out for rattlesnakes because the bluffs on the west bank of the creek were full of snake dens. After several incidents involving rattlesnakes the oil company dynamited the dens. Nothing was ever done about the dens on the east side of the creek, though, and the area around the Heltzel cabin continues to be one of the "snakiest" places I know of.

The larger ranches along Powder River had their regular ranch hands who worked the year around. Extra help was hired for seasonal jobs, such as lambing and calving, irrigating and haying, grain harvest, or fence building. With the discovery of oil, ranchers suddenly found themselves unable to hire help of any kind because everyone had gone to work in the oil patch, including the owners of some of the smaller ranches! Who wanted to work for ranch wages when the oil company was paying big money, especially if you worked overtime? Ranch work always involved overtime during the busy season, but you got paid the same, regardless.

By 1954 the population of Linch and the camps that had been built, such as West Sussex, stood at about 1,000. The quonset-style school building had been replaced with a modern brick school, complete with a gym. Various businesses connected directly to the production of oil were part of the town. In addition, filling stations, cafes, grocery stores, and garages came and went over the years.

Woody's Bar and Recreation Hall achieved nationwide notoriety when two cowboys transporting a Mexican steer in a trailer stopped for some refreshment. As the evening progressed they decided it would liven things up to turn the steer loose in the bar. It certainly had the desired effect! Before the fear-crazed animal crashed out the door to freedom it managed to do an amazing amount of damage, including trampling the bar owner.

According to the *News Record*, a Gillette, Wyoming newspaper, "A bar patron, unamused, called one of the ranch hands outside and expressed his displeasure with two crowbar blows to the head."

One of the two deputy sheriffs investigating the incident said, no, the two men hadn't been drinking Wild Steer malt liquor. The bar, however, was immediately dubbed the Wild Steer Saloon, and it carried the name for as long as it remained in existence.

After the first years of frantic activity and ceaseless noise in the "oil patch" things leveled off. This is not to say it was quiet because it wasn't. There were always the sounds of pickups driven by the pumpers, trucks performing various services, bulldozers, drilling or workover rigs, the creak and groan of the pumps bringing the crude oil up out of the bowels of the earth. The field was dotted with tank batteries where the crude oil was processed before it was sent by pipeline to the refinery at Casper.

Raleigh moved to lambing camp as one of the lambing hands in the spring of 1949, and I guess one spring of midwifing a bunch of ewes was enough to convince him there must be better things to do. As soon as lambing was over he enlisted in the army and was sent to Fort Riley, Kansas. After he enlisted, we were surprised to learn he was a super-brain. No one would ever have guessed it to look at one of his high school report cards! A year later, on the day we came in off the trail to our summer camp, we turned the radio on and learned we were at war with North Korea. I had the same sinking feeling I'd had when Fred got his induction notice during WW II.

Raleigh was an indifferent correspondent at best, but he had written before we left on trail that he was being sent to Fort Lewis, Washington. We had no access to mail on the trek to camp, but hadn't expected to hear from him again before late summer. Then we heard on the radio that Raleigh's unit was among the first ones sent to Korea. When we heard that his unit was suffering heavy casualties we headed for Sussex to get our three weeks' collection of mail.

There was no word from or of Raleigh, so all we could do was wait. Two more trips down, a week apart, produced no word of any kind, so we contacted the commanding officer at Fort Lewis. That was when we learned Raleigh was not in Korea. On arriving at Fort Lewis he had been transferred to an artillery unit when it was learned he could type. Later he convinced them to transfer him from his clerk-typist job to communications, where he worked as a switchboard operator, attended radio school, and learned Morse code.

This unit was moved to Camp Hanford, Washington, to guard the atomic facility there. Raleigh spent the rest of his enlistment time there. Because of the nature of their assignment, they had the same status as combat troops.

By the time we got off the mountains the fall of 1950 the division of the Meike land was complete, with new fences marking the boundaries. With the range fenced, the livestock could be turned loose so winter herders were no longer necessary. Now our duties included checking the fence and repairing it if necessary, keeping an eye out for predator problems and sheep bogged in the quicksand along Salt Creek. In winter we fed cake every day to the sheep and to the cattle, too, if they happened to be in the same area. Whenever we took care of the cows, that included opening water holes every day for them, either on Salt Creek or Dead Man. If we had a bad spell of weather, we often hauled the cows baled straw to supplement the range feed.

We continued to use the GI as a work horse, pulling sheepwagons and hayracks with it. Eventually, Brookie cut down the body back from the front seat, level with the bottoms of the side windows, making a pickup out of it. Still later, he cut the whole body off behind the front seat, welded a back in it to form a cab and put a flatbed and rack on it, converting it to an even more useful vehicle.

The only drawback to the little jeeps was lack of hauling capacity. We compensated for that by buying an extension box for one of them. After we sold the GI to Glen and Alvin Lohse we built a small, two-wheeled trailer to pull behind the sheepwagon to haul all the things needed on trail.

In this rough country there is a lot of terrain that simply cannot be negotiated by anything but a saddle horse, so jeeps never totally replaced them. Brookie never was without a good horse, but he was never without a jeep vehicle either, from 1949 until his death in 1981. We certainly covered countless miles in them, both on the mountains and on the Meike range south of Powder River, searching for lost livestock, gathering and trailing cows and sheep, checking fence, putting out salt, and numerous other ranch chores that would have required horses in "the good old days." We had several CJs (the "little jeep"), jeep pickups and one station wagon, which we used to transport Pete and several of the neighbor kids to and from Buffalo on the weekends when they attended the high school there.

Brookie could pile as much baled straw on our pickup as most people would haul on a farm truck, usually three layers higher than the pickup cab. I always cut the strings and dumped the straw off the pickup because the cows would mob us when we started to feed and I was not an aggressive enough driver to get through them. Instead of unloading from top to bottom, I always unloaded from back to front so I had the bed of the pickup for solid footing.

There are steep hills on both sides of Dead Man where the road crosses, especially on the north side. Halfway up, the road makes an elbow-bend switchback to reach the top of the bluff. One morning we started to feed on the north bank of the creek, but we ran out of room before I had half the load off.

"Hang on!" Brookie hollered back through the open window. "I'm gonna have to climb out on top." I put my back against the wall of bales and braced my feet.

The next thing I knew, the top layer of bales, which was higher than my head, started falling on me as the whole load began to slide toward the tailgate. I was powerless against the weight of all that straw, and there wasn't a thing to grab hold of. I had my open pocketknife in my right hand for cutting strings and my hay hook in my left for unloading the bales. Instinctively I snapped the blade shut on the knife and slipped it in my pocket, just as I and all the straw parted company with the truck. There were bales under me, on top of me and all around me, and a few had rolled back down the hill.

As I clawed my way out and brushed straw off my head and face I realized I was about to be swarmed by a whole herd of cows. In a panic I struggled to my feet and started climbing straight up the bluff to where the pickup was sitting on the switchback. Brookie had jumped out and was coming to my rescue.

"Are you okay?" he kept asking as he kept hugging me and picking straw out of my hair and telling me how sorry he was.

I wasn't hurt, but I couldn't decide whether to be mad or hysterical or laugh about the whole thing. The more I thought about it the funnier it seemed, especially after Brookie described the way I looked fighting my way out of the straw. He said he had no idea what was happening until he suddenly realized he could see daylight through the back window when he made the bend. He looked down at the heap of bales and didn't realize I was in the middle of it until he saw me fighting my way out. The same instant he saw the cows making a run for that nice big pile of straw and he was afraid they would trample me before he could get there. About then, we realized that somehow I had managed to hold onto my hay hook through all the excitement. We sat on the edge of the road and laughed till we could laugh no more.

Brookie pioneered jeep trails through timber patches, rock piles, and sagebrush where a deer could hardly find passage and around mountainsides so steep I had to get out and cling on the high side to keep the jeep from tipping over. He loved nothing better than to take unsuspecting "flat-land furriners" straight up the side of a mountain. One of his aunts from Wisconsin told us after he took her sightseeing that the claw marks from her fingernails would be in that jeep as long as it was in existence. Mom, on the other hand, rode with him all over the mountain camp and enjoyed every minute of it. I asked her once if his driving ever scared her.

She looked surprised. "No, why should it?" she replied. "He's a good driver."

He must have been, too. He would zero in on some distant spot and head for it. I don't think it ever occurred to him that he might not make it. With blind confidence I rode wherever he drove, up the steepest mountains, down into canyons I was sure we'd never get back out of. But he always made it, except where snow was involved.

In winter, loaded with hundred-pound sacks of cake for the sheep or cows, he plowed off into the snowdrifts with that same "we can make it" philosophy, with the result that the two of us probably shoveled more snow digging ourselves out of snow banks than the combined residents of Johnson County have cleared off their driveways and sidewalks in the last fifty years. As the bloom and optimism of youth were left behind it seemed to me he used less and less good judgment when it came to snow banks. I may have grown stronger from the exercise, but my patience grew thinner each time we got stuck! I used to think if he buried the jeep in one more drift I would just walk off and leave it, but

I never did because it was easier to dig it out than to walk ten miles back to the ranch through the snow!

As it became more and more difficult to find anyone to help range lamb, Brookie and Peto became the mainstays of the lambing operation. By the mid-50s we considered ourselves lucky to have Trum Shaw and my uncle Bill Eldridge to help.

By this time, Trum was well past his prime, and Uncle Bill was downright ancient! Talk about a study in contrasts! Trum stood well over six feet and I would guess weighed in excess of 300 pounds. Uncle Bill was like a wizened-up little gnome! He was barely five feet tall and probably wouldn't have tipped the scales at 120 pounds soaking wet! They were both seasoned range hands, though, and each had spent years working with sheep, so they had a lot of know-how, but anything of a physical nature was beyond their capabilities.

The spring of 1957 found us with a lambing crew made up of Trum, Bill, Brookie, and myself since Peto had joined the army the fall before. As well as doing the cooking, I was pressed into service nearly every day as a lambing hand. Thanks to our little jeep and the accessibility the oil company roads gave us to every part of the range, Brookie was able to almost be in two places at once!

One afternoon I was just ready to put a salmon loaf in the oven to bake for supper when the jeep pulled up in front of the wagon in a cloud of dust. "Grab your shovel and come on!" Brookie hollered. "We've got a whole bunch of sheep bogged in Salt Creek."

The drop herd had been left to noon on Salt Creek on a stretch of creek bank that was considered solid. A few had wandered downstream a short distance, and when they went to the creek for a drink they walked into a patch of quicksand. When Bill and Trum discovered the bogged sheep after dinner, one of them had to ride a considerable distance horseback to where Brookie was working with ewes and lambs to let him know what had happened.

When we reached the bend of the creek where the sheep were bogged we found Trum and Bill carrying sticks, tree limbs, and anything they could find for us to stand on while we extricated the sheep. Pulling off our boots and socks and armed with the shovel from the wagon and the one we always carried in the jeep, Brookie and I began to dig.

When sheep bog in quicksand they usually sink until their bodies are resting on top of the sand. As they struggle to try and free themselves the water in the sand rises to the top, so they are surrounded by a small pool of water mixed with urine and manure. The sand around their legs and feet sets like hardened cement, and because a sheep's foot is quite a bit larger than the leg above it, it's necessary to dig clear to the bottom of the hoof to free it. You dig out one leg at a time, carefully, so as not to break the leg with the shovel. And you hope the freed legs don't bog again before the last one is loose.

While you dig down, the liquid from around the sheep's body drains back down around the leg, which helps loosen the quicksand. As soon as you have enough space around the leg you force your hands down each side of the leg as deep as you can go, grab hold and with all your strength manipulate the trapped part back and forth, up and down until spots dance before your eyes, your vision blurs, and your hands cramp. While you straighten your aching back, flex your numb hands, and get your breath back you probably need to pull your own feet and legs out of the quicksand because whatever you were standing on has long since sunk and you're in the sand up to your knees. This process continues until you have finally freed all four legs; then the animal is dragged to solid footing.

In this case, as soon as we had a ewe loose we slipped the lariat loop over her head and Trum or Bill pulled her out onto the bank with his horse. Bill finally had to leave to head the herd to the bedground while Trum continued to help us. When it got too dark to see, Brookie positioned the jeep so we could use the headlights to light our rescue operation.

Some of the sheep were able to get up and stagger off after they rested a while, and a few more managed to leave during the night after they had recovered somewhat from the trauma. Daylight revealed seven casualties out of the twenty-three we dug out.

By the time we got back to the wagon that night I figured there was a real possibility of me being on the casualty list! I was totally exhausted and chilled to the bone from standing in quicksand and water up to my knees. My fingernails all felt as if they were going to fall off from digging in the sand. Our pants legs were stiff with sand, which had chafed our legs as effectively as if we'd been sandpapered.

After we cleaned up and got some dry clothes on I still had to fix supper for all of us. I dumped the uncooked salmon loaf into a greased skillet and cooked it like an omelet, opened a can of pork and beans and a can of peaches. With bread and butter, that was supper!

The following spring all our efforts to find a lambing crew failed and once again we ended up hiring Bill and Trum. In an effort to save as many lambs as possible, the Meikes had acquired two large army tents. We built holding pens in strategic locations so if bad weather threatened we could set up the tents inside whichever of the pens was closest. The plan was to corral the sheep and as quick as a ewe lambed, get her and her offspring inside the tent where it was dry before the lamb chilled.

One of our corrals had been constructed not far from an oil company tank battery west of the bridge on Salt Creek. A little distance to the north, natural gas was being burned at a "flare." The gas was piped away from the battery and escaped through an upright pipe about two stories high, where it was ignited and burned continually like a giant pilot light, illuminating the area around it.

Late one afternoon, with bad weather approaching, we set up the tents in the corral by the flare. A drizzly rain had begun to fall at dusk, so the crew corralled the sheep before they came into the wagon for supper. Trum and Bill volunteered to take the first shift, so Brookie jeeped them back to the corral and helped them tent the ewes that had lambed while they were eating. After they were set up he drove back to camp, leaving the "two old boys," as he called them, to check the herd every fifteen or twenty minutes and tent the ewes that had given birth.

The plan was for Brookie and me to sleep until midnight, then take over so Bill and Trum could sleep until morning. We went to bed as soon as Brookie got back to camp but neither of us was the least bit sleepy. We laid there and worried about how the two old boys were doing. Brookie said the footing was terrible because it was so slick from the rain. There was a lot of brush growing in the corral as well as inside the tent itself. While the flare lighted up the area, it also caused the brush to cast shadows that made it almost impossible to tell what was underfoot. The more we stewed and fretted, the more wide awake we became. At eleven o'clock it was apparent we weren't going to get any sleep, so we got dressed, put on our slickers and climbed in the jeep.

The two old boys were pathetically glad to see us, and they looked about done in. Since neither of them drove, Brookie took them back to the wagon they shared and built a fire for them because they were so chilled. Meanwhile I checked the herd and took several ewes and lambs to shelter.

As soon as Brookie was sure Trum and Bill were warming up, he came back to the corral and we began one of the longest, most boring nights I ever spent in my life. As long as we were busy it wasn't bad, but there would be lulls when nothing was happening. We sat on the ground inside the tent with our backs against the sidewall because there was nothing to sit on. Though we had a flashlight we were in total darkness because we were saving the flashlight for emergencies. Every fifteen minutes or so we'd make a tour of the herd in the rain, which came down steadily. I was so bleary from lack of sleep that as soon as I'd sit down, I'd relax and conk out. Brookie would hold me so I wouldn't fall over, then rouse me when it was time to make another check.

I was so tired when we arrived at the wagon I have only a foggy memory of fixing breakfast for everyone. As soon as we finished eating, the men took off to the pen to turn the drop herd out to graze and Brookie began trying to pair up ewes and lambs after he turned them out of the tent into the corral. After washing the dishes, I laid down on the bed fully dressed and slept until the alarm woke me at 10:30 so I could start preparing dinner.

Using the army tents as emergency lambing sheds did not prove to be a very successful venture. In this windy country it took more than one person to set them up, and with our limited crew that in itself presented an almost insurmountable difficulty. When we turned the ewes and lambs out of the tents after a storm was over it was total chaos. Ewes with twins usually got separated from one of their lambs in the confusion so we were left with several "bums" or orphan lambs. The only hope of saving them was to give them to ewes whose lambs had died. The dead lamb was skinned and the hide put on the bum so the mother, smelling it, would think it was hers, a ploy which worked more often than not. After a brief experiment we returned to using lambing tents.

About the time we abandoned the army tents, lamb jackets were put on the market. Constructed of waterproof canvas and lined with a light flannel type material, they were very similar to the jackets we see small dogs sporting today. They were held in place by three elastic bands, one that went under the neck, one that went under the body behind the front legs and a third that reached under the body from flank to flank.

After Peto got out of the army, he, Brookie, and I made up the lambing crew each spring with Don commuting from the ranch when we needed him. As the ewes lambed we left them behind with their offspring while we moved on with the drop herd. Little by little they would gather together to form a herd. When the drop herd dwindled down to around a hundred head they were trailed in to the river bottom across the road from our place where there was feed, water, and shelter and left to finish lambing more or less by themselves while we began gathering the ewes and lambs into bunches for docking.

While the ranch was one unit I was the lambing cook for five to seven men and that was my only responsibility. Once a week a camptender brought wood, water, groceries, and hay and grain for the horses. After the ranch was divided Pete was busy with calving, plowing, planting, and irrigating, so I took over the job of camptender. As the help situation became more critical I became jack-of-all-trades, doing everything from pulling bog to moving the camp to a new location.

Before the labor shortage became acute, problem ewes were tied to a sagebrush or whatever was handy with a length of lambing rope (quarter-inch sisal rope). One of the lambing hands had to ride by three or four times a day to suckle the lamb until the ewe accepted it and could be released. Now Peto and Brookie hauled the ewe to camp in the jeep, set up a lambing tent, put the sheep in it and drove off. It was up to me to cope with whatever the difficulty might be, whether it was a ewe with a jacketed lamb, a sheep with so much milk her teats were too big for the lambs to suck or, in some cases, a cantankerous old renegade that simply didn't want the responsibility of motherhood!

Most of the things I've learned in my lifetime, I've learned the hard way. My first experience suckling a lamb in a tent provided me with some additional knowledge! Hunkered down on my hands and knees I opened the tent flap just enough to stick my head in so I could assess what needed to be done. The next instant I saw a myriad of colorful stars as something slammed into my head, knocking me sprawling backward on the ground. It took a few seconds before I could gather my scrambled wits together and realize what had happened. When cornered, ewes with young will react by either panicking or attacking. This one happened to be an aggressive type, and she butted me head-on. If we hadn't been at such close quarters she might have broken my neck! I never stuck my head in a lambing tent after that without first testing the temperament of the occupant by sticking my hand in. If she was feisty I would slap the side of the tent and while she was distracted, grab her by a hind leg and throw her.

It was surprising how quickly a ewe would develop a maternal instinct when her whole world was encompassed by the walls of that little tent and the only living thing she could see was the lamb. It was easy to test how the relationship was progressing by taking the lamb out of the tent. It would bleat frantically for its mother, and if the ewe responded I knew she had claimed the lamb. In the case of a jacketed lamb I would then remove the jacket and put the lamb back in with the ewe for an hour or so to make sure the bond was not going to be broken by the different appearance and smell of the lamb.

Other sheepmen, faced with the scarcity of help, were resorting to turning their sheep loose in fenced pastures and letting them lamb themselves, so Pete, Don, and Peto decided to give it a try.

During the years of 1962 and 1963 no organized lambing was done at the ranch. The sheep were put in bunches of five to six hundred to a pasture and left to lamb on their own on the range. After lambing was over the sheep were gathered in the various pastures and the lambs docked and branded prior to heading for the mountains. By the end of the lambing season of 1963 it was clearly evident that this was not the solution to the problem because our lamb percentage was down considerably to what it had been when we supervised the process. It was decided to abandon range lambing altogether and go to a straight shed lambing operation.

The Meikes tore down the old straw shed that had been used for shed lambing and in its place built a large new shed that would hold the entire drop herd at night. Existing sheds were enlarged, also. The irrigated fields were fenced into pastures and sheds were built in each to accommodate a couple hundred ewes and their lambs at night and during bad storms.

The drop herd was under supervision twenty-four hours a day. At night, the drop herd was kept in the big night shed and watched over by a night man. The night man's job was to keep checking through the bunches and as soon as a ewe lambed, to put her in a jug and check her milk supply. If she had given birth to two lambs but had only enough for one, the extra lamb was put in the bum pen under a heat lamp. A ewe that had produced a single lamb with enough milk to raise two was immediately given a second lamb from the bum pen. Many ewes have such a mothering instinct during and immediately after giving birth that they will claim any lamb as their own. If a ewe seemed skeptical, several methods could be used to confuse her natural instincts, such as dunking both her own lamb and the graft lamb in a bucket of warm salt water. Probably the easiest and best way was to "smear" the bum around in the ewe's afterbirth to give the lamb the same smell as her own. Sometimes it was necessary to suckle lambs that were weak or had mothers that would not, for some reason, allow their lambs to suck. This involved climbing into the jug with the ewe and using whatever measures were necessary to get a nipple in the lamb's mouth and milk into its stomach. Most lambs are born with the instinct to suck, but in some this function, so necessary to survival, is missing and must be learned.

The jugs were formed by two lines of thirty-six-inch-high by twelve-foot-long wooden panels wired together end to end and stretching almost the width of the shed. These made the sides of the jugs. An individual jug was made by placing a four-by-four-foot wooden panel between the side panels to make a small pen, about four feet square, just large enough to hold a ewe and her offspring. Double rows of these jugs separated the shed into sections, two large ones to keep the drop herd in (the drop herd was broken into two sections to make it easier to handle), and a third, smaller section to hold ewes and lambs when they were turned out of the jugs. Later, an extension was added to the night shed and the drop herd was broken up into four groups instead of two.

The mother and her babies were kept in the jugs long enough to make sure there would not be problems, then turned out into the ewe and lamb pen at the far end of the shed.

In the morning the drop herd was turned out of the night shed into a big lot that separated the night shed from the day shed and the day crew took over. The person who ran the night shift ate breakfast with the Meike family, then returned to the night shed with whoever ran it during the day, usually Peto, and clued him in on any problem sheep in the night's drop, after which the night person went home and to bed.

The day shed's arrangement of jugs was somewhat different from the night shed. For one thing it was smaller and did not have floor space for shedding the drop herd. The sheep were fed out in the lot, with water available from a well at the east side of the lot. The day crew walked through the sheep and as soon as a ewe lambed the lambs were picked up by the front legs and carried to the shed with the ewe anxiously following. If the ewe was flighty the lamb might have to be laid down several times so she could renew her contact with it. If a ewe refused to cooperate sterner methods were used, such as roping her or catching her with a sheep hook and dragging her in. As in the night shed, each ewe was jugged and the same procedures followed.

The night's drop was docked each day just before noon. The docking was now done in a totally different manner from range docking, where a whole crew of people were involved. One person went up and down the rows of jugs putting small rubber rings on all the lambs' tails and on the scrotums of the male lambs with an elastrator. The rings cut off the blood supply and in a few weeks the shriveled up tails and scrotums would just fall off, along with the rubber ring, leaving a neat, clean amputation with no blood loss and very little shock involved.

The elastrator is a simple tool about ten inches long with handles in an open position at one end. At the business end are four small prongs grouped together. A small rubber ring is slipped over these, the handles are squeezed together, which spreads the prongs and the ring, allowing it to be slipped over the tails and scrotums. When the handles are released the prongs close until they are against the tail, for instance, the ring is slipped off securely circling the tail.

The ewe lambs were no longer earmarked for age. Instead, an ear tag bearing the name of the ranch and the year were clipped into their ears with another little tool. The ear tags came in a variety of colors so one color would be used one year, another the next, so a ewe's age could be determined at a glance without reading the year stamped on the tags.

By mid-afternoon the shed boss began branding out, which means each ewe and her lamb or lambs were branded with a number from one to a hundred. Any ewe and lamb pair that were not doing well were skipped and left in the jug for another twenty-four hours. The branded ewes and lambs were moved to larger pens at each end of the shed for twenty-four-hour observation. The next day they were moved again to sheds and pens adjacent to the lambing sheds. At this time any pair that wasn't doing as well as they should was held back for further care and might even be taken back to a jug for more critical care.

Finally, when a hundred ewes and their offspring were numbered with one color of paint they were combined into one bunch and moved out to a shed in one of the fields.

The process was then repeated using another color of paint. The outside bunches were taken care of by Brookie and me. We kept them fed and watered, doctored sick sheep, and kept an eye out for lambs that were not thriving and tried to determine why. If a lamb died we hauled the ewe back to the shed so they could jacket a bum for her. If a ewe died we took the lamb back to the bum pen to be used for grafts. At that time we had a total of twelve sheds to look after by the time lambing was finished. Water was furnished by wells, for the most part, so troughs had to be kept filled.

Feed and water had to be carried to all the ewes in jugs twice a day. As soon as the jugs were emptied, fresh straw was put down for the next night's occupants, the main shed had to have fresh straw for the drop herd to bed on the next night, bums had to be fed milk replacer from a bottle, and always there was suckling to do! Everything that was being done in the night shed was being duplicated in the day shed with each day's drop of lambs. I always thought of it as perpetual motion because you did the same things over and over, though maybe it was more like a tidal wave. The first ewe that lambed started the little surge that swelled to a hundred lambed ewes, then two hundred and on and on until there were several thousand ewes with lambs!

Shed lambing involved a tremendous amount of work, but it paid off in the number of lambs that went to market every fall. Range lambing invariably involved losses because sheep are given to multiple births. Twins and triplets are common, and, depending on the breed, even quadruplets aren't unusual. A 90 percent lamb crop on the range was considered excellent and a lot of ranchers, including Pete Meike, gave the lambing boss $100 bonus if he brought in 100 percent or better. With shed lambing, at least 150 percent was normal.

Each year saw changes in the shed lambing procedure as different ways of doing things were tried. If they produced good results they became part of the program; if not, they were discarded. But the basic operation never changed.

Living with Brookie was never boring—sometimes aggravating, often frustrating, but never boring! He could not be idle for any length of time. During the summers on the mountains we built new corrals and remodeled or relocated existing ones. We put in miles of new fence as the mountain camps were being fenced in.

After we moved off the mountains in the fall the sheep were put out on winter range in fenced-in pastures. They were free to roam and were soon split up into smaller bunches by canyons and ridges. Every day we checked on them, making a rough count of the different bunches. Not knowing where or when we'd show up helped discourage people from butchering sheep or hauling off a pickup load to sell. Whenever the sheep were watering along Salt Creek there was always the possibility of some bogging in quicksand, so we had to keep an eye out for that.

Usually we moved our sheepwagon out to some central location so we could eat our noon meal there if necessary. If we were lucky in finding the sheep we might be back in at the house by noon; more likely it would be early or mid-afternoon, which meant that we had some free time every afternoon before darkness put a stop to outdoor activities.

As sure as I would think I was going to have a couple of hours to bake some pies or do some house cleaning he'd say, "You know, I always thought there oughtta be a gate in the drift fence out there by that reservoir. Let's go build one this afternoon." And he'd be loading gate posts and wire while I was trying to shift my mind from domestic pursuits to fencing pliers and wire stretchers.

Or we'd be coming through the hills past the Pine Knobs and he'd make the off-hand remark that we'd always needed a docking pen there so we didn't have to move the ewes and lambs clean over to Dead Man at docking time. I knew I might just as well prepare to start digging post holes the next day because once he zeroed in on a project it was as good as done!

So I don't know why I should have been surprised when he walked into the house one afternoon in the fall of 1957 and announced, "Let's build a room onto the house."

"We don't know anything about building a house," I protested feebly.

"I built my own homestead cabin, and it's still standing," he replied very logically, as he always did in such instances. "We'll build it out of logs so it'll be warm," he went on enthusiastically while I was still trying to think of some suitable rejoinder, "and we'll have double picture windows on the south looking toward the Pine Ridge. I saw an ad in the Buffalo Bulletin the other day for machined house logs that are squared on three sides and are tongue and grooved for a windproof fit."

In forty-eight hours he not only had drawn a blueprint complete with doors and windows, he had figured how many rafters it would take, how many ceiling beams, and on and on. Next he consulted Pete Meike to see what he thought of the idea. Not only did Pete approve of the plan 100 percent, he came and helped Brookie lay out the measurements for the foundation for a room sixteen by twenty-four feet, adjoining the old house on the south.

In three days we were in Buffalo ordering house logs and lumber, cement, spikes, electrical wiring, and plumbing supplies, not to mention box after box of nails in more sizes than I'd ever dreamed existed.

Our foundation was poured, seasoned, and ready when a truck from the lumber company finally arrived and began unloading the building material. We were ready to start construction, or at least, Brookie was. I was still muddling along wondering if we had any idea what we were doing! He had one distinct advantage over me: he could see the completed room in his mind's eye, whereas all I had was an out-of-focus blur!

Pete came nearly every afternoon to check on our progress, offer suggestions, and if he had time, help. My brother Fred was working in the oilfield at Linch that winter and living at our place. If he got home early enough in the evening he took over for me while I cooked supper, and he usually put in a full day whenever he had a day off.

The weather cooperated beautifully with very few stormy days. Brookie was jubilant. "We'll eat New Year's dinner in the new room!" he predicted confidently. "In a year or so, as soon as we can afford it, we'll tear down the old house and build on to the new room."

I had a lot more confidence in what we were doing by this time, so I endorsed the idea whole-heartedly. How nice it would be to have a house with straight walls and level floors and no snow blowing in under the doors!

Brookie was a meticulous carpenter; everything had to be absolutely level and square. Sometimes I got a little irked when a log didn't fit the way he wanted it to and we had to keep raising it and putting in shims made of thin strips of wood to level it until it suited him. In spite of his being so finicky, the walls went up faster than I ever dreamed they would, and soon we were fitting his ceiling beams in.

The seventeen-foot beams had been cut and machined to his specifications: squared on three sides the same as the house logs but with no tongue and groove. Installing them created a lot of extra work, but the end result was well worth it. Over the years many people have commented on the uniqueness of them and how much they add to the room. They really set off the ceiling, which was made of eight-inch knotty pine boards.

When Christmas Day arrived the outside construction was finished, the windows and doors had been installed, and we were ready to cut the doorway through from the old house. We had positioned the new room so that the double windows of the old dining room would be cut out to make a double-width door between the new room and the old house.

What a hard, dirty job that turned out to be! It was comparatively easy to remove the window sashes, but when we began tearing the framework loose it released clouds of dust. Every time we ripped off a board we were showered with dead flies and millers mixed with mouse manure! Finally, the logs had to be sawed out below the windows to complete the doorway. This involved a lot of elbow grease because these old cottonwood logs were big. We had to do all the work down on our knees. What a simple task it would have been if we'd had chainsaws in those days.

December 31 found us with most of the interior finish work yet to do on the new room, but we triumphantly carried the food through our newly completed connecting door on New Year's Day and ate in the new room!

In the early spring of 1958 we learned that Uncle Bill Eldridge had an old sheepwagon for sale. He had bought it several years before and made a deal with his nephew Harry who was to repair it for the use of it. Harry's ranch was several hours' drive down Powder River from Kaycee, and since Bill didn't drive, they seldom had any contact with each other. Somehow, Bill learned that Harry had never done anything with the wagon and it had sat for so long that the wooden running gears had practically disintegrated. Bill hired someone to lift it off the running gears onto a flatbed trailer and haul it to his place at Kaycee.

It looked like a total wreck to me the day we went to look at it, so I could hardly believe my ears when Bill said he wanted $150 for it and Brookie said we'd take it. The canvas top was in tatters, I pointed out as we drove home, the floor was rotted out, and the stove was a rusted wreck. Brookie's years of repairing wagons at the Meikes had given him the expertise to look past the superficial things to the basics and the structure of the wagon was sound, he assured me. Also, it was a Shulte wagon, he said, as if that gave it the *Good Housekeeping* Seal of Approval for sheepwagons. It would take a lot of work to restore the wagon, he told me, but it would be worth every cent we put into it in the long run.

Several days later we hauled it home on one of the Meikes' rubber-tired hayracks and parked it out by our garage shop. We didn't have time to do anything with it before going to lambing camp, so it sat there until we came off the mountains that fall. Then we began working on it in our spare time.

Our first priority was to get a top on it, so we ordered enough sheet aluminum from Sears to cover it. At some time someone had covered the entire top with sheets of thin plywood in place of the usual oil cloth and blanket that was put on before a new top went on. Brookie wanted the entire wagon top insulated, so he left the plywood in place and covered it with fiberglass wool before the metal went on. Accomplishing this was no minor feat, out in the open, in this windy country, I might add. The aluminum was put on in lengthwise strips starting at the bottom of the wagon top. The bottom edge of each new strip overlapped the top of the one below it to make it leakproof. A line of caulking compound under the lap-over guaranteed a waterproof seal. Then began the tedious job of drilling small holes through the double thickness of metal an inch apart and screwing in countless dozens of little metal screws to secure the aluminum.

Redoing that wagon took us the entire winter, and Brookie enjoyed every minute of it. Because it was ours he was able to modify and innovate as he went along. Most wagons were gloomy affairs, with a window in the back over the bed and occasionally a small window either in the top door or over the water bucket stand to shed a little more light on the stove on stormy or cold days when the doors were closed. Brookie outdid himself on making our wagon lighter. As well as a window in the door and one above the stove he had installed a glass in the overjet ventilator panel on the right side of the wagon.

The great day finally came when our "new" wagon was carefully slid from the hayrack onto the running gears of a Chevrolet pickup we had bought after the owner totaled it one Saturday night on his way home from a Sussex dance. We secured it to the running gears and began the move in. On March 12 we were ready to move the wagon to the hills so we could start gathering all the sheep into one area for shearing in April. At the last minute, Brookie decided to frame the side window on the inside to give it a more finished look. He had a strip of beveled molding which would do nicely, but he decided it was too wide. Well, it wouldn't take long to cut a strip off it with Warren's electric saw, which we'd been using on our rebuilding project and hadn't yet returned. Soon he had his measurements made and a line marked on the molding where it was to be sawed. He plugged in the saw and began his cut.

Neither of us was ever sure afterward what happened. His index finger almost hit me in the face as it went flying past. I was so horrified I was frozen for a few seconds. He jerked his hand back and grabbed it with his other hand before I could see the extent of the injury. I had enough presence of mind to unplug the saw. When I turned back, Brookie had wrapped his handkerchief around his hand and was heading for the jeep, which was backed up to the wagon but was not yet hooked on.

"Take me to Pete's," he said and didn't speak another word until we were halfway to Buffalo.

This was long before we had an ambulance and EMTs in our area; in fact I don't believe there was even an ambulance in Buffalo at that time because I remember the hearse from the funeral home being sent out to rural areas in the county in lieu of an ambulance. The Meike ranch had been designated as a first-aid station by the Red Cross, and as such was equipped with first aid necessities, including a stretcher.

As I drove to the ranch a jumble of thoughts ran wildly through my mind. Was Brookie going to bleed to death before we could get him to a doctor? Had I actually unplugged the saw, or had the thought only crossed my mind? What if I found no one at the ranch? Would I be able to drive the seventy miles to Buffalo? What about money? I didn't even have my checkbook with me. What became of Brookie's finger?

When I drove in to the ranch the crew was in the midst of "pulling the well," a dirty, messy job involving pulling all of the "innards" out of the well to correct a malfunction of some kind. Everyone was wet and muddy, including Pete.

I jumped from the jeep and ran over and told him what happened. He threw down the pipe wrench he was using and snapped, "Take him to the house."

I helped Brookie inside and told Naomi what had happened. She stood frozen to the spot, the blood draining from her face, and I thought she was going to faint. Just then Pete rushed in, taking in the situation at a glance.

"Just wrap a clean bath towel around his hand," he told Naomi while he hurried to the bathroom to clean up and on to the bedroom to change clothes.

In addition to his pickup Pete had what we all referred to as his "town car," a late model sedan that was used exclusively for going to town. Within minutes we were on the road with Brookie and me in the back seat. At one point Brookie opened the towel and took a quick look at his hand.

"You can slow down a little if you want to," he remarked. "It's not a matter life and death. I'm not bleedin' at all."

"Thank God," said Pete.

I glanced over Pete's shoulder and saw that the speedometer needle was hovering just under 100 miles an hour. It didn't scare me a bit—me, the nervous rider! I'm sure we must have set a new speed record that day that was probably never broken if there had been any statistics for comparison.

Much later, I realized Brookie and I were both in a state of shock following the accident. It was hours before any details of the trip really registered and even after all these years there's still a feeling of unreality about the whole episode. My diary entry for this day says, "Brookie was in the operating room from 3:45 P.M. to 7:00 P.M. They saved all his fingers but the one that went flying past my face. I stayed at the hospital and sat up with him."

The time I spent in that waiting room seems quite unreal to me, even now. At one point I realized tears were running down my face, but I was not crying in the sense that I was sobbing. Most of the time the waiting room was deserted because we had arrived about the time afternoon visiting hours were over and evening visitors began coming just as he was taken to the recovery room.

My memory of the next several days is so incoherent that without my diary for that period I would now have no idea what took place. Our son, Pete, who was boarding with a family in town and attending high school, was with me every evening. Pete Meike came several times to check on Brookie's progress. Family members and friends were at the hospital every day during visiting hours. No matter what was going on, in the back of my awareness was the sound of that saw and Brookie's finger flying past my face.

Brookie's recovery was amazing, considering how badly mangled his fingers had been. Nine days after the surgery the doctors removed the stitches, and we were able to go home for the weekend. I felt as if my sanity had been restored. Monday morning we were back at the hospital so his hand could be put in a cast, and he was officially released except for routine check-ups.

Once we were home again nothing had changed except we were two weeks behind schedule. The date for shearing the sheep was fast approaching, so we didn't bother to move the wagon out. Instead we concentrated on getting the sheep gathered and moved in to the shearing pens. As soon as the sheep were sheared we moved sheep, wagons, horses, and lambing gear to where lambing would start at the Heltzel place on Salt Creek. Peto, Brookie, and I were the lambing crew with Don commuting back and forth from the ranch to help and Pete working on the weekends when he was out from school.

Pete and I had many a laugh afterward about our sheep butchering experience while we were camped there, though it wasn't all that laughable at the time. Brookie and Peto hauled a big wether into camp after breakfast one morning, unloaded it on a nice grassy spot, cut its throat, and left us to butcher it. We had both helped Brookie dress countless deer and sheep and even a few elk, so we had a good idea of how it was done. Actually doing it, we soon discovered, was something else! Two hours later when we finally completed the job of skinning and gutting it we were both covered with blood and mutton tallow and the carcass was bristling with green grass so we spent another hour picking all the grass stems off. I've dressed quite a few sheep since then, but always where I could hang them up while I was doing it, which certainly simplifies the job.

When the doctor removed Brookie's cast before lambing, he cut it in half lengthwise so it resembled the two halves of a clam shell. He told Brookie to wear it while he was working, especially while he was riding, and to take it off at night. After lambing wound down, a check-up with the doctor showed the hand was completely healed and Brookie could discard the cast.

We hit the trail for the mountains on June 5 with me trailing the sheep and Brookie pulling my camp. Peto and our Pete pulled out with the second herd a day behind us, with Pete trailing and Peto camptending. I was thankful we had good weather all the way because this was Pete's first trailing job, though he'd made the trail countless times while he was growing up.

June 18 we were two days' trail from camp when my brother Dan arrived during the night with the shocking news that Brookie's father had died. Dan had brought two men up with him, one to move our wagon while Dan trailed my herd and the other one to take over trailing for Pete.

We left camp immediately, arriving in Kaycee at 2 in the morning to find all the family members from the area sitting up with Brookie's mom, who was in a state of shock. The next few days passed in a blur of activity. Funeral arrangements were made; relatives in Wisconsin and Illinois were notified and met as they arrived.

The day of the funeral was fair and quite warm, so a record number of people turned out to pay their respects and attend the get-together at the Turk home following the services. Harvey had always loved pomp and ceremony. As we were leaving the church to drive to the cemetery, one daughter-in-law smiled through her tears and remarked, "Harvey would have loved all this!"

Plans had to be made for Mary. Her health had been deteriorating for several years, complicated by diabetes. The diabetes required insulin shots every day, which she was unable to administer herself. Like many women in her age bracket, she had never learned to drive, and she was

too unsteady on her feet to walk to the post office and grocery store on
Main Street. Since her doctor was in Casper it was decided that the
sensible thing was for her to live with Brookie's sister Evelyn and her
husband, Claude Key, in their home there. The morning after the funeral
Claude, Evelyn and Mary left for Casper, accompanied by some of the
in-laws, while the rest of us disposed of all the leftover food, cleaned out
the refrigerator, and put the house in order for closing it up.

For some reason, unplugging that empty refrigerator and propping
the door ajar suddenly brought home to me the finality of what had
happened. This house that had always been like a second home to all of
us, was dead, as surely as Harvey was. Mary's warm smile would never
greet us at the door again as she bid us come in and sit a spell, or have
something to eat. I was overcome with sadness and escaped to the
bedroom, where I finally cried all the tears I had been unable to shed up
to now.

By early afternoon Brookie, Pete, and I were on our way to the
mountains along with the in-laws who had not gone to Casper with
Claude and Evelyn and Mary or returned home.

Once we arrived at camp we had no time to mope around. Both
herds of sheep had come in off the trail, so lambs that had been born on
the trek to the mountains needed to be branded and docked and the
herds had to be counted and settled on the camps. In three days the
relatives and the relief crew had left the mountains, Peto had brought up
a herder for the second herd, and we were busy showing him his camp
boundaries, putting out salt for all the sheep, gathering the neighbors'
cows and putting them back on their own range and repairing fence so
they would stay where they belonged.

Trum always wintered at his uncle's ranch in Nebraska, coming back
to the Meike ranch each spring in time for lambing and summer
herding. The spring of 1958 he decided he was too old to help lamb so
he took a job herding sheep for a Natrona County rancher. Ben Romero,
who replaced him that summer, was a Hispanic from Colorado, a retired
man in his seventies who had never worked with sheep. The Stanley
camp, which he would be herding, was fenced on two sides so even
though he'd had no experience he had no trouble herding and really
enjoyed himself.

Pete spent the summer on the mountains with us except when he
was down on the flats attending 4-H Club meetings. Pete Meike had
been a dedicated 4-H leader for years and as soon as our Pete was old
enough he started him in 4-H. At the Johnson County Fair and Rodeo in
August he won a first place ribbon on his forestry project, two red
ribbons on his colt, Ginger, and a red ribbon on his conservation project.

We built a new sheep-working corral during the summer and Pete helped us on that, plus herding sheep for us when we went to Sussex to get the mail and groceries once a week.

In mid-summer Mary Turk put her house up for sale, and the family gathered to help her sort a lifetime accumulation of possessions. We had made an appointment with an ear specialist in Casper for Pete, so we hauled a load of things Mary was keeping when we went over. After examining Pete the specialist told us there was nothing he could do for him, and his suggestion was to get him the best hearing aid we could buy. He called the Beltone Hearing Clinic and made an appointment for us for that afternoon. We were quite impressed with the competent manner in which they tested him and evaluated his hearing. He had a hearing loss of over 50 percent in each ear, and his hearing would diminish as he grew older, they said. On their recommendation we had him fitted for hearing aid glasses. The new hearing aid was more powerful than any of his previous ones, and for the first time he had almost normal hearing capacity.

The sale of Harvey and Mary's household goods took place July 25 in their yard in Kaycee. Mary told the family members when they were helping her sort her things for the sale that if any of us wanted any item as a keepsake we would have to bid on it at the sale because she had seen families torn apart by jealousy and greed over the distribution of family heirlooms.

"If I give something to one of you that someone else wants there'll be hard feelings over it," she said with her usual Scottish wisdom. "If you have to bid on what you want everyone will have an equal chance at it."

We all agreed this made sense. Mary made an exception in Brookie's case. All he wanted was his dad's barber tools. She gave them to him, because no one else in the family could use them and she doubted if they would sell at the sale.

As it turned out, no two of us wanted the same thing so our only worry was some outsider running up the bid on us. I had my heart set on the antique Seth Thomas wall clock that Harvey had bought at an auction several years before. Brookie and I agreed as we drove off the mountains to the sale that morning that $35 was as high as we could go on the clock. That late in the month we were always scraping the bottom of our bank account and that month we were especially hard-pressed after our visit to the specialist and the Beltone people!

Brookie told me since the clock was going to be mine it was up to me to bid on it. This was only the second time in my life I had ever been to a sale, so I was a bundle of nerves by the time the clock came up for sale.

The auctioneer opened the bid at $5.

"$7.50," some fellow in the crowd bid before I could open my mouth.

I raised it to $10. He went to $12. We see-sawed back and forth, raising the bid two or three dollars at a time until he bid $30.

I raised it to $32.

"$34," he said, after a pause that seemed to go on forever.

"$35." I bid my limit and held my breath.

The auctioneer looked expectantly at my "opponent." "I've lost it," I thought. Then the guy shook his head and turned away. "Going once, going twice, at $35 to the lady over here!" I went weak with relief.

The sale was a huge success. The Turks had been widely known, the event had been well publicized, and Mary's large collection of antiques drew collectors from as far away as Billings. The auctioneer said the crowd was in a buying mood, so everything sold high. The house had been snapped up as soon as it was put on the market, so the end of the sale that day certainly marked the end of an era in the Turk family history in the Kaycee area.

*Pete has outgrown his mom, 1958*

# THE MARCH OF TIME II
## (1959-1972)

That fall Brookie was once again in the hospital for his hand. His middle finger had been almost totally severed at the second joint in the accident with the saw. Although the doctors had managed to reattach it, the circulation in it was so bad it always had a faint bluish color and increasingly turned an alarming purple color when it got cold. Whenever this happened we were told to get it in warm water as soon as possible and massage it to prevent gangrene from setting in.

Dr. John Knebel had said it might be necessary to amputate the finger, and by the time we moved off the mountains Brookie was in complete agreement. He entered the hospital the evening of October 28 and had the finger amputated the next morning, five days after his fifty-second birthday.

Brookie always made the most of any situation, and those two stumps offered endless opportunities for laughs. He loved to impress kids by pushing the ends of the stubs up against his nostrils so it gave the impression that he had his fingers up his nose to the middle joints. One time some friends were visiting us. They had a five-year-old son who sucked his fingers. All their attempts to get him to stop had met with failure, the parents told us as the kid sat there defiantly slurping on his fingers.

Brookie put on a very serious face and told the boy, "I used to have the same problem. I wouldn't stop sucking my fingers and look what happened."

He held up his hand for Little Ed's inspection. Disbelief was replaced by a look of horror on the little guy's face as he carefully checked out the stumps and convinced himself it was not some sort of hoax. He questioned Brookie closely about how it happened. Brookie gave him lurid details of how the fingers began to wither and finally just fell off.

Little Ed *never* sucked his fingers again, his parents told us later.

Mary was so devastated by Harvey's death it seemed unlikely to the family that she would ever be able to live by herself, especially since she could not give herself the daily insulin shots she needed. When her doctor suggested she might be able to switch to oral medication Brookie and I were skeptical, for the simple reason we'd never heard of controlling diabetes with anything but insulin. A trial period proved she did not need the shots, and her mental attitude improved miraculously, much to the delight of the family.

Her announcement that she was going to move to an apartment in Buffalo, however, took everyone by surprise. Family reaction ranged from consternation to disbelief, with the exceptions of Brookie and Bo, who thought it was a great idea. Bo and Doris lived in Buffalo and would be able to check on her every day. As Mary pointed out, most of the friends she'd known since the Turks' homesteading days had either retired in Buffalo or came to town frequently to shop and do business. With the exception of the doctor for her diabetes, she had always done her doctoring in Buffalo until she had to move to Casper.

While the family members were arguing for or against her move, she went briskly ahead, renting an apartment within walking distance of downtown and settling in. For the first time in her life she was totally independent, and she thoroughly enjoyed it. Nearly every day she made the trip down Main Street, almost always encountering friends from the Kaycee-Sussex area.

I think we all had totally underestimated the inner strength of this pioneer woman, who had come west in 1917 with Harvey and their five offspring to live in a tent at their isolated homestead site until a log cabin could be built. After their marriage in January 1907, Harvey and Mary were staying temporarily with his parents, James and Martha Turk, while they looked for a place to live. She and Harvey considered their marriage a partnership, rather than a master-servant relationship, which didn't set well with James, who believed women should be seen and not heard. A certain amount of friction had already developed between him and Mary because she had staunchly stood up against him for equality of the sexes.

One evening after the "old folks" had retired, Harvey told Mary to pick out a dress and hat from a catalog (I failed to ask which one) and he would mail the order next morning on his way to his barber shop. When they went to bed they left the sealed envelope on the dining room table. When Mary came downstairs the next morning to help Martha fix breakfast she was dumfounded to find James waiting for her with the opened envelope in one hand and the order in the other. He informed her that she was in no need of anything as frivolous as a new hat and gown.

Trying to control her anger, she told him it was Harvey's decision to order the things and Harvey's money that was paying for them.

As long as she and Harvey were living under his roof, James told her coldly, they would abide by his decisions.

He was unaware that Harvey had walked into the room behind him and witnessed the whole exchange. Walking up to James he extended his hand for the order and envelope. Without a word, James marched over to the heating stove and dropped them in the fire.

Mary looked Harvey in the eye and said, "I'm leaving."

"Go start packing," Harvey told her, "while I go find a place to live." In less than two hours they were setting up housekeeping in two small furnished rooms over a hardware store.

Later that spring, Mary was walking home from a social function of some sort, proudly wearing her new navy blue hat when she was caught in a sudden shower. Before she could take shelter the dye from the hat ran down her face and onto her white blouse. The stain never did come out of the blouse and for a day or so Mary's face had a strange, bluish tinge.

"James Turk would have been so pleased if he'd known about it," she laughed when telling the story. "He'd have been sure the Lord was punishing me for my willful ways!"

Her life in Buffalo ended abruptly when she suddenly developed glaucoma in one eye and was rushed to the Casper hospital for surgery. The loss of the sight in that eye impaired her sense of balance so, reluctantly, she moved back to Casper.

Hoping to remain independent, Mary bought a small trailer house which was parked in the Keys' back yard. After it was discovered that she was totally ignoring her diabetic diet, her doctor insisted she have her meals at the house so Evelyn could monitor what she was eating, much to Mary's annoyance. From that point on her health, both physical and mental, deteriorated rapidly. She was experiencing what the doctor termed "mini-strokes," most of them unnoticeable except for a momentary lapse of memory or a slight faltering in her speech. We were warned that each one would do a tiny bit of brain damage, which would manifest itself in a gradual personality change.

Brookie and I had not seen her for several weeks when we went to the Keys' to help Mary celebrate her birthday September 28. The deterioration of her physical health was obvious in a marked weight loss. It took only a few minutes to discover, to our shock, that our loving, witty, high-spirited Mary was now sarcastic, quarrelsome, and spiteful, especially toward Evelyn, whom she referred to as "my boss."

We spent a miserable day listening to her verbally attack Evelyn whenever she dared to join the conversation. Brookie was nearly in tears as we drove home. "If Sis had said black was black, Ma would have argued that black was white," he observed.

How our hearts ached for Evelyn, facing the daily hostility and the constant worry that Mary would light a burner on the propane stove in the trailer and catch her clothing on fire or scald herself as she made a cup of tea. One day Evelyn glanced out the window and saw smoke billowing from one of the garbage barrels that sat along the back fence. Mary was tossing something into the fire from a box at her feet. When she saw Evelyn hurrying out of the house she hastily picked up the box and dumped everything in the barrel.

Seeing snapshots, photos, and papers with Mary's handwriting on them being consumed by the blaze, Evelyn asked what she was burning.

"None of your business!" Mary snapped. "Just a bunch of crap I cleaned out of the trailer!" Later it was discovered she had destroyed a lifetime collection of family pictures and all of her original poetry, essays, artwork, and copies of a newspaper column she wrote for the *Sheridan Press* newspaper over a period of several years, a loss of family history that was irreplaceable.

Before snow and cold weather came Claude and Evelyn moved Mary into the house because her health was failing day by day. In mid-April she was hospitalized, and Evelyn let the family know that the end was near. The Casper family members had been taking turns sitting with her, so Brookie and I went to help out.

Poor Mary! Most of the time she lay in a comatose state, eyes closed, her breathing so shallow sometimes it was difficult to determine if she was still alive. Occasionally she would mutter or move restlessly, her eyes would open momentarily, showing no recognition of anyone.

After two days the doctor told us there was not much point in sitting with her twenty-four hours a day because she might linger for weeks. Her condition was being monitored by qualified people, and any change would be reported to Evelyn immediately. Brookie and I had ewe and lamb bunches at the ranch waiting to be moved to the hills, so we decided we would stay until evening and then come home.

As I sat with Mary one last time, holding her limp hand, she suddenly squeezed my hand, opened her eyes and looked straight into mine. "Louise," she said in a weak but distinct voice, "you must be tired from working through lambing."

I assured her I'd been sitting there resting and was doing great.

With a wry little smile she said apologetically, "I'm just like an old ewe: feed me all winter and then when green grass comes I die."

Her eyes closed, her face and hand relaxed, and for one startled moment I thought she'd died. Then I saw she was breathing slowly and lightly as before.

I didn't tell the family about it at the time because I thought it would only make them feel worse. As time passed, it got shuttled into the dim recesses of my mind and forgotten until recently.

On April 20 Mary died peacefully, leaving behind three sons (Carlton, Brookie's youngest brother, had died in 1954 from a heart attack), one daughter, one sister, one brother, fifteen grandchildren and thirty-three great-grandchildren. Funeral services were held in Kaycee, and we laid her to rest beside her beloved Harvey.

I always felt they were true Wyoming pioneers, even though they hadn't come west in a covered wagon.

Vivian and her husband, Warren, and their three-year-old daughter, VeNancy, moved back to Wyoming in 1957 after his job in Nebraska played out. He went to work in the oil field at Linch and continued to work there until his retirement years later. We gave them four acres of our land, and they had a well drilled and built a home of their own.

Their son, Floyd, was born in July 1958. As Christmas 1959 approached, Vivian was awaiting the birth of another baby. They had no phone, and she began having pains on December 14 while Warren was at work. She picked up baby Floyd and with little VeNancy tagging along she walked the 200 yards to our place to tell us she needed to get to the hospital. We were just sitting down to our noon meal when they arrived, so we jumped up and left everything sitting on the table and raced the stork to the hospital in Buffalo, where we left Vivian. Warren got home from work about the same time we got home from Buffalo, so we let him know what had happened.

There was a phone at the Sussex store across the river from us and the plan was for the hospital to call there when there was something to report and the message would be delivered by Al Lohse, the storekeeper. Warren ate supper with us, then went home and gathered up the kids' clothes and brought them over to me. The night passed with no news, so Warren took off for Buffalo early the next morning and spent the day sitting with Vivian. Her "condition" had stabilized and nothing was happening, so he came on home. When he called from the store the next morning he learned Vivian had been dismissed and was staying at the home of her aunt and uncle in Buffalo.

The days passed, with us keeping VeNancy and Floyd and Warren working each day. On Christmas morning Warren took the kids, went to

Buffalo, and brought Vivian out to spend the day. We had a big Christmas supper, then Warren took Vivian back to town. The evening of the 27th Al finally brought the news that Vivian had delivered little Warren Scott and that mother and child were doing great.

The year 1959 had dealt us some low lows, but ended on a positive note with the arrival of another healthy grandchild.

Some of my most vivid memories, both good and bad, pertain to trailing sheep. One of the things I liked least about the spring trail was getting up in the cold, predawn dark, getting dressed by flashlight, and getting the camp ready to move.

We always picketed our saddle horses at night so we wouldn't have to hunt them in the dark in the morning. Our work horses were good camp horses, as a rule, and wherever the camp was, that was home to them, but sometimes they strayed while they were grazing. If that happened we would have saddle horses go hunt them when it got daylight. We couldn't picket the work horses because they didn't have the chance to eat during the day that the saddle horses had, so we hobbled them.

The hobbles were two wide leather cuffs joined by a few links of chain with a swivel in the middle. The cuffs were buckled around the front legs just above the hooves. A horse quickly learned to manage the hobbles by either taking short, mincing steps with the front feet or by hopping with their front feet. The muffled thump of hobbled horses grazing at night was a sound that every sheepherder and camptender went to sleep by.

Whenever Brookie was camptender, we slept in a bed roll in a teepee and the herder slept in the wagon. When we were herding and someone else was tending camp, it was the other way around. By the time the bedroll and teepee had been rolled and loaded in the supply wagon, the sheepwagon packed, and the horses harnessed and saddled, and picket ropes and hobbles taken care of, it would be light enough to see and the sheep would start moving.

I would be thoroughly chilled by that time, and it seemed as if the sun would never get high enough to warm me, especially if there was a cloud bank in the east as there sometimes was at daybreak. If the day turned into a scorcher later, I wondered why I couldn't have just a little of the heat in the early morning and some of the chill at mid-day!

Once we left civilization on the spring trail we had to have enough supplies of all kinds to take us to camp. We had no refrigeration of any kind, not even ice chests, but we managed to have eggs on the trail and even fresh meat. We usually butchered a mutton the first night we were on the mountains. The nights were pretty cool, if not downright chilly that time of year, so the carcass was hung up at night in the cold, then rolled up in a piece of canvas in the morning and put in the supply wagon. We unwrapped the meat and cut off what we needed for a meal and the rest was rewrapped. Fresh meat was kept this way all summer on the mountains. A herder would butcher either a sheep or a deer and share the meat with one or two neighboring herders.

Eggs will keep much longer without refrigeration than most people realize. An eggshell does a remarkably good job of insulating its contents. We always started out with a twenty-four-dozen case of eggs. They were usually kept in the cubbyhole back under the bed in the wagon where the temperature was a little cooler.

Water on trail was used very sparingly. Between Sussex and Kaycee, if anyone felt the need for a bath, the Sahara Ditch or Powder River made a good place to cool off and wash off the trail dust. The day we nooned on North Fork by the Brock Ranch, we replenished the water supply in the barrel, and that had to do us until we reached Bear Trap. I always looked forward to the day we pulled down onto Bear Trap, where I could do the accumulation of laundry and spread it to dry on the clean, green grass. I could wash my hair and use all the water I felt like carrying from the creek. From there on, water was a fairly available commodity, as we were crossing creeks and passing springs nearly every day.

One of the bonuses of trailing sheep was finding Indian relics. On the mountains you were apt to find arrow heads, scrapers, and stone knives almost anywhere, and especially where there was water, since the Indians often killed game on water and there were also campsites on some of the creeks. We usually had a tidy collection by the time we got to camp, and the summer would yield a lot more.

When Brookie and I trailed by ourselves, he was always cook and camptender and I was the herder. After we started moving wagons with vehicles, I tried both jobs, and I got into a lot less trouble trailing. I never got stuck with a herd of sheep, but I had a real talent for bogging our wagon and pickup in a mud hole or a snow drift!

Because I'm a glutton by nature, my best memory of trailing sheep is of breakfast! If we had made an extra-long trail to get to a stockrest before stopping, it might be ten o'clock before we had breakfast. My appetite would be honed to a razor-sharp edge by the time I rode up to the wagon. The smell of boiled coffee, frying bacon or ham, and sourdough hotcakes on the morning air completely overshadowed any other smell on earth. Brookie always said the same thing when I rode up to the wagon: "Light and eat, stranger! Breakfast's ready!"

The weather always had a direct impact on trailing. Warm weather simplified the job unless it got hot too early in the day. If sheep get too warm, there's no way of moving them. That was the main reason for our early starts. When it was cold and rainy, the sheep were miserable and wanted to walk all day, so it kept everyone busy holding them up so they would graze. Then there could be blizzards or thunderstorms or fog. I hated all three equally.

If there was a blizzard, you could move the sheep into a timber patch if there was one handy; if not, into sage or rock outcroppings. Thunderstorms usually caught us after we'd started moving in the afternoon and about all you could do was hope and pray the lightning would miss you.

Once, in the lane between Sussex and Kaycee, the lightning struck a power pole between the lead of my sheep and where Brookie was moseying along ahead with the wagon. It was a spectacular sight! There was a blaze of blue flame where it struck, then blue fire went racing along the power line both ways from the pole. It caused an immediate power outage because the wire burned in two, but as I passed by with the tail end of my herd, I could see no damage to the pole at all.

Over the years, I've seen quite a few sheep killed by lightning. Once in a great while, a herder would be a victim, but most herders had a healthy respect for it. If he couldn't do anything else, he'd tie his horse to anything he could find, get as far away as he could, and lay down.

Fog always held a fascination for me, possibly because I'd had very little experience with it until I started living in the mountains. Fog is a fairly rare occurrence on the flats, but quite common in the high country. There's something so stealthy about it as it comes wisping up the canyons in innocuous-looking tendrils. One moment the sun may be shining brightly and the next, it has been blotted out by the soft, silver down of the fog. Other times it can come rolling across the tops of the higher mountains and lie there all day, obliterating them from view while the valleys and slopes remain untouched.

If the fog comes in from the east, it can last for several days because it is accompanied by what the meteorologists call an upslope condition. A west or north fog is usually followed by clearing within twenty-four hours. At our camp, you not only see the fog coming in, you can smell it and feel it. As it comes up the east slope, it picks up the scent of the mountain mahogany that grows in abundance on the canyon sides and mountain tops, a fragrance unlike any other I know. I can find only one word to describe it: *fresh.* You can feel the fog caressing your face with its clammy fingers, and eventually it leaves tiny, crystal droplets on your hair, your clothing, and your horse's ears and mane. I didn't like the fog when we had to spend all day in it. After the camps were fenced so we didn't have to worry about the sheep straying away, I learned to love the fog, except when I had to go out in it at night when nature called!

One fall, we had been camped at the forks of Blue Creek for several days waiting for the fog to lift so we could start down on trail with our herd. On this particular evening, the fog seemed even thicker than usual. I had put off going out "to see a man about a dog" until it became an absolute necessity. This was a temporary camp, so there was no outhouse; you just walked the prescribed fifty paces from the wagon and did your duty. The light from the Coleman lantern was cutting a big swath out into the fog through the glass in the door, so I decided I could probably see well enough without the flashlight. I stepped off the front of the wagon and stood for a moment, waiting for my eyes to adjust to the light.

I walked away, following the path of light and looking down so I wouldn't stumble over a rock or bush. I had taken almost all of my fifty paces and the light from the wagon was dimming when I looked up and froze in my tracks. Crouching in the fog ahead of me was a dreadful apparition. It was indistinct, yet I saw it with great clarity. It looked to be ten feet tall and had the shape of a gorilla: too-long arms dangling to its knees, head too small for the massive shoulders and torso. I stood there too paralyzed by fright to move, my mouth too dry to scream for Brookie.

Finally I took a careful step backward and the creature moved cautiously one step toward me. I stopped. It stopped. I took two steps forward and it took two steps back from me. It began to penetrate my fear-frozen brain that it was a reflection of me. The light shining from behind me was casting my distorted shadow against the dense fog.

Shakily, I performed several arm maneuvers to convince myself I was facing my own shadow, quickly accomplished the mission I had come for, and began a slow, backward retreat to the wagon, watching in fascination as the monster followed me, mimicking my movements in a weird, mechanical fashion. When I was about ten steps from the wagon, blind terror overcame me and I turned and bolted. I leaped the last half of the distance onto the doorstep, landed with a crash, wrenched open the door, and fell wild-eyed into the safety of the wagon.

"Something after you?" Brookie inquired mildly.

"No, not really," I panted, "but I want you to go out and see what I saw."

Moments later he came back in grinning. "That's enough to spook anybody," he laughed. "I think you're a lot braver than you think you are!"

In the years since, I've tried several times to duplicate that phenomenon, but have never seen another "monster." I don't know what set of circumstances created that scary illusion.

Another fall, our departure with the sheep had been delayed for a week by dense fog. We were holding the sheep on the head of Irish Creek, ready to throw out onto the trail. At last we awoke one morning to a clear, blue sky. We spent the forenoon getting the camp ready to move and gathering the sheep. As soon as dinner was over and the wagon packed, we hit the trail, headed for Chittem Springs, where we would spend the night.

When I got to where I could see off into the Big Horn basin, I didn't like what I saw at all. The entire basin lay under dense fog, looking for all the world like a huge ocean with whitecaps on it. My hope that the fog was stationary in the low country was short-lived. Where I was the sky was brilliantly blue, the autumn sun quite warm and there was not a breath of breeze, but a west wind was moving the fog slowly into the mountains. I hadn't gone a quarter of a mile before I saw a solid wall of fog coming up out of Canyon Creek toward the trail.

Just before it reached the lead of the sheep, they all stopped and stood with their heads lifted, sniffing curiously. I have never seen sheep react to the fog that way in all the years since. Usually the leading front of a fog bank will be broken, but that was such a solid wall, it looked impenetrable.

It swallowed my herd, then me. Even my horse's ears were indistinct and from there to Chittem Springs, I was trapped in a strange twilight where I could not even see the ground from atop my horse.

Instead of blowing on through like a west fog normally did, it kept us trapped in the pasture at Chittem for two days before we were able to hit the trail for home.

I always hated trailing in the fog. For one thing, I was always lost unless I was in a lane! It's bad enough to get lost, but when you're lost with two or three thousand sheep, that can complicate the situation, especially if you are trying to avoid another herder with another two or three thousand sheep!

One fall, we had trailed the sheep to the foot of the mountains where we cut out and trucked the lambs from Blue Creek Ranch's corrals to market. After the last of the lambs had been loaded, we started the ewes back up the mountain. Night overtook us at the top of the slope where we put the ewes into another corral so they wouldn't go back looking for their lambs. Next morning, we awoke to a pea soup fog, much to my dismay. We went from the corral into Blue Creek Ranch's Carr Springs pasture where they had a herder with a band of sheep.

Brookie assured me there was nothing to worry about, as the herder knew we were coming through and would have his sheep back out of the way. Brookie would be in the lead with the wagon, and if he saw any of their sheep, he had his saddle horse, so he could move them before I got there with my herd.

I watched him disappear into the fog with great misgivings. "All you have to do is follow the road," I told myself. And I did, except that instead of coming to Carr Springs with Blue Creek's camp by it, I crossed a deep draw that was completely alien to me. Then I came to a recently built reservoir in a smaller draw.

I sat there on my horse staring at the raw, earthen dam, wondering when someone built a reservoir by Carr Springs without my knowing about it. Then my herd stopped moving. I rode around them and found out why: they had come up against a fence with an iron gate on the road, and a sign saying, "Please Close Gate."

The light dawned! When the road forked, I had taken the road to Beaver Creek instead of the one to Carr Springs. Instead of following a southwesterly course, I had gone almost straight north. Once I knew where I was, all the landmarks I could see in the fog looked like their old familiar selves!

Quickly, I turned the sheep back, hoping to get where I belonged before Brookie found out I'd been lost. I wouldn't admit to such a dumb blunder! I hadn't gone half the distance when Brookie came riding out of the fog looking for me. He said he came back because he met the Blue Creek herder looking for his herd, which had vanished in the fog. Brookie thought they might come to my sheep, so he came back to help me. I managed to make the rest of the trip back to our camp without getting lost again, and we didn't pick up the Blue Creek sheep, either.

The spring trail was a great event after we got the GI. Besides Vivian and Pete, we usually took one of Brookie's nephews along to help trail. In addition to an assortment of people and their gear, we were apt to have bum lambs and goats, and always at least two cats, which were hauled in a cage while we moved. When we camped for noon or night, they were picketed with several feet of small nylon rope attached to their collars. Their picket pins were bridge spikes pushed into the ground. When we camped for the night the kids each set up their orange nylon pup tents to suit themselves and whoever was helping us slept in a teepee. We usually found snow drifts after we got in the high country so we took the hand-cranked ice cream freezer with us so we could make ice cream. We always left the chickens at the house and moved them up after we got to the summer camp. The Davises' camptender,

Chub Corn, always used to have his little chuckle by asking me each summer if I had much trouble trailing the chickens to the mountains.

After Vivian married and left home and Pete was old enough to have a summer job we began trailing by ourselves again, and it was certainly a lot less complicated! Just as we used to do, I was always the sheepherder and Brookie was the camptender.

Most of the trails were uneventful to the point of being boring, and that was the way I liked it: no bad storms, no bad roads, no mix-ups. But occasionally we did have things out of the ordinary happen, both good and bad.

As I trailed up the road behind my herd of sheep Memorial Day morning in 1965 I was already looking forward to breakfast. It was our first full day out on the trail; we had trailed to the American Watergap from the ranch the afternoon before and spent the night there. It was a clear, beautiful morning, and I was pushing the tail end of the herd because I expected it to get warm early in the day and it was a long way to the Fifteen-Mile bridge, where we would be nooning.

I rode my horse down over the highway embankment to move a bunch of stragglers along. Just as she stepped back up onto the pavement she either slipped or stumbled and fell. Instinctively I kicked my foot loose from the stirrup, but I didn't have time to get it out of the way as she went down flat on her side on the highway with my leg under her. I kicked my other foot loose before she scrambled to her feet, and managed to hold onto one rein. If my leg was broken I didn't want to be left afoot, though how I planned to get back on her hadn't entered my mind.

I pulled her over to me by the reins, reached up and got hold of the stirrup and managed to stand up. I felt faint from pain and shock, but after a few moments the faintness passed and I made myself step gingerly on my crippled leg. Everything held together and since I neither heard or felt any bones grating I decided nothing was broken.

By the time I managed to get on my horse I was sweating from pain and feeling faint again. Brookie was a mile or more ahead of me with the wagon, and it never occurred to me to ride up through the sheep and overtake him to let him know I'd been hurt. A good soldier never deserted his post of duty, and I guess I thought the same applied to sheepherders. I rode along in a haze of pain, hoping someone would come along the road so I could let Brookie know I was in trouble, but since it was a holiday, there had been no traffic at all, and no one ever came. I was in such a state when I finally got the wagon with the tail end of the sheep that the smell of coffee and pancakes for once didn't do a thing for me!

Brookie helped me off the horse after he learned what had happened. His first concern was that my foot might be so swollen we couldn't get my boot off. I had been afraid to remove it after the fall because I had a confused feeling that it was holding my foot and leg together!

I gritted my teeth and tried not to flinch or groan as he worked my boot off. I don't know which of us was the more shocked when we saw my foot and leg. From my knee to the ends of my toes I was the color of grape juice, and the impact had been so great it squeezed the blood out from under my toenails! Brookie was horrified! After lecturing me soundly for not riding into one of the ranches to get help, he unhooked the pickup from the wagon and headed for the Meikes' to bring someone up to take over the sheep while he took me to the doctor.

Sweat continued to pour off me from the pain, a phenomenon I had never experienced before. I couldn't think of eating, but I drank large quantities of water.

In a short while Brookie drove up with Pete and Naomi right behind him in their car. They would take over the afternoon move while Brookie took me to town in their car. My leg was terribly swollen by now, and I couldn't bend my knee, so getting me in the car was fun! We finally accomplished what was beginning to seem like the impossible by having me back up to the doorway of the car and just fall in backward. Once on our way I told Brookie I was going to have to stop at Kaycee so I could go to the bathroom! He said we would stop at Aunt Della's.

My Aunt Della still lived in the little house east of Kaycee where Julie was born. She was beginning to fail in her old age and was also diabetic. Mom had been at loose ends since Dad's death in 1960, so she had come to live with Aunt Della and look after her.

Mom was very upset when she saw my awful-looking leg. She and Brookie tried to get me out of the car so I could use the old outhouse that sat behind Della's garage, but the pain was so excruciating every time I tried to move my leg that I finally told them I'd have to wait till we got to the hospital. Mom brought me a big glass of cold water, which I gratefully gulped down before we proceeded on.

Because it was a holiday we went directly to the emergency room at the hospital. When the nurse saw my leg she exclaimed, "Oh, no! The doctor on duty just left for home after doing an emergency appendectomy on a little girl from Kaycee. Wait a minute and I'll call his wife and have her send him back down." As if we were going any place!

The nurse and Brookie finally got me out of the car by pulling me around so my feet were on the ground. They each took one of my hands and pulled me to my feet. I nearly passed out, and sweat poured off me.

I was so nearly out of it by the time they got me in a wheelchair I only vaguely recall being pushed up the ramp to the emergency room. The nurse handed me a cold, wet washcloth to wipe my face with, and I came back to reality.

The doctor would need x-rays, the nurse said, so we went to the x-ray room. I noticed some large paper cups sitting on a sort of sideboard and I told the nurse I was so thirsty I wished I had one of those full of cold water. She left and in a few moments was back with one full of water and chipped ice. By the time the doctor arrived I had drunk nearly all of it.

Dr. Tom (Nicholas) was a little peevish at being called back to the hospital, but he needled me good-naturedly as he prepared to x-ray my leg. "How come you horseback people are always giving us skiers a bad time about broken limbs?" he asked. "It seems to me I'm called on to patch up way more horse-related injuries than I ever do ski accidents."

The x-rays showed no broken bones, which surprised me. The way my ankle hurt I figured I must have at least one fracture. All the pain in the knee area was from pulled ligaments, Dr. Tom told us, and he would put my leg in a cast from above the knee to the ankle.

"Will I be able to ride with a cast?" I asked.

"No!" he said emphatically.

"But Brookie needs me to trail the sheep," I protested. "Isn't there some alternative to a cast?"

"I can put you in the hospital for two or three days," he sighed, with either exasperation or resignation, "and treat your leg with moist hot packs. If we can get the swelling down I can wrap it with an elastic bandage."

So I was admitted to the hospital, and Brookie left to go back to his trailing job. An aide took me to a room in a wheelchair and helped me get undressed and into a hospital gown. As soon as she had me in bed she gave me some pain medication and brought me the standard hospital pack: bed pan, bath pan, soap, Kleenex, thermometer, and a pitcher of ice water and a glass.

I poured a glass of water and drank it, and was suddenly uncomfortably aware of how full my bladder was. When I told the aide I needed to go to the bathroom she said the doctor's orders said I was not to get out of bed. In fact, I was not to move my leg if I could avoid it.

I have never been on good terms with bed pans, and the minute the aide slid this one under me my brain suffered a short-circuit of some kind. My bladder kept receiving the message from my brain to relieve myself, but the message stopped right there and nothing happened. I remembered hearing someone say, "I couldn't have peed a drop if my bladder had been bustin'!" Here I was, faced literally with such a situation!

The aide assumed it was because she was in the room so she left, telling me she'd be back in a few minutes. She returned to find me getting rather desperate. When I told her I hadn't been to the bathroom since early morning and she learned how much water I'd drunk, she got concerned, too. She turned the water on in the washbowl so I could hear it, thinking that might prime me. It made the urge to go even greater, but still nothing happened.

"We'll probably have to put a catheter in you," she told me.

"Oh, no!" I protested. "I know I could go if I could use the bathroom. It's the thought of this bed pan that shuts me off."

"But I can't go against the doctor's orders," she said.

"Can't we bend them a little?" I asked. "If we had a commode we could put it right here by the bed and all I'd have to do is slide off the bed."

"Tell you what," she said, "I'll run next door to the nursing home and borrow one of their potty chairs."

She came back carrying what looked like an ordinary, straight-backed chair with arms, but when she removed the seat cushion, a cover lifted off and it was a potty chair! Between the two of us we managed to get me out of bed, onto the floor and on the potty chair without a disaster. And it had the desired effect, too! The chair was a fixture in the room as long as I was there!

If I hadn't been so worried about Brookie I would have enjoyed the next two days. No getting up in the chilly dawn, nothing to do but lie there and be waited on. The meals were good and I really caught up on my sleep, especially when they had the steam heat on my leg. It was very soothing and was really reducing the swelling. I hadn't had any pain medication since the morning after I was admitted. Word of my accident had gotten around the Sussex-Kaycee area, so everyone from our neck of the woods who came to town dropped in to visit.

By Wednesday morning I was getting itchy to get out of there. Dr. Tom told me that morning that my leg was looking good and I could leave as soon as I could make arrangements for someone to pick me up. Then, like the answer to a prayer, Brookie's nephew Dallas Turk and his wife, Pat, arrived. They had come off the mountains that morning from their summer range on Arch Creek. Brookie was at the Hibbard Stockrest, so they had stopped to talk to him and had promised to bring me out if the doctor would release me. They thought he missed me and was anxious to get me back home!

He was doing fine, they assured me. Sonny Jarrard had been coming every morning and afternoon to trail the sheep for him. Sonny had a small ranch on North Fork and had made a deal with Pete to run his little band of sheep with the Meike sheep that summer on the mountains. We were to pick them up with our herd as we passed by. Sonny had come to the rescue when Brookie called him and told him he was in a bind.

Dr. Tom showed me how to wrap my knee with an elastic bandage so I wouldn't shut the circulation off and told me to stay off my leg as much as I could until all the swelling was gone. I assured him it felt fine. I didn't tell him my ankle still hurt almost as much as the day Brookie brought me in. I figured it would heal eventually, and I didn't want anything to keep me from going back to camp!

As we drove from Buffalo to Kaycee we could see thunderstorm activity all along the top of the mountains. The Turks stopped only long enough at the wagon for Brookie to help me out of their pickup because they were hoping to get home before it rained. When the rain came it was a "goose drownder!" In a short while the storm went grumbling on off toward the east and we were left sitting in a quagmire of adobe and bentonite. Brookie said it was a good thing he had decided to lay over at the stockrest for the night because we couldn't have moved anyway. The sheep couldn't escape because the stockrest was fenced, so we spent a leisurely evening catching up on everything that had happened. Brookie cooked me a good supper, insisting that I stretch out on the bed and take it easy. I was so glad to be home!

We waited next morning until the mud was starting to set up before we hit the trail. Sonny had arrived earlier, saddled Tress and was gathering the sheep so he could put them out on the trail. I got down off the bed and was going to go sit in the pickup while Brookie packed the wagon for moving. After assuring him I didn't need any assistance, I stood on the doorstep debating whether I should step on the wagon tongue with my good foot or my bad one. The wagon tongue, made of two-inch pipe, was covered with mud where Brookie had been stepping on it. Failing to take note of that, I finally decided to step down with my game leg first. The next thing I knew, my foot slipped off the muddy tongue and my ankle snapped loudly as I hit the ground with my entire weight on my bad foot. For one horrible moment I thought I'd broken my ankle. Then I realized that the pain was gone! We decided something had dislocated when Tress fell on it, and when I fell it popped into place.

The night we camped at the foot of the mountains I convinced Brookie and Sonny I could take over the trailing, so Sonny went home. My knee had limbered up surprisingly since I'd started using it and I could ride with no problem by not using the stirrup. The rest of the trip to camp was uneventful. I never did go back to the doctor for a checkup and the knee made a complete recovery.

Exactly a year later, Memorial Day morning found us climbing the slope of the mountains. I don't recall why, but I was riding Brownie, the big, chocolate-colored horse Brookie had been using for several years. I seldom rode Brownie. He was so tall I could hardly mount him on flat ground because I couldn't reach the stirrup. I cheated by using anything I could find to stand on to give me the extra reach I needed. Besides his size, he didn't like me. With everyone else he had a calm, tractable disposition but with me he was impatient, nervous, and downright mean. Usually when I trailed sheep I walked almost as much as I rode. If I led Brownie he either stepped on my heels or bit me, and I don't mean playful nips—he meant to do damage!

The trail from the Little Park to the Big Park unnerved me because the trees were so dense I always felt claustrophobic. Brownie seemed to delight in trying to brush me off on the lower-growing tree branches. Even when I stayed on the road I had to watch him every minute. Whoever the enterprising souls were who built the road years before, they'd had to clear rocks and trees to allow passage of wagons, and they hadn't made it a bit wider than necessary. The trees growing along the edge had been trimmed so all of them had snags sticking out where limbs had been hacked off.

I relaxed my attention long enough to scan the trees for stragglers above the road and the next instant, Brownie rammed my knee into one of those jagged limb ends with such force it broke loose from the tree and I was nearly unhorsed! I was almost afraid to check the damage because I could feel blood running down my leg into my boot. There was a big rip in my almost new Levis and a matching one in my knee. The snag had glanced off the inside edge of my kneecap and torn through my flesh toward the inside of my knee.

By the time I got my handkerchief out of my hip pocket and wadded it over the wound, my pant leg was soaked with blood. Just as I came out of the trees I met Brookie riding back to help me with the sheep. Blood was seeping between my fingers where I was pressing the bloody hanky against my leg. Brookie looked horrified at the sight of all that blood, and I tried to assure him it was not as bad as it looked.

As soon as we got to the wagon he cleaned up the blood, and it was easy to see I had a pretty nasty gash. His attempts to pull the edges together and tape them weren't very successful, and blood continued to seep through the gauze pad he put on it.

We'd have been in a real predicament if Pete—our son, this time, not Pete Meike—and his college buddy Norbert and their girlfriends hadn't arrived just then from Casper. Norbert volunteered to stay and help Brookie make the afternoon move while Pete and the girls took me to the doctor.

Of course, the doctor on call that day was Dr. Tom! "What's this thing you have about Memorial Day?" he asked me as he prepped my leg for stitches—seven of them. "Come back in a week and I'll take the stitches out," he told me as he bandaged my knee.

"In a week I'll be too far down the trail to come back," I replied.

"Well, Brookie can take them out. Tell him to cut the stitches with a pair of manicure scissors or his nail clippers and pull them out with tweezers. Be sure to sterilize everything first, including the wound."

It was after dark by the time we got to the camp. The kids left for Casper immediately and I was so pooped from the day's events all I wanted to do was go to bed.

The day the stitches were to come out I noticed a strange reluctance on Brookie's part to get at the project. We had made our morning move, breakfast was over, and the sheep were contentedly digesting their morning's feed. I assembled scissors, tweezers, and antiseptic, bared my leg for the procedure, and sat waiting for him to get going.

He gave the stitches what seemed like an unnecessarily long scrutiny. "Don't you think we ought to wait another day?" he asked.

"Go ahead," I ordered, getting fidgety with all this delay.

Meticulously he swabbed antiseptic on my knee with a piece of cotton, dipped the scissors, then the tweezers in the little bowl of peroxide. At last he picked up the scissors and bent over my leg, which he had stretched across his lap. I suddenly felt a trifle unnerved and I looked away. I felt a tiny little prick as the point of the scissors went under a stitch, and a slight pull as he removed the stitch.

Then Brookie laid down the tweezers, lifted my leg off his lap, and stood up. I looked up at him and saw his face was pale under his tan.

"You'll have to do it," he said. He abruptly wheeled and went outside.

I sat there, dumbfounded by this turn of events. Brookie certainly wasn't squeamish by nature; people who worked with livestock couldn't be. I'd watched him suture cuts that were pouring blood, pull lambs that had been dead long enough they stank to high heaven; he'd even cleaned the gore off my leg when I got hurt!

"Well," I thought, "I guess I can do it if I have to."

Actually, it was kind of fascinating, working the sharp point of the scissors under a stitch, snipping it, then gripping one of the loose ends with the tweezers and pulling it out. As I pulled each one I dripped peroxide in the tiny puncture holes and watched it fizz. When I finished I put a bandage over it, cleaned up the "operating area," and went to the door.

"All done," I said cheerfully.

Brookie was fiddling with something on his saddle. He strode over and put his arms around me. "I'm sorry. I just couldn't do it. I was afraid I'd hurt you when I pulled the stitches. I had to pull so hard on that first one."

"They all pulled a little, but it didn't really hurt," I told him. I couldn't resist teasing him a little. "What would we have done if I hadn't been able to take them out, either?" I asked.

He grinned his lop-sided grin. "Then I could have done it."

One little trailing episode that I never told Brookie about had nothing to do with the sheep. In fact, I never told anyone about it until just recently. I was trailing through the Sawmill Lane one fall afternoon on our way off the mountains. A sheepman named Woosley had the range on both sides of the lane.

As I came abreast of his sheepcamp, which was about fifty yards from the trail, his little Mexican herder, Juan, came from the wagon and intercepted me. Juan was a very small man, with a leathery face that gave little clue as to his age. He could have been forty or seventy. All the years I'd been passing this way with sheep, I'd been meeting him, and he'd always been friendly, polite, respectful. He'd also always been sober. As he walked up alongside my horse, I realized he was very drunk.

As he stood looking blearily up at me, he reached out and grasped my leg. My first thought was that he was so unsteady on his feet he was clutching at me for support. This idea took flight, however, when he said, "Your man, he old?"

Brookie was probably forty-five at the time. I shook my head and said "No," sidestepping my horse away from him and his boozy breath.

"He no good in bed," Juan declared. "You need real man. You come back my wagon tonight. I take care you."

I was outraged and wheeled my horse to ride away.

He stumbled after me and produced a Hershey bar and a Milky Way from his coat pocket. "Here, here," he implored me. "You take. In winter I live in Worland. You need man, you come see me."

I hurried after the tail end of my herd, overwhelmed by a variety of feelings—anger, outrage, disgust. "That dirty little creep!" I thought. "How dare he assume I was that kind of woman! To proposition me so crudely—and for two candy bars!"

As I rode along behind the sheep fuming, I thought, "I'll tell Brookie when we camp this evening and he'll go back and kill him; or at least threaten him!"

Then I began to visualize Brookie's reaction. It was the kind of incident that would tickle his funny bone, and I could almost hear him telling it, as over the years it became one of his stock of little anecdotes. And that was the reason I've kept it to myself for so long.

Vivian got married during her sophomore year of high school, but Raleigh and Pete both graduated and went on to college. Pete's high school graduation in May 1962 turned out to be even more memorable than we had anticipated.

Pete's hearing aid developed a problem just days before graduation. After he notified Beltone in Casper, they sent someone to Buffalo with a "loaner" for him to use and took the ailing one back for repairs. Two days before graduation we were notified that Pete's hearing aid was ready. It had rained steadily for the past twenty-four hours, and everything at the Meike Ranch was at a standstill, so we decided to take the day off and go to Casper and pick it up.

The rain continued to pour down as we drove to Casper, transacted our business, visited some of the relatives, and drove home again. The road from the highway to our house was a sea of mud and water as we drove in just after dark.

Tired by the long day of driving in the rain, we went to bed early. The next thing I knew I was startled awake by a loud banging on our front door. Then the door crashed open. "Turks, are you awake?" Don hollered. "Get up! Powder River's running past the corner of your yard!"

"We're awake!" Brookie yelled back, and indeed we were!

I don't remember either of us saying a word as we fumbled into our clothes, grabbed a flashlight, and hurried outside. I've had a lot of nightmares but nothing as frightening as those first few seconds when we stood there with the rain pouring down and saw water swirling and gurgling wherever Brookie swung the beam of the flashlight. To me the most frightening thing was the darkness and the roar of the water. That was when I discovered that flood water has a disgusting odor. I have no words to describe it because I have never smelled anything else that has that stink!

I felt totally bewildered, like an old hen that had been thrown off the roost in the middle of the night. I had always prided myself on being level-headed in a crisis, but this was unlike any crises I'd ever been faced with. "What'll we do, what'll we do?" I kept saying. If I wasn't wringing my hands I should have been!

Brookie suggested we ought to go back in out of the rain and pick everything up off the floor. Once we began to do something constructive I began to feel a little more in control of the situation and less like I was in a bad dream. We jerked out all the lower dresser drawers and stacked them on the beds. In the kitchen we piled cupboard drawers on the table and emptied lower shelves of pots and pans and piled them in the sink. The lower shelves of the bookcases had to be emptied, the living room drapes tied up so they wouldn't be in the water if it got in the house.

Finally, having picked up everything we could see, I voiced the question that had been nagging at me. "Where are we going to spend the night?"

Brookie, as usual, came up with a logical solution: we could hook onto the sheep wagon and pull it out to the highway and go to higher ground. We planned on moving to the mountains to start repairing fence as soon as graduation was over, so I had been stocking the wagon with groceries. Over the years I had managed to get the wagon completely equipped with bedding, dishes, and so on, which greatly simplified moving into the wagon in the spring and back into the house in the fall. All I had to transfer were our clothes, perishable food, and canned goods.

While Brookie got the jeep I filled two gallon jugs with water and splashed my way out to the wagon, which was parked behind the house. To my relief I discovered that the flood water was only four or five inches deep. Getting the wagon hooked to the jeep was an exercise in frustration! Brookie couldn't see where he was backing unless I shone the light on the front of the wagon. Then I couldn't see to hook the wagon to the trailer hitch. Finally, after several tries and some shouting back and forth—"If you'd shine the light so I could see what I'm doing!" and "If I do then I can't see what I'm doing!" I got lucky and made connections.

Once we left the area of the buildings we could only guess where the road was, since there was nothing between us and the highway but water—lots of water! Because the house site was a little higher than the rest of the river bottom, we were now in much deeper water, and the current was strong enough I could feel it pushing against the side of the station wagon. Dimly we could make out the gate posts in the highway fence where our access road joined the highway, so we aimed for that. I breathed a great sigh of relief as we pulled up onto the highway because the beam of the flashlight had showed the water almost up to the bottoms of the doors on the jeep.

We followed the highway out past the Longs' and turned off into the Johnson Creek pasture across from their place. We didn't get far because it was so muddy, but at least we were up away from the river. The wagon was fairly level so we unpacked, stripped off our wet clothes, and crawled into bed. As we laid there listening to the rain drumming on the wagon top we suddenly realized that in all the confusion we'd left the dogs at the house! I wanted to go back and rescue them, but Brookie vetoed that. As strong as the current was when we came out, he said, it had probably gouged out holes in the roadway by now. If we fell in one it would drown the motor and we might end up washing away in the jeep. He assured me the dogs would be all right, especially if they stayed in the yard, but even so I laid awake a long time imagining all kinds of dismal scenarios.

When we awoke before daylight the next morning the rain had quit, which was encouraging. Daylight had come by the time we finished breakfast and revealed not the clear day we'd hoped for, but a leaden gray cloud cover threatening more rain at any minute.

We unhooked the jeep from the wagon and drove down the road to our turn-off. What an awesome sight! The old saying about Powder River being a mile wide certainly looked to be true, but it was very definitely more than an inch deep! I had hoped against hope that the river wouldn't get in the house, but we could plainly see that the water was up to it.

The dogs were nowhere to be seen. We tried calling them, though I doubted they'd be able to hear us above the roar of the river. To our relief they came sloshing around from behind the house. They responded to our attempts to call them out by wagging their bedraggled tails but stayed on the front door step.

Jack Andrew and his teenage boys, Elton and Art, drove up just then and volunteered to wade in and rescue them. Brookie decided to go along so he could see how things were at the house. At the last minute I decided to go, too, because my dog, Willie, was never very friendly to anyone but Brookie and Pete and me. We weren't thinking very clearly or we would never have attempted anything so foolhardy. The fact that the water was up around the house should have told us it was much deeper than when we came out the night before because it wasn't even up in the front yard when we left. The current was now very strong between the highway and the house and before we had gone very far we were in knee-deep water, then thigh-deep, and in some places hip-deep. Several times the cross-current nearly washed my feet out from under me, but I was afraid to turn back because I was having a real problem with my equilibrium. The water swirling around me gave me the sensation that I was falling over. The only way I could maintain my balance was to keep my eyes off the water and on the house.

A quick look through the windows showed the floors were covered with water, and I wondered sadly what it was doing to my beautiful off-white, patterned vinyl linoleum on the floor of the new room. Earlier in the spring I had set out three little apple trees in the front yard and spaded up and seeded a new piece of lawn at the west end of the old part of the house. The grass had germinated well and had begun to look like grass rather than frog hair. Now it was under several inches of water.

Brookie's dog, Skipper, was old and fat and placid, and when we started to wade away from the house she willingly followed. Then the current caught her and started carrying her away even though she paddled frantically. I began calling her as I tried to overtake her. Wading through water that deep was like wading through cold molasses. At the sound of my voice she managed to turn toward me and began trying to reach me. By this time the current had carried her around the corner of the yard and into a kind of backwater formed by the buildings where I managed to reach her. Holding on to her collar I maneuvered her back to the corner of the yard, both of us panting from our exertions and near panic.

Brookie suggested that if I held on to her collar while she swam across it would keep her from washing away and would also help keep me upright. Once more we waded into the swirling murky water, keeping fairly close together so if someone got in trouble the rest of us would be near enough to give assistance.

Willy had ignored all our coaxing, sitting stolidly in the water on the door step, but when he finally realized Skipper was leaving he plunged into the flood and swam after us. As he caught up with us, Jack, thinking he needed help, reached out and grabbed his collar. Before I could yell a warning, Willy wrenched free and snapped at Jack's hand, drawing blood. The dog swam so strongly that he outdistanced us and was waiting at the jeep when we all sloshed up on to the highway. Jack's dogbite looked pretty bad, so after emergency first aid at the Meike Ranch, he drove to Midwest where Dr. Hart, the oil company doctor gave him proper treatment.

The rain that had threatened all morning didn't materialize and by afternoon, not only did the clouds begin to move out but the water began to drop. The next morning the river was back in its banks, leaving the river bottom a mess of sand bars, mud flats, water holes, and drifts of debris.

We were able to drive to the house, where we began the monumental task of cleaning up. We were severely handicapped by the lack of clean water. Our water system, consisting of an electric pump and storage tank, is six feet below the surface of the ground in a "cave" about six feet by six feet. This is covered by a slope-roofed structure about four feet high at the front and slopes to the ground at the back. The door to the well house is in the front; the top and the three remaining sides have a two foot layer of dirt covering them as insulation to prevent freezing in the winter. The well house had filled with flood water, so our water system was a lost cause.

The Meikes had a flowing well that supplied water for the livestock over across the highway, so we hauled water from there to start our clean-up. The whole yard was under a layer of gray, slimy mud. The floor in the house was under a similar layer, we discovered when we opened the door; the water had seeped away, leaving an inch or so of residue behind.

When we built the new room on the house we abandoned the furnace under the house as a heat source and installed propane gas heating stoves in the new room and in the lean-to. We no longer needed to store coal under the house, so we had covered up the coal chute and the area directly out from that was where I had planted the lawn. The flood water had washed away the fill-in dirt in the chute and filled the basement with water. As the water poured down the chute, it mixed with all the loose dirt that made up the basement floor, creating a mud soup that came up through the cracks in the floor of the old part of the house. So we had a lot more mud to contend with than if we'd simply had plain flood water.

Cleaning up turned out to be a worse nightmare than the flood itself. All forenoon we scooped up soupy mud and dumped it in buckets and carried it out of the yard. When we broke at noon to fix a bit to eat, I was so discouraged I almost wished the house had washed away—at least we wouldn't have been faced with this seemingly hopeless task.

In mid-afternoon we quit, got ourselves cleaned up, put on our good clothes, and headed for Buffalo for the graduation ceremonies, which were scheduled for 7 P.M. at the high school gym. I managed to put the disaster at home to the back of my mind and enjoy the momentous occasion. It hardly seemed possible that baby Pete was standing up there, six feet tall, accepting his high school diploma! "Where had the time gone?" I wondered. Whenever we were involved in some disagreeable task, Brookie would say, "How time flies when you're having fun!" For some reason this old cliché flitted across my tired brain, and I had to forcefully quell the hysterical laughter that welled up inside of me when I thought of what was waiting for us at home.

We had driven Don's car to the graduation, and Pete Meike told us when we arrived at the high school that he needed to ride back out with us. When the festivities were over we headed for home with Pete driving. I had crawled in the back seat, hoping to sleep, but my mind jumped from one thing to another, always coming back to what was still to be done at the house before we could move to the mountains.

A lot of my pictures were in albums in a drawer, but I had run out of space and neglected to buy more albums. All the extra snapshots plus all my negatives were in a box under our bed—the one thing we missed when we put everything up off the floor. I discovered them the next morning when I was cleaning the bedroom floor. All the negatives were stuck together in a big, sticky mess, as were the pictures.

That day, someone brought a sump pump over from Linch and pumped out all the basements. When they got to our place they pumped out the well house first, then drove the vacuum truck around to our west yard fence. When I looked out, two men with big, rubber boots were clomping across what was left of my little patch of new lawn, dragging the hose, which they put down the chute into the so-called basement.

That was the last straw! I went in the bedroom, closed the door, and sat on the bed among all my ruined snapshots and negatives and cried and cried. Later, I was able to replace most of the pictures, as I always had extra prints made to send the relatives. My mom had several albums full of the pictures I'd sent her over the years, so we had negatives made from them.

As soon as we had the floors cleaned we moved to the mountains to start repairing fences. What a disheartening summer that was. We were without clean water at the house until after we moved off the mountains that fall. My sister-in-law June Brown had volunteered to haul water for the little apple trees so I wouldn't have to do that on our trips down. One day we noticed the leaves were turning yellow on the trees. Brookie thought June had forgotten to water them, so he filled a barrel at the flowing well so he could give them a good soaking. In a few minutes he called me to come look. He had poured a bucket of water at the base of each tree. Instead of sinking into the ground it just lay there. Apparently the flood run-off had brought so much bentonite down from the bentonite beds that it had effectively sealed the top of the ground and no water could penetrate.

Brookie got an iron rod and punched holes all around the trees and we used most of that barrel of water before we had the roots saturated. From then on the little trees thrived. I'm sure our theory was correct because by the following spring, many of the cottonwoods that lined Powder River had died.

The kitchen linoleum was a casualty of the flood. It had been completely saturated, and as it dried out, the vinyl checked and cracked just like the mud did in the yard. After we moved back in the house that fall we decided we would have to discard it and put down new linoleum. When we tried to pull it up we discovered it was glued to the floor with a thin layer of dried mud. We ended up stripping it off in pieces. Brookie decided not to put down more linoleum. Instead he put down masonite in a big, checkerboard pattern after he found out he could get it in two colors—a light tan and a darker brown. Several coats of varnish gave it a mirror finish that was very pretty.

Russ Streeter retrieved our pump from the well house during the summer and tried to clean it up, but it was so badly damaged we had to buy and install a new pump.

Before cold weather came we had to take the heating stoves apart and clean the mud out of the burners. Though the bottom of our propane water heater was full of mud, the burner itself was high enough that it escaped.

During the summer we dropped off our dirty clothes at the laundry in Kaycee on our weekly trips to the house and picked them up on the return trip in the afternoon, all washed, dried, and folded. This was pretty handy for me, since the alternative would have been to go back to a wash tub and a scrub board. Though it was a nice vacation from doing laundry, I was more than happy when we finally got everything working again at the house so I could do my own washing.

The Sussex store building was so badly damaged by the flood that it was abandoned. Since the building also housed the post office and living quarters for whoever was running the store and post office, it meant some drastic changes to the Sussex community. Al Lohse had retired as storekeeper and post master in 1960 due to ill health, and his son Alvin and daughter-in-law Wanda had taken over. After the flood my folks' homestead cabin was moved in north of the abandoned store building. The post office reopened in it with Dana Lohse, wife of Al's oldest son, Glen, acting as post master. The following spring all of the patrons of the Sussex post office were notified to install mailboxes at their turn-off from the highway and on May 24, 1963, the post office was officially closed. Sussex became a ghost town.

I don't think any of us had ever really appreciated what an important role the store and post office played in our community. Going after the mail was always a break in routine, and there were usually several people there picking up their mail to exchange news with, comment on the weather, or speculate on some piece of gossip.

The absence of the store certainly changed our buying habits. If you discovered ten minutes before a meal that you needed a loaf of bread, it meant you went without because no one was going to make the forty-mile round-trip dash to Kaycee for a loaf of bread. Some of us die-hards speculated hopefully that maybe someone would start up a new store, though we all knew deep down there just wasn't enough business in our small ranching community to make such an undertaking pay.

*Skipper, George, and Louise on the mountain, 1959*

*Trailing off the mountains via Barnum, the modern way, 1970.*

*Brookie and Louise, September 1959*

# TRAIL'S END

## (1973-1981)

During the winter and spring of 1973 I noticed that Brookie seemed to have no energy at all, and he looked bad. During lambing he was often too tired by evening to eat supper and went to bed almost as soon as we got home from work. I suggested he ought to see a doctor, but he insisted he was just older and the work was harder for him.

Once we got to the mountains things would be better, I thought, because we wouldn't be under the daily pressure we were during lambing. Instead, things got worse. Climbing up and down mountains fixing fence was just too much for him, so I did all the fence repairing where he couldn't drive to it with the pickup. He was always so exhausted when we arrived back at camp he would climb on the bed and fall asleep while I was fixing a meal. As often as not he was too tired to eat when I had it ready.

Just as I would be convinced he had to see a doctor, he would take a turn for the better. My fears would subside until he had another spell of lethargy, listlessness, and drowsiness. I was so concerned about his health that I was very relieved when we left the mountains earlier than usual with the livestock that fall.

We had only been at the house a few days when I made an appointment at the clinic in Buffalo for Brookie's annual flu shot. The day he was scheduled to go he woke up nauseated and was running a temperature, so we decided we'd better stay home. A little later he came out of the bedroom dressed in his "town clothes" and announced he was feeling better, so I hurriedly got ready and we left for Buffalo.

Several miles north of Kaycee he suddenly pulled over to the edge of the road and said, "You'll have to drive. I'm too sick." I knew he must be terribly ill to ask me to drive. He would never ride in a car with anyone else driving because he always got carsick.

After we got in town he complained of being terribly thirsty, so I took him to Carol and Halsey's house. He wouldn't go in because he was afraid he had something contagious, so I brought a big glass of water out to the pickup.

He gulped it down and said, "It doesn't help a bit. The water just slides over my tongue and down my throat and my mouth is as dry as ever."

Since Brookie's appointment at the clinic wasn't until one o'clock, I decided to go do our little bit of business so we could leave immediately after he got his shot. I drove to one of the service stations and bought a new battery for Pete's old Volkswagen Bug. At that time a new battery had to have the acid solution added when you bought it. They told me it would be about half an hour before it was ready.

As we sat in the pickup waiting, Brookie noticed the pop machine in front of the station.

"I'm so thirsty," he said hoarsely. "Maybe a can of root beer would quench my thirst."

He drank several swallows. "I'm so sick I've just got to lie down," he said. "Could we go down to the park where there's some shade?"

I quickly drove to the park after telling the station attendant we would come back and pick up the battery later—much later, as it turned out.

I helped Brookie stretch out on the grass in the shade of some bushes, and it was then I realized just how sick he really was. His eyes stared past me, glassy and unseeing. When I tried to rouse him he mumbled incoherently. With fear-induced strength I managed to get him to his feet and to the pickup, but loading him in was almost beyond my capability. He was like an empty sack. Just as I despaired of lifting his bulk—he weighed close to 250 pounds at that time—he rallied a bit and was able to help himself enough that I dumped him sprawling into the seat. I slammed the door and ran around to the driver's side and drove to the clinic in a panic.

It was 12:30 and everyone had gone to lunch except for one girl who was manning the desk and answering the phone. I explained the situation to her.

"Take him to the emergency entrance at the hospital," she said. "I'll call them and tell them to get one of the doctors."

The next hour was like a bad dream. Brookie was helped from the pickup by three white-coated people, put in a wheelchair, and wheeled up the ramp into the emergency room, where he was transferred to a table. I sat there holding his hand, waiting for a doctor.

At one point the county coroner came walking through. "You're too early, Bill!" Brookie croaked when he saw who it was. "I ain't dead yet."

The doctor arrived at last and began firing questions at us while he made a quick examination of Brookie. In a few minutes they moved him to a room and left me sitting there. I was so unfamiliar with hospital procedure that I had no idea what was expected of me. I just sat there, thinking someone would come back and tell me something.

After half an hour passed I went looking for information. I found the nurses' desk and the nurse on duty said Brookie had been admitted by Dr. Pat.

"What room is he in?" I asked.

"You can't go in," she informed me crisply.

"Well, what's wrong with him?"

"I can't release that information."

At last I got her to tell me I would have to ask the doctor about his condition, and, oh yes, the doctor had already gone to the clinic to begin his afternoon of seeing patients. If I wanted to talk to him I'd have to see him there.

I walked across to the clinic and explained to one of the receptionists what I wanted. In a few minutes Dr. Pat came out. "I'm sorry," he apologized. "I thought someone would take you to Brookie's room. He has diabetes, and he's pretty badly dehydrated. I've ordered an I.V. to get his body fluids back to normal, and I've given him insulin to get his blood sugar back down where it belongs. He'll be in the hospital several days until we get his condition stabilized, but he should be feeling better by the time you get back over there. I suspect he's been a borderline diabetic for quite some time, possibly a year or more. Has he been unusually tired and run down? And do you recall if eating sweets made him even more lethargic instead of giving him a boost?"

I thought of the day we left camp at daylight, without breakfast, to go to the Bar C Creek corrals where one of the sheep outfits would be shipping lambs. Brookie, as brand inspector, had to be there to give clearance on the lambs and check what strays were in the herd. What we had anticipated to be a three-hour job at most lasted well into the afternoon. The owner had two large bands of sheep in the corrals, and he had so many strays it looked as if he was running community herds. Even making a three-way cut we had to run the sheep through the chute several times to separate everyone's sheep.

Brookie looked positively gray with exhaustion by the time we headed home with a pickup load of sheep belonging to one of our neighbors. We were barely out of sight of the corral when Brookie pulled over and asked me to drive. In two minutes after changing places he was asleep. He didn't even wake up when I drove into the neighbor's pasture and unloaded the sheep.

At camp he roused himself and crawled wearily onto the bed. "I don't know what's the matter with me," he mumbled, "but I'm completely done in."

"For one thing you haven't head anything to eat since supper last night," I told him. "For another, we've both run 500 miles over there in that corral. Here are a couple of candy bars to hold you until I fix something to eat."

He was asleep almost instantly after he finished the two small candy bars I gave him. When the meal was ready I couldn't awake him sufficiently to get him to eat.

"Later," he muttered. "I'm too tired and sleepy right now."

I could hardly believe the difference in him when I got back over to the hospital. His lips were still cracked and dry looking, but he had color in his face, his eyes were no longer glazed, and he smiled when he saw me. When he was released from the hospital a few days later he said he felt better than he had in years.

I was afraid he might have to have insulin injections, but Dr. Pat said he should be able to control his diabetes by diet alone for the present. We took a crash course in diabetes by studying all the pamphlets, leaflets, and booklets we were loaded down with when we left the hospital.

Brookie had been steadily gaining weight for a number of years, and I had worried about him having a heart attack, but it never occurred to me he might become diabetic. His diabetic diet was so well-balanced that we both began losing weight. Over a period of several months his weight dropped from 250 pounds to 200. Dr. Pat said as long as he kept his weight at about 200 pounds he should be fine.

Brookie looked and felt better than he had for several years, and he had so much energy I could hardly believe it. Projects he had kept putting off because he was always too tired to work on them now became a challenge. We lived as if there would be no tomorrow, even though Dr. Pat had warned us diabetes is a progressive disease and sooner or later Brookie would have to take oral medication to stimulate the pancreas to produce insulin. After three years I convinced myself that his pancreas must be producing insulin normally, which showed how little I really knew about diabetes.

Without warning, Brookie began having trouble keeping his blood sugar down to a safe level no matter how carefully we followed his diet, and the chronic tiredness was back. At last we were forced to face reality. After a thorough check-up, Dr. Pat put him on oral medication. Immediately his blood sugar level stabilized and his energy was back. Eventually the oral medication began to lose its effectiveness, and the doctor put him on stronger pills. The next step, he told us, would be insulin. Brookie vowed he would never use insulin because he couldn't bear the thought of giving himself injections.

Brookie had chronic bronchitis from the time he was a kid, and as long as I had known him he had a little dry, hacking cough. This became more persistent as he got older, so that if he laughed or exerted himself it brought on a paroxysm of coughing. Then he began having problems with what we loosely termed "the flu." At least once every winter he landed in the hospital with pneumonia. He developed a faint wheezing sound if he breathed hard, and finally it was there all the time, due to the bronchitis, the doctors said.

During the summer of 1978 a tourist woman spent a couple of days visiting at our camp on the mountains. While she was eating breakfast with us the morning she planned to leave she complained of a sore throat. By the time she was ready to go she was running a temperature and having chills. She felt so rocky she decided to stay until she felt better. The next morning when she left she was still really under the weather.

Twenty-four hours later Brookie and I both came down with her bug. When my chills and fever began to respond to the aspirin I was taking, and my sore throat eased to where I could swallow without bringing tears to my eyes, I was suddenly aware of how sick Brookie was. He lay on the bed, mumbling incoherently. His lips were dry and cracked from fever, and he constantly shook from chills. I begged him to let me take him to the doctor, but he stubbornly refused, saying he'd be all right as soon as the aspirin worked.

About nine o'clock that evening he sat bolt upright in the bed and said, "I think I'm having a heart attack. I have such pains in my chest!"

"Keep calm," I kept telling myself as I chained the two dogs and put out enough food and water to last them a couple of days. With Brookie loaded in the pickup I headed off into the gathering dusk. Every bump brought a groan from him as I picked my way along the rocky road, until I felt like screaming. The saying "Make haste slowly" kept going around and around in my mind.

It was totally dark long before I reached the foot of the mountains. I breathed a sigh of relief; at least I was on a paved road now, and I could make better time. Or so I thought. Every deer for miles around must have been grazing in the highway lane that night. As I picked my way carefully through them at fifteen miles an hour I kept checking my gas gauge, which was creeping toward empty. I hoped the gas station in Kaycee wouldn't close before I got there. I didn't want to have to get someone out of bed so I could get gas.

After a seeming eternity of watching the glow of eyes in the headlights and trying to guess which way the deer would jump, I reached the intersection at the north edge of town. I saw with relief that the lights were still on at the service station. In a matter of minutes, with a full tank of gas, I was on the interstate headed for Buffalo. After I nearly hit a big buck deer, I was again forced to make haste slowly, straining my eyes for deer feeding in the highway right of way. My nerves were quivering from tension, and my eyes felt as if they were bulging from their sockets by the time I drove up in front of the hospital.

Brookie had subsided into an uneasy sleep or stupor, I wasn't sure which. Occasionally, when he shifted and muttered I asked him how he felt. I never received an answer, but at least I knew he was still alive. When he realized where we were, he insisted on walking into the hospital on his own.

How things had changed since the day I sat in the emergency room wondering what had happened to Brookie. In the ensuing years of doctoring his diabetes I had learned all about hospital procedure. While the doctor on night duty examined him, I filled out and signed admittance papers.

As I sagged in a chair in the waiting room the admitting nurse appeared in the doorway.

"I need your husband's given name," she said sharply, "not some nickname!"

After all I'd been through, her tone of voice immediately raised my hackles, but I made an effort to reply politely, "That is his given name."

"Well," she snapped, "it's certainly a strange name!" She turned to march back to her desk. "Whoever heard of such a name!" she muttered.

At last the doctor came to the waiting room to tell me that Brookie's heart was fine, but he had double pneumonia and was in serious condition. He was being given oxygen, so he should be showing some improvement by the time I came back in the morning.

Shortly before 2 A.M. I stumbled out to the pickup and climbed in the cab, dazed by exhaustion. Should I wake Carol at this time of night or rent a motel room? Suddenly my ability to cope with any decision seemed beyond me. I folded my jacket for a makeshift pillow, laid down in the seat, and sank into oblivion.

Traffic in the street behind me startled me awake a little before six. Except for my eyes being a little dry and scratchy, I felt surprisingly rested. I felt even better after an astonished Carol fed me breakfast and several cups of coffee. She also scolded me soundly for sleeping in the pickup instead of coming to her house.

Back at the hospital the doctor said Brookie was improving, but he would be hospitalized for several days. He was still too ill to care whether I was there or not, so I decided to go back to camp for a couple of days.

This was my first experience of being by myself on the mountains, and I was a little uneasy, aware of how far I was from civilization. What if I should break a leg?

"And how many legs have you broken in the past thirty-seven years?" I asked myself.

"There's a first time for everything," a little voice nagged.

Putting such ridiculous thoughts behind me, I loaded salt and made the rounds of the salt stations. On Davis Mountain I was met by a disturbing sight. In the area between the salt trough and the fence 200 yards away, the coyotes had killed four big black-faced lambs. As I followed the trail of dead lambs I noticed that none of them had been opened up after their throats were cut. A fifth lamb had apparently crashed into the fence in blind panic and was hanging there dead, his head still caught in the mesh of the wire. Tufts of wool had been jerked out of its pelt and scattered about the immediate area. The body had been disemboweled and the choice parts eaten. The entrails were scattered through the grass along the fence.

I called Don on the radio and told him what I'd found. He said he would have the predator control man, Bill Dixon, up there as soon as he could contact him. Just after dark Bill drove into camp and while he drank a cup of coffee I pointed out the location of the kills against the starlit sky. At daylight he was back at my camp. He was pretty sure, he told me, we had a pair of coyotes teaching their pups to hunt. He expected to find the den farther down Beaver Creek.

Two days later I called Don from the hospital to update him on Brookie's condition. Bill had killed the female coyote and four pups, Don told me. The male and one pup escaped. We had no further coyote problems the remainder of the summer, so they apparently relocated after the mother and pups were killed.

Brookie was improving, but he still had a lot of congestion. He was going to be hospitalized for several more days, so I went back up to camp to keep an eye on things. Four days later Dr. Pat reluctantly released Brookie from the hospital. He agreed we could do the same things for Brookie at home that were being done in the hospital. Besides, Brookie was getting downright insistent about going home!

X-rays taken several days earlier showed shadows in the lower parts of both lungs. A tuberculosis test had been negative, and new x-rays taken the day he was released showed the shadowed areas had diminished a little, so we all just assumed it was going to be a slow healing process.

This bout of illness had really weakened Brookie, and he was so slow getting his strength back that I could still see the effects of it when we left the mountains that fall.

While Brookie was in the hospital, Dr. Pat told us a pneumonia shot would be available later in the fall, so in November he went in and was given one. He was pretty much back to normal by this time, except for a persistent cough, which never did completely clear up. Because he seemed to feel good I finally dismissed the cough as bronchitis.

Late one afternoon Brookie was sitting in his big easy chair reading when I plunked myself down on the chair arm, intending to ask him what he'd like me to fix for supper.

"What in the world happened to your finger?" I exclaimed. A water blister covered almost the entire area between the first and middle joints on the back of one of his fingers.

He was as surprised as I was, and he had no idea what caused it. A burn seemed unlikely because, as he pointed out, he would certainly have been aware of a burn that severe. It was not painful, and after a day or so it began to heal. But every few days more of the mysterious blisters appeared on the backs of his hands or fingers.

A trip to the clinic in Buffalo left the doctors as baffled as we were. They told Brookie to soak his hands two or three times a day in a warm Epsom salts solution to help dry up the blisters and ward off infection. Periodically he checked in with the doctors, but nothing changed. The blisters continued to form, and it was sometimes painful for him to bend his fingers when the backs were covered with the scabs the blisters left. The salts dried up the blisters, but his hands were so dry they sometimes cracked and bled.

Early in December Dr. Pat called and said he thought maybe he was on to something. He had been discussing Brookie's case with a Sheridan dermatologist who was pretty certain he knew what was causing the blisters, so Dr. Pat had made an appointment for Brookie. Our trip to Sheridan was nerve wracking. The highway was snow-packed and slick as glass. The streets in Sheridan were no better, and by the time we reached our destination I was wishing we had stayed home.

The doctor took one look at Brookie's hands. "Well, I know what your problem is," he said, "but I'll need to do a blood test to be sure."

The test confirmed his diagnosis, the name of which escapes me all these many years later. The blisters are a symptom of a genetic liver problem which is passed on from father to son and can be present one generation after another without ever surfacing. It manifests itself when the liver produces an oversupply of iron in the blood, which in turn causes sensitivity to ultraviolet rays. The result is blisters, which form on skin exposed to sunlight.

Once the specialist had diagnosed the ailment he turned the case back over to our doctor in Buffalo. The treatment consisted of having a pint of blood taken, a phlebotomy, at least once a month so the body would draw on the oversupply of iron as it replaced the blood. Each time he had blood drawn the iron content was checked, and if it had not lessened since the last time he would have to go back in two weeks instead of a month and have another phlebotomy.

When Brookie had his first pint of blood drawn on December 20, 1978, we came home armed with a carton of thin, white cotton disposable gloves. The doctor had emphasized there was to be no exposure to ultraviolet rays, either outdoors or indoors. If we had fluorescent lights in the house, which we did, we either needed to get rid of them or Brookie would have to wear the gloves and a hat when he was exposed to them. He used to chuckle about what anyone would think if they looked in the window and saw him sitting reading decked out in his white gloves and his old Stetson pulled down to shade his face.

Because I worked with Brookie during the day, I spent the evenings catching up on household chores, such as baking, cooking, and laundry. Brookie liked to read in bed, so unless there was something on TV that he particularly wanted to watch, he always went to bed before I did—in the buff, his customary way of sleeping. Even our reading light in the bedroom was fluorescent. Sometimes when he'd hear me heading for the bedroom he'd fling the covers off so when I walked in he'd be studiously reading, clad only in his white gloves and his old black Scotch cap, making a startling contrast against the white pillow case.

In just a few weeks the existing blisters had completely healed, and no new ones popped up so we knew the treatment was working. Brookie had always worn gloves and a hat or cap when he was working outdoors, but it irked him to have to wear them when he was in the house, especially at mealtime. He swore food didn't taste the same when you fed yourself with gloves on. Eventually he abandoned the indoor protection, saying if he started blistering again he'd go back to it, but he was never bothered by the blisters again.

We had the idea that after three or four phlebotomies the iron would be reduced to a normal level, but this was not the case. I began to really dread the seventy-five-mile trip to Buffalo, especially during lambing when he suddenly found himself having to go every two weeks after it was determined that instead of the iron level dropping, it was rising. I always had to go so I could drive home because he always came out of the clinic as pale as a ghost and feeling completely washed out. It usually took him about thirty-six hours to completely recover.

After we moved to the mountain camp in May it meant we had an eighty-seven-mile drive, one way. At last, in late August, his blood test was normal. A check-up two weeks later showed it was still stable, so he was released from the doctor's care. I felt as if a great weight had been lifted from us. But, as Brookie pointed out, it could have been worse if we'd had to drive to Sheridan for each treatment.

Brookie had a couple of routine blood checks during the next several months, and they were completely normal. In spite of all the health problems he had in the next couple of years, there was never a recurrence of the liver malfunction.

Pete's first marriage had ended in divorce by mutual agreement, with the two of them sharing custody of their three children, Brook, Kari and Clinton. One day in January 1980, he called us from Casper where he was living and working. He had a special girl he wanted us to meet, he said, so he would bring her out on Sunday. Her name was Maggie and they planned on getting married.

We were stunned! Who was Maggie? We'd never even heard of her, and here Pete was telling us he was going to marry her. When the day finally arrived I was in a fine state of nerves speculating on what kind of person she was going to be.

When they drove in I walked out to greet them, and my first thought when she got out of the car was that this small person must be the fiancee's daughter. While I was looking for a third person Pete said, "Mom, I want you to meet Maggie."

When I reached to embrace her she gave me a bear hug that made my ribs creak. "Hi, Mom," she said, and in an undertone, "It's all right if I call you Mom, isn't it?"

The rest of the day I just kept feasting my eyes on her. She was so cute! She was also so pretty with her long, dark blonde hair. We learned she was from California but had been living and working in Worland. Pete had met her during the summer, and they had been corresponding until she moved to Casper to find a better job. I could see why Pete had fallen in love with her. Her sharp wit and good humor totally endeared her to Brookie. In the months ahead I thanked God so many times for sending us Maggie.

In late February Brookie landed in the hospital again with his congested lung problem. Though he was home again by the time lambing started the first of March, he was far too ill to work, so I worked by myself. Pete and Maggie came out from Casper nearly every weekend and helped me. Maggie had a natural instinct for working with sheep, even though she'd never been near one before.

Pete and Maggie had hoped to be married before lambing started but that didn't work out. They wanted to be married by Brookie's and my Episcopal minister. They were both divorced, so our minister had to wait for permission from the bishop of the Episcopal Diocese of Wyoming. Eventually all the formalities were taken care of and the wedding was set for the evening of March 29 at our house with Reverend Dean Addington officiating.

Dr. Pat had scheduled Brookie for additional x-rays March 27 so I took the day off from work and took him in. While he was at the hospital I went to a beauty parlor and got a perm so I would look halfway presentable at the wedding. After seeing the x-rays the doctor told Brookie he really should hospitalize him, but he let him go home so he could see Pete and Maggie married.

Brookie had hoped to give Maggie away, but he was too ill to be on his feet, so he watched the ceremony from the couch and Don Meike did the honors. We had a small reception after the ceremony, featuring a beautiful traditional wedding cake baked by Cathy Pryor, wife of one of the Meike ranch hands. The festivities didn't last long because everyone had to work the next day. Brookie was exhausted by the time the wedding ceremony was over, so I helped him to bed as soon as he watched the bride and groom cut the first piece of cake.

Dr. Pat was very concerned about Brookie's x-rays so he made an appointment for him with a cardiopulmonary specialist in Casper for April 10.

When the day arrived Don took Brookie to keep his appointment while I stayed home to make the rounds of my ewe and lamb bunches. All day I tortured myself with doomsday thoughts about what the doctor would find. There was no doubt in my mind that there was something terribly wrong with Brookie, I just didn't know what.

Don practically had to carry him in from the car when they arrived home that evening. After he left, I realized Brookie was not only on the verge of collapse, he was so indignant he fairly sputtered when he told me about the interview with the specialist.

According to Brookie the doctor was so aloof he barely acknowledged Brookie's presence. Brookie handed him the big envelope of x-rays Dr. Pat had sent. While the doctor went away to view them Brookie sat in the office and waited.

His first words when he returned were, "You're a coal miner. Where did you work?"

"I've never been a coal miner. I'm a sheepherder," Brookie told him shortly.

"Same difference," the doctor replied cooly. "You've been exposed to a lot of dust in your job."

Brookie had to admit he had. I thought of trailing sheep in such clouds of dust you couldn't see the herd, or working sheep in corrals so dusty everyone looked like they'd been made up for a minstrel show by the time we finished.

"Did he examine you?" I asked.

"Nope. He said he read Dr. Pat's report and looked at the x-rays and he said I have miner's disease. He will call Dr. Pat and they'll get back to me. Well, I got news for him—I ain't goin' back! He's a big horse's katoot and he doesn't know what he's talkin' about!"

"Horse's katoot" was a term Brookie used to convey his utmost contempt for someone. It fell in the same category as someone else's "bastard" or "son of a bitch." I was never sure which part of a horse's anatomy it referred to, and I never did ask!

The bad feelings I'd had all day became reality when Brookie mentioned miner's disease. There'd been a lot in the news in recent years about miner's disease or black lung, about the lives it had claimed. I knew it was the same as a death sentence unless the doctor was mistaken. I wanted to cry and scream and yell that it wasn't so. I knew I didn't dare do any of those things, that I was going to have to be strong enough for both of us.

"But what am I going to do?" my mind cried. My common sense answered, "You'll do what you have to do. You'll take one day at a time and make the best of it."

Dr. Pat let us know that Brookie was scheduled for exploratory surgery at the Casper Hospital May 12, which was almost three weeks away. Brookie was feeling better but was still not up to going with me to work. He spent the days at the house and unless he was having a bad day he cooked for me.

His nerves would be so frazzled by the time I'd get home from work in the evenings he would take his frustration out on me. I was always bone weary, physically and mentally exhausted from the worry that ate at me every waking hour. Sometimes I had to bite my tongue to keep from snapping back. If it got too bad I'd step outside and feed the chickens or gather the eggs while I regained my composure. In bed, he would hold me in his arms and cry and say he was sorry.

To divert him I'd tell him about my day, what bunches of sheep I'd moved, if we'd processed any lambs, what the rest of the crew was doing.

"I oughtta be there helpin' you!" he'd cry out in frustration.

It seemed as if my whole world had fallen apart. I had spent my whole adult life with Brookie. Somehow I could not imagine living without him. He always told me, half joking, half serious, that I would outlive him by years because of the difference in our ages, and because of that I needed to learn to be self-sufficient. In all our years together I had never even considered one of us without the other. Some days, I convinced myself it would be a relief to get the exploratory surgery over with. At least then we'd know what we were faced with.

Brookie's nephew Scott Key and his wife, Beth, planned on me staying with them while Brookie was hospitalized. I was too inexperienced a driver to cope with Casper's traffic, so they drove out to our place the afternoon of May 10 and picked us up. I knew I would need to come home again as soon as possible, so Scott drove our pickup back to Casper so I'd have transportation home later. Brookie rode with him, and I made the trip with Beth.

The next afternoon we checked Brookie into the hospital, a very uncomplicated procedure as we had done all the paperwork by mail a couple of weeks earlier. This was when we learned that the specialist who had read the x-rays and recommended surgery did not do the operating himself, sort of like an architect reading the blueprints while someone else did the actual work. After Brookie was settled in his room on the third floor the surgeon who would be operating next morning came in and visited with us. He explained the operation and made it sound very routine. I found myself feeling more relaxed than I'd felt for weeks. We could come back in the morning and be with Brookie until he went to the operating room. This evening they would be doing blood tests, urine tests, and so on, preparing for tomorrow's surgery.

Pete and Maggie had taken the next day off from their jobs so they could be at the hospital with me. When we checked in at the nurses' desk we were told that a different doctor would be doing Brookie's surgery. Brookie's doctor had flown to Denver during the night with his wife after she was stricken with a near-fatal heart attack. The surgeon who would be operating was just as qualified, we were assured. We didn't get to meet him, however, because he was already in the operating room.

When we got to Brookie's room we found him sedated to the point where he was only half awake, so we didn't find out if he knew about the change of doctors. Very shortly he was loaded on a gurney and wheeled away.

There was a waiting room on the ground floor adjacent to the recovery unit where Brookie would be brought after the surgery, so we went there to wait. For some reason everything that happened the rest of that day is so jumbled in my mind that I have no clear recollection of anything. The waiting room was not very large and was quite crowded with people waiting for word from the recovery room. People were summoned from time to time, disappeared through a door in the end of the room, then reappeared to gather up coats and purses and leave. A uniformed delivery man came in and restocked a vending machine with sandwiches but I don't recall eating anything the entire day, though I suppose I must have. At some point Pete and Maggie must have left because when a nurse finally told us we could see Brookie only Beth went in with me.

The nurse led us to a curtained-off cubicle and for a moment I didn't recognize the person lying in the bed. Brookie's face was so gray I thought he must already be dead. Just then he gave a gut-wrenching groan and moaned, "Oh, I hurt!" Then Beth was leading me out to her car and the rest of that day has mercifully been blotted from my memory.

I'm not sure how long Brookie was in Intensive Care before he was moved back to his room. The doctor who did the surgery talked to me briefly during this time. Brookie was going to be in a lot of pain, so he would be under heavy sedation for the next several days. Biopsies had been sent off to a lab because there seemed to be quite a lot of scar tissue in the lungs. Until the results came back there wasn't much else he could tell me except that Brookie had come through the surgery in good shape.

Once he was back in his room my brain began to function again, and I returned to reality from the nightmare that had held me in its grip.

A couple of days later I asked at the nurses' desk if Brookie's doctor would be in to see him that morning. I wanted to talk to him and see if he'd gotten the results back on the biopsies. The nurse informed me the doctor had left the day before on vacation. I asked about the specialist and she said he was also on vacation.

"So who's looking after Brookie?" I asked.

"He's receiving the best of care," she assured me. "If there's any kind of a problem there are doctors available. Right now he just needs to be kept quiet so he can heal."

I know how it must feel to be set adrift in the middle of the ocean. When I started to go into Brookie's room the nurse stopped me and said that now that the situation was no longer critical I would have to observe hospital afternoon and evening visiting hours.

When Beth picked me up to take me home to lunch I told her what had happened. I decided this would be a good time for me to go home for a few days. I called Pete and he said he and Maggie would keep an eye on Brookie until I got back.

As soon as we ate lunch Scott drove my pickup to the edge of town and Beth and I followed in her car. After I thanked them for all their help I bade them good-bye and headed for Sussex. As I drove north the terrible depression that had weighed me down began to lift, and I began to feel more optimistic about the future.

Vivian had been caring for the cats, dogs, and chickens in my absence, and I could hardly wait to get home to them. A homing instinct has always been so strong in me that I know just how a pigeon must feel as it arrives back at its cote. The three dogs were hysterical with joy at being let off their chains, and the three cats came and wound themselves around my feet so I could hardly walk. The first thing I saw when I walked in the yard was the tulips, a dazzling array of different colors and shapes. How I wished Brookie could see them! He was always so proud of my yard and especially of the tulips every spring.

As soon as I sorted through the accumulation of mail Vivian had left on the kitchen table I changed into my work clothes. With the dogs bouncing excitedly around in the back of the pickup I drove to the ranch. Don was repairing a piece of machinery at the shop, so I filled him in on what had happened. When I asked about the sheep he said no one had had time to do anything with them since I left.

Once lambing was over Brookie and I always had full responsibility for the sheep so the rest of the crew was freed up to start on the other spring work, such as plowing and preparing the soil for planting. In addition to alfalfa the Meike Ranch raised a lot of barley and oats. There were miles of ditches to clean before a crew of at least two men could begin their full-time job of irrigating. Sandwiched in with all this was calf branding and moving cows and calves to summer pasture. My being gone had thrown the usually smoothly run operation out of kilter because they couldn't start irrigating until the sheep were out of the fields. Don was visibly relieved when I said I'd start moving ewe and lamb bunches to the hills next morning.

What a comfort it was to be back in my own bed that night! Our queen-size bed felt awfully big with just me in it, but I was so wrung out by all the stress that I went to sleep as soon as I laid down and didn't wake until morning.

The dogs were as delighted to be working again as I was. We spent the day moving sheep from the alfalfa meadows to various pastures out in the hills.

Maggie called that night and gave me a report on Brookie. He refused to eat except at noon when Maggie used her lunch break from her job to go to the hospital and feed him. He was almost totally uncommunicative, and she worried that he was not making the progress she thought he ought to. She was glad to hear I would be back over in a couple of days. Dana Lohse had called me and said she would be going to Casper and I could ride over with her.

The day Dana and I went to Casper I got up half an hour early so I would have time to pick a big bouquet of tulips to take to Brookie. I arranged them, along with a few sprigs of fragrant white plum blossoms from our little plum tree, in an oversized ceramic beer mug with Brookie's name on the side, a gift from Pete several years before. When I arrived at Lohse's at eight o'clock, our scheduled departure time, Dana took time to go pick some of her tulips to add to the bouquet.

In Casper Dana let me out at the hospital with the mug full of flowers and said she would pick me up at noon and take me to lunch. Then she would bring me back to the hospital and I could visit with Brookie until we left for home in mid-afternoon.

I checked at the nurses' desk to see if I could visit Brookie at this unscheduled time. She said I could because the other bed in the room was presently unoccupied. I asked if the results of his tests had come back and she said I'd have to get that information from either the surgeon or the specialist, and neither of them was back from vacation yet.

When I opened the door and stepped into Brookie's room he was lying on his back staring into space. His gaze moved to me at the sound of the door closing, but his face registered no sign of recognition or emotion when I said, "Hi."

I placed his tulips on his bedside table and leaned over to kiss him. Suddenly his eyes blazed with rage, and he shoved me away so violently I staggered backward. "Get away from me!" he hissed.

I stood there completely speechless.

"What are you doin' here?" he snarled. "Get out of my room! I don't want you in here! Get out!"

His behavior was so irrational I was frightened, not for my well-being but for his sanity. Could something have caused brain damage during the operation? I realized now that I had not really conversed with him since the afternoon he was admitted.

I tried talking to him as if nothing unusual had happened. I told him how pretty the yard was, about moving sheep, how the summer birds were all back along Powder River. In the middle of my one-sided dialogue he carefully turned his back to me and closed his eyes. I sat there in numb silence until my watch said it was time to meet Dana in the hospital parking lot.

Rising, I leaned cautiously over Brookie and murmured, "I'll see you after lunch, sweetheart." If he heard me, he gave no sign.

Of course Dana wanted to know how Brookie was doing and what he thought of the flowers. I was still so stunned by his reaction to my presence I hardly knew what to think or say, so I told her he'd slept most of the time I was there.

When she dropped me off after lunch I went back to his room with great misgivings, but to my surprise he was, if not enthusiastic, at least civil. I was almost afraid to say anything for fear I'd break the spell. Seeking a safe subject I remarked that his roommate had gone home since last time I was there.

"He's gone, alright," Brookie said, "but he didn't go home!"

Some inflection in his voice made me look closely at him. "You mean he . . . died?" I asked hesitantly.

Brookie's voice dropped to a conspiratorial murmur. "I pretend I'm asleep so they don't know I know anything. They're spiriting people out of here at night! They just disappear!"

His choice of words made a little chill run down my spine. What could he have seen that gave him such an idea?

"That whole piece of wall at the head of that other bed is a sliding panel," he said. "The night they took him away they slid it open and there was a van backed up outside. They put him on a stretcher, loaded him in the van and drove away, and the wall slid shut again."

I remembered the man's wife visiting him. "What about his wife?" I asked. "She wouldn't stand for something like that."

"She was in on it!" he exclaimed.

"This is the third floor, so they couldn't have backed a van in and loaded anyone," I said reasonably.

"You don't know anything about it!" He was getting angry now. "So just shut up!"

I was pretty sure he'd been hallucinating. The next thing he said convinced me of it.

"See that door?" He motioned at a door in the wall across from the foot of his bed. "Do you know what's in there?"

As it happened, I did. The first day Brookie was back in the room I had asked a nurse where I could find a rest room. She indicated the door and said there was a toilet in there, to go ahead and use it since Brookie wouldn't be, and there was no patient in the other bed. I'd opened the door to find a toilet and washbowl in such a cramped little space that I almost had a claustrophobia attack before I could use it and escape.

"Yes," I told Brookie, "there's a toilet and washbowl."

"Ah!" he exclaimed. "That's what they want you to think! But it doesn't really work. It slides to one side and there's a shaft there that they lower people down to the basement and they haul them away from there."

Now I knew he was unbalanced, and I knew it would be unwise to try to talk sense to him. Curious to see what his answer would be, I asked him who was behind all this.

"The Mafia!" he whispered dramatically.

Hoping to distract him I asked if a doctor had ever been in to check him.

"I don't know, but they did take me to the x-ray room one day." To my surprise, he started grinning. "Have you seen the big black guy that works in here?"

As a matter of fact, I had. I'd ridden up in the elevator with him one day and if he hadn't been wearing hospital whites I would have thought he was one of the Harlem Globetrotters by the height and build of him!

"Another guy on this same floor was having x-rays that day," Brookie told me, still smiling, "and they sent a white guy and this big Negro to take us to the x-ray room. The black guy bet the white guy that he could pick me up and carry me in his arms and run down the three flights of stairs faster than the other guy could take his patient down in a wheelchair in the elevator.

"Surely he wouldn't dare do that with that incision not healed!" I protested.

"Well, he did," Brookie exclaimed belligerently. "And we won, and he never hurt me a bit!"

Presently a nurse came and gave him a shot. He was soon asleep and had not wakened when Dana came up to the room to tell me she was ready to go home. I wrote him a note and propped it against the mug full of tulips. I explained to him that I had to go home because there were still several bunches of sheep to go to the hills and they needed me to move them.

Two days later I had just gotten home from work and was fixing supper when the phone rang.

"You'd better get over there and find out what they're doin' to Brookie!" Glen Lohse said.

He was very upset. He and Shine Devoe had been in Casper that day and had gone to visit Brookie before they left for home. He said the first thing Brookie asked them was if they'd seen me lately. Glen told him he talked to me the morning I went to Casper with Dana but he hadn't seen me since.

"She's quit me!" Brookie said sadly. He said he hadn't seen me since the day they operated on him.

"See that bouquet of tulips sittin' right there on the table, Brook? She brought you those day before yesterday when her and Dana came to Casper."

Brookie didn't know where the flowers came from, he told Glen, but he did know he hadn't seen me since the day he had the surgery. "She's quit me!" he repeated and proceeded to call me some pretty choice names.

Glen pointed out that Brookie's name was on the mug the flowers were in, whereupon Brookie turned his back on them, closed his eyes, and ignored them.

"He acts as if he's lost his mind!" Glen sounded like he was almost in tears.

Warren had the next day off from work, and he and Vivian and I had planned on going to see Brookie anyway. I decided I'd better be prepared to stay all night, so I packed a couple of changes of clothes in my suitcase and took it along.

The nurse on duty told us when we arrived in mid-morning that we couldn't go in until visiting hours because there was another patient sharing the room, but she could bring Brookie out to the lounge. When she wheeled him out in a wheelchair I got the shock of my life! He had deteriorated so badly since I'd last seen him that I hardly knew him. He was so weak he was tied in the wheelchair so he wouldn't fall face forward. His head hung down so his chin was on his chest, and his eyes stared unseeing at the floor. His face was emaciated and had the waxy pallor of a dead person.

Vivian put her arms around him and kissed him on the cheek, but there was no indication that he was aware of anything. We tried talking to him but there was no response. Soon the nurse came and wheeled him back to his room. As soon as she was out of sight Warren and Vivian both burst into tears. I was too numb to cry.

"We've gotta get him out of here before they kill him!" Warren said, drying his eyes.

I promised Warren I would do something, though I wasn't sure what. They left to do some shopping and would go directly home when they finished. There was a good restaurant within walking distance of the hospital, so I went there after stowing my suitcase in Brookie's room. While I waited for afternoon visiting hours I drank numerous cups of coffee and ordered a meal I had no appetite for at all.

As I passed the nurses' desk one of them called to me and said the specialist was back from his vacation. "He's in the hospital now. When he comes back past I'll have him stop and see you."

Brookie was lying with his eyes closed, apparently asleep, so I sat on the visitor's chair and waited impatiently for the doctor to put in an appearance. Having never seen the man I was beginning to think he was the figment of someone's imagination . . . one of Brookie's hallucinations, perhaps!

Before I had time to get too fidgety the door opened and a tall, well-dressed man introduced himself as the doctor and said he understood I wanted to see him. I asked him if the results from Brookie's biopsies had ever come back.

He looked at me in astonishment. "You mean no one told you his condition's terminal?" he blurted out.

He told me the name of the disease, but I was so stunned by his brusque manner and total lack of compassion that it never penetrated my brain. My first thought was for Brookie, but when I looked around he was lying there, staring vacantly into space and I learned afterward he had no recollection of the doctor being there. Brookie might as well have been invisible for all the attention he paid him.

It took my brain a few minutes to shift gears after he left, which was probably just as well because the more I thought about it, the angrier I got. How dare he act as if Brookie was so insignificant he could totally ignore him! I wondered if it was because Brookie told him he was a sheepherder and he classed sheepherders as a subhuman species. Much later it occurred to me that Brookie might have been downright belligerent the day the doctor called him a miner! Even now, though, I think it was unpardonable of him to treat me in such a callous fashion.

After I calmed down a little I thought about what the doctor had said. I'd had very little experience with the word *terminal* except in connection with batteries and airports, but I was pretty sure it meant a person was going to die from whatever ailed him. Seeing Brookie in his present state it was easy for me to believe he was in the process of dying.

I kept thinking if I could just get him back to the hospital in Buffalo where he knew the doctors and nurses he wouldn't feel so isolated, and I would be able to go see him without having to depend on someone to drive me. I had no idea how to go about that, or even if I could get permission to move him to another hospital. It all seemed so overwhelmingly hopeless I wanted to cry, but I knew that wouldn't solve anything.

"Lord, please help me," I said instead. "I don't know where to turn or what to do next."

A few minutes later there was a rap on the door, it opened and there stood Don Meike. My prayer was answered! He would know what to do!

He soon realized it was hopeless trying to talk to Brookie. "Let's go out in the hall," he said in an undertone.

"What happened to him?" he asked sharply once we were out of the room.

I told him the whole story, including what the specialist had said about his condition being terminal.

"I'd like to get him out of here and back to Buffalo," I said, "but I don't know what to do."

Don was on his way home from a Woolgrowers' meeting in Casper. "I'll call the Kaycee ambulance as soon as I get home and see if they can come over here in the morning and transfer Brookie to Buffalo. You get hold of the doctor and arrange to have him release Brookie when the ambulance arrives."

Later in the evening Don called and said the ambulance would be there at nine o'clock the next morning. I had left a message at the desk for the doctor that we would be transferring Brookie to the Buffalo hospital the next morning and would need him to release him. Maggie and Pete came to the hospital that evening and were so relieved when they found out we were going to move Brookie. They had become more and more worried about his condition, but the nurses had assured them this was to be expected after such radical surgery.

I spent the night with Beth and Scott, and she had me at the hospital the next morning at eight o'clock because I wanted to be sure I was there when the ambulance arrived. I didn't want to risk being left behind!

Jim Zimmerschied, our Kaycee deputy sheriff, was driving the ambulance when it arrived shortly after nine. Bunny Taylor, who owned the Exxon station in Kaycee, was riding shotgun. His sister Alta was Brookie's sister-in-law, so Bunny always seemed like family. I was so glad to see them!

It was close to ten before we got all the paperwork done. When Jim and Bunny wheeled the stretcher into Brookie's room I saw a spark of interest in his eyes, and I began to hope that whatever had gone wrong with Brookie's mind would right itself when he was back on familiar territory.

It was a gray, overcast day with a fine, misty rain falling, but nothing could dampen my spirits as we headed toward Kaycee. I rode up front and Bunny rode beside Brookie, keeping an eye on him. Bunny talked to him, but I couldn't understand anything he said. Once, though, I was almost sure I heard Brookie laugh. Remembering the condition he was in yesterday, I decided I must have been mistaken.

We finally drove out of the rain, but the sky was still heavy with clouds when we reached Kaycee, where we stopped at Bunny's station for a potty break. Everyone in Kaycee must have known the ambulance was transporting Brookie to Buffalo because the rear door kept popping open as people stuck their heads in to say hello and wish him a speedy recovery. He seemed much more alert as we resumed our journey, and I could even hear him talking to Bunny occasionally. My heart lifted.

While we were still a few miles out of Buffalo, Jim called the hospital on the radio and told them the ambulance was transporting a transfer patient from the Casper hospital, and gave them Brookie's name and all his vital statistics. A hospital team was waiting for us when we pulled into the emergency entrance. When Brookie saw Karen, his favorite nurse, he positively beamed, and I could have cried with joy that he was at least recognizing people again.

I waited in the hall with my suitcase while they got Brookie settled in a room. Jim took all the transfer papers to the admitting desk and stopped to talk to me on his way back to the ambulance.

"He looks and sounds better already," he said cheerfully, and I agreed.

The nurse came out presently and told me Brookie was pretty well done in by the long trip. She suggested I might want to wait until evening visiting hours to come see him because he had been given a pain killer and was being fed a belated lunch. He would probably sleep as soon as he finished eating.

It had been a long time since I'd eaten breakfast but I didn't feel the least bit hungry. I needed to let Halsey and Carol know we were in Buffalo, so I called them and Carol came and got me. I filled them in on everything that had happened except I didn't tell them about his condition being terminal. Halsey's health had been deteriorating steadily for months, and I didn't think they needed to be burdened with that bad news.

By the time evening visiting hours came every relative in Buffalo knew Brookie was at the hospital and nearly all of them were there to see him. There were too many of us to all go in the room at once so they visited in shifts while the rest of us waited in the hall. No one stayed longer than a few minutes, to avoid tiring him. Standing out in the hall with Carol and Halsey, listening to the joking and friendly heckling going on in the room, it was hard for me to believe Brookie was the same person who had slumped speechless in the wheelchair only yesterday.

When there were only a couple of people left in the room Carol, Halsey and I joined them.

When Brookie saw me standing by his bed his smile changed to a look of pure hatred. Using language I'd never heard him use in all our years together he ordered me out of his room, out of his sight, and out of his life.

"I don't ever wanta see you again!" he spat at me.

I retreated to the hall while everyone stood in stunned silence.

Halsey followed me out. "Well," he remarked awkwardly, "he's really got a bee in his bonnet, doesn't he?"

I had told them during the afternoon about his reaction the day I took him the tulips. "I feel so helpless," I sobbed with tears streaming down my face. "He's totally irrational. He acts as if he'd like to kill me!"

His outburst brought the visit to an abrupt end. Everyone went home and as soon as we got back to Turk's house I went to bed.

I didn't sleep. I was completely exhausted, both mentally and physically, but I couldn't shut my brain off so I could relax. Brookie had seemed so like himself until he saw me. The only thing I could think was that his mind had slipped where I was concerned. If he was going to be an invalid the rest of his life, how could I care for him when the very sight of me sent him into a rage? I would have to put him in a nursing home and how could I handle that, financially? Finally I slept, but I was awake next morning as soon as I heard Carol stirring about.

I was just getting dressed when the phone rang. I heard Carol say, "Just a minute," then she was at the bedroom door.

"Oh, no!" I thought. "More bad news!"

"Brookie wants to talk to you," she said.

I braced myself for more abusive language as I picked up the phone.

"Louise?" he asked in a very subdued voice.

"Yes."

"Are you coming to the hospital this morning?"

"If you want me to."

He must have heard the hesitancy in my voice. "I want you to!" he said. "I have to talk to you."

I was still very skeptical when I walked into his room later that morning. I was dismayed to see the other bed in the room now had an occupant. Someone had been brought in since we left last night. Almost holding my breath I walked over to Brookie's bed, expecting to be met by more abusive words. Instead, when I was close enough he reached out and grabbed one of my hands in both of his. When I looked in his eyes I saw such anguish and pleading it nearly broke my heart.

"I'm so glad you came," he said. "I'm okay this morning. I've been trapped in some kind of a nightmare."

He introduced me to his roommate, Max. Max explained that he had emphysema and his wife had brought him to the hospital about 9:30 the night before after he experienced breathing difficulty.

He started grinning. "We had quite a little excitement here just after I was admitted," he said. "We had a bunch of midget Mexicans in here trying to set fire to Brookie's mattress!"

I looked from one to the other to see if this was supposed to be some kind of joke.

"It sure seemed real to me!" Brookie explained. He smiled sheepishly. "These little Mexicans about two feet tall came walking in and went under my bed and started lighting matches, trying to set fire to the mattress!"

Max took up the story. "He got pretty excited. He was hollering at the guys under his bed and yelling at me to ring for the nurse. I did because I thought I had a real loony on my hands!"

The nurse came and realized Brookie was hallucinating. She gave him a tranquilizer and explained to him that the pain killer they had been giving him at Casper could cause hallucinations. As soon as Dr. Pat saw in the transfer papers what they were giving him he put him on a different medication.

Later, when Brookie and I had a chance to talk privately we came up with what we thought might be the explanation of why they had continued to administer a drug that had the effect it did on him. Before the doctor who did the surgery left on his vacation he probably prescribed heavy and frequent doses of pain medication to get Brookie through those first days of almost unbearable agony. When he no longer needed such "heavy-duty" medication there was no one there to change the order.

When we received the hospital bill and an itemized statement several pages long our theory was pretty well proved. I wasn't familiar with drugs, but Maggie had been a nurse's aide and had a working knowledge of them. She and I were wading through the pages and pages of items charged to Brookie's account, including a Band-Aid and a safety pin, when Maggie exclaimed, "Look, Mom! Here's the villain!"

We started at the beginning and noted one particular drug each time it appeared, the amount of the dosage and how often it was administered. He had received the drug every few hours, every day except the last day he was there.

"This drug causes hallucinations, deep depression, personality changes, and can be very addictive," Maggie explained. "It's a wonder they didn't make a drug addict out of him!"

It had apparently taken nearly forty-eight hours to get the effects of the drug out of his system. He had no clear recollection of anything that happened during the twelve days following his surgery, except for the hallucinations! They were as sharp and clear as if they'd really occurred. He remembered Don being there, but he said he didn't try to talk to him because Don was sitting in an old-fashioned rope swing at the foot of Brookie's bed gently swinging to and fro. Brookie thought it was so ridiculous he shut his eyes so he wouldn't have to watch him. When he opened his eyes again, Don was gone.

"Was the swing still there?" I asked jokingly.

"No," Brookie laughed. "I guess he took it with him."

The speed of his recovery was amazing once he was back in the real world. In four days he was up, prowling the halls, wanting to come home. Pete and Maggie had brought my pickup to Buffalo so I'd have transportation. I came home for a couple of days to water the yard, do laundry, and check the mail. When I went back, Dr. Pat released him. The doctor at Casper had put Brookie on insulin at the time of the surgery and Dr. Pat concurred. He had told us earlier that it was only going to be a matter of time until he would have to be on insulin anyway.

Before we left the hospital I had to learn to give the insulin shots. I was a little nervous at first, but in a few days the procedure became completely routine. The shots never seemed to bother Brookie at all, and he often praised me on how painless they were.

There was never any logical explanation for the remarkable recovery he made, not only from the surgery but in his overall health. He had lost a good deal of weight during his ordeal. Now he had such a good healthy color and seemed to feel better than he had for a couple of years. He was under the impression that the operation had been remedial rather than exploratory, and I didn't see any reason to tell him differently. The incision was slow to heal, partly due to his diabetic condition, but also because there was a drain in it. Once the drain was removed he healed rapidly, and before too long he was even riding horseback.

Brookie was fretting that we were late getting moved to the mountains so as soon as Dr. Pat was satisfied that the insulin injections were causing no problem and the incision was healed we made the move.

Brookie always said he had two great loves in his life: the Big Horn Mountains and me. Once when I kidded him about always putting the mountains first, he said that was because he loved the mountains first, not because he loved them more.

That was probably one of the best summers we spent together on the mountains. Whenever any of the livestock needed to be moved we saddled our horses, gathered cows or sheep, and trailed them to fresh pasture. We fished and explored and hunted Indian relics.

When Brookie got out of bed one morning in mid-July he almost fell when his left leg collapsed under him. "My leg's asleep," he complained by way of explanation.

As I watched him hobble to the outhouse and back again I realized something was wrong. He climbed back in the wagon with some difficulty and remarked that not only was his leg still asleep, but his left arm and hand and the side of his face felt "funny." We discussed the possibility of it being a stroke and decided we'd better go to the doctor. I was thankful that his speech was normal.

The numbness had left his face by the time we reached Buffalo, and he said his leg felt stronger as we walked into the clinic. After hearing his symptoms Dr. Pat promptly hospitalized him for observation and treatment in the form of physical therapy.

To my surprise, Brookie took a very optimistic view of the whole thing. As he pointed out, we'd planned on spending that weekend in Buffalo anyway, at a two-day family reunion and fiftieth wedding anniversary celebration Halsey and Carol's kids had planned for them. The opening day of the festivities was still two days off, so we decided I'd better go back to camp and take care of cats, dogs, and chickens and check sheep and gates.

Brookie had hoped Saturday morning he would be so improved that Dr. Pat might release him temporarily at least, so he could go with me to the big reception at the Wesleyan Methodist Church that afternoon. When I got to the hospital I was greeted by a less than happy husband. Because his recovery had been slower than anticipated, Dr. Pat had vetoed releasing him, even temporarily. I stayed at the hospital and had lunch with Brookie. By the time I left for the church he was in a much better frame of mind.

The reception had been carefully planned and was beautifully carried out. Such a multitude of family and friends came to congratulate Halsey and Carol that at times I was almost claustrophobic in the crush of people.

Following the reception the family members gathered at Howard and Bonnie Turk's home to visit and later share a buffet supper, which we ate out on the lawn. During this time, groups of three or four relatives took turns visiting Brookie, so he got to share some of the fun.

Sunday morning everyone headed for the Big Horns west of Buffalo for an all-day picnic. I decided to spend the day with Brookie instead before going back up to camp that afternoon.

When I came down again several days later he had made such great progress Dr. Pat released him. Other than a slight weakness in his left hand, Brookie was left with no noticeable effects from his stroke.

We were driving up Main Street in Buffalo one day in early September and saw a lot full of snow machines. Next to the sidewalk there were also several small motorcycles and a three-wheeler with "Sale" signs prominently displayed on them. It would never have occurred to me to even stop and look at them, let alone buy one. Brookie was very interested in the three-wheeler because they were quite popular as all-terrain vehicles. The salesman assured us the price had really been cut on the trail bikes, as he called them, and also on the three-wheeler. They were putting the snow machines on display for the winter sports trade and needed the floor space. When we left town we were the owners of the three-wheeler, which was riding proudly in the back of our pickup.

Brookie was like any kid with a new toy; he spent hours each day playing with it. Although he bought it for me, my first experience with the three-wheeler convinced me I wanted no part of it. It felt very unstable, and every time I got on a side hill (which was most of the time in the mountains!) I felt as if it was tipping over. Because I had ridden bikes all my life my reaction was to put my foot on the ground for balance. I didn't know this was a no-no on a three-wheeler until the hind wheel ran over my heel, tore my shoe off and nearly crippled me. Brookie got along great with it because he'd spent all his younger days on horses rather than bikes.

A week later he insisted we had to go back to Buffalo and see if there were any of the little trail bikes left so I could have one. When we went back to camp that day I was the proud owner of a neat little yellow trail bike. What fun we had with them! We rode miles on them to our favorite relic hunting sites or just traveling around the area for the fun of it.

The day we bought the yellow bike we ran across our mountain neighbor, Ross Buckingham. Ross, who had also spent all his life astride a horse, was almost unbelieving when he learned we planned to herd sheep with it.

"Well, I hope you plan to ride it in a round corral first before you take it out on the open range!" he commented, shaking his head. When horses were being broken to ride they were ridden in a round corral before finally being ridden out in the open.

I had reason to remember that one day when Brookie decided to try out my bike. The gas was controlled by the hand grip on the right handlebar; the brake lever was on the left. He made a big circle out away from camp and did fine until he was almost back at the wagon. Something cross-threaded in his brain, he said later, and instead of using the brake he used the opposite hand and gave it more gas.

I had been standing in the doorway watching his sedate approach when everything went out of control. I realized what had happened. I leaped out the door. "Use the brake! Use the brake!" I yelled.

I have never seen such a look of sheer desperation in my life! He was headed for a broadside crash with the wagon, and I knew he'd break his neck, not to mention smashing my bike! At the last second he turned the wheel, barely missing the back corner of the wagon, and dived into a sagebrush patch directly behind it. The bike stalled in the thick brush and keeled over with Brookie still grimly astride!

As soon as I determined that very little damage had been done to either him or the bike I collapsed on the ground because my knees were too weak to hold me up. Then I began to laugh. I couldn't have stopped if I'd known he was going to kill me!

"Remember what Ross told you the day we bought it?" I gasped. I went off into another fit. "I wish you could have seen your face!" I shrieked. "I know now exactly how a bronc rider looks coming out of the chute on a bucking horse!"

By now Brookie was laughing almost as hard as I was. We chuckled and giggled all through dinner, reliving the whole episode. He thought it was almost as funny as the day I slid out of the back of the pickup with a load of baled straw on top of me. I thought this was by far the most hilarious!

After we moved off the mountains for the winter Brookie's health began to deteriorate again. He often complained that the TV picture was fuzzy. I was so burned out on TV that there were only a few shows I watched. More often I was at the kitchen table writing or reading in bed, so at first I didn't pay any attention to his complaints about the picture not being clear.

"I wish K-2 would fix their picture," he grumbled one night when we were both watching a show. "It's so blurry it's driving me crazy."

We always had great TV reception, and this time was no exception. My suggestion that it must be his eyes and maybe he needed to see the eye doctor made him downright surly.

SHEEP!291

"I can see as good as I ever could!" he grumped. He had always had exceptionally good eyesight and had never had to wear reading glasses.

When we began to move the sheep out to the winter range after bucking was over it was soon apparent to me that he really was having a problem with his vision. Finally it was so obvious he could no longer deny it. Reluctantly he went and had his eyes checked and was fitted with glasses. He refused to wear them where anyone would see him, but he did wear them to watch TV.

Halsey's death three months after the golden wedding celebration was a terrible shock to Brookie. Even though we had known for several weeks that Halsey was dying, we still were not emotionally ready for it. Poor Brookie was grief-stricken, and at first I didn't find this disturbing. I tried to ignore little signs that indicated he was not able to put it behind him. Hardly a day went by when he didn't cry and say it wasn't right that he had outlived Halsey.

Gradually he lost his appetite for his favorite foods, so before I'd prepare a meal I'd ask him what he felt like eating. His reply was always the same: "I don't care. Whatever you want. I'm not very hungry."

All the vitality he had during the summer and fall ebbed away and left him tired and listless. At first I tried to convince myself that the insulin wasn't working as it should, but a twice-daily check of his blood sugar showed no problem there.

As the winter dragged by I yearned for spring. He would feel better when we had sunshine and warmer weather, I told myself. Sometimes I would almost be convinced that he was getting better, or at least holding his own. Then I would compare his present condition with the way he'd been just a few weeks ago and I knew it was only wishful thinking. Because of his poor appetite he'd lost quite a bit of weight, which made his face thin and haggard. His breathing was so shallow that the least exertion brought on a coughing spell that left him gasping for air.

In January 1981 I finally persuaded him to go see the doctor. He hadn't been to the clinic since he'd had a routine blood check the day we bought the three-wheeler. He was still looking and feeling so good then I know Dr. Pat must have been shocked when he saw how much ground he'd lost.

The doctor hospitalized him at once and put him on oxygen. New x-rays were taken, and I was horrified when Dr. Pat showed them to me. The clear space in his lungs had dwindled alarmingly compared to the x-rays taken a year ago before he had the exploratory surgery.

After they did blood tests Dr. Pat and the respiratory therapist explained to us that Brookie wasn't getting enough oxygen to keep his body going, so he would have to be on oxygen from now on, at least part-time. Rick told Brookie he would be able to tell by the way he felt when he needed oxygen.

Dave Kennedy, who owned an oxygen supply business in Buffalo, rented out and maintained all types of oxygen equipment, so when I brought Brookie home he followed us out and installed an electric unit that manufactured oxygen. Because I am mechanically and electronically deficient, I was terrified of this "thing," even though it looked quite benign. Sitting there hissing softly it could have posed for a medium-sized propane heater. I was afraid it might malfunction and I wouldn't be smart enough to realize something was wrong. Dave assured me it was almost fool-proof. (It was that "almost" that worried me!) Either he or Rick could almost always be reached by phone. (That "almost" again.)

The difference the oxygen made was nothing short of miraculous. Brookie's face lost the gray look almost immediately, and his mental attitude improved 100 percent. He felt so much better he went with me most days to check on the sheep. He had learned he could be without the oxygen comfortably for about three hours if he didn't exert himself.

The oil company pipeline that carried water from a hot water spring near the foot of the mountains to the oil field crossed miles of the Meikes' rangeland. At strategic points along the line, valves had been installed so tanks or reservoirs could be filled for the livestock. The sheep were in a pasture where they depended on oil company water so I had to check every day to make sure the valves were running enough to supply the sheep with water. At the same time I checked gates and fence and watched for any signs of predator problems.

One day we found a little bunch of the sheep had escaped through a hole in the fence into the neighbor's pasture. They were already about a mile from where they'd crawled out and were heading into really rough country. I knew I was going to have to walk them back to where they belonged and repair the fence. When I asked Brookie if he could follow me with the pickup I learned how blind he had become. He nearly panicked, fearful that he would drive into a washout or over a rock pile. Finally I convinced him that he could follow me and the sheep down the long ridge that ran back to the pasture fence and if I saw anything that might cause him trouble I would guide him around it.

We arrived at the fence without any problem. I put the sheep back in and repaired the fence, which had apparently been torn down by a bunch of antelope. We were only about half a mile from the oil company's shale road, but because of an uncrossable draw I had to follow the ridge back the way we'd come in.

When I got in the pickup I was surprised to find Brookie almost in a state of collapse.

"I've got to get back to the oxygen!" he gasped.

I managed to maintain a calm appearance though my brain shrieked *Hurry!* Should I follow the shale road to Linch where it joins Highway 192 and comes right past our place, or should I come through the hills on the dirt road which would cut off miles but was much rougher? I decided on the dirt road. Soon I noticed the closer we got to home the less agitated Brookie seemed. Actually, we hadn't been gone from home as long as we usually were, so I decided the problem had been caused by the stress of his having to drive. I thought that episode might discourage him from going with me, but it didn't.

In our spare time we embarked on several projects at the house, including reroofing the utility room and building shelves under our big, south-facing picture windows in the living room. Though I did most of the actual labor, he was able to oversee the job and even did all the cutting with the electric saw.

When lambing started Brookie went with me nearly every morning and drove while I fed cake to the various bunches of pregnant ewes waiting to go in to the "maternity ward." Putting pride aside, he wore his glasses and could see well enough to avoid running over the sheep as they mobbed the pickup to get at the cake. As soon as we finished feeding I took him home, where he spent the rest of the day reading or puttering around the house. Most days he even had a hot meal ready for me when I came home at noon.

He became more and more dependent on the oxygen, and his gradual physical deterioration was very evident. When lambing was over I knew I had to make some decisions about our immediate future. It seemed quite obvious to me there was no way we could go to the mountain camp when it was time.

As if reading my thoughts, Brookie said, "I'm going to the mountains again this summer."

"How would we manage about the oxygen?" I asked.

"I don't know. We'll talk to Dave," he replied.

Dave said he could fix us up with a large oxygen tank with a gauge on it that would show us when we needed to take it to Buffalo for a refill. I wasn't sure what Don would think about us going to the mountains, but he said the decision was entirely up to us. If we were comfortable with the idea, that was all that was necessary. So we moved to the mountains again.

During the summer, whenever we made a trip off the mountains I secured the oxygen tank in a corner of the pickup bed behind the cab and ran the plastic tubing through a crack in the sliding rear window to where Brookie was sitting. When we were in camp the tank sat behind the wagon and we ran the tube in through a hole I drilled in the back wall.

It was a constant worry to me all summer that something might happen—a cloudburst, vehicle trouble, or some disabling accident to me so I couldn't drive, and he would run out of oxygen, but I never let Brookie know this. None of these things ever happened, thank God!

Brookie was so happy to be at the camp that for the first few weeks he was quite cheerful, even though I was out all day working on the fence. When they began trucking the sheep up, he even went with me to the unloading site, but this brought home to him the fact that he couldn't ride or do anything else for that matter.

Every day he became more depressed until I was afraid to leave him alone in camp for fear he might kill himself. As had been his habit for years, his pistol, a .38 Smith and Wesson Police Special in a sheepskin-lined leather zipper holster, was in the seat of the pickup whenever we went anywhere, and when he was in bed it was under his pillow.

The fence repair was all done except for a short span behind Davis Mountain. It was only a short distance from camp but out of sight of the wagon. He knew this was all I had left to do, but every day I made excuses not to go.

"Why don't you go finish your fence?" he asked me one morning after breakfast.

"No problem," I answered. "I can do it any time and there's no livestock in these pastures yet."

He looked me right in the eye and said, "Go finish your fence. I won't do anything while you're gone, I promise." He knew exactly what I had been thinking! We knew each other so well we often shared a sort of mental telepathy. I knew he wouldn't break his word, so I got busy and finished the fence.

By mid-summer Brookie was so weak he couldn't walk from the wagon to the outdoor toilet. I would help him off the bed, out of the wagon, and onto the three-wheeler, which we kept parked right by the front of the wagon. The toilet door was fastened open so he could drive right up to the doorway. He had enough strength to get in the toilet, then get back on the three-wheeler when he was ready to come back to the wagon.

During the years we'd lived together if one of us had trouble sleeping the other usually sensed it, so we'd be sleepless together! Now Brookie seemed never to sleep at night, partly because he dozed off and on during the day, and partly, I decided, because he was afraid if he went to sleep at night he might die, though he never said so. To pass the long night hours he would put our little battery radio under the end of his pillow away from me. He kept it turned so low I couldn't distinguish what songs were playing, which irritated me no end.

"If you're going to listen to the radio, at least put it between us and turn it up so I can hear it!" I exclaimed in exasperation one night. From then on we listened to a clear-channel, all-night truckers' station out of Detroit that played country music, took phone calls from truckers, and gave road and weather conditions for the entire United States. Sometimes the music would lull me to sleep, but if Brookie stirred the least little bit I was instantly wide awake. I doubt if I ever got over four hours of sleep at a stretch.

As the days of summer grew shorter and Brookie grew weaker, I prayed every day for continuing good weather. Some years September brought Indian summer to the mountains with warm sunny days, brilliant blue skies, and brisk, frosty nights. Other years one storm after another would blow through, and at this elevation it was more often snow than rain.

My prayers were answered. September passed with only a few spells of unsettled weather that brought no snow. I was so relieved when it was time to bring the sheep down. Jerry Pryor and Peto were going to trail the sheep, and I would be the camptender since Brookie would be confined to our wagon.

Two days before our departure date Brookie became so ill that I decided I'd better take him to the doctor. Dr. Pat insisted on hospitalizing him for a few days until his condition stabilized. I wanted to stay with him, but Brookie wouldn't hear of it.

"You go on back to camp and come down with the sheep," he told me. "You have people depending on you to do your job. Maybe I'll get out of the hospital in time to come part of the way with you."

Reluctantly I went back to camp and made preparations for the trail down. The barrel of gas had to be loaded just behind the cab of the pickup so I could siphon gas directly into the tank when needed. Along with the Handyman jack, a shovel, and the tool box there were two spare tires for the sheepwagons, two metal garbage cans that I used for storage (one for dog food, the other for extra coats, gloves, slickers, and overshoes). The propane bottle for the sheep wagon stove along with the water can and two ice chests containing perishable food were loaded at the back of the pickup where I had easy access to them.

We were two days' trail from home when Vivian brought Brookie out from the hospital. Even in the few days we'd been apart I could see he'd failed. He was too done in to spend the day riding in the pickup, so

I made a place for him on the bed. Vivian and I unloaded his oxygen tank out of her car and set it in the wagon. When we camped that night I put it outside.

How relieved I was when we got home the next afternoon so I could get Brookie settled in bed. And what a blessing it was to have the bathroom within a few steps of the bed! We had a hide-a-bed couch in the living room that I kept made out into a bed so he could lie out there in the daytime. He had lost all interest in television, so he spent his days dozing and reading while I was at work.

Pete and Maggie came faithfully every weekend as they had all summer, and this helped make life more bearable. Maggie waited on Brookie like a devoted slave, plumping his pillows, getting fresh water, bathing his hands and face, and badgering him to eat.

All summer he had lived on hot dogs and buttermilk, the only food he could tolerate. On one of his trips to the clinic for a checkup, Dr. Pat, concerned about his weight loss, asked him about his diet.

"Are you sure you're not pregnant?" he chuckled when Brookie told him. They had a good laugh over it.

Brookie was almost completely bed-bound now except for trips to the bathroom. He was so unsteady on his feet I worried that he might fall while he was alone, but he steadied himself from one piece of furniture to another and made the trips without mishap.

Brookie's seventy-fourth birthday on October 24 haunts me still! Propped up with pillows he was pale as a ghost as Pete, Maggie, and I piled his birthday gifts beside him on the hide-a-bed. Even the slight exertion of trying to open them was too much for him. He tried to show enthusiasm as we opened them for him, but moments after he thanked us for them he closed his eyes and sank into exhausted sleep.

For the next two days I stayed home from work. He was so ill I truly expected him to die. The second night as I lay in bed beside him I thought his breathing had stopped. I put my hand on his chest to see if I could feel a heart beat. He stirred and murmured, "I was asleep."

"I want you to take me to the hospital," he said the next morning. "I don't want to die here at the house because I'm afraid it would haunt you the rest of your life."

I assured him it wouldn't, but he was adamant. I went to the ranch and told Don I didn't know when I'd be back. For some reason, as soon as he was admitted and settled in bed at the hospital he began to perk up. I spent the rest of the day with him, then went to Carol's house for the night. I arrived at the hospital about nine o'clock the next morning, not sure I would be allowed to see him that early.

"Oh, I'm glad you're here!" a nurse's aide greeted me. "Brookie says no one can give him a bath except you, and I can't change his bed until he's bathed." Each morning after that I made it a point to be there shortly after eight to give him his bath so as not to throw their schedule off!

Within a week I had him home again. His old wit was back, and he even had some color in his face. In fact he looked better than he had since we had moved to the mountains the past spring. Before I took him to the hospital we had been sleeping in the living room because he was too weak to move back to the bedroom at night. Now he insisted on sleeping in the bedroom, so every night I moved the oxygen machine from the living room to the bedroom.

I don't know how long this state of remission, if that's what it was, might have lasted if disaster hadn't struck. I got up a little after six one morning, put the coffee on, and got dressed. When Brookie called me from the bedroom the sound of his voice told me something was wrong.

"The oxygen machine isn't working!" I could hear panic in his voice.

For a few moments I thought he'd had a bad dream; the machine was humming reassuringly and the light was on, indicating it was producing oxygen.

"It's working," I assured him.

"No it isn't! There's nothing coming through to my nose!"

I checked. He was right; there was nothing.

No problem, I told myself. The line has gotten kinked. Quickly I checked but found no kink in the line.

I ran to the phone and dialed Dave's number. The phone rang and rang, but there was no answer. My hands were shaking so badly I could hardly find Rick's home number in the phone book, let alone dial it. On the second ring he answered, and I was weak with relief.

When I told him what had happened he said Dave had gone to Sheridan early. "Call the Kaycee ambulance," he told me. "They can get there quicker than I can, and they'll have oxygen."

To my consternation I had to call four different numbers before anyone answered, then I got the wife of one of the EMTs. She said her husband had already left for work but she would call until she rounded up an ambulance crew. Meanwhile all we could do was wait. Silently I prayed.

Brookie was making a determined effort to stay calm. He insisted on getting dressed, even though I protested. He had me help him to the living room so he could lie on the hide-a-bed, "so I'll be that much closer to the door when they get here," he said. He even had me get his electric razor so he could shave. He combed his hair and laid his dress Stetson on the bed beside him. I wanted to laugh, but I didn't dare; I was too close to hysteria!

I went in and unplugged Dave's "almost foolproof" machine while we waited. I hadn't realized how totally dependent on the oxygen Brookie was now. His breathing was so labored I was sure he would die before the ambulance got there. Glen Lohse happened to stop by, so he sat with Brookie and talked to him, which helped distract him.

It was forty minutes after I called before the ambulance arrived. This is no discredit to our volunteer ambulance crew. They are all working people, and my call came about the time they were on their way to jobs or opening up businesses. I could see Brookie go limp with relief when they brought the portable oxygen tank in and got him hooked to it before they did anything else.

When they loaded him on the stretcher Jim Zimmerschied looked at Brookie's hat and said, "I don't think you'll need that in the ambulance, Brookie. Louise can bring it with her."

I was going to drive our pickup in so I'd have transportation. I didn't leave immediately. I knew Brookie was in good hands, and I needed a few minutes to pull myself together, though what I really felt like doing was having hysterics and then collapsing!

Vivian called after she saw the ambulance leaving to find out what had happened. I hadn't called her earlier because she has a tendency to get emotional in a crisis. She said she would care for the cats and dogs and pick up the mail while I was gone. I changed my clothes, gathered up some of Brookie's things, packed a suitcase, and was on my way, without his hat. He never wore it again.

Brookie was resting comfortably when I checked in, so I went to the Busy Bee cafe and got something to eat since I'd been too unnerved to think of eating at home. Then I took my suitcase to Carol's house and moved into her spare ground-floor bedroom.

Dear Carol! What a comfort she was in the weeks that followed. Her house became a second home to me and later for Pete and Maggie, who took up residence in her basement bedroom.

When the ambulance delivered Brookie to the hospital, Dr. Pat wasn't there. Dr. Pete admitted him so Brookie automatically became his patient. When I talked to him he said he was not satisfied with the diagnosis of pulmonary fibrosis; he thought it was entirely possible he had tuberculosis instead, so he was going to pursue that theory.

For a moment hope sprang up in me. Then I thought, surely Dr. Pat and the doctors in Casper wouldn't have made such a misdiagnosis! Tuberculosis tests in Buffalo had been negative and it didn't seem likely the biopsies would have missed it later. When I suggested this the doctor said older doctors were apt to be complacent about TB because it had become so rare. For this very reason it was on the rise again, so he wanted to make sure.

Brookie was moved into an isolation room. Only immediate family members were allowed to visit and then only one at a time in sterile gown, mask, and gloves. Poor Brookie was totally bewildered! "I can't tell one of you from another," he complained querulously.

The old standard TB test again came back negative, so the doctor went on to his next test. Fluid was to be suctioned from Brookie's lungs by means of a tube inserted down his windpipe. The nurse could not get it inserted, which caused him to have such a gagging and coughing spell I thought he was going to choke to death.

"We just need a larger tube," the doctor explained. "The other one was too small, so when it hit an obstruction it folded up and shut his air off."

I thought to myself, "The small one shut his air off, so he's gonna use a bigger one? I can't watch this!"

I bolted from Brookie's room into the little anteroom where we donned and removed our sterile things. I ripped off gown, mask, and gloves and fled to the visitors' lounge where I burst into tears. By the time the doctor emerged from Brookie's room a few minutes later I had myself under control—until he said, "Everything went great with the larger tube. If this doesn't show me what I'm looking for I'll do a similar procedure that will clip a sample of lung tissue for testing."

Suddenly I was shaking with anger. "No! You're not! I brought Brookie in here where he could have good care and live out his last days in peace and quiet. If all you're going to do is torment him I'm taking him home!"

The poor doctor was completely flabbergasted by my outburst.

"I'm sorry," he apologized. "I didn't realize I'd caused you such distress. My problem is that I've been trained to try to keep people from dying. I'll have Brookie moved out of isolation as soon as possible."

When we came back after lunch Brookie was "back among the living," as he put it. He was given a new lease on life, it seemed. Friends were constantly dropping by to see him.

His brother Bo, and Bill Skiles, Buffalo's brand inspector, came several nights a week to visit. On the nights they came I would usually go eat a leisurely supper because I knew he'd be royally entertained while I was gone. The three of them spent the time regaling each other with funny experiences from their pasts. I've often thought it was a pity someone didn't tape their sessions together. Some of the stories were so ribald I would come back to find the nurses had discreetly closed the door to Brookie's room! If laughter has the power to heal, Brookie should have been cured!

Dr. Pete went on vacation shortly after he took Brookie out of the isolation room and was replaced by Dr. Heistand. He was one of the newer doctors at the clinic, and we didn't know him at all. The first thing he did after getting acquainted with Brookie and familiarizing himself with Brookie's case history was to meet with the family.

He told us what to expect in the next few weeks in such a kind way that I was immediately at ease with him. When I said Brookie had a fear of smothering he told us people with respiratory illnesses usually die from heart attacks. The heart labors so hard to try to compensate for the lack of oxygen that it finally gives out. He assured us if Brookie was in danger of asphyxiation at the end he would be sedated so he wouldn't suffer anxiety and he would not be kept alive by any artificial means except for the oxygen. I felt greatly reassured after talking to him.

Brookie, who had always enjoyed good food, now found everything so unappetizing he had to force himself to eat a few bites at each meal because he feared if he didn't they would nourish him intravenously. Remembering Dr. Heistand's promise, I tried to convince Brookie that would never happen, but he was skeptical. What little food he put in his stomach disagreed with him almost as soon as he swallowed it, giving him indigestion or nausea. Consequently there was an ever-present roll of antacid tablets on his bedside table. I sometimes wondered if he wasn't getting more nourishment from them than he was the food!

By Thanksgiving Pete and Maggie were staying in Buffalo full-time. Pete had taken a leave of absence from the office where he worked and Maggie was between jobs. We spent our days at the hospital except when we went to eat, and if Brookie was having a particularly bad spell we took turns sitting with him through the night. While one of us was on shift two of us slept in the visitors' lounge.

Carol's younger son Jack was a life saver. After working an eight-hour shift as an electrician for his brother Howard, he would eat supper, then come and sit with Brookie while we took three or four hours away from the hospital atmosphere. It gave us a chance to unwind by eating supper without hurrying, usually at a cafe. From there we went to Carol's and took showers and visited with Carol until it was time to go back.

There were two big couches and a large recliner chair in the visitors' lounge. We would come back to find a stack of blankets and pillows waiting for whoever was not sitting with Brookie. There was hot coffee available to us twenty-four hours a day in the nurses' kitchen, too. The Lord richly blessed us with all those wonderful, caring people.

Even though I could have eaten with Brookie whenever I wanted to, I never did. I reasoned that if the sight of food sickened him, watching me eat would really upset his stomach. On Thanksgiving Day I made an exception when one of the nurses asked me if I wouldn't like to share Thanksgiving dinner with Brookie. He said he would really like that.

As the morning progressed the tantalizing odors drifting up from the basement kitchen made my mouth water. At noon we were served a delicious traditional turkey dinner: white and dark meat, dressing, mashed potatoes and gravy, cranberry sauce, sweet potatoes, and pumpkin pie.

"It sure looks good," Brookie said, surveying his tray, but he ate only a bite or two of the turkey and barely tasted the other things. When he saw I had cleaned up everything on my tray he tried to get me to eat what was on his. Suddenly I was almost sick to my stomach as guilt flooded over me. How could I sit there gorging when Brookie was slowly starving to death?

I don't think visitors realized how desperately thin he was. Seeing him lying in bed in a sloppy hospital gown and covered with bedding from the waist down it was hard to tell how wasted his body was. He always had an angular face, even when he weighed 250 pounds. It was a fresh shock to me every morning when I bathed him to see how emaciated he was.

Brookie always told me my birthday came so soon after Thanksgiving people were still picking turkey out of their teeth. This year was no different, of course. I was so depressed I hoped no one would remember it.

"Happy birthday!" Brookie greeted me when I walked into his room. "What a heck of a place to have to spend your birthday!" he added ruefully. He suggested I ought to go to one of the restaurants and treat myself to a great birthday dinner.

"It wouldn't mean a thing without you there," I told him. "I'd rather be right here with you."

Maggie and Pete came about the time I finished giving Brookie his bath. As a rule we all stayed with him during lunch, trying to encourage him to eat something, then we would go out while he had a nap. That day they said they would go to Carol's and eat lunch at noon, then come back at one so I could go eat. A little after one the door of Brookie's room was opened by a nurse and in walked Carol, Pete, and Maggie with a beautiful birthday cake, ice cream, and a neat wicker basket full of all kinds of dried fruit. They had all gone in together on this surprise party for me. Carol had baked the cake, and Brookie had suggested the fruit basket, knowing I loved dried fruit. I was completely overwhelmed! Brookie was as pleased as a little kid.

Shortly after that Raleigh flew in from his home in Racine, Wisconsin, and spent several days with his dad. Every evening Raleigh, Bo, and Bill held forth in Brookie's room. Listening at the door you would have thought there was a stag party in progress, complete with booze and floozies! Even with the door closed the hilarity reached such a pitch at times a smiling nurse would have to stick her head in the door and ask them to hold it down a little!

Laughter really is great therapy. Brookie positively bloomed during those few days. Raleigh's visit had done him a world of good emotionally, if not physically. Afterward I realized Brookie had run on sheer nerve while Raleigh was there because there was a real let-down after he left.

Our nice weather had held on into early December, and I was so grateful for that. Once a week I drove to the house to pick up the mail and give the poor old dogs a few hours off their chains. The cats were always so glad to see me; I'm sure they all felt as if their world had somehow gone askew.

Every year Brookie and I sent about seventy-five Christmas cards to relatives and friends. I always tried to have all the out-of-state cards in the mail by the tenth of the month. I was so emotionally dragged down I dreaded the very thought of Christmas. I just wished we could skip it, but one morning Brookie said to me, "Shouldn't you be getting your Christmas cards ready to go?"

I was so sure he was not going to live to see Christmas that the thought of sending Christmas cards sickened me. Nevertheless, I dragged myself downtown and bought several boxes of cards and began the task of addressing them, sitting in a corner of Brookie's room in a chair using a magazine as a lap board.

Brookie's food consumption had dwindled away to almost nothing because everything he ate nauseated him. He was still able to drink buttermilk in small quantities, so they brought him several small glasses a day. He was also able to tolerate a liquid diet supplement that he said tasted like a milk shake. One afternoon the dietitian came to ask him if there was anything at all he felt like he might eat.

To my complete surprise he replied, "Yes. I think I could eat some Campbell's beef soup."

"I'll fix some for you right now," she said, giving him a big smile.

When she returned minutes later with a big bowl of steaming soup I expected him to swallow one spoonful and then push it away. Instead, to my complete amazement, he ate every bit of it plus the crackers she'd brought. I knew he would spend the rest of the afternoon eating antacid tablets, but he never once complained of an upset stomach. For breakfast the next morning he ate almost a whole bowl of oatmeal and a piece of toast.

"You must be feeling much better," I remarked.

"I do!" he answered emphatically. "In fact I was wondering if you'd go downtown after you give me my bath and get me a crossword puzzle book."

We were both avid crossword puzzle fans, but it had been months since he'd had enough energy to even look at a puzzle. Pete and Maggie and I had passed the long, wearisome hours in the hospital working crossword puzzles, so I offered him one of our books.

"No," he said. "I want a brand-new one of my own, a virgin."

So I went to the drug store and got him a puzzle book and a soft-leaded pencil.

His condition improved so much in the next couple of days he began talking of going home for Christmas. Dr. Heistand approved the idea, provided his condition remained stable. For the trip home we planned to put a mattress in the back of Pete's station wagon and bed him down on that with a portable oxygen tank. I would haul an oxygen machine out in the back of my pickup for him to use at the house.

I mailed all the Christmas cards, bought groceries to restock the cupboards at home, and we even did Christmas shopping. The night before the Big Adventure we were all like kids on Christmas Eve. Brookie said he didn't need anyone to sit with him, so we went to Carol's and went to bed.

Early the next morning I went to the hospital so I could help Brookie with his breakfast and give him his bath before we left for home. My spirits were dampened a little by the change in the weather that had occurred during the night. A cold north wind was blowing, it was spitting snow and the Big Horns were obscured by heavy clouds.

As I passed the nurses' desk the RN on duty called to me. I knew before she said a word that the Big Plan was over.

"Brookie had a real bad spell early this morning," she told me with tears in her eyes. "Just as we were about to call you his condition stabilized and he's been resting comfortably ever since."

Brookie was awake and watching the door when I walked into his room. His face had such a waxen pallor that with his silver hair he seemed to blend right in with the whiteness of the pillow.

He clutched my hand when I leaned over to kiss him. "I'm sorry, kid," he whispered.

"Kid" had been his pet name for me until Raleigh and Vivian began living with us. I guess he didn't think it was an appropriate name for the stepmother of his kids, so he began using my given name. His use of the name now after all these years broke my heart. "It's all right," I told him, and we held each other and cried, knowing we were about to write the end to our love story.

It would have been over that afternoon if Dr. Heistand had been at the hospital when Brookie suffered a full-blown heart attack. The doctor on duty, unaware of our wish to let him die, managed to resuscitate him.

A nurse I didn't know had taken over night duty that week and she did not hold with family members spending the night in a patient's room. There were hospital personnel to take care of what needed to be done and family members were disruptive. So, for the last few nights of Brookie's life we left when visiting hours were over, went to Carol's, and went to bed.

The night of December 18 I sent Pete and Maggie home at supper time and told them I'd be along when evening visiting hours were over. At nine o'clock the announcement came over the loudspeaker for visitors to clear the hospital.

"I wish you wouldn't go," Brookie said when I stood up and put my coat on. "I don't feel good."

"Do you want me to get the nurse?" I asked.

"No, not yet. I just feel—unnecessary," a term he'd used ever since I'd known him to cover everything from a headache to appendicitis.

I took my coat off and hung it over the back of my chair and sat down again. "I guess they won't throw me out bodily if I stay," I joked.

Brookie closed his eyes and I sat holding his hand. Presently he murmured, "I think it's indigestion. Would you give me a couple of antacid tablets?" "It's his heart!" My mind screamed while he chewed and swallowed.

Soon he said, "It's getting worse. Maybe you'd better call the nurse."

I pressed the buzzer and soon an aide appeared in the doorway. After I explained the problem she said she'd tell the nurse.

"I'm to take his blood pressure and his pulse," she said when she appeared in the doorway again. Whatever she learned galvanized her into action. "I'd better get the nurse!" she exclaimed as she disappeared down the hall.

Apparently she hadn't told the nurse I was in Brookie's room, because when she stepped in the door and saw me she stopped short.

"Didn't you hear the announcement on the loudspeaker? Why are you still here?"

"Because I think Brookie may be having a heart attack, and I couldn't just walk off and leave him!" I snapped.

"The front doors have been locked for the night! Now you'll have to go out the emergency entrance at the back and walk clear around the building to your car!"

She checked Brookie's pulse, and her aggressive demeanor changed noticeably. "We've just had three car wreck victims brought in, and the only doctor in the hospital tonight is checking them over. I'll go see if he can see Brookie."

Brookie was becoming more distressed by the minute, groaning and pressing his hands to his chest. At last the doctor and the Dragon Lady appeared. Quickly he checked Brookie's chest with the stethoscope, stepped out in the hall, and murmured some instructions to the nurse, who disappeared down the hall. The doctor came back in and talked to Brookie while we waited for the nurse to return with the medication he had ordered. She gave him an injection in the upper arm, and the doctor assured Brookie it would soon ease the pain. I knew when it took effect because I could see him relaxing.

"Better?" asked the doctor.

"Yeah, much better!"

The doctor smiled and left.

I told the nurse I would sit with Brookie for a little longer, then I'd leave.

"I guess you can stay if he wants you to," she said grudgingly.

As soon as Brookie fell asleep I put on my coat and walked out into the hall. As I turned toward the back of the building the nurse called to me from her desk, "I can let you out the front."

Ordinarily I'm a pretty even-tempered person, but my nerves were so frazzled that I was still doing a slow boil at her earlier attitude. I turned and marched to the front door.

"I thought you were going to stay," she said as she unlocked the door.

"I wouldn't want to break any hospital rules!" I snapped. "If you need me I'm at Carol Turk's. Thanks for unlocking the door."

I stomped down the steps, got in the pickup, and left.

Carol was waiting up for me.

"You haven't had any supper, have you?"

"No, but I'm too upset to eat." I began telling her everything that had happened.

Carol paid no attention to my refusal to eat. She set a cold lunch out on the table for me. By that time I'd simmered down and begun to realize I'd acted pretty childishly.

Carol said to me while I ate a sandwich and some salad and drank hot tea, "I think Brookie is like Halsey. He had such a strong will to live he just couldn't die. I used to come home from the hospital at night and pray he'd die before morning. When morning came I'd feel so guilty for wishing him dead. A friend of mine came and talked to me about losing her husband to Alzheimer's. She said she decided it was wicked to pray for him to live when he was in such terrible shape. I never felt guilty again about praying for death to set Halsey free from the agony he was in."

With tears in my eyes I admitted that I'd been doing the same thing: praying Brookie would die before morning, and then feeling so guilty in the light of day.

"There are so many things worse than death," Carol told me as we cleared away my supper.

It was after eleven before we went to bed. I felt totally drained from being so angry earlier, but I also felt so comforted by Carol's words that I fell asleep immediately.

The ringing of the telephone finally penetrated the deep sleep I was in.

"I'll tell her," I heard Carol say.

I was already half dressed when she got to my bedroom door. "The hospital?" I asked, though I didn't need to.

"Yes. They said they thought you'd better come. Do you want me to wake Pete and Maggie?"

"No, not yet. If he's critical I'll call back as soon as I get there. If you don't hear from me in fifteen minutes go on back to bed and get some sleep." I had already checked my watch and knew it was just a little after 3 A.M.

The nurse was waiting at the front door to let me in.

"How bad is he?" I asked.

"The doctor says his heart is giving out. He may live for several hours, but he could go any time. That's why I called; he keeps asking for you."

He was watching the door when I walked in and he tried to smile. His voice was so weak I had to lean over to hear him. "I'm glad you're here."

I moved the visitor's chair over by the bed and sat down. He groped for my hand, and I smoothed his wispy hair back away from his forehead with my free hand.

The minutes passed. Then he opened his eyes. "I hope you'll forgive me for all the times I was ornery," he murmured.

"Nothing to forgive," I assured him. "Everybody feels ornery when they're sick."

"No! No!" he was so emphatic his voice had a little more strength. "I mean all the times I was ornery to you back through all our years together!"

He sounded so distressed I squeezed his hand. "Nothing to forgive!" I replied. "I think it was always pretty much a fifty-fifty situation. I hope you've forgiven me."

"We used to have some pretty good rows, didn't we?" He grinned at the remembering. "I think I used to pick fights with you because it was so much fun making up!"

More time went by. His eyes would close and I would think he was sleeping, but then he would say something and we would talk for a few minutes.

"How's old Chub?" he asked once.

Chub was his old retired sheepdog, blind and deaf but still healthy. He was part Border collie and part who-knew-what.

I told him about the dogs and cats, especially his old Spotty-Cat who had shared many of Brookie's invalid hours on the hide-a-bed; about the day I came home from Casper after Brookie's surgery and Spotty went all through the house looking for Brookie after he didn't find him on the couch. When Spotty couldn't find him, he let out a cry so mournful it stood the hair up on the back of my neck!

Brookie thought the world of the people who made Johnson County Memorial Hospital the caring, well-run place it was. When the day shift came on that morning his door was opened by the only person he didn't like, one of the aides. I suspect the reason Brookie didn't get on well with her was that she had absolutely no sense of humor. Many times I heard Brookie's mother say, "I can forgive anyone a world of sins if they have a sense of humor." That was pretty much his philosophy, too.

The aide came in with a brisk "good morning," then stopped to read his chart.

"Oh, oh!" she said. "No urine output for the past ten hours. Did someone forget to chart it?"

"I don't think so," I told her. "I was here until after ten last night and since three this morning, and there's been no urine to chart."

"Well," she said cheerfully, "we can remedy that with a catheter!" And she bustled out the door.

"Oh, please," Brookie pleaded, "don't let them put a catheter in me!"

"I won't," I promised, and headed for the desk. The aide was nowhere to be seen, but Dr. Heistand was there going over charts with the day nurse.

"You won't put a catheter in Brookie, will you?" I asked.

"No," he assured me, "but we are going to hook him up to an I.V. so we can administer pain-killing medication more efficiently. His heart is giving out, so we need to keep him sedated so he's comfortable but not unconscious."

Greatly reassured I went back and relayed this information to Brookie. He was terribly upset about the I.V.

"What do I have to do to die?" he cried out. "Could you unplug the oxygen?"

"I could," I answered, "but I would probably be sent to the pen for doing it!"

After I explained why they were going to put him on an I.V. he said with weary resignation, "I guess it's all right" and closed his eyes.

Dr. Heistand and the nurse came in with the I.V. and he again explained to Brookie the reason for it. Just as they finished hooking it up, Brookie gasped and clutched his chest with his free hand. "Oh! I'm having those chest pains again!"

The doctor rapped out an order, the only word of which I heard was "morphine." The nurse ran from the room and in moments ran back in with a syringe. The contents were injected into the I.V. tube. Brookie began to relax, and the doctor motioned me to follow him out to the hall.

"If there are any family members you want here before he dies, you'd better call them now. Also, I need to tell you that I promised my son two weeks ago that I'd take him skiing today and we had planned to leave about an hour from now. Dr. Pete is back and says he will take over if it's agreeable to you. If you're not comfortable with that I'll call my son and tell him we'll go skiing next weekend."

"Don't disappoint your boy," I told him. "Dr. Pete will be fine. I know Brookie won't mind because he really likes him."

Dr. Heistand told me how sorry he was about Brookie, how much he'd enjoyed him, even though he'd been so ill. Then he went back into the room and talked to Brookie, explaining that Dr. Pete would be taking over and why.

Just then, Pete, Maggie, Carol, and Jack arrived. I talked to them out in the hall and explained what was going on. We called Warren and Vivian and told them they'd better come. Next I called Brookie's sister Evelyn and her second husband, Henry, at their home in Sheridan.

Dr. Heistand left as Dr. Pete arrived and ushered us into Brookie's room. Someone brought chairs so we could all sit down. I sat by Brookie's head and held his hand. Maggie sat beside me, occasionally patting my arm or shoulder. Pete and Jack sat across from us by the I.V.

There was such a feeling of unreality about everything that I felt as if I was in a dream. I was aware of what was gong on, but it was as if I was not connected to what was happening. Evelyn and Henry arrived, and there were tears and hugs and more chairs were brought in. People conversed in low voices. Occasionally someone left to go to the rest room or get another cup of coffee and returned. Through it all, Dr. Pete sat near Pete and Jack, totally removed from all the conversation.

Sometimes I closed my eyes and tried to pray; mostly I sat and looked at Brookie's face. He looked so peaceful I wondered if he had died and no one was aware of it. I concentrated on his chest and could make out a barely discernible movement of the bed spread.

Almost as if he read my thoughts Brookie opened his eyes and looked into mine. "I'm so afraid to leave you alone." His voice was faint but his words were clear. "What's going to become of you?"

"Don't worry, sweetheart, I'll be okay," I put so much conviction into the words that for a moment I almost believed them myself even while my heart was crying, "I'll never be okay again!"

"We'll take good care of her, Dad!" Pete said.

"Brook, we all love her very much!" Jack added. "We'll look after her!"

Brookie looked at me a moment longer, then, as if reassured, he closed his eyes.

\*　　\*　　\*

Two days before Christmas we buried Brookie in the Kaycee Cemetery while the first winter storm of the season lashed us with a bitter north wind that made the snow sting like buckshot pellets. After the months of anguish I was exhausted, and my emotions felt as frozen as the bleak day.

Brookie's beloved Big Horn Mountains, a few miles to the west of us, were obscured by the storm, but I knew they were there even though I couldn't see them. And I knew spring would come again, even though in my present state of mind it was hard to imagine. The coming of spring would bring a renewal of life and hope. With God's help I would live one day at a time and be able to face the future alone.

No, not alone; the Lord would be walking with me, maybe even back to Brookie's mountains!

*The house after the new room was built.*

*Brookie in July 1981, six months before his death.*